CROSSED PATHS

CROSSED PATHS

Labor Activism and
Colonial Governance
in Hong Kong, 1938–1958

LU YAN

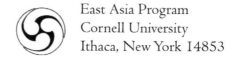

East Asia Program
Cornell University
Ithaca, New York 14853

The Cornell East Asia Series is published by the Cornell University East Asia Program (distinct from Cornell University Press). We publish books on a variety of scholarly topics relating to East Asia as a service to the academic community and the general public. Address submission inquiries to CEAS Editorial Board, East Asia Program, Cornell University, 140 Uris Hall, Ithaca New York 14853-7601.

Cover Image: Queen's Road, Hong Kong, 1930s. Used with permission.
Back cover: Police blockade at Russell Street, January 28, 1950. Courtesy of HKFTU.

Number 195 in the Cornell East Asia Series.
© 2019 Lu Yan. All rights reserved.
ISSN: 1050-2955
ISBN: 978-1-939161-05-5 hardcover
ISBN: 978-1-939161-95-6 paperback
ISBN: 978-1-942242-95-6 e-book
Library of Congress Control Number: 2018966294

Contents

Acknowledgments

This book would not have reached its finish line without the help of many. I owe special thanks to four people for starting and sustaining my research in Hong Kong. In 2007, Allen Smart first mentioned the file by British labour officers archived in the Hong Kong Public Records Office; his comment that more ROC and Guomindang flags than the PRC flags were flown on Chinese national holidays in mid-twentieth-century Hong Kong impelled me to investigate attentively Chinese partisan influence entangled with labor activism and colonial governance in this former British colony. Chau Yick, a youth and labor activist in Hong Kong during the 1940s and 1950s and writer on the movements he participated in and researched, opened the door to the archive at the Federation of Trade Unions (FTU) in Hong Kong. His generosity in sharing knowledge and source materials, as well as his prompt replies to my numerous inquiries, significantly enhanced my understanding of the lives and work of Chinese labor in Hong Kong that otherwise cannot be learned from books. Wong Shuk Mei gave critical help with FTU materials and continued her support even after her retirement. John M. Carroll generously gave encouragement and support; he made sure I had access to the Special Collection at the University of Hong Kong in my research trips, suggested useful sources, and shared his insights to grassroots society in Hong Kong and Hong Kong history.

Thanks are due to the late Mr. Lo Fu and Mr. Lo Hoising for granting me interviews, to Mrs. Wu Shu San for leads to useful sources, to Professor Lu Weiluan for an interview that opened a special window to early 1950 Hong Kong through her memory of the bloody event at Russell Street, and to Professor Choi Wai-kit for generously sharing his source materials with me in Hong Kong and the United States. I learned much through conversations with Lee Pui-tak, Christopher Munn, Suzanne Pepper, Qian Jiang, and Elizabeth Sinn. Yoko Miyakawa's cheer and conversations made those working days in Hong Kong's sultry summer bearable and joyful. Henrietta Harrison's hospitality added delightful surprise to my trip to Oxford. I also thank Professors Liu Weikai and Zhou Huimin for conversations and help at the National

Chengchi University, and Peter Zarrow for facilitating my research at the Institute of Modern History at the Academia Sinica. I would not have completed research there and at the Guomindang History Archive without timely help from Chen Chisong and Ye Chiou-ling.

My thanks also go to archivists and librarians whose help to locate needed source materials was indispensable. I am particularly grateful to the librarians at the Department of Interlibrary Loans in the Dimond Library of the University of New Hampshire (UNH), who responded promptly and effectively with results to my countless requests for books, maps, and microfilms. Special thanks are due to Bernard Hui at the Hong Kong Public Records Office, Iris Chan and her team at the Special Collection of Hong Kong in the Main Library of the University of Hong Kong, Ma Xiaohe at Harvard-Yenching Library, Wei Qingrong at the Law Library of Harvard University, and Xue Zhaohui at Stanford University Library, who often went beyond the call of duty to locate source materials for me.

In the course of writing the manuscript, Chen Jian has given constant encouragement. Sherman Cochran continues to be an inspiration even after his retirement; he read the penultimate version of the introduction and gave most helpful advice. Chi Man Kwong, Hanchao Lu, Caroline Reeves, and Jan Zeserson read parts of the manuscript and made useful comments. Karen Alexander provided generous help that improved the style of this work. Thanks are due to Wake Forest University for the invitation to present part of this book, and to Qiong Zhang for her interest in this work and her support. I especially thank my colleagues Jan Golinski and Lige Gould as chairs and Molly Girard Dorsey, Cathy Frierson, Judith Moyer and Lucy Salyer at the Department of History at UNH for support in various ways, and Tu Lan at the Department of Geography for patient guidance in map making. Generous support of the Wheeler Fund, Rutman Fund, and Dunfey Fund from the Department of History, funds from the Center for International Education and the Center for the Humanities at UNH made the many research trips to Hong Kong, Taibei, London, and Oxford possible. Assistance by Christine Aiello for map making was prompt and efficient. The constructive comments and recommendations by three anonymous reviewers for Cornell East Asia Series (CEAS) helped me make it a better book. Mai Shaikhanuar-Cota of CEAS deserves special thanks for her impeccable professionalism and guidance through the phases of book production. While help came from so many to make this book a reality, I alone am responsible for any remaining mistakes and shortcomings in it.

Last but not the least, my unending gratitude goes to four women: to aunt Yan Bo, for her inexhaustible inspiration and understanding; to Chen Zhihui, for her generosity; to Fan Xiaoming, for her support; and to Xiao Min for her friendship.

Note on Names

All Chinese names are rendered in pinyin, except for two (both transliteration of Cantonese pronunciation), Chiang Kai-shek and Sun Yat-sen, which have been popularized in English books. Names known in English sources by Cantonese transliteration appear in parentheses marked with *Ct.*

Place names in Hong Kong are rendered in either English or in Cantonese transliteration, following local custom.

Newspaper titles in Hong Kong are rendered as they appear in the masthead, which do not always use Cantonese (such as *Sing Tao Jih Bao*); those without are rendered in pinyin.

British spelling of "labour" is used throughout for official positions and titles.

Tables and Charts

Illustrations

Abbreviations

CMU   Chinese Mechanics Union

CNRA   Chinese National Revolutionary Alliance (Zhonghua minzu geming tongmeng)

FRUS   Department of State (United States), *Foreign Relations of the United States*

GDGM   Zhongyang dang'anguan and Guangdongsheng dang'anguan (eds.), *Guangdong geming lishi wenjian huiji*

GDZZSZL   Zhonggong Guangdong shengwei zuzhibu, Zhonggong Guangdong shengwei dangshi yanjiushi, and Guangdong sheng dang'anguan (eds.), *Zhongguo Gongchandang Guangdong sheng zuzhishi ziliao*

GHZJ   Yuan Xianggang wenhua jiaoyu yishu shetuan qingzhu Xianggang huigui zuguo (ed.), *Guanghui de zuji (Brilliant footprints)*

GMDCRC   Guomindang Central Reform Committee

HGGJDD   Guangdong qingyunshi yanjiu weiyuanhui yanjiushi and Dongzong GangJiu dadui duishi zhengbianzu (eds.), *Huigu GangJiu dadui (Recollections of the Hong Kong–Kowloon Independent Brigade)*

HKAR   *Annual Report of Hong Kong* (Hong Kong Government)

HKFTU   Hong Kong–Kowloon Federation of Trade Unions

HKNSA   Hong Kong Resisting-Japan National Salvation Association (Xianggang kangRi jiuguohui)

LDAR   Commissioner of Labour (Hong Kong), *Annual Departmental Report*

QCJXQ   Guangdong qingyunshi yanjiu weiyuanhui yanjiushi (ed.), *Qingchun jinxingqu: huiyi Xiangang Honghong geyongtuan (March of youth: recollections of the Rainbow Choir in Hong Kong)*

SCMP   *South China Morning Post*

TUC   Trades Union Council

WKYP   *Wah Kiu Yat Po*

XGBZJYZL   Fang Jun, Mai Xiaolin, and Xiong Xianjun (eds.), *Xianggang zaoqi baozhi jiaoyu ziliao xuancui* (*Selection of articles on education from early newspapers in Hong Kong*)

XGFJWJ   Zhongyang dang'anguan and Guangdongsheng dang'anguan (eds.), *Zhonggong zhongyang Xianggang fenju wenjian huiji, 1947.5–1949.3* (*Collection of documents at Hong Kong branch bureau of the Chinese Communist Central Committee*)

XGFYZL   Guangdong funü yundong lishi ziliao bianji weiyuanhui, *Xianggang funü yundong ziliao huibian* (*Collection of materials on women's movement in Hong Kong*)

ZELWX   Zhonggong zhongyang tongyi zhanxian gongzuobu and Zhonggong zhongyang wenxian yanjiushi (eds.), *Zhou Enlai tongyi zhanxian wenxuan* (*Selected articles by Zhou Enlai on the United Front*)

ZGZYNJJ   Zhonggong Jiangsu shengwei dangshi gongzuo weiyuanhui et al. (eds.), *Zhonggong zhongyang Nanjingju* (*The Nanjing Bureau of Chinese Communist Party*)

ZGZYWJXJ   Zhongyang dang'anguan (ed.), *Zhonggong zhongyang wenjian xuanji* (*Selected documents by the central committee of the CCP*)

Introduction

All these divisions and inequalities due to differences in social or provincial origin or in methods of recruitment soon vanished, however, in the face of the shared hardships of working-class life.
—Jean Chesneaux (1968)

Clearly there is no simple equation between the development of industry, the formation of the working class, working-class consciousness, and revolutionary activity.
—Emily Honig (1986)

Hong Kong ... was decolonised in substance, if not juridically, in the early 1950s at the same time as most of the remaining colonial territories in East and South East Asia.
—John Darwin (1997)

Writing nearly a quarter century apart, the two labor historians cited in the epigraphs reached radically different conclusions on the modern Chinese working class and working-class consciousness.[1] Industrialization as a critical phase in global history arrived in China after it had transformed Europe, making inroads into a society with a high level of urbanization and demographic mobility. In his pioneering study on Chinese labor activism, which developed along with anti-imperialist political protests during China's tumultuous 1920s, French historian Jean Chesneaux argued for the revolutionary power of industrialization in creating a new working-class solidarity. In particular, the "merciless effects of long working hours, frequent accidents, brutal treatment by foremen, and strict discipline enforced by overseers" within modern industrial establishments were instrumental for the making of "a genuine and united proletariat." U.S. historian Emily Honig disagreed and proposed an opposite argument through a case study in which she carefully probed the "warp and weft" of women workers' lives and work in Shanghai's

---

1. Chesneaux, 70; Honig, 245.

I

cotton industry. Instead of seeing a "united proletariat" emerging from the "shared hardships of working-class life," Honig argued that modern industrial establishments did not automatically transform peasant girls into members of a united working class. Nor did it separate them from old, traditional bonds. Instead, she found them still involuntarily held in the grip of traditional secret societies that directly controlled their employment and voluntarily attracted to sworn sisterhoods that cushioned them with mutual help in a city of strangers. Regional and dialect differences persisted and divided workers. Imperialism did not unite them, but often "exacerbated" the workers' existing particularistic divides.

Not alone in her interpretation among labor historians of China, Honig spearheaded an approach that was later captured by political scientist Elizabeth Perry in the phrase "politics of place."[2] In the city of Tianjin, historian Gail Hershatter found that workers during the first half of the twentieth century kept "close bonds to kin," and their position remained "marginal and transient" in the economy.[3] In modern Beijing, where the economy retained its preindustrial quality, political scientist David Strand discovered working people whose lives and collective actions were dictated by parochial interest: labor bosses controlled the workplace and brokered the relationship between workers and employers, while workers formed their own regional-dialect groups or gangs. Even at a time when a nationalist movement swept the city, the power of parochial interest could tear it apart with turf fights among laborers. Traditional guilds often overlapped with regional associations and, in place of industrial unions, provided organizational bases for workers' collective actions.[4]

Although seeming to have followed a divergent argument, this school of local studies has pursued some of the issues identified by Chesneaux, who first pointed to the influence of traditional social organizations among Chinese workers and to regional differences as a cause of uneven development in labor activism across China. Taking cues from Chesneaux, who attributed the weakness of labor activism in Shanghai to its predominantly female and child labor force and that in Beijing to its preindustrial economy, Honig and Strand

---

2. Perry, part I.
3. Hershatter, 7.
4. Strand, esp. chapters 7, 8, and 10.

pursued these issues further and discovered the still vigorous and powerful regional divides and traditional social organizations in these industrializing urban centers. Their differences with Chesneaux began there. Rather than treating regional divides and traditional forms of social organization as external to industrial labor, their works viewed these seemingly external forces as internal to it and demonstrated their implosive potential to cause labor fragmentation. As a result, their studies rejected Chesneaux's sweeping argument of the lineal progress from industrialization to working-class awakening. The concepts of class solidarity and class consciousness central to Chesneaux's work give way to regional affinity, secret societies, and labor bosses, which have all taken center stage in the depiction of the workplace and the life of Chinese labor by the school of local studies.

This approach, which deemphasizes workplace dynamics in the creation of class consciousness, is not without challengers. At least two substantial studies point to the importance of class-based antagonism. Sociologist Chan Wai Kwan, in exploring class formation during early colonial Hong Kong, presents the case of seamen who came to grasp the idea of class difference on ocean liners, where discriminatory treatment of Chinese and white seamen created a humiliating and widely recognized hierarchy of classes.[5] In studying the arms industry in wartime Chongqing, historian Joshua H. Howard points to the divide between manual and mental labor as the objective basis for class difference, from which a subjective expression of class consciousness rose in protest against managers representing the state who exploited and mistreated them. Partisan leadership, particularly from the Communists, became important in helping workers organize and transform their latent feelings of class antagonism into class consciousness.[6] These studies advance our understanding of labor history in China in at least two ways. First, historical experiences of Chinese labor varied across China's vast territory and therefore need to be placed within specific temporal and spatial frames. Second, class formation, as both studies emphasize, was not a static given but an ongoing process demonstrated through labor action.

In this study of labor activism in Hong Kong from the 1930s to 1950s, I intend to return to the question of labor politicization that Chesneaux high-

---

5. Chan Wai Kwan, chapter 5.
6. Howard, esp. chapters 4, 7, and 8.

lighted, but at the same time give equal attention to conditions beyond the workplace that, as suggested by other labor historians, could keep working Chinese from or push them toward large-scale collective actions. I choose Hong Kong because of its demographic similarity to other modern Chinese cities, which offers opportunities to examine both the capability of the working class to take collective action in solidarity, which Chesneaux and Chan Wai Kwan emphasized, and the potential for fragmentation (or lack of capability for collective action) among working people who were immigrants. I choose Hong Kong also because of its political difference from other modern Chinese cities. Ruled by Britain as a crown colony, colonialism became an inescapable force in the life and work of Chinese. A study of Chinese labor under colonial rule in Hong Kong therefore foregrounds the problem of foreign dominance and presents a meaningful comparison to the case of imperialism that fragmented Shanghai textile workers as documented by Honig.

Hong Kong has had a rich history of labor activism. In particular, the Seamen's Strike in 1922 and the Hong Kong–Guangdong General Strike-Boycott of 1925–1926 have attracted contemporary and scholarly attention for their importance to the development of the Chinese labor movement. Chesneaux views these two strikes in Hong Kong to be of national importance by inspiring (in the first case) and strengthening (in the second case) a nationwide labor movement.[7] But Hong Kong was also a modern Chinese city with a social composition similar to other large urban centers on the mainland, such as Shanghai, Hankou, Chongqing, and Beijing. It was and still is a city of migrants with distinctive regional origins and dialects. If the objective "body" of

---

7. Chinese authors have presented at least three different discussions of the Seamen's Strike. The first was by Deng Zhongxia, who wrote in 1928 while in Moscow as a representative of the All-China Federation of Trade Unions to the Red Workers International, though his writing was apparently published much later. The second was by Chen Da, a U.S.-trained sociologist teaching at Tsinghua University in Beijing, whose major analysis of Chinese labor problems was published in 1929. A decade later, in May 1939, Liu Shaoqi, one of the top Communist leaders and a veteran of the labor movement, presented a talk to students at the Workers School in Yan'an on the development of the Chinese labor movement. Most likely, Liu was the only person who knew both Deng's and Chen's works. All three reached similar conclusions on the causes and significance of the Seamen's Strike. See Deng Zhongxia, esp. chapter 4; Chen Da, esp. 182–95; Liu Shaoqi, passim.

Chinese labor in Hong Kong was made of the same material as that in other major cities, what enabled them to overcome regional and other particularistic differences? No scholarship in Western languages has been published to explore further developments in labor activism in Hong Kong since Chesneaux's discussion. In exploring the development of labor activism there beyond the well-known events of the 1920s, the present study, with its attention to colonial Hong Kong in the British Empire, is an attempt to look at Chinese labor activism anew in its Chinese and global contexts.

My research began ten years ago on official documents housed in the Public Records Office in Hong Kong. I encountered internal reports by British labour officers who left a thick stack of records resulting from day-to-day contacts and observations of Chinese workers and union activists. Some reports vividly described how ordinary Chinese workers drew "a heap of satisfaction" in response to the southward advance of the "Red Army" in 1949. Other analyses traced the history of labor unions in Hong Kong. Without exception, they emphasized the political character of Chinese labor unions as well as their close connection to the mainland. As I searched further, I found loud echoes similarly characterizing this politicized labor activism in the internal dispatches and memoirs of other colonial officials. Other contemporary sources, such as news reports, internal documents by Communists and Guomindang Party members, and memoirs by labor activists, reinforced these two themes in the British records. Except for a ten-year lull following the General Strike-Boycott of 1925–1926, Chinese workers in Hong Kong had brought forth wave after wave of activism, positioning themselves in the center of a national salvation movement, armed resistance against Japanese invasion, clandestine operations in support of the Allies in the China theater and, above all, social activism and industrial disputes throughout the second half of the 1940s and early 1950s. As the record shows, workers and laborers in Hong Kong appeared to be far more active than their contemporaries in Shanghai or Beijing who, as depicted by existing scholarship, were preoccupied with securing immediate, particularistic interests and had to be mobilized by outside forces before they joined national movements. Why was the "local hold"—be it foremen or secret societies—missing in Hong Kong? Or, were Chinese workers there more easily manipulated by external forces?

Existing scholarship provides very limited answers to these questions. Popular protests by grassroots societies in Hong Kong first appeared in the 1884–

1885 Sino-French War, when boat coolies (laborers) boycotted work on French ships anchoring in Hong Kong. According to historian Jung-fang Tsai, behind this protest were the Triads, a secret society that assumed an organizational role for the protesting workers.[8] That the Triads exerted influence over manual laborers has also been confirmed by a recent study of rickshaw pullers, who made up only a small fraction of Hong Kong's working Chinese.[9] Another case study of one of China's labor leaders, Deng Zhongxia, argued that direct involvement of Communists in organizing workers was key for successful labor mobilization in Hong Kong during the General Strike-Boycott of 1925–1926.[10] These studies on different topics echoed the points made by local studies of labor in mainland cities because they highlighted the importance of nationalist sentiment, the organizational potential of secret societies, and the appeal of the Communists as an outside force. Chronologically, their discussion sheds light on the years before and up to the 1920s, but not after. Explaining later developments in labor activism, particularly observations by British labour officers on the continued politicization of Chinese workers decades later, awaits further research.

If traditional forms of social organization and external forces wielded influence on Chinese labor in Hong Kong before the 1920s, did such influences continue and remain the same in later decades? Certainly, the power of secret societies, ubiquitous in grassroots communities and reaching high in political and economic circles as well, cannot be ignored. But it needs to be considered in context. Despite its widespread presence, the influence of secret societies was neither identical nor uniform across China. Existing studies on Shanghai's Green Gang, which featured prominently in Honig's study of cotton workers, provide useful comparisons.

The Green Gang reached its zenith under specific historical conditions. In semicolonial Shanghai, jurisdiction was divided among three authorities: the Chinese city, the French Concession, and the International Settlement administered by a coalition of several foreign powers. The Green Gang built its power by taking advantage of all three authorities as outsiders in the city without a deep reach into local society. It supplied the French Concession with

---

8. Tsai, esp. chapter 5.

9. Fung, esp. chapter 2.

10. Kwan, chapters 3 and 4.

police detectives and helped enhance the Concession's official revenue through a semiofficial agreement over opium sales. In return, Green Gang leaders gained prestige and continued their monopoly on the illegal but lucrative narcotics trade. By assisting the Guomindang's anti-Communist coup in 1927, during which the French Concession and the International Settlement provided easy passage for Green Gang thugs, the gang sealed its collaboration with China's national government. "In the process," as historian Brian G. Martin indicates, Green Gang leaders "parlayed their standing with one group into increased influence with the other and thus encouraged perceptions among both groups of their indispensability."[11] Beyond transient personal connections, relations between the Green Gang and officialdom became institutionalized over time as gang leaders acquired important positions in the foreign-controlled municipality and the Guomindang state.

The reverse must be said about the secret societies in Hong Kong, a territory annexed from China in 1842 through British imperialist conquest and administered by a single colonial master. The pervasive presence of secret societies (or, sworn brotherhoods) in city neighborhoods and the absence of their influence in Hong Kong's colonial establishment was the combined result of foreign control of the city and its sociogeographical membership in South China.[12] Despite British annexation, Hong Kong remained geographically part of South China's Lingnan macroregion. No border control existed for more than a century. Continued easy movement within the greater Lingnan macroregion enabled the Triads, the predominant secret societies in South China still committed to anti-Qing rebellion, to establish headquarters in Hong Kong. In the late 1840s, they participated in popular anti-British uprisings in South China after the Opium War. Before the fall of the Qing dynasty, they repeatedly gave support to major political movements, including the Taiping Rebellion and the 1911 Revolution. Their network had been critical in garnering grassroots support for Sun Yat-sen and his revolutionary organi-

---

11. Martin (1992), citation from 286. Also see Martin (1995), 64–92, and Martin (1996).

12. For geographical and cultural connections between Hong Kong and South China, see Davis, esp. introduction and chapter 14. For similarity of legal practice in land ownership between rural Hong Kong and China, see Hase; for Hong Kong's demographic and social membership in the Lingnan macroregion, see Salaff; Lu Yan (2014b).

zation that was later renamed the Guomindang in 1912. As colonial masters, the British had every reason to be vigilant against the rebellious Triads with their record of antiforeign resistance in South China. Suppressing the Triads became law in the earliest days of British rule in Hong Kong. Issued as the No. 1 Ordinance of 1845, the Triads and Secret Societies Ordinance made Triad members "guilty of felony" and subject to branding on the right cheek, three years' imprisonment, and deportation. Over time, this ordinance became a major instrument against Chinese political activities in Hong Kong, including labor organization. The ordinance was revised in the wake of each major political upheaval on the mainland with repercussions in the colony, such as the coolie protests during the Sino-French War of 1884–1885, the 1911 Revolution, and the Communist victory in 1949.

British suppression severely limited the Triads' territorial reach. Without the opportunity of collaboration with or cooptation by the authorities, the Triads in Hong Kong became far weaker than the Green Gang, and this induced further fragmentation. After the 1911 Revolution, according to police records, the Triads lost their common goal of nationalism, splintered into smaller groups, and operated "under the guise of various trade guilds, benevolent associations, or sports clubs." They evolved into "the type of criminal organisations that we know today."[13] Thus degenerated, Triad criminal activities were no match for the Green Gang's, whose operations spread beyond Shanghai to other provinces through narcotics trafficking with the complicity of the Guomindang state.[14] With no coherent operational network or unifying ideal, in twentieth-century Hong Kong the Triads disintegrated into small bands of neighborhood gangsters.[15] Without the political clout and social networks comparable to those of the Green Gang in Shanghai, the Triads never acquired the same monopolistic power over Chinese labor in Hong Kong.

Because the Triads lacked political power in Hong Kong, the issue of the secret societies' influence on Chinese labor needs to be viewed differently from what happened in Shanghai. Triad movement toward fragmentation and crim-

---

13. Morgan, citation from 66.

14. Cai Shaoqing, esp. 233–40, for collaborations of the Green Gang and the Red Gang on the middle-upper Yangtze valley over the narcotics trade. See also Wakeman for a penetrating analysis on the collaboration of the Guomindang's antidrug bureau and the Green Gang.

15. Morgan, 65.

inality did not lead to the same notorious contract labor system the Green Gang had. But it had a different kind of impact on the Chinese labor movement in Hong Kong. In chapters 2, 4, and 6, I trace the pattern of Triad activities in contrast and intersection with Chinese labor activism in Hong Kong and describe their criminal proclivities when they took actions of consequence. Although their strength and projected power fluctuated in opposite direction to vacillating British strength in the colony, the Triads' entanglement with partisan politics—as during Sun Yat-sen's early phase of revolutionary activities and party organization—continued under new circumstances of war, local anarchy, and political conflict.

If the Triads, as a traditional, internal force within Chinese society, were unable to achieve predominant control of Chinese labor in twentieth-century Hong Kong, what organized and mobilized Chinese workers there into actions with "visions of change" beyond their localized and particularistic interest? British colonial documents offer two opposite interpretations. The first appeared in the early 1930s, when a colonial governor pointed his finger at "communist agitators" for instigating a major popular protest. The second explanation came from a low-ranking British official in the late 1940s, whose direct contact with Chinese workers and labor activists led him to argue about the genuine desire for economic improvements as the motivation for labor activism. My research in both Chinese and British records steered me to discover two large forces that emerged in tandem and developed in parallel during the 1930s. Partisan leadership's appeal to local society and labor's desire for economic improvements, however genuine, required both forces to translate into legitimate collective actions in colonial Hong Kong.

The first force, civic activism for national salvation, became an outstanding theme in local records and was echoed in British official documents. Contemporary sources—such as reports from major Chinese newspapers, Communist Party internal documents, and personal memoirs by activists and observers that surfaced later—depicted a restless society from the 1930s to the early 1950s. The popular impulse toward voluntary action first arose in response to the impending Japanese invasion of China, and it involved Chinese of different classes and occupations. Still without coherent political leadership, ordinary Chinese spontaneously rallied in public protest. They formed groups that met frequently for reading, singing, and discussion of contemporary affairs. Voluntary associations appeared on factory floors, in neighborhoods among the young, within various professions, and among students from grade school to middle school and college. Those formed by workers became the most energetic. The spirit of civic voluntarism intensified when total war broke out on the mainland; even business leaders began to donate to the Chinese government for its national defense. Chapter 1 depicts the emergence of civic activism as a departure from a decade-long political quiescence in Hong Kong.

A striking feature of this upsurge in civic activism in Hong Kong during the 1930s and 1940s was the prominence of working people as key agents. With a shared agenda of national salvation, civic activism in Hong Kong did not begin with elite leadership, as it did on the mainland, but started in grassroots society with workers at the forefront.[16] Other social groups, such as students and business elite, entered and left the movement at different points, but Chinese workers were most active in taking initiative and most persistent in efforts to support China's national struggle for survival. Their voluntary associations in choirs, reading groups, recreational clubs, or athletic organizations offered conduits for working Chinese to join wartime resistance. Some voluntary associations developed directly from regional-dialect groups, yet their purpose was not to divide the city into separate regional turfs but to gather all possible energy and resources together in a national effort to resist foreign invasion. The unity of regional associations in the national cause was surely not unique to Hong Kong.[17] What mattered was the closer connection, through expression and action, between Chinese in British-occupied Hong Kong and their homeland. What became consequential were the organizational links established by Chinese activists in Hong Kong with partisan leadership on the mainland, which reconfigured labor organization in Hong Kong. From prewar to postwar times, the organizational links continued and, to a certain extent, shape the course of labor activism in Hong Kong.

The second new force did not originate in Hong Kong, but in London as an imperial initiative to intervene in labor affairs throughout the empire. It was a major departure from Britain's longstanding laissez-faire approach to

---

16. For political and intellectual elite leadership in initiating the National Salvation Movement, see Coble; for social leadership by business elite, see Chen and Mao.

17. For a case study of regional associations providing an important organizational base of mobilization for the May Fourth movement in Shanghai, see Goodman (1992).

colonial governance in economic and social realms. In the late 1930s, London took a pivotal step toward interventionism in labor affairs, placing the responsibility of managing industrial relations on colonial states throughout the empire. This momentous departure from tradition, so far, has been presented in a different framework in British imperial history or discussed only in passing in studies on labor movements in Africa and West Indies. For old-school British imperial historians, London's turn to interventionism in colonial governance in the 1930s was a reaffirmation of the British tradition of "good government." For labor historians, it was a policy adjustment to changing colonial economies and to labor protest, rather than a major departure from established colonial governance tradition.[18] The commonly recognized point of British departure toward direct state involvement in colonial affairs has been its 1940 Colonial Development and Welfare Act, which committed the imperial government to greatly increasing financial resources to aid social improvements in the British colonies. Viewed from the perspective of colonial labor in the British Empire, as I show in chapter 1, London crossed a threshold toward interventionism when it decided on setting up labour departments across its global empire three years before the 1940 act. This caused radical changes in governing structure and governing methods in the colonies. By granting legal status to labor unions, which had been outlawed in many colonies, including Hong Kong, this move opened new possibilities in reforming colonial relations.

In separate ways, Chinese civic activism for national salvation and British intervention in colonial labor problems helped rouse Hong Kong from political dormancy and, when the two crossed paths, launched it on a track of transformation. Civic activism among the Chinese in Hong Kong gave expression to deeply held, widely shared sentiments among the predominant majority of local residents that they were Chinese and, more precisely, Chinese sojourners in Hong Kong. In that regard, Hong Kong society was not too different from other modern commercial and industrial centers such as Shanghai, Xiamen, and Qingdao. These urban centers were made by what

---

18. For interpretation of British intervention in traditional imperial history, see Wicker, J. M. Lee. For a more inclusive take on this policy change within the framework of imperial need for colonial resources, see Constantine; for policy change in response to labor protest, see Cooper, "Introduction" and chapter 3.

historians call "internal migration," where millions sought employment or other economic opportunities in places far from home.[19] Most Chinese residents in Hong Kong came from the neighboring Guangdong Province. Other regional groups included Hakka, Fujianese (known locally as the Hoklo), and provincials from Jiangxi, Hunan, Zhejiang, Jiangsu, and Shandong. Opportunities and desires took them to Hong Kong, just as others went to different Chinese cities. Like many contemporaries, such as those in Shanghai where the sojourner's mentality has received the most documentation, these internal migrants never viewed life in their new place of employment as permanent.[20] However far they went, they planned to eventually return to their birthplace— if not in life, then in death with their ashes (if the distance was too great) or their bodies shipped home.[21] Despite British rule since 1843, the sojourners' mentality in Hong Kong strengthened again and again, because Chinese needed no passports or travel documents to enter and leave until the midtwentieth century.

Unlike other modern Chinese cities, Chinese labor experiences in Hong Kong were shaped by colonial rule and developed major differences. Living under alien rule did not simply reinforce the sense of sojourning for working Chinese; official practices in this annexed Chinese territory sharpened their awareness of alienation. An observation by Sir Alexander Grantham, governor of Hong Kong during the critical decade after the war and after Chinese labor activism took dramatic turns under his watch, best captured the "otherness" of working Chinese in Hong Kong in this statement: "The majority of Chinese in the Colony also had little loyalty to Hong Kong. Like the Europeans, they came to Hong Kong to work until they retire home to China, just as the

---

19. See Ge Jianxiong (et al.), vol. I. Although Ge et al. did not use the phrase "internal migration," their analysis made it clear that migration throughout China's vast territory over centuries had far surpassed migration overseas. In his study of overseas Chinese, Philip Kuhn observed that Chinese emigration was "a subset of a vaster scene of human movement of which the major part was internal migration." See Kuhn, 4.

20. Wakeman and Yeh; Goodman (1995). It is certainly wrong, however, to mistake better documentation as reflection of the strongest sojourner mentality, "more than any other place in China." See Paulés, citation from 146.

21. Sinn (2007); Henriot, 76–79.

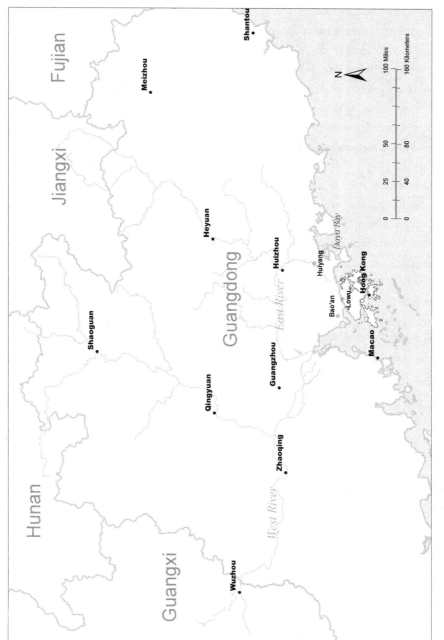

Map I. Hong Kong in South China. By Tu Lan.

Europeans returned home to Europe."[22] Here the phrase "little loyalty" was key. It marked "the majority of Chinese" as an untrustworthy Other, as opposed to the Europeans and a small number of Chinese elite who collaborated with the British state and viewed colonial Hong Kong as their home.[23] Grantham's statement did more than reveal a broadly shared official view; it registered a reality of antagonism created through official and private practices in colonial Hong Kong. In an extensively researched study on court practice and policing, historian Christopher Munn has documented accumulative "repressive legislations" in early Hong Kong, which had generated incrementally "a general criminalization of the Chinese community … in the official assumption."[24]

In workplaces where private companies reigned, racial discrimination against Chinese stimulated consciousness of class antagonism. As sociologist Chan Wai Kwan has documented in his study on class formation in Hong Kong, prejudicial treatment at workplaces where white seamen on the same job received much better accommodations and higher wages was the root cause of the Seamen's Strike in 1922. In shared grievances with the seamen—particularly in reaction to repressive actions by the colonial state in closing down the Seamen's Union—other working Chinese rallied for a sympathy strike that soon involved nearly all trades in Hong Kong.[25] Labor activism faced harsh repression in the wake of the 1925–1926 General Strike-Boycott. Not only did the colonial state introduce the Illegal Strikes and Lockouts Ordinance in 1927 to severely circumscribe collective labor action, print media controlled by business elites helped drum up a Red Scare that generated a culture denouncing social protest.[26] But the impending national crisis of foreign invasion again turned working Chinese to look toward their homeland. Through civic activism, they revived long-held traditions of supporting China, just as they had done in earlier national crises.

---

22. Grantham (1965/2012), 112.

23. For Chinese business-professional elites as the only social group to acquire a Hong Kong identity, see Carroll, esp. chapters 3 and 4. For their cooptation into the colonial establishment, see T. C. Cheng.

24. Munn, 12.

25. Chan Wai Kwan, chapter 5, and 194–95.

26. Chan Lau Kit-ching (2000).

The dramatic turn of official intervention in industrial relations introduced a new dynamic into the relationship between the colonial state and working Chinese. When Hong Kong joined eleven other colonies to answer London's call for reform and established a Labour Office in 1938, the colonial state halted its antagonistic approach to Chinese labor, revoked the antilabor laws, and stepped into industrial disputes as a mediator. Politically, direct state intervention in labor affairs also began to alter the existing approach of indirect rule in the Crown Colony. For nearly a century, the British colonial state had relied on Chinese business-professional elites to manage the Chinese community in Hong Kong.[27] Establishing the Labour Office, later upgraded to Labour Department, meant that the function of Chinese elites would be significantly reduced (if not totally eliminated) in dealing with the largest segment of the Chinese population. That function shifted in part to a Labour Advisory Board, which had been set up in the wake of the 1925–1926 General Strike-Boycott but was rarely functional (chapters 1 and 4).

Socially, state intervention in labor affairs opened a new "contact zone" where the colonial state and Chinese labor came into direct interaction.[28] The policy from London, of course, had to be implemented through layers of colonial establishment to reach the ground. As the imperial center continued the practice of having the "men on the spot" take charge, reformist intervention depended on local practice and particularly on the human agency of colonial officials. British labour officers visited and inspected factories and workshops

27. See three pioneering studies by sociologist Henry Lethbridge on the function of Chinese business elite in three key organizations for British indirect rule in Hong Kong, "A Chinese Association in Hong Kong: The Tung Wah," "The Evolution of a Chinese Voluntary Association in Hong Kong: The Po Leung Kuk," and "The District Watch Committee: The Chinese Executive Council of Hong Kong?" in Lethbridge (1978), 31–51, 52–70, 71–103. All appeared in the *Journal of the Royal Asiatic Society Hong Kong Branch* before they appeared in his collected volume. Also see Sinn (1989/2003); Carroll.

28. Literary scholar Mary Louise Pratt used the phrase "contact zone" for her analysis on political-literary discourse and knowledge production in the former Inca Empire under Spanish rule. Although her emphasis was on cultural interactions in that particular social space, I use the phrase more literally to mean a social space under Hong Kong's colonial situation. See Pratt (1991). Also see Pratt (1992), "Introduction."

regularly, met workers and labor activists, and encouraged them to unionize. They sat at negotiation tables to recommend constructive solutions for business owners and Chinese workers when industrial disputes broke out. In addition to influencing affairs on the shop floor, colonial officials in Hong Kong's institutional hierarchy from the governor to the labour commissioners held critical power to make major decisions on the spot and shape colony-specific policies in London. Being earnest civil servants of the Crown did not guarantee identical interpretations of all official policies or agreement on approaches to Chinese labor. In any case, once the imperial center made the pivotal move toward interventionism, colonial states began to wield direct and decisive power in labor affairs.

Thus, the dual nature of Hong Kong as a Chinese society under British rule renders it inadequate to confine this study to only the "inner side" of Chinese labor—their traditional bonds, in particular—as other local studies do. Whereas issues of nationalism and colonialism could be secondary to labor in other locales or at other times on the mainland, they became outstanding themes interwoven with the rise and fall of Chinese labor activism in Hong Kong. This was not just the case for the 1920s, as existing studies demonstrate. It became more so as war, revolution, and colonial intervention came to be entangled with the resurgence of Chinese labor activism from the 1930s onward. The themes of nationalism and colonialism were pushed to the forefront through the unfolding course of history as Hong Kong's fate took dramatic turns. From a colony occupied and managed by the British for nearly a century without major challenges to a Japanese-occupied territory, within weeks Hong Kong became fully integrated as a zone of Chinese guerrilla resistance in the China theater. At the end of the war, British forces restored the colonial state in Hong Kong, which was expected to continue the prewar imperial initiative of intervention to reform colonial industrial relations. Where would this reformist initiative lead?

In many parts of the British Empire, the long-term consequence of the imperial interventionist turn was negligible in economy but distinctive politically. Instead of making colonial labor more productive for the empire, as London had hoped, colonial labor was emboldened by the legal right to unionize and merged their struggle for better social-economic treatment with their struggle for national independence. This phenomenon was well analyzed by scholars of African, Caribbean, and Middle Eastern histories and labor activism.[29] Despite the intensity of the labor movement in Egypt and Palestine, the Middle East nonetheless does not make a comparable case for understanding the British imperial initiative in reforming colonial labor affairs. With the exception of Cyprus, nearly all Middle Eastern territories were either British mandate or protectorate during the time concerned.[30] It was not the imperial center in London but the indigenous governments or authorities—however firmly Britain might have controlled them—that decided and practiced labor policies in this region. Hong Kong's experiences with the imperial initiative to reform colonial labor relations may be better understood in comparison to those in British Africa or British West Indies. Not only did Britain hold important colonies in both regions, but labor protests there, especially, created so great a pressure that directly forced London to make a historic change of labor policy in the 1930s.

Admittedly, each colony in those regions had its own peculiarities in socioeconomic-demographic structure that shaped its political climate, a topic I avoid elaborating so as to not get too far afield. But two outstanding features are worth highlighting in the political experiences of British West Indies and Africa for comparing with Hong Kong: labor activism converged with the national struggle for independence in nearly all the British colonies, and the postcolonial governments there took the British model. Gradually enlarged local participation in political process had been part of the decolonization process in both West Indies and Africa still under British rule. Nonetheless, there was a notable difference between the two regions, however important the contribution of labor movement was to the rise of self-government. In the West Indies, labor leaders in their anticolonial struggle eventually assumed national leadership in the decolonization process. One of the celebrated cases was Alexander Bustamante (1884–1977), a well-known labor leader in Jamaica who was imprisoned by the British for his anticolonial activism. Busta-

---

29. For British Africa, see Gutkind, Cohen, and Copans, esp. the article by Stichter on trade unions in Kenya; and Cooper. For British West Indies, see Post, Sewell. For Middle East, see Beinin and Lockman (1987) and Lockman (1996). These two works on the Middle East working class, however, take British policy and practice as a context without further discussion or analysis.

30. A useful overview of British official approaches to the Middle East can be found in Darwin (2009), esp. chapter 10. More recently, Harrison offered a comprehensive survey of British imperialism in the Middle East.

mante eventually became the first prime minister of Jamaica when the country finally achieved independence. This pathway from labor activism to political activism for independence was not limited to Jamaica—it was common in the Caribbean region. It made one labor activist note that "the labor movement played a major role" in these colonies' "social revolution" toward self-government. When universal suffrage became effective in Jamaica and Trinidad, as well as other smaller territories in British West Indies, "trade union leaders were voted into political office, and self-government found expression in and through the trade union movement."[31]

The phenomenon of labor leader–turned–political leader in the British West Indies did not happen in British Africa. National leadership of anticolonial movement there emerged from the educated elite. Ghana, the first African country to win national independence from colonial rule, was a case in point. Known before independence as the Gold Coast, it was a British colony with the best developed and most prosperous economy in Africa. Organized labor among miners and railway workers became a distinctive feature there in the 1930s. From the late 1930s to the late 1940s, recurrent strikes forced London to admit that "immediate constitutional advance is necessary."[32] By then, new political leadership from the modern intelligentsia had overshadowed the tribal chiefs and their once indispensable role in Britain's indirect rule. Kwame Nkrumah (1909–1972), who returned in 1947 after extensive education and experiences abroad in the United States and Britain, became a leader in the colony's first political party, the United Gold Coast Convention, before he organized another, the Convention People's Party. The British noted that Nkrumah was able to "catch the public imagination," with his influence "spreading not only into the countryside but also into the trade unions."[33] As Britain prepared its retreat from the Gold Coast, argues historian Frederick Cooper, keeping it on the British side was London's central concern. In the British view, by his political moderation Nkrumah proved to be a better choice than the more radical communists, who were gaining considerable influence

---

31. Daniel, citation from 163, 169, 171.

32. Cabinet Paper CP (49) 199, October 8, 1949, cited in Cooper, 259, 550 n.99.

33. Cooper, 257, citing official minutes on May 10, 1949, from CO 537/4638.

among the population as the country moved irreversibly toward independence.[34]

Caribbean and African experience of labor activism and anticolonial political struggle aiding one another surely found a loud echo in the history of labor activism in Hong Kong. Yet the aspiration of organized labor in Hong Kong stopped short of demanding the end of colonial rule by the mid-twentieth century, and labor did not play a critical role when Hong Kong finally shed its colonial status in 1997. In an essay published that year, British historian John Darwin recognized that Hong Kong appeared to be a unique case in the history of British decolonization. Unlike other former British colonies, Hong Kong did not have an "*indigenous* nationalism" rallying its residents to create a new country and become "a chip off the old British block in its political institutions and values." To explain Hong Kong's colonial longevity, Darwin suggested considering it an outcome of Chinese–British diplomatic accommodation. He likened Hong Kong after World War II to the treaty ports in China formed on the basis of international agreement. China after 1949, in his view, tried to not end British rule in Hong Kong despite its capability of doing so. Under this mutual accommodation, he concluded, Hong Kong "was decolonised in substance, if not juridically, in the early 1950s at the same time as most of the remaining colonial territories in East and South East Asia."[35]

As much as I agree with Darwin that Hong Kong's colonial status was embedded in the international relations between China and Britain, I find his point of Hong Kong's decolonization "in substance" in the early 1950s problematic. This is a view by an imperial historian, thinking through the "official mind" and framing the colonial rule in Hong Kong more in what British diplomatic and colonial officials thought from the center, but not so much in what the colonial state did on the ground. It would be more convincing had Darwin critically considered the momentary and long-term consequences of retaining and exercising foreign control and dominance juridically to an indigenous majority population. To say that the Chinese and British governments accommodated one another to allow British control of Hong Kong did not make that fact of foreign rule disappear. Whether British governance of

---

34. Cooper, 202, 432–34.
35. Darwin (1997), citation from 16, 30; emphasis original.

Hong Kong retained or rejected the colonial "substance" must be measured not only by how the officials in London thought but more by what the colonial state and its supporting establishment did to the majority of Chinese in Hong Kong.

When it began to attend the labor question in the 1930s, did the colonial state in Hong Kong have decolonizing British rule in mind? Over time, did that reformist intervention in this British colony intensify Chinese labor's nationalism (as it did in British West Indies and Africa) or attenuate it? From the point of departure in the late 1930s, the answer to the first question was a clear "no," and the answer to the second was far beyond a foreseeable horizon. What were known to all then were a manifested sentiment of attachment by working Chinese to their homeland and an imperial will to redeem the pitfalls in colonial governance. As this study chronicles the practice of Hong Kong colonial state in London-initiated reform of industrial relations and its interactions with mobilized working Chinese, it presents an evaluation of Hong Kong's status "in substance" from the ground.

Throughout the book, I most often use the phrases "working Chinese" or "laboring Chinese" but not so often "working class" to refer to the collective body of Chinese skilled workers and unskilled laborers. It is a relatively loose term but describes more accurately the reality of the objective being of the working class in Hong Kong. As a "class in itself," it recruited from all kinds of labor sources—from farmers in the New Territories to migrants from South China and further north.[36] For this study of labor activism, I find Charles Tilly's definition of the European proletariat—"people who work for wages, using means of production over whose disposition they have little or no control"—to be useful in describing the overwhelming majority of Chinese workers and laborers in Hong Kong.[37] My inclusion of street hawkers in work-

---

36. For an example of farmers who joined the industrial workforce, see Wu Weichi, 12–19. Wu was born into a farmer's family, became orphaned at age twelve, and survived by serving neighbors as a cowherd. In his late teens, he found a job at a seamen's lodge before working on ocean liners. When war ended, Wu was one of the leading activists who formed the Preparatory Committee in September 1945 to revive the Hong Kong Seamen's Union. Yuan Sheng, "海員工人的燈塔: 介紹香港海員工會" (The beacon for seamen: Hong Kong Seamen's Union), in *Gongren wenhuashe* (ed.), 18–20.

37. Tilly, citation from 1.

ing Chinese—following Hong Kong's first labour officer—may have gone slightly beyond Tilly's definition. Although not industrial workers, these people possessed virtually nothing, and their "way of life" in industrializing Hong Kong was comparable to, if not worse than, that of manual laborers. They became "disposed" to act together with industrial workers when civic activism appealed to their sense of being.[38] Although the labor activism discussed herein centered on actions of industrial workers, readers will find that their collective actions took varied forms and involved Chinese who lived and worked in close proximity to industrial labor.

In six chapters, this book chronicles the rise and fall of Chinese labor activism in Hong Kong from the 1930s to the 1950s, which took place in the context of wars, revolution, colonial reform, restoration, and intervention. Chapter 1 describes the first British effort to understand labor conditions in Hong Kong and the revival of labor activism amid Chinese civic activism aiding China's resistance before the Pacific War. Chapter 2 turns to wartime experiences and highlights the importance of armed resistance as a further development of prewar civic activism and a training ground for future labor activists. Chapter 3 discusses the tension between British reoccupation of Hong Kong and the prevailing global consensus against colonialism in the first half of the 1940s. It also underscores the delicate position of Chinese resistance forces in Hong Kong between high-level political bargains and ground-level colonial restoration. Chapter 4 focuses on the postwar labor movement from 1946 to 1948. It examines the changing leadership and structure of labor unions, the relationship between the colonial state and Chinese workers, and the deviation of Hong Kong's restored colonial state from London's reform agenda. Chapter 5 describes the labor-related efforts in lawmaking by the colonial state, its confrontation with mobilized Chinese labor in Hong Kong, and the approach to labor activism in Hong Kong by the new Central Government in Beijing. Chapter 6 discusses the adjustments by organized labor on the left and right sides in a changed political climate in Hong

---

38. These terms in quotation marks are taken from political scientist Ira Katznelson, who suggests considering class as a concept in "four connected layers of theory and history: those of structure, ways of life, dispositions, and collective action." The first two explain the objective conditions shaping a class, or "class in itself," the third, its cultural expression, and the last becomes closest to "class for itself." See Katznelson, 3–41.

Kong and in Asia, which in part had the unintended consequence of the bloody 1956 riots.

The great upheavals of wars, foreign invasion, and revolution that reshaped many parts of the world at the time, particularly in Asia, were lived experiences of the working Chinese in Hong Kong during the two decades examined here. If past labor strikes had made Hong Kong a city with rich tradition of labor activism, the rise of civic activism among Chinese residents and the advent of reformist state intervention by the British presented a favorable climate for renewing that outstanding tradition. The existing, "internal (or traditional)" forms of social grouping, be it secret societies, sworn sisterhoods, or regional/dialect associations, had the potential to either strengthen or weaken labor unity. External forces, such as direct intervention of the colonial state or Chinese partisan leadership, could also enhance or undercut Chinese labor activism in Hong Kong. None of these forces, internal or external, caused an identical consequence in labor movement. What imperial intervention in reforming colonial labor affairs might produce, after all, was anyone's guess when it all began in this sleepy colony at the far eastern frontier of the British Empire. The particular course that labor activism took here is the story of the following pages.

I

Departures

Belying its quiescent appearance, Hong Kong in the 1930s had arrived at a threshold of dramatic changes. A new wave of vigorous industrial expansion had begun to restructure the once limited industries serving trade and urban needs locally, reshape the urban landscape, and transform the city's demographical composition. Already by 1931, the sixth decennial census of Hong Kong noted that the number of people employed in manufacturing had surpassed those engaged in trade, commerce, insurance, and banking.[1] A new industrial area emerged in the northeastern part of Hong Kong Island, known as Shaukeiwan. Across Victoria Harbour to the north, more factories and workshops were being erected on the Kowloon Peninsula. Leading this industrial expansion were mostly Chinese-owned light industries producing for distant markets. Quantitatively they were more numerous but were often small in size. European firms continued to dominate the economy.

Hong Kong embraced the industrial age at an extraordinary time in the city, in China, and in Asia. In September 1931, the first gunshots of World War II were fired in Asia when Japan's Kwantung Army attacked garrisons in northeast China and soon occupied all of Manchuria. Hong Kong immediately felt the repercussions of Japan's aggression as creeping invasion developed into total war in 1937. Chinese industrialists along the coast relocated factories westward to the hinterland and southward to the British colony. Chinese political dissidents, condemning their government's policy of appeasement, set up bases in Hong Kong. Young Chinese arrived in Hong Kong from the mainland, either fleeing political suppression of national salvation activism or moving through Hong Kong to join the guerrilla resistance in North China.

---

1. Hong Kong Government, "Report on the Census of the Colony of Hong Kong, 1931," 101–2, 152.

Map 2. Hong Kong and Kowloon. Coastlines based on Army Map Service (U.S.), "Hong Kong and New Territory," 1945.

Working Chinese in Hong Kong held mass rallies to protest the Japanese invasion of their homeland, raised funds to support China's defense, and boycotted Japanese goods and Japan-related jobs.

The mounting sense of crisis among the Chinese population, however, did not affect everyone in Hong Kong. Through much of the 1930s, as it had been for most of the previous century, this city in South China was a divided world between its small, complacent European expatriate community and its restless majority. The divide was measured by race, of course, and by wealth and power. The towering, 1,800-foot Taiping Mountain, called Victoria Peak by the Europeans, physically embodied the vertical order of this great divide for nearly a century under British rule. The famous Peak—a mountaintop area where, during South China's sultry summers, temperatures are at least five degrees cooler than in the lowlands—had been reserved, by law, for Europeans only. Below the Peak, the Mid-Levels held mansions and houses built by rich Chinese, Europeans, and Eurasians, as well as European missionary establishments. The bottom section, the Taipingshan area, was crowded with migrants from South China whose residences, shops, restaurants, theaters, sing-song clubs, and brothels made up Hong Kong's lower town.

The colonial state was still small then, and government deskwork could be tedious in its formality. Most of the time, the colonial state was indifferent to this Chinese society and preferred to leave the messy business of managing the "natives" to the collaborating Chinese business-professional elite. Yet by the late 1930s, colonial Hong Kong had to put aside its aloofness and take action. It did so not by choice but in response to an empire-wide crisis that alarmed London. Urged by the imperial center, Hong Kong departed from tradition and made new attempts to manage Chinese labor affairs.

Interventionist Turn from London

Far away from Hong Kong, repeated disturbances and protests had been rocking other parts of the British Empire since the early 1930s. Particularly in British Africa and the Caribbean, the empire's need for food and industrial materials turned former agriculturalists, who once lived self-sufficient, self-contained village lives, into wage earners in copper mines and on sugar plantations. As Great Britain continued the traditional, laissez-faire approach to colonial governance, big companies dominated economies in these overseas "possessions," extracted maximum profit, and ignored the very basic needs of local labor.[2] When the Great Depression shook the world, the combined forces of drastic price drop, social change wrought by industrialized production, and ossified colonial management of the "natives" created a new, volcanic climate of politicization.

Willing acceptance of unbearable employment conditions came to an end during the interwar years. Although the small middle class in the British Caribbean began to initiate a nationalist movement in the 1920s, anticolonial protest by the working population took center stage there and in Africa in the following decade. In 1934, labor protests and strikes erupted in sugar estates on Trinidad, followed by those in Northern Rhodesian copper mines and the sugar industry on St. Kitts and British Guiana the next year. In 1935, a sudden outbreak of strikes among African miners in the African copper belt brought to the surface decades of suffering from below-subsistence-level wages, poor employment conditions, assault and abuse by Europeans, and police brutality.[3] In 1937, widespread disturbances broke out in the wake of strikes in oil fields and sugar estates on Trinidad and Barbados and spread to British Guiana and Jamaica. In 1939, labor strikes surged in Mombasa, on the docks of Dar es Salaam, and on railways. Some of the protests had union involvement. Personal networks, dance societies, religious organizations, and mass meetings provided organizational links for these collective actions.[4] Protesters focused on the incredibly low and dehumanizing wages. In a petition to the governor of Jamaica in 1938, protesters' anger was palpable in these words: "We are the Sons of Slaves ... We are still economic slaves, burdened in paying rent to

---

2. In a study of the entwined relationship of race, labor, and colonial rule in British Jamaica, historian Thomas C. Holt presents an informative analysis of the ways powerful international companies transformed the Jamaican economy while creating a wage structure, with seasonal workers receiving less than subsistence wages as the major labor force, that ensured the greatest benefit to business owners. See Holt, esp. chapter 10.

3. Parpart, esp. chapter 3, and 57–61; also see Henderson.

4. For West Indies strikes and disturbances, see Daniel; Holt, "Epilogue," esp. 384–86; Sewell, chapter 2, esp. 13–22. For labor protests in Africa, see Cooper, 58.

Landlords who are sucking out our vitalities."[5] These protests were different from previous disturbances led by the middle class. Through broad participation, the working class demanded changes in governance in response to economic crisis.[6] When protests showed no sign of letting up, work stoppage in colonies providing important foodstuffs and other strategic matériel, such as oil, threatened to cut off supplies to Britain when it was facing the looming war of Axis aggression.

The worldwide labor protests forced London to seriously reconsider and revise its traditional laissez-faire approach toward local societies across the empire. In a semi-official capacity, Lord Malcolm Hailey started his famous tour of Africa in the mid-1930s to identify problems on the continent. His investigation produced the massive *African Survey* and led him to recommend changes to indirect rule.[7] The Labour Party became more insistent on the need for reform in colonial labor affairs and for state intervention. Its members in the House of Commons demanded that the Colonial Office take responsibility for education, health, and housing in the colonies. Their view, nonetheless, was framed in imperial trusteeship and did not endorse rising demands for self-government among colonized peoples.

Labour opposition pressure compelled an otherwise reluctant Colonial Office to establish the position of labour advisor to oversee colonial labor problems, which became the first step toward reformist intervention from the imperial center.[8] In 1938 the secretary of state for the colonies, Malcolm

---

5. Cited in Hart, 15. Hart was a trade union activist and secretary of the Trade Union Advisory Council in 1939, president of the Jamaica Government Railway Employees Union in 1942–1948, vice president of the Trade Union Congress of Jamaica 1949–1953, and secretary of the Caribbean Labour Congress 1946–1953.

6. Sewell, 20.

7. One of Lord Hailey's eloquent presentions was at Chatham House in December 1938, in which Hailey argued the need "in securing early association of educated Africans with our administrative institutions." See Hailey. For a penetrating assessment of Lord Hailey as a propagandist for British rule, see Louis, passim; also see Cell, chapters 15–16; Wolton, 38.

8. Malmsten; Constantine, chapters 8 and 9, explores internal disagreement between the Colonial Office and the Treasury over where to allocate financial resources, hence the reluctance of the Colonial Office to aggressively expand colonial development.

MacDonald, admitted that the "primary cause underlying the unrest is the very low standard of economic and social conditions among the colonial communities," and proposed a Royal Commission for the West Indies to investigate the situation.[9] Sent at the end of 1938, the Royal Commission to the West Indies produced a report that enabled the Colonial Office to successfully promote the Colonial Development and Welfare Act of 1940. In making its case to Parliament, the Colonial Office defined its "primary aim" as being "to protect and advance the interests of the inhabitants of the Colonies" with a "first emphasis" on "the improvement of the economic position of the Colonies."[10] Malcolm MacDonald, a critical force behind the act, defended this extraordinary reformist intervention and denied that it was a "bribe or reward for the colonies' support in this supreme crisis." He argued that the act "breaks new ground" and "establishes the duty of taxpayers in this country to contribute directly and for its own sake towards the development in the widest sense of the word of the colonial peoples for whose good government the taxpayers of this country are ultimately responsible."[11] Superseding a similar act passed in 1929, the new act conceptualized an imperial responsibility for Britain's overseas possessions and allocated more funds for welfare programs in the colonies.[12]

Although the official debate focused on whether Britain should assume more financial burden for the colonies, eventually reaching a favorable consensus, the primary problem causing the move was a changed colonial labor policy. Well before the act was passed and became law, the Colonial Office had made a quiet, but radical shift in colonial affairs by issuing the Colonial Office Circular Dispatch in 1937. In it, the secretary of state for the colonies, W. Ormsby-Gore, urged "the larger and more important Dependencies" to make establishing Labour Departments their "ultimate aim." His tone remained conditional, though, as he acknowledged the objections of some colonies to assuming direct responsibility for colonial labor. As if conceding to their ob-

---

9. Memorandum by the Secretary of State, June 1938, CO 318/433/1/71168, cited in Cooper, 68; "Cabinet meeting conclusion, 15 June 1938," CAB 28 (38), 12–13, 17; "Cabinet Meetings, 29th July 1938," CAB 36 (38), 20.

10. Colonial Office, *Statement of Policy on Colonial Development and Welfare Presented by the Secretary of State for the Colonies to Parliament by the Command of His Majesty*, citations from 4, 6.

11. House of Commons Debate, May 21, 1940, House of Commons, 5:361, col. 42, col. 45.

12. J. M. Lee (1967), citation from 13.

jections, the secretary said he had "no desire to insist on the application of a uniform system to varying conditions."[13] Nonetheless, in 1937 eleven colonies responded positively to the circular and set up labour offices, including the British Solomon Islands Protectorate, Ceylon, the Federated Malay States, Johore, Kedah, Kelantan, Kenya, Malta, Sarawak, the Straits Settlements, and Uganda. Hong Kong followed in their footsteps the next year. By 1941, thirty-three labour offices with a total staff of 150 were in operation across the British Empire.[14] By setting up labour offices throughout the empire and designing labor laws, the imperial center departed from the established laissez-faire approach to take up a new path of social engineering.

As one of the colonies that first responded to London's interventionist initiative, Hong Kong moved to recognize the changed reality on the ground. By 1938, Hong Kong was well along in its transition from trading port to budding industrial center. The official census of 1931 recorded that 13 percent of the population of 850,000 were employed in manufacturing, although the actual number was far greater because outworkers without formal contracts also worked in existing industries. Contemporary sources estimated at least 800 factories operated in 1930 and 1,000 during 1938–1940, about a quarter of the total in Kowloon.[15] At the time, Shanghai was China's leading industrial center. But Hong Kong was catching up as war loomed and eventually engulfed the mainland. In 1938, Hong Kong witnessed yet another influx of new investment by mainland industrialists. More than twenty new factories from Shanghai alone, each employing more than 200 workers, could be counted in the colony shortly after war broke out.[16]

---

13. Colonial Office, *Labour Supervision in the Colonial Empire, 1937–1943*, 1; for Ormsby-Gore's 1937 circular, see Colonial Office, *The Colonial Empire in 1937–1938*, "Appendix II," 78–79.

14. Colonial Office, *Labour Supervision in the Colonial Empire*, 4.

15. Ngo, 122, 126; these figures are based on a Chinese source, which gives the lowest figure. Ngo also cites official records registering 1,523 factories in 1927 and 1,142 in 1940, and an unofficial directory in English enumerating 3,000 factories and workshops in 1927 and 7,500 in 1940. Another Chinese source estimates 2,000 factories existing in 1940. See also "香港華資工業史" (Chinese-owned Industry in Hong Kong), in Chen Datong and Chen Wenyuan (eds.), n.p. At the time, Shanghai had the highest concentration of mainland industrial establishments. Butters cites 22,376 factories and workshops with about 600,000 workers in Shanghai in 1937.

16. *GDGM* 44:239.

Labor Conditions in Hong Kong

Well before the empire-wide labor revolt in the 1930s, economic grievances
and reactions to racism and imperialism had motivated Chinese workers in
Hong Kong to strike and protest. Labor organization had begun to emerge
among skilled workers, particularly carpenters in the shipping industry and
mechanics across the colony, around the turn of the century.[17] Collective labor
actions took a militant turn in the 1920s when three waves of strikes ushered
in the era of industrial conflicts. In 1920, 6,000 mechanics held a nineteen-
day strike that ended victoriously with a pay raise. In 1922, a strike led by the
Seamen's Union lasted for more than a month, culminating in a general strike
by more than 120,000 industrial workers, domestic servants, and even office
staff. Three years later, the sixteen-month-long General Boycott-Strike, protesting the killing of Chinese demonstrators in Shanghai and Guangzhou
(Canton) by British police, paralyzed the colony. Nearly all Chinese workers
and laborers, 200,000 in total, left Hong Kong and returned to their homes
in Guangdong province.[18] At that time, the colonial state was not ready to
consider permanent solutions to labor problems. After the General Strike-
Boycott, a Labour Subdepartment was created ad hoc under the Secretariat for
Chinese Affairs, but it disbanded less than two years later.[19]

Thus, appointing a labour officer to the Secretariat for Chinese Affairs in
1938 became a major official step toward assuming direct responsibility over

---

17. Existing studies provide two different dates for the beginning of industrial
workers' activism. Ming Chan, who studied the Hong Kong labor movement as a part
of labor activism in greater Guangdong, emphasizes the importance of trade and
nonagricultural employment that gave rise to an industrial working class in the Canton Delta. He views the formation of the Chinese Mechanics Union in 1909 as a
marker of industrial worker organization in Hong Kong. See Ming Chan (1975), part
III. Chau Yick, a journalist who authored a detailed narrative of collective labor actions in Hong Kong, puts the date earlier, citing the "Shipbuilding Craft Workshop"
formed in 1896 as the earliest industrial labor organization in Hong Kong. See Zhou
Yi (Chau Yick) (2009), 19–20.

18. For the mechanics' strike in 1920, the Seamen's Strike of 1922, and the General Strike-Boycott, see Zhou Yi (2009), 22–51, 62–82; Ming Chan (1975), 268–
356; also see Carroll, chapter 6, on the Chinese business elites' role in brokering the
final compromise between organized labor and the colonial state.

19. Butters, 126.

labor affairs. The appointee, Henry R. Butters (1898–1985), had been in Hong Kong for sixteen years, since his arrival in 1922 as a Far Eastern cadet and graduate of Glasgow University. He served as a district officer, as an assistant to the secretary for Chinese affairs, and then as chief assistant to the secretary. In these posts, Butters was in frequent contact with local Chinese.[20] By the time of his appointment as the colony's first labour officer, he was second assistant colonial secretary. He served as labour officer for only a year before being promoted to the position of financial secretary.[21]

As the first labour officer in the colony, Butters faced the challenge of sizing up the labor conditions in Hong Kong without basic data. For nearly a century, the colonial state had shown no interest in the lives of working Chinese except during local epidemics that threatened the well-being of the European community. Taking up London's recommendation for local surveys, Butters went in person to larger and small industrial sites, including four mines. Unusually for a colonial official of his times, he even took to the streets to interview coolies, hawkers, laborers, and workers. The end result was a seventy-page document, "Report on Labour and Labour Conditions in Hong Kong," divided into twelve chapters. It is framed by a general introduction about the population and industrial development, and concludes with a summary and recommendations. The body of the report is made up of chapters under the headings of "China," "Societies in Hong Kong," "History of Social Legislation in Hong Kong," "Legislative Interferences with Freedom of Contract, and Emergency Legislation," "Factories and Workshops," "Wages and Cost of Living," "Housing," "Accidents, Medical Treatment and Compensation," "Education," and "Cases" of the twenty working Chinese

---

20. For example, see various reports on Butters's deliberations on court cases as a magistrate in Kowloon and Victoria: "Scene at Kowloon: European Charged with Riotous Conduct," *SCMP*, October 9, 1930, 8, a report on Butters's deliberation at the Kowloon Magistracy concerning a fine of HK$10 against a drunken European, who refused to pay a rickshaw fare to a Chinese puller and assaulted him with the help of an Indian Police Sargeant; "Assault Charge: Watchman Sentenced at Kowloon Court," *SCMP*, March 31, 1933, 9, a report on Butters's deliberation concerning sentencing a Chinese man, who slapped a Chinese woman in a dispute over money, to two months in prison.

21. Miners. Also see Colonial Office, *The Dominions Office and Colonial Office List*, 1939, 665.

whom Butters selected "at random" to interview on the streets of Hong Kong and Kowloon.

Emerging from this first official record is a panoramic view on ground-level conditions of working Chinese, whose lives and work were framed by Hong Kong's close connection with the mainland and by the laws in the colony. Recognizing Hong Kong as "geographically a part of China" and its society as predominantly Chinese (who made up 97.7 percent of Hong Kong's civilian population), Butters first noted the Chinese sojourning mentality. Most of them "regard themselves as only temporary resident [*sic*] in Hong Kong" and preferred to include the phrase "sojourning Hong Kong (*Kiu Kong*, or *qiao-Gang*)" in the names of their associations.[22] The strong roots that linked the majority of Hong Kong's Chinese to places back home were confirmed in Butters's "random" interviews. Of the twenty people he interviewed, all but one farmer in the New Territories were born outside of Hong Kong. They came to Hong Kong because surviving on the land became impossible or the factories that had employed them in Guangzhou closed down. At least half of them were still sending monthly remittances to folks at home on the mainland.[23]

In the 1930s, this great mass of sojourning Chinese worked in an economy making the rapid expansion to light industry. Cotton spinning and weaving, knitting, electric torch and metalware production added to established shipbuilding and ship repair facilities, sugar refineries, and public electric power, gas, and telephone utilities. The colonial state kept data on registered factories and workshops employing twenty people or more. These alone had increased more than 100 percent in just five years, from 403 to 829 between 1933 and 1938. By early 1939, the total was 857, of which 303 were located in Hong Kong and 554 in Kowloon.[24] A different estimate cited more than 2,000 Chinese-owned factories a year later, possibly including unregistered operations.[25] However difficult it was to ascertain accurate numbers of factories, available data enabled Butters to select twenty-six as the "more important in-

---

22. Butters, 107, 108.

23. Butters, 157–63.

24. Butters, 109, 132.

25. "Xianggang Huashang gongyeshi" [A history of Chinese-owned industry in Hong Kong], in Chen and Chen (eds.), a three-page chapter in this unpaginated book.

Table I. Workforce employed in Hong Kong's major industries, 1939

Number employed	Industries
10,400+	Shipyards
6,000+	Knitting, spinning and weaving
5,000–6,000	Rubber factories (including outworkers)
4,000–5,000	Printing factories
3,000–4,000	Metal wares
2,000–3,000	Electric torches, tobacco
1,000–2,000	Confectionery, biscuits, preserves, public utilities, shirts—garments
500–1,000	Batteries, electroplating, furniture, engineering, glass and mirrors, cork and felt hats, joss sticks, newspapers, green peas processing, stockings, sugar refineries
Below 500	Brewery, cement, oil refineries

Source: Butters, 133.

dustries." Table I, based on Butters's statistics, conveys a rough sense of the spread and concentration of the industrial labor force in different production lines.

The 54,690 workers in registered industrial establishments, including 28,470 men and 26,220 women, were only a fraction of the workforce in Hong Kong. Numerous Chinese worked in the many unregistered industrial establishments. There were also "casual workers," such as coolies, stevedores, and street hawkers. Butters found it impossible to estimate the population of these workers. Instead, he illustrated the possible number of casual workers by taking the case of hawkers, whose registered number was 11,722 in 1938, though "there were probably five unlicensed hawkers for every licensed one" in 1938, making the total around 70,000.[26] There was no way to determine how many did outwork beyond factory premises, like stitching rubber shoes at home for 1.5–2 cents a pair or working as weight-carrying coolies for confectionery workshops.[27] The actual number of working Chinese was certainly several times larger than the workers in registered factories and workshops. The abundant supply of labor, where job changes from casual work to factory

26. Butters, 134.

27. See Butters, 158, and chapter 2, where I discussed a young coolie's life at a candy workshop.

work were easy and frequent, gave an ambiguous shape to the industrial work-force. The power of the contractor system remained stronger in some established trades, such as shipyards, where job demands fluctuated, or in the rick-shaw business; but it was negligible in newly emerging light industries, because these required only low-skilled workers.

With a progressive view and a personal mission to improve labor conditions, Butters singled out substandard industrial establishments as his "chief concern" with Hong Kong's rapidly expanding industries. It was a particular problem in recent, Chinese-owned light manufacturing facilities. Many such operations set up in tenement houses designed for residential use. This practice enabled investors to start quickly and save costs, but it endangered workers' health and safety. Hong Kong alone had 409 "converted tenement floors" in industrial operations. Conditions in Kowloon were worse, with 1,041 converted tenement floors serving industrial needs, particularly in the Shamshuipo, Taikoktsui, and Mongkok areas.[28] In one extreme case, an overcrowded tailoring workshop that Butters inspected, "one male worker engaged in ironing was found suspended from the roof on a beam with his ironing board suspended in front of him." He found that many Chinese newspapers in Hong Kong Island's downtown area, called Central, were printed under "bad" conditions in "old property" not designed for industrial use.[29]

Preferring to leave economic matters to business management, the colonial state thus far had passed no legislation regulating working conditions, such as factory overcrowding, working hours, and minimum wage. Long working hours became the norm for Hong Kong's working Chinese. In factories, the standard workday was nine hours, from 7 am to noon and then 1 to 5 pm. But many workers, especially in knitting, rubber shoe, and electric torch factories, chose to work overtime (until 8 pm) so they could "eke out the low wages" on piece rate. Among the different pay scales of piece workers and laborers, permanent workers, tramway and bus drivers, and transport coolies, wages could vary from as high as HK$150 a month for a printing artisan to as low as 0.20–0.60 cents a day (i.e., HK$6 to HK$18 a month) for a female worker at a rubber shoe factory or spinning and weaving establishment. In the city's large shipping and ship repair industry, where the majority of employees were

---

28. Butters, 136.
29. Butters, 135.

men, wages for electricians, sail makers, turners, and pattern makers ranged from HK$1 to HK$1.40 a day, and the best coppersmiths and fitters could make HK$1.55 to HK$1.60 a day. Wages for sawyers, boilermakers, and blacksmiths were lower, between HK$0.70 to HK$1.20 a day. This average monthly wage of HK$30–42 was comparable to that for tramway workers and bus drivers, ranging from HK$30–39 for conductors to HK$36–$45 for tramway drivers. Skilled male workers took these jobs. Their earnings would allow them to support a wife and a child. For male coolies in government departments, wages of HK$13 a month meant they could afford the low rent for bunk beds in shared lodging rooms. Supporting a family was out of the question. Such self-sustaining rates of pay, however, were comparable to the wages of most female workers, the predominant labor force in the light industries, such as rubber shoe and metalware manufacturing. They earned between HK$6 and HK$15 a month, without overtime.[30]

How did wages of HK$30–45 for a male worker with a small family and HK$6–18 for a female worker fare in the city? Butters compared these wages to the cost of housing, food, and clothing for the Chinese workers and considered it far from adequate. Although the diet for working Chinese consisted mainly of rice and vegetable and some salted fish, the lower the income, the greater proportion of it had to be spent on food. Even for relatively better-off workers whose monthly wage exceeded HK$30, income was insufficient to pay housing expenses. Rent was so high that working Chinese were not living in apartments, let alone houses, but in tiny portions of subdivided flats. The "most common type" of Chinese residence, Butters noted, was the "old-fashioned … tenement house" of three to four stories, with a footprint of forty-four feet deep by fourteen feet in width. It was not uncommon to find twenty-five adults crammed in a subdivided flat on every floor. A couple would typically rent a "cubicle," which cost HK$5–6 a month. A single worker usually chose a "bed space" or a "cockloft." Some had to share a tiny space to reduce the rent to HK$2.50. Even by squeezing their living space to the extreme, Butters noted, the cost still exceeded a reasonable proportion of their income, as "in the case of a family frequently more than a third of the income is expended on housing."[31] Women workers, who received very low wages in

30. Butters, 142–48.
31. Butters, 139, 149.

Fig. 1. Taikoo Dockyard, 1938. Courtesy of Information Services Department, Hong Kong Government (SAR).

Fig. 2. Queens Road, 1930s. Courtesy of Information Services Department, Hong Kong Government (SAR).

light industries, could only assume a supplementary role in the family economy or subsisted alone.

This image of working Chinese toiling long hours for low wages and surviving in less than rudimentary housing accommodations found its reflection in the interviews Butters conducted. Of the ten women and ten men, eight were employed in various kinds of industrial establishments, such as the European-owned Taikoo Dockyard, the Chinese-owned Lo Kwok Po weaving factory, the large Fung Keong Rubber Factory, and the Chung Hwa (Zhonghua) Book Company. Wages for these workers varied greatly. The highest paid was a forty-eight-year-old plater at the Taikoo Dockyard who received HK$45 a month. He could afford to rent a whole floor, subdivide it into cubicles and bed spaces, keep one for his family (a wife and two daughters), and sublet the rest for extra income. The lowest paid was a thirty-one-year-old woman working in a battery factory who earned only HK$0.21 a day for working eleven hours (i.e., HK$6.3 a month). She lived in a cubicle with her often-unemployed seaman husband and three young children. Other workers had earnings ranging from HK$0.20–0.30 a day for a seventeen-year-old weaver, to HK$0.35 a day for an electric torch factory worker, and HK$1.26 a day for a woman worker with five years of experience in a rubber factory. Their living spaces did not differ greatly. For the unmarried, it was usually a bed space, sometimes shared with a mother or a sworn sister. For the married, a cubicle accommodated the whole family.

The remaining twelve interviewees were mostly what Butters called "casual workers," including one outworker, four coolies (two men and two women), a rickshaw puller, a worker at a rice oil shop, a female domestic servant, and a hawker. In addition, Butters interviewed a salesman at the Wing On Department Store, a fisherman who lived aboard a ship owned by his master, who also lived aboard with his family, and a woman farmer cultivating in the New Territories. In comparison to the casual laborers in urban Hong Kong, the Wing On salesman lived in luxury, earning HK$30 a month with free food and living quarters and wearing Western clothing. The highest earning among the casual workers was a tea-carrying coolie who could receive HK$5–6 a week when jobs were available. When the tea ships were gone, he made only HK$0.30 a day carrying vegetables. The sixty-year-old woman hawker earned only HK$0.15 a day. She had to squeeze her little income by eating less and often missed payment of HK$1 monthly rent for her bed space. Usually, the young and able-bodied fared better with relatively higher earnings. One sixty-year-old coolie was once a painter at the Taikoo Dockyard but quit his job because he found it "too hard and dangerous."

The rationale that an abundant labor supply drove wages down only partially explained the poor labor conditions. In devoting a significant portion of his report to the role of regulation and the state, Butters subtly blamed official negligence for these fundamental labor problems. Under the headings of "Societies in Hong Kong," "History of Social Legislation in Hong Kong," and "Legislative Interference with Freedom of Contract, and Emergency Legislation," he laid bare the history of a colonial state that was most active in suppressing any suspected Chinese association. Although it occasionally made paternalistic gestures of investigation, it never followed through on any of the recommendations for social improvement.

Vigilant in guarding this annexed territory within the sociogeographical China, from its earliest days the British colony had designed a legal framework that never legally guaranteed its Chinese population the right to unionize. Butters singled out three major ordinances—the Societies Ordinance of 1845 (which underwent revisions in 1887 and 1911), the Emergency Regulations Ordinance of 1922, and the Illegal Strikes and Lockouts Ordinance of 1927—as the chief instruments that outlawed any Chinese association undesirable for the colony. Under the Societies Ordinance, all societies must register or obtain exemption from the registrar-general, whose title was later changed to the secretary for China affairs. This anti-Triad ordinance thus established a critical mechanism for state surveillance. In the 1920s, the state evoked the Emergency Regulations to outlaw the Chinese Seamen's Union when its strike developed into "the first general strike" in Hong Kong, and then outlawed the General Labour Union of Hong Kong after the General Strike-Boycott of 1925–1926. A further preemptive measure against Chinese labor unions was the promulgation of an Illegal Strikes and Lockouts Ordinance of 1927, which became "the first enactment … dealing expressly with trade unions." In the wake of vigorous enforcement of these laws, as Butters noted with sarcasm, "the surviving Hong Kong unions became little more than friendly societies concerned more with the provision of funeral expenses for the dead than the improvement of the conditions for the living."[32] Of the

---

32. Butters, 116, 117.

300 associations in Hong Kong at the time of Butters Report, there were eighty-four labor unions with a total membership of 44,000. Craft or merchant guilds, clan associations, regional associations, seamen's lodge houses, and social clubs were among the rest known to the police.[33]

In contrast to these severe and forbidding laws, other measures that Butters discussed demonstrated the extent of official attentions to labor-related problems. Of the three branches of the governing body in the colony, the Urban Council was the more active and more attentive to social problems but the least powerful in comparison to the Executive Council and Legislative Council. The Urban Council, still named the Sanitary Board in 1919, made by-laws to prevent overcrowding in factories. Another notable official measure was the appointment of a commission in 1921 to investigate the problem of child labor. The commission was alarmed by "the employment of children outside factories in casual and unskilled work, and especially in burden bearing, in particular the carrying of bricks and other materials to the Peak and Hill Districts." It viewed working hours among Chinese as "universally excessive," and "wages were paid almost entirely by piece rates." It blamed the use of child labor for "depress[ing] the general standard of remuneration of adults."[34]

Thanks to the recommendation by this commission on child labor, the colony passed the Industrial Employment of Children Ordinance in 1922, which forbade employment of children in dangerous trades, set an age limit of ten as the minimum in all factories, limited working hours to nine each day, and mandated one rest day for every seven days for a child laborer. Under a provision of this ordinance, the secretary for Chinese affairs was appointed protector of juvenile labour, while two new positions of inspectors, one male and one female, were established. This ordinance opened the way to other amendments and at least two labor-related new ordinances, the Factories Ordinance of 1927 and the Factories and Workshops Ordinance of 1932. These laws institutionalized the labour protector and the inspectors and placed women in the category of protected workers, along with children and young persons, to prevent them from being employed in dangerous trades and on night shifts.

---

33. Butters, 119.
34. Butters, 120.

These were well-meaning gestures of paternalism. Yet the real problem in Hong Kong was not in the evolving legal regulations regarding industrial labor, but in the absence of official will to enforce most of the regulations. For example, the earliest by-laws written by the Urban Council to regulate over-crowding in industrial establishments "never received the confirmation of the Legislative Council." Only the office of secretary for Chinese affairs was designated for dealing with industrial disputes through conciliation or arbitration. After the General Strike-Boycott, a Labour Advisory Board was appointed, with the secretary for Chinese affairs chairing the board and his chief assistant serving as its secretary. The board included officials and management representatives only from major European companies.[35] It had no Chinese or labor representation, and it rarely convened after its formation.

Without the right to unionize, without the legal protection of a minimum wage and maximum working hours, and without even a symbolic voice in any official body dealing with labor problems, it was not a surprise that Chinese workers in Hong Kong had to struggle with "housing congestion, poverty, disease, unemployment," as Butters described their situation.[36] Although he attributed these problems to "excessive immigration" from the mainland, his narrative of the laws and their enforcement put the colonial state in the spotlight. He urged the state to assume more active roles in protecting labor rights and eliminating some of the repressive laws that he viewed as obsolete. Quite extraordinary for a member of the establishment but in line with London's determination to pursue a "forward policy," Butters argued that the colony should not treat the working Chinese as merely "workers segregated in cantonments" but "must regard them as citizens in the first instance."[37]

In the last section of "Summary and Recommendations," Butters outlined what the state could and should do in two regards. One would be legislation on working hours and conditions as well as collective action. He considered the most recent Factories and Workshops Ordinance of 1937 too limited because it dealt with only "a fraction of the total working population" in registered factories and workshops, therefore he recommended expansion of its

---

35. Butters, 125.
36. Butters, 110.
37. Butters, 164.

coverage to include workers and laborers in the service industry, fishing, and agriculture. The second recommended action was an institutional reform by repositioning the labour office within the administrative structure. Butters pointed out the absurdity in the existing "diarchy" arrangement, where the Urban Council and the protector of labour dealt with labor issues. "The Urban Council is empowered to make by-laws defining the duties and powers of the Protector while the Protector is empowered generally to overrule the by-laws and recommendations of the Urban Council."[38] In its stead, he suggested four new ordinances: a Trade Union Ordinance, a Workmen's Compensation Ordinance, a Trade Boards Ordinance replacing the existing Minimum Wage Ordinance, and an Ordinance replacing the existing, narrowly defined Factories and Workshops Ordinance. Together, he believed, these new laws should help develop "genuine" trade unions following the British model without encouraging labor toward "participation in Chinese politics and their own aggrandizement."[39] With these changes, the colony might be safe from losing ground to the mainland.

Butters's recommendation for legislation protecting workers' collective action is worth noting because, had it materialized, the change would have been a major departure from past colonial practices and a positive reform in Hong Kong's legal framework. Ordinances concerning collective action, such as the Emergency Regulations Ordinance and the Societies Ordinance, were "mostly obsolete" in Butters's view. They needed to be reviewed and possibly replaced by a trade union bill to "bring the position of trade unions in Hong Kong into alignment with that of English trade unions."[40]

As London looked for ways of dealing with the labor question throughout the empire, Butters's vision of organized labor in Hong Kong added substance to the imperial center's vision of reform through direct state intervention. He wrote and presented a trade union bill for consideration by the Legislative Council but, just as they did before, the colony's lawmakers looked the other way and never put it on their agenda. Not until a decade later, in March 1948, did a Trade Unions and Trade Disputes Bill go through first reading before

---

38. Butters, 165.
39. Butters, 166–68.
40. Butters, 165–66.

the council. By then it had become quite different from the one envisioned by Butters.

Civic Activism for National Salvation

While the core colonial establishment dragged its feet, labor in Hong Kong did not wait. Surprisingly, "[m]any unions which for ten years have appeared to be extinct have been recently revived" after a decade of sleepy quietude. They were, noted Butters, "moved by patriotism to renewed activity chiefly of a political and nationalist character."[41] For some, it was the renewal of their well-established tradition of political engagement with mainland affairs; for others, it became a rediscovery of this tradition under the national crisis of foreign invasion.

In 1938, China had been at war with Japan for a full year, the culmination of Japan's incremental and intensifying aggression since the late 1920s. In the election of 1928, Japan's hawkish opposition party Seiyukai defeated the incumbent Minseito party, winning on an assertive foreign policy platform of using military means to protect Japanese interest in China.[42] After the election, Tokyo sent marines to China twice to deter the Chinese army's northward march to unify the warlord-divided country. Further north, the Japanese Imperial Army openly advocated protecting Japan's interests in China by excluding other powers by means of war when necessary. In 1931, Japan's Kwantung Army took the daring step of engineering the Manchurian Incident and succeeded in occupying China's northeastern provinces, therefore beginning what Japanese historians call the Fifteen-year War with China.

The Chinese in Hong Kong reacted with alarm and anger to Japan's first major military move against China. In 1928, the massacre of 2,000 Chinese civilians by Japanese marines in China's northern city Jinan, known as the Jinan Tragedy, became a major news event in Hong Kong. Merchant elite-controlled newspapers, particularly the *Wah Kiu Yat Po* (*Overseas Chinese Daily*) and *Kung Sheung Daily News* (*Industrial and Commercial Daily News*), gave the event

---

41. Butters, 118.
42. Jansen, 364–72.

extensive, multipage coverage for weeks, with reports on the event and its repercussions in China and around the world. In defiance of colonial law, some
unusually brave Chinese made public speeches on the streets calling for mass
protests against the Japanese invasion. They were quickly arrested, fined, and
sentenced to hard labor. These flashes of protest became preludes to the sustained movement that followed. In September 1931, just a few days after the
outbreak of the Manchurian Incident, tens of thousands of Chinese in Hong
Kong responded with huge rallies in assembly halls and on the streets. Their
peaceful protests turned violent during a mass rally in downtown Wanchai
when a few Japanese publicly sneered at Chinese indignation. Infuriated, some
Chinese vented their anger with their fists. They attacked Japanese shops and
Japanese pedestrians as proxies for the invaders of their homeland. Protesting
Chinese clashed with police called in to stop the disorder. As protests spread
throughout the colony, the colonial government found the police inadequate
to quell the disturbance and mobilized regular troops to maintain order.[43] At
the end, the governor's official report cited fourteen deaths, six Japanese and
eight Chinese. But information circulated within the colonial administration
indicated that British troops had killed at least 400 Chinese demonstrators.
At least 200 rioters were arrested and thrown into jail. Alexander Grantham,
the second police magistrate in Hong Kong, considered anti-Japanese feeling
among Hong Kong Chinese to be "very bitter indeed."[44]

Bitterness against Japanese invaders alone was not enough to cause widespread and sustained protest. Authorities identified the Ko Shing Theatre, one
of the three most popular stages for Cantonese opera performance, as a venue
that facilitated anti-Japanese activities and suspended its performances for
three days in early October. The Barbers Guild (Huanran gongshe, Ct. Wun
Yin Kung She), accused of "actively fomenting disaffection in connection with
the anti-Japanese movement," was outlawed.[45] Actual organizational nodes,

---

43. Lu Yan (2014a).

44. "The Governor's Statement in Legislative Council on 1st October 1931, in
regard to the Anti-Japanese Agitation," CO 129/536/6, citation from 62; Grantham
(1968) transcript, 8.

45. "Order by the Governor in Council, No. 617, 1st October 1931," in CO
129/536/6, 51; "Order by the Governor in Council, No. 686, 9th October 1931," in
CO 129/536/6, 52; William Peel to J. H. Thomas, 16 October 1931, in CO
129/536/6, 23–25.

however, were too many for the alien regime to identify. In fact, each neighborhood had an informal network with links that stretched beyond to mobilize fellow Chinese. Their indignation and sorrow had been so widely shared that a boycott of one store would always draw a large crowd of pedestrians, whose cheers and shouts merged with the smashing and burning of Japanese goods. Liang Keping, a second-grader at the time of the Manchurian Incident, remembered seeing such boycotts in her neighborhood in Wanchai, where many dock workers lived. Under the severe press censorship, newspapers often had "empty windows" where articles with anti-Japanese content had been deleted. But the Chinese found ways to circumvent the official censorship on anti-Japanese expression. They sent out New Year's greeting cards featuring mainland heroes who fought the invading Japanese army. In choosing these images to replace the usual greetings of "wishing you a great fortune," the Chinese in Hong Kong made a loud statement that they supported their homeland in her resistance.[46]

While working Chinese spearheaded the broad participatory civic movement in Hong Kong, powerful, officially recognized merchant elites in the colony also joined in, demonstrating their desire to aid in China's defense. In a sense, this effort continued their engagement in Chinese politics in the first quarter of the twentieth century.[47] The Eurasian millionaire Robert Ho Tung took actions on several fronts in support of the mainland's war effort. Quietly aiding the rise of a strong Chinese state since the turn of the century, he sent his son to England and France for military training. Once his education was completed, the young man returned to serve in the Chinese army. Ho Tung himself was the principal donor when the Chinese government announced a "donation for airplane campaign" on the occasion of Chiang Kai-shek's birthday in 1935. Others in the business community contributed as well, though they observed the legal boundary delineated by the colonial state and discretely collected donations for the campaign. When the war broke out in 1937, the business community, led by the Chinese Chamber of Commerce and the Tung Wah Hospital, immediately started a new campaign for war relief. The chamber became the semi-official organ that transmitted donated funds to the

---

46. Liang, 1–2.

47. For Hong Kong business elites' involvement in Chinese politics in 1900–1925, see Chung.

Chinese government.[48] By then, national salvation had become a colony-wide movement in Hong Kong, involving rich and poor, famous elites and humble hodgepodge. Actors and actresses in the film industry, singsong girls in entertainment, factory workers, street hawkers, shop clerks, teachers, and students from primary to middle school and from the government-sponsored University of Hong Kong all formed their own associations for national salvation.[49] One observer counted 150 such organizations that suddenly appeared in the colony in the second half of 1937.[50]

This upsurge of national salvation activism in the late 1930s also reflected Hong Kong's new political environment as colonial repression moderated under historical exigency. In 1936, British Asia began to feel a direct threat when Japan signed the Anti-Comintern Pact with Germany. With imminent war looming in Europe, Britain wished to avoid a two-front fight by provoking Japan. Sympathetic to Chinese resistance while adopting a calculated "benevolent neutrality," Britain gave China "moral support and limited material aid, but at the same time avoided confrontation with Japan."[51] It allowed more than thirty official and semi-official establishments from China to operate in Hong Kong, which channeled funds and purchased strategic matériel from abroad.[52] As a result, around 60–70 percent of overseas war matériel passed through Hong Kong and reached the mainland via railways connecting the colony to southern China.[53] Hong Kong's colonial state also slightly relaxed its anti-Communist stance when the Guomindang formed a united front with the Communists to fight their common enemy. One gesture British Hong Kong made was to allow the Communist-led Eighth Route Army to set up a liaison office in Hong Kong after the Communist request was made through the British embassy in China's war capital of Chongqing.

All these, however, were tacit acquiescences, achieved with a handshake and a nod of the head, and therefore easily retractable. Under close police surveil-

---

48. Zhou Jiarong, Zhong Baoxia, and Huang Wenjiang, 53–55.

49. English-language sources on the National Salvation Movement in Hong Kong are rare, although Chinese memoirs abound. For a recent study on student participation in aiding China during the 1930s, see Cunich, 387–93.

50. *GDGM*, 44:211.

51. Bradford A. Lee, 18; Chan Lau Kit-ching (1990), chapter 6.

52. CO 129/580/3, 36–38.

53. Snow (2003), 29.

lance, compounded by an anti-Communist culture that the merchant elite helped mold through their control of the press,[54] the Eighth Route Army Liaison Office failed to elicit strong support from local people. It closed down in early 1939 after a police raid, having operated only for one year. Guomindang operations in the colony remained illegal, but it enjoyed much greater tolerance from the colonial state. That tolerance had its limit, however, defined by constant pressure from the Japanese Consulate General who demanded that the British put down anti-Japanese activities in the colony. Governor Geoffrey Northcote, himself sympathetic to the Chinese resistance, made a gentle but firm point to the governor of Guangdong, Wu Tiecheng, when Wu visited Hong Kong to mobilize support for China's war efforts. If "prominent Chinese" like Wu and T. V. Soong did not "actively repress" anti-Japanese activities here, reminded Governor Northcote, "the situation might become very difficult and might easily re-act upon" the many Chinese agencies that operated legitimately in Hong Kong.[55]

Three Avenues of Partisan Leadership

With or without Japanese pressure to suppress "anti-Japanese activities" in Hong Kong, the British had good reason to worry about social activism among the Chinese, for the devastating experiences of the General Strike-Boycott remained fresh in their memory. But the colonial state had chosen poor targets when it anxiously watched high-flyers like Wu Tiecheng or the Eighth Route Army Liaison Office parachuting into Hong Kong. Times had changed. "Instigators" of popular activism were no longer the same as the labor movement activists of the 1920s. While the working Chinese had already begun their own anti-Japanese protests in the early 1930s, three forces—the Guomindang, leading political dissidents, and the Communists—provided potential leadership to Hong Kong's masses. Their approaches varied, and their appeal to local Chinese came to be defined by how they responded to the crisis of foreign invasion as well as by the strength of different organizational links to the grassroots.

---

54. Chan Lau Kit-ching (2000).

55. "Memorandum of Interview," from Northcote to Colonial Office, September 25, 1939, CO 129/580/3, 43.

The Guomindang, one of the two most important parties that organized the General Strike-Boycott of 1925–1926, no longer sought to change the political order, but defended the order it had established. As the party controlling the government on the mainland, the Guomindang's relationship with Britain had changed from one of confrontation to one of conciliation and cooperation. Their collaboration was most successful in hunting down Communists in Hong Kong and deporting them to the mainland to be tried and executed.[56] Nonetheless, British Hong Kong prohibited any political party from operating in the colony, and the Guomindang never gained legal footing there. In fact, its general branch in Hong Kong and Macau, which once operated two branches with 139 cells and claimed 20,000 members in both colonies, had been forced to disband in 1926, partly because of resolute deportations by the colonial state.[57]

Operating illegally in British Hong Kong, the Guomindang's connection with grassroots society, particularly with labor in the colony, had not changed significantly from its early days. In the years when Sun Yat-sen secretly organized the China Revival Society (predecessor to the Guomindang), Hong Kong's Triads helped him muster grassroots support. Reliance on secret societies to reach local labor appeared to continue after the Guomindang became the party in power. Its lack of direct contact with working people and its established connections with the Triads can be illustrated by the Guomindang's most celebrated "labor leader," Ma Chaojun.

Despite his credentials as a worker from Hong Kong, Ma Chaojun (1886–1977) spent only two years in the colony as a teenage apprentice in the Ma Hong Ji Machine Workshop (Ma Hongji jiqichang) near the Kowloon Dockyard. He left for San Francisco to work in Chinese-owned shops and later in a machine factory. There he joined the Zhigong Tang, a leading Triad organization among overseas Chinese. At age eighteen, Ma met Sun Yat-sen, who turned the youngster into an enthusiastic anti-Qing revolutionary and sent him to Japan as party liaison. Since then, Ma had become a professional poli-

---

56. Chan Lau Kit-ching (2000), 1044–61.

57. Chen Xihao, 150–51. Chen Xihao was head of the Training Department of the (Guomindang) Party Affairs Steering Committee in the Special Municipality of Shanghai (上海特別市黨務指導委員會訓練部部長). The book derives from his lecture notes for a training course in the department.

tician in the party, an effective mediator between party factions, and an energetic organizer in rallying the party's right wing to fight Communism.[58] Even though Ma held leading positions in the Guomindang, directed the party's labor affairs, and participated in the International Trade Union Council as China's labor representative, he had minimal experience as a worker and no experience as a labor leader in Hong Kong or anywhere in China.[59]

The Guomindang's two branches in Hong Kong and one in Macau nevertheless continued to hold influence over the labor unions of seamen, butchers, dockhands, and workers in other industrial and service lines, including the tramway, bus, electricity, water, gas, Kowloon-Canton Railway, hotels, restaurants, and domestic service. Even though the colonial policy of repression eliminated Guomindang party organization there after 1926, Hong Kong's Chinese workers viewed the party leading the Chinese government as their legitimate leader. When the Guomindang General Branch of Hong Kong reformed again in July 1939, it quickly claimed 5,000 members in the colony.[60]

As formal Guomindang organization phased out in Hong Kong during much of the 1930s, an opposing force set up base there and became a rallying point for concerned Chinese who were frustrated by government appeasement toward the Japanese invasion. It began to emerge in the 1920s when internal conflict rattled the Guomindang. Eventually in the 1933 mutiny in Fujian, dissident politicians and generals made a daring attempt to organize a political alternative to Nanjing's power. Rejecting Chiang Kai-shek's leadership and policies, these dissidents founded a Chinese republic, announced socialeconomic reform programs, including "land to the tillers," and called for national resistance to Japan's invasion.[61] Their rebellion lasted two months before the government army quashed it. Fleeing to Hong Kong, these political

---

58. Guo Tingyi, Wang Yujun, and Liu Fenghan, 5–8. This oral history interview makes it clear that mediating factional struggles after Sun Yat-sen's death was Ma's central task, and his role in labor leadership was more symbolic than real.

59. Guo Tingyi et al., 63, 80–81.

60. "駐港澳總支部黨務沿革概要" (An outline of the development of Hong Kong–Macau General Branch), in Zhongguo Guomindang zhongyang weiyuanhui disanzu (ed.), 201–8, citation from 203–5.

61. For extant documents on the domestic and foreign policy of the Chinese Republic (ZhongHua gongheguo) founded in Fujian, see Fujian sheng dang'anguan. Also see Jiang Ping and Luo Kexiang, 107–19; Wu Minggang.

and military leaders—most of them from South China—formed the Chinese National Revolutionary Alliance (CNRA, Zhonghua minzu geming tong-meng) in 1935. Li Jishen (1885–1959), the former governor of Guangdong province, was made its president. Among the CNRA's top leaders were widely popular military leaders Cai Tingkai (1892–1968) and Jiang Guangnai (1888–1967) of the Nineteenth Army, who in 1932 led arduous resistance against the Japanese invasion of Shanghai and were viewed by Chinese in Hong Kong and across the country as national heroes.

Operating from Hong Kong, the CNRA became a major organization for national salvation, connecting activists in south and southwestern China through expansive networks in Guangdong, Guangxi, and Fujian provinces. Its public statement in December 1935 announced eight tasks, five of them aimed at mobilizing the armed forces along with people of all circles in China for a war of resistance.[62] When Mme. Song Qingling (widow of Sun Yat-sen) and other social and political elites formed the National Salvation Association in Shanghai in June 1936, the CNRA sent representatives and formed a South China branch of the National Salvation Association in Hong Kong. Echoing the National Salvation Association agenda, the Hong Kong–based CNRA called for a united front in the war against Japanese invasion. It went a step further than the National Salvation Association by appealing to all parties to join forces and overthrow Chiang Kai-shek's government in Nanjing.[63]

This national salvation and antigovernment agenda made the CNRA and the Communist Party allies, while their members maintained close contact as friends. Individual Communists who lost contact with the party and acted on their own initiative also reached out to this anti-Guomindang force. Between 1934 and 1939, CNRA leaders published a daily newspaper titled *Dazhong Ribao*, with *Public Herald* as its English title.[64] Although its formal organiza-tional reach was limited, regular contact with other dissenting political forces enabled the alliance to function as a transitional base from which future grass-

---

62. Jiang Ping and Luo Kexiang, 122.

63. Jiang Ping and Luo Kexiang, 123.

64. The catalog for the libraries at the University of Hong Kong, which housed a Special Collection of Hong Kong, the paper appears as *Public Herald* for its English title; another source shows its English title as *Public Daily News*. See Kan Lai-bing and Grace H. L. Chu (eds.), 133. I use the title from the university catalog because it keeps copies of the newspaper.

roots activism gathered force.[65] The *Public Herald* in particular provided an important forum that helped concerned Chinese in Hong Kong connect. By publishing their essays and voicing their views in the *Public Herald*, individual activists began to converge in a vigorous movement.

The early 1930s were the years when Communists suffered under devastating, nationwide government repression. Free of direct official Chinese intervention, Hong Kong initially provided a safe haven for the party organization in South China. But the colonial state's anti-Communist policy, the broadly anti-Communist culture in Hong Kong, and the Communists' political immaturity and imprudent tactics caused more casualties to their organization and a failure in generating popular support. Directed by radical leaders, political speeches on street corners in the so-called hit-and-run rallies (*feixing jihui*, literally, flying rallies) only invited police action. Party leadership focused on radical actions driven by Communist theory and ignored strong popular sentiment among the Chinese in Hong Kong against the Japanese invasion. Although Hong Kong's governor firmly believed that Communist instigators were behind mass rallies in 1931, internal Communist Party documents prove the opposite.[66] By 1931, historian Chan Lau Kit-ching notes, Communist Party organization in Hong Kong was "nothing more than an empty shell" after repeated police raids. By the end of 1932, it was "so weakened that there was no need for further intensive police action." By 1934 it had been totally annihilated after repeated police raids, arrests, and betrayals.[67] Destruction of Communist organization in Hong Kong paralleled that in Shanghai, where the Communist Central Committee had been located, and formed part of a broad pattern in the Chinese Communist Party (CCP)'s nationwide setback. When the Red Army was forced out of its base in the Jiangxi Soviet and embarked on the Long March in late 1934, underground Communist organizations throughout urban China and in Hong Kong were completely quashed.[68]

---

65. Fang Shaoyi, 101–9.

66. CO 129/586/3, 78–79.

67. Chan Lau Kit-Ching (1999), chapter 10, describes rapid destruction of the Communist organization under repeated police raids in Hong Kong. Citations from 168, 174, 175.

68. Stranahan, chapter 3, discusses the destruction of the underground organizational network in Shanghai.

Initiatives by individual party members and by party leadership soon revived connections between the Communist center in northwest China and
various locations in the second half of the 1930s. Upon arriving in the northwest at the end of the Long March in late 1935, Communist leadership reviewed and readjusted policy after the devastating defeat. It turned away from
radical approaches to moderation in "White Areas"—that is, Guomindang-
controlled areas and, by extension, areas such as Hong Kong and Macau
controlled by forces friendly to the Guomindang. This self-adjustment coincided with new instructions from Moscow. There, Chinese delegates to the
Comintern drafted "A Public Letter to All Chinese Compatriots for Resisting Japan and National Salvation," calling for a united front, and published it
in the Chinese-language *National Salvation Daily* issued from Paris.[69] The delegation dispatched Lin Yuying (a.k.a. Lin Zhongdan, 1897–1942), a labor activist
and one of the first Communists in China, to reconnect with their comrades
in northwestern China. Disguised as merchant "Zhang Hao," Lin reached
Yan'an in November 1935 via Xinjiang and Mongolia.[70] The directive to form
a united front with all other parties, particularly the Guomindang, became a
new policy proclaimed in a conference resolution of the party's Political Bureau in December 1935.[71] Liu Shaoqi, a pragmatist and veteran labor leader
since the 1920s, was given the task of directing the operation in North China's
White Areas.[72]

---

69. Zhongguo Suweiai zhongyang zhengfu and Zhongguo Gongchandang zhongyang weiyuanhui, "為抗日救國告全體同胞書" (A Letter to All Chinese Compatriots for Resisting Japan and National Salvation), in Zhonggong zhongyang shujichu
(ed.), I:679–82.

70. Li Weihan, "回憶張浩回國時的一點情況" (Recollections on the situation
when Zhang Hao returned to China), in Zhonghua quanguo zonggonghui Zhongguo
gongren yundongshi yanjiushi (ed.), 21; Wang Heshou et al., "忠心為國雖死猶榮"
(Dedicated to the country, glory remains after eternal departure), in Zhonghua quanguo zonggonghui Zhongguo gongren yundongshi yanjiushi (ed.), 3–13, citation from 9.

71. "中共中央關於目前政治形勢與黨的任務決議；一九三五年十二月二十五
日中央政治局通過" (A resolution by the Central Committee of the Chinese Communist Party on current political circumstances and Party's tasks; passed at the Political
Bureau on December 25, 1935), in Zhonggong zhongyang shujichu (ed.), I:734–45.

72. Another major articulator of new policies and tactics in White Areas was Luo
Fu (pen name for Zhang Wentian, 1900–1978), a central leader of the Political Bureau before the party eventually recognized Mao's indisputable leadership and used

Although annihilation of the nationwide party organization left many members in White Areas leaderless, the two-year lacuna opened up ground for a new generation to take a more active role. They were either individual Communists without party connections or local activists who rallied around the cause of national salvation. The Hong Kong Resisting-Japan National Salvation Association (HKNSA; Xianggang kangRi jiuguohui) was probably the earliest national salvation organization with a working-class base led by individual Communists. One major leader, Zhou Nan (1907–1980), came from a poor peasant family in Guangdong and began working after finishing primary school. In 1927, he joined the Communist Party while working in a battery factory in Hong Kong, but he lost organizational connection when his contact was captured in a major police raid in 1930.[73] Surviving on odd jobs, Zhou became an avid reader and studied works by Marx, Lenin, and Ai Siqi, who popularized Marxist thought for Chinese readers. Zhou began to contribute articles for the *Public Herald*. His articles attracted the attention of like-minded youth. In fall 1935, these young men and women formed a study group. By the end of the year, more than 100 had joined the group and decided to form the HKNSA. It remained a voluntary mass organization without contact or instruction from any political party, and its membership continued to grow. These Hong Kong Chinese—estimated at 400 to 500—were mostly workers, plus a smaller percentage of students, teachers, and shop clerks. In September 1936, the HKNSA suffered a fatal blow when police raided its meeting as

---

the title "chairman" for his position. For examples, see Liu Shaoqi, "肅清立三路線的殘餘; 關門主義冒險主義" (Eliminating the remaining influences of exclusiveness and adventurism under [Li] Lisan Line), in Zhonggong zhongyang shujichu (ed.), 1:754–59; this was first published in the Northern Bureau's *Frontline* (火線 Huoxian) on April 10, 1936; Luo Fu, "關於白區工作中的一些問題" (Some problems in our work in the White Areas), October 18, 1936, in Zhonggong zhongyang shujichu (ed.), 2:79–98; Luo Fu, "白區目前黨的中心任務" (The central task in the White Areas for our party), in Zhonggong zhongyang shujichu (ed.), 2:126–44.

73. This was a major incident for the South China Bureau of the CCP; Zhou Nan's contact, Mo Shubao, was arrested and betrayed many of his comrades. See *GDGM*, 19:1–2. The following discussion on HKNSA and its leader Zhou Nan is drawn mainly from a memoir written by He Jinzhou. I have cross-referenced two contemporary sources in the 1930s, Communist internal reports made by Dasheng (alias of Li Fuchun) in early 1931 and "Report on Youth Work in Hong Kong" made in Yanan by Wu Youheng in 1941, to verify key information in He's memoir.

members held a commemoration of the Manchurian Incident. Its major leader, Zhou Nan, was in Shanghai attending the All-China Conference of National Salvation Associations and escaped arrest.[74]

In the wake of the destruction of the radical and inexperienced HKNSA, another secret National Salvation organization appeared in Hong Kong. He Sijing (1896–1968), a sociology professor at Guangzhou's Sun Yat-sen University who joined the party in 1932, fled to Hong Kong after his friends in the CNRA warned him of impending arrest. In May 1936, He participated in the All-China Conference of National Salvation Associations in Shanghai, then returned to Hong Kong to set up its South China branch (Huanan jiuguohui) with friends from the CNRA.[75] In the hands of these politically experienced people, the South China branch adopted a more cautious approach while providing a meeting ground for national salvation activists and for the recruitment of future Communists.

Among the youth who became attracted to the South China branch of the National Salvation Association were those who later joined the Communist Party and assumed important leadership roles in Hong Kong. Wu Youheng (1913–1994), a student activist from Guangzhou, arrived in Hong Kong in spring 1936 in hopes of boarding a ship for Manchuria and joining the armed resistance in the northeast. Instead he connected with the South China branch and remained in Hong Kong. In September, the twenty-three-year-old Wu became a fresh member of the CCP and was appointed almost immediately to head the recently formed City Branch after local party members reconnected with the Central Committee in the north. As representative of the NSA's South China branch, Wu made contact with the remaining members of the recently crushed HKNSA.[76] Before he left for Yan'an in 1940 as Hong Kong's

---

74. The record in the Communist Party's internal report, probably made by Wu Youheng based on his recollection in 1941, indicates that the police raid on the HKNSA meeting took place in 1937. See "Xianggang qingnian gongzuo baogao," in GDGM, vol. 44, esp. 130. In Wu's report, Zhou Nan was cited as Hong Biao (洪標), the name he used during years in Hong Kong as an underground Communist. He Jinzhou's memoir uses 洪飆 for the name. In cross readings of other relevant materials on the events in Hong Kong, He Jinzhou's dates appear to be more accurate.

75. He Sijing, 19; Fang Shaoyi, 100–109; Fang was a student at Sun Yat-sen University in 1933.

76. Most of the information regarding Wu are gleaned from Anonymous, "香港

representative to the CCP's Seventh National Congress, Wu had become a keen observer of mass movements in Hong Kong.[77]

Young, passionate, and patriotic, Zhou Nan and Wu Youheng were among many who transformed from national salvation activists to Communists and linked the two movements. They added fresh blood to a party that was moving from infancy to maturity and from radical inexperience to pragmatic policies, all while maintaining vitality with grassroots support. The emergence of this new generation of leaders demonstrated a sharp difference from the Communist leadership in the 1920s labor movement. They were not outsiders with more book knowledge than local experience, parachuting in from Moscow or major metropolises in China to lead the masses.[78] Even people like Wu, with his early intellectual background, were a new kind of leader in Hong Kong's Communist Party. They came from and continued to keep close touch with the grass roots by working with and within it. That gave the CCP an edge over the Guomindang and the Chinese National Revolutionary Alliance in the colony. The Guomindang needed to go through the Triads to reach the masses, whereas the CNRA remained a coalition of mainland political and military elites. In 1938, as the Chinese government declared war against Japan and adopted a united front with other parties, CNRA leaders returned to the mainland and dissolved the organization in Hong Kong. But the Communists in Hong Kong, with their deep connections to the grassroots, stayed.

Labor Activism and the "Labor Question"

That workers, students, shop clerks, and office staff would join hands to form a secret national salvation association is revealing of a new social reality

---

青年工作報告" (Report on youth work in Hong Kong), and "吳有恆關於香港市委工作給中央的報告" (Report by Wu Youheng to the Central Committee on the works of the City Committee in Hong Kong), both in *GDGM*, 44:127–517, and Wu Youheng, 243, 247.

77. *GDGM*, 44:41. In addition to Wu, there were four more representatives, including three workers and a party secretary of the district branch of Kowloon.

78. See Ming K. Chan (1975) for an analysis on the difference between CCP leaders and Guomindang leaders in labor movement of the 1920s.

in British Hong Kong.[79] The escalating Japanese invasion pushed hundreds of thousands to flee from the Chinese mainland. It made the national crisis a personal one. After the war broke out in 1937, the colony's total population increased from 800,000 in 1931 to 1.8 million in 1938. When greater Guang-zhou fell in October 1938, so many more fled to Hong Kong that as many as 50,000 poor people could not afford shelter and slept on the streets. In fact, over half of them were not recent refugees but local workers who either lost jobs or had wages reduced when factories cut operations.[80] In a saturated labor market, working Chinese were hit hard by the domino effect of rapidly in-creased population, shortages of goods, inflation, and stagnant or decreasing wages. Among those looking for jobs were youth forced out of middle or high school by the advancing enemy. Wu Youheng estimated that a quarter of the colony's workers were young, including many school-aged youths. They strug-gled to survive on a monthly wage of HK$8–10 and worked fifteen to sixteen or even eighteen hours a day.[81] War conditions and refugee status narrowed the gap between students and workers in this extraordinary time. Their personal struggle for survival and their political activism for national salvation became one because the individual and the nation were both in peril.

Leaderless since 1927, workers regrouped with rapid speed in the less re-pressive political climate of late 1930s Hong Kong amid colony-wide civic activism. Among the newly revived labor organizations, the Seamen's Union, which had led the first general strike in Hong Kong but was banned after the

---

79. This issue is ignored by the limited existing scholarship on the National Sal-vation Movement, which tends to emphasize either partisan instigation (Lin Yunhan; Israel) or intellectual/student leadership (Coble).

80. Anonymous, "香港職運工作報告" (Report on labor movement in Hong Kong), GDGM, 44:13; the reporter estimated that about half of the 50,000 were lo-cals. Also see Wu Youheng, "Report by Wu Youheng to the Central Committee on the works of the City Committee of Hong Kong," February 16, 1941, in GDGM, 44:237–517; citation from 239, 363, hereafter cited as Wu report.

81. Anonymous, "Report on youth work in Hong Kong," January 25, 1941, in GDGM, 44:127–236, citation from 206–7. It was most likely authored by Wu Youheng, because some of the information reappeared in the Wu report, and the writing style is similar to that document. He probably drafted individual reports on the labor movement in November 1939 right after arriving in Yan'an, including this report on youth work, before he completed the much longer report on party work by mid-February 1941.

General Strike-Boycott of 1925–1926, once more became the most prominent and active. Former union members who had survived anti-Communist repression quietly played key roles in organizing fellow Chinese seamen into the recreational clubs tolerated by the colonial state. The seamen's Music Society for Leisurely Entertainment (Yuxian yueshe), for instance, was just this kind of labor union in the guise of a recreational society. This society was formed in 1929 by seamen on the ocean liner *Empress of Japan*, with some labor activists-turned-Communists, including Zeng Shoulong and Zhang Dongquan, in the lead. The society organized Chinese seamen to perform Cantonese drama while at sea and helped them in times of sickness and unemployment on shore. In 1937, the seamen made two attempts to register as a union with the colonial government. Their first application was flatly rejected. But the second try, with more than a thousand signatures, succeeded and the society was registered as the Hong Kong Seamen's Union. By then, there were more Communists among seamen. One of them was a college student-turned-seaman Zeng Sheng (1910–1995), who had fled arrest in Guangzhou for national salvation activism, found a job as a bellboy on the *Empress of Japan*, and became part of the union's leadership.[82]

Regrouped Chinese labor in Hong Kong again marched at the forefront to aid China's struggle against the Japanese invasion. Soon after total war broke out, the 3,500 Chinese seamen working on Japanese ships left their jobs. Among those working on the four renowned Empress ocean liners owned by the Canadian Pacific Line—*Empress of Japan*, *Empress of Canada*, *Empress of Russia*, and *Empress of Asia*—845 left the ships, boycotting the shipment of war matériel to Japan. Seamen's activism spread further on shore. In the second half of 1937, approximately seventeen boycotts by seamen and dockhands marshaled support from 8,399 participants.[83] Between November 1937 and February 1938, four strikes with 3,000 participants broke out at Hong Kong dockyards. One nine-day strike occurred at the Hong Kong and Kowloon Wharf and Godown Company when 2,000 dockhands refused to unload Japanese goods and prevented them from coming ashore. At Standard Oil, 500 workers refused to load a shipment for Japan, forcing the company to cancel the contract. Communists played an active role in some of the strikes and boycotts,

---

82. Zhou Yi (2009), 89–92; Zeng Sheng, 59–63.
83. Wu report, 399.

but the workers themselves also initiated anti-Japanese boycotts. At Hong Kong's largest Chinese grain firm, Hongji, 400 dockhands refused to load grain for shipment to Japan. On their own initiative, other dockhands dumped tungsten ore into the sea rather than load it on a ship bound for Japan. Five thousand workers at the Taikoo Dockyard refused to repair Japanese ships and convinced replacement workers hired by the company to boycott as well.[84] Under censorship and the attentive watch of the Japanese consul general in Hong Kong, news of Chinese workers' anti-Japanese strikes and boycotts could not appear in local newspapers. Nevertheless, their activism appeared in internal reports by Communists who participated in or attentively watched these collective actions. Coming to light after several decades and now available to researchers, these reports show a rapid surge of anti-Japanese boycotts by Chinese workers in Hong Kong between 1936 and 1939.

Beyond subversive boycotts and strikes against Japan, working Chinese in Hong Kong contributed to China's resistance through fundraising. The year 1938 saw their most enthusiastic participation, epitomized by an impressive campaign started by hawkers. It started at a small scale at Shamshuipo, an emerging industrial area on the Kowloon Peninsula. In the wake of a colony-wide commemoration of July 7, the day of the Lugou (Marco Polo) Bridge Incident that marked the outbreak of total war, three vegetable hawkers decided to hold a three-day charity sale. Among the poorest of the poor, with only a slim profit margin from the daily sale of perishable produce, the hawkers' heroic decision to put the country's well-being before their own became contagious. Word went out to textile workers in the neighborhood, who immediately followed with their own fundraising. The ingenious textile workers challenged the factory owners to match their donation, and they complied under public pressure. Other hawkers and workers quickly emulated this strategy across the colony. As a result, "every market held charity sales." Factory workers devised a surprising way to move the public. They gathered in groups of several hundred to march through Hong Kong's streets on quiet nights, shouting in unison with a "mountain shaking" voice: "Help our country [*jiu-guo ya*]!" In just three weeks they raised HK$700,000. On the first anniversary of the Shanghai Incident, known among the Chinese in Hong Kong and on

---

84. Anonymous, "Report on labor movement in Hong Kong," *GDGM*, 44:11–40, citation from 16–18; Wu report, 387–90. Also see Zeng Sheng, 83.

the mainland as the August 13 Resistance, hawkers alone raised HK$1,180.[85] Their charity sale continued through the following year and raised a grand total of HK$300,000.[86] An observer described the campaign's crowning moment, when nearly 20,000 people showed up in parade at Shamshuipo to send funds raised that day to the Chinese Chamber of Commerce, which collected funds for transmission to Nanjing:

> All kinds of people from neighborhood areas and factories arrived. Workers held big signs showing the names of their factories or shops and the total sum of their donation. They sang songs of national salvation as they marched. The Guangzhou Boy Scouts who are taking refuge in Hong Kong marched at the forefront. The members of Association of National Martial Arts and other athletic organization joined them and performed along the way. ... It was really the first time that Hong Kong witnessed such a great mass parade.[87]

The hawkers, many of whom were illiterate and had limited social connections, could not have made such a broad impact with patriotic enthusiasm alone. The quiet support from activists in the colony's grassroots national salvation organizations was critical in linking the hawkers' activism with the larger network of Hong Kong society. Youths from a supporting group of the radical HKNSA, now registered with the colonial state as the Society of Extracurricular Activities, helped hawkers spread the news, design charity sale settings, and make posters. They also helped circulate the story of the three hawkers' charity sale and the factory workers' donation challenge through their network in the colony. These educated youth earned the hawkers' "boundless trust." It is interesting to note that the young activists were far more cautious of public attention than were their hawker friends. Some of these young people had become underground Communists. They still remembered the quick demise of the HKNSA just a year earlier. Although they hes-

---

85. "瓜菜贩义卖赈款昨交华商会" (Donation from hawkers of vegetable and fruit sent to the Chamber of Commerce yesterday), *Sing Tao Jih Bao*, August 13, 1938, 10; Wu report, 345–46.

86. "今年'八一三'义卖小贩主张自办" (Hawkers want to manage fundraising themselves this year for "August 13th"), *WKYP*, June 7, 1939.

87. Anonymous, "Xianggang qingnian gongzuo baogao," *GDGM*, 44:213–14.

Table 2. Estimate of unemployment in selected industries, 1939

Industries	Total Workforce	Unemployed
Seamen (ocean liners only)	30,000	16,000
Textile	60,000	5,000
Automobile drivers	6,000	3,000
Printing	7,000	500
Tobacco	5,000	2,000
Shipbuilding and repair	50,000	10,000
Construction	50,000	10,000
Total	208,000	46,500

itated to hold the grand parade, the enthusiastic hawkers prevailed in the end.[88]

Boycotts and fundraising by working Chinese in those years was extraordinary, not just in sheer scale but also in the enormous sacrifices of the participants. Whereas Henry R. Butters noted the imbalance between workers' excessive working hours and generally very low pay, underground Communists attentive to social ills provided corroborating evidence. Boycotting Japanese ships and shipments caused many Chinese seamen to lose their jobs. An internal report by the Hong Kong city branch of the Communist Party estimated that "at least 5,200 seamen lost their jobs due to their anti-Japanese struggle since the war began." The number amounted to about a third of Hong Kong's 16,000 unemployed seamen in November 1939. At 53 percent, the unemployment rate for seamen was the highest among all workers. The report estimated an overall unemployment rate of 22 percent in the seven principal industries, listed in Table 2.[89]

Communist observers provided more details on various practices that kept labor costs low. Employers had an edge in the glutted labor market and continued the general practice of piecework, which maximized their profits. At some factories, employers chose not to lay off workers but kept them waiting on call. Workers could "wait at their factory for a whole day without earning a penny." When there was an order, they "would work for more than twenty hours nonstop." This practice lowered their regular income at a time when

---

88. "Report on youth work in Hong Kong," *GDGM*, 44:214.
89. "Report on labor movement in Hong Kong," *GDGM*, 44:11.

Hong Kong's cost of living had doubled or even tripled.[90] Young workers, who amounted to about a quarter of the employed workforce, made up an even higher proportion of shop clerks, textile workers, and domestic servants. Their unemployment rate was lower than average, but a quarter of them were apprentices receiving lower wages while working on jobs that required skilled workers.[91] This tactic kept costs low for employers, while threatening experienced and middle-aged workers with unemployment or underemployment. In some industries where business remained robust, workers successfully resorted to collective bargaining. One site of labor activism in the late 1930s was the Hong Kong branch of Chung Hwa (Zhonghua) Book Company, officially designated in 1932 as the printer of Chinese currency.

Anticipating war with Japan, Chung Hwa built its Hong Kong branch in 1933 and relocated workers from Shanghai to the new site, offering free lodging and relatively higher pay to permanent workers. Even so, workers found that their pay hardly kept up with the pace of inflation in Hong Kong. Various disputes between the company and the workers occurred throughout 1937. One major conflict took place in September when the company decided to increase production by 20 percent. To that end, it lengthened the night shift from six to nine hours and canceled the usual bonus and two rest days (*shanggong*) per month. Seven hundred workers from Shanghai—both temporary and permanent—went on strike for ten days. They succeeded in forcing the company to agree to an eight-hour shift. In March 1938, another strike erupted after workers' negotiation over unfavorable conditions in the new contract failed. This time, more than a thousand workers joined the strike. Mediation by Labour Officer Henry Butters helped end this two-month-long industrial dispute with favorable conditions for the workers.[92]

In December 1938 came the second wave of industrial conflict at Chung Hwa, triggered by two incidents: two workers were dismissed for fighting at work, and a larger than usual fine was laid on workers for ruining three bank

---

90. "Report on labor movement in Hong Kong," *GDGM*, 44:13.

91. Anonymous, "Report on youth work in Hong Kong," in *GDGM*, 44:207–8.

92. Zhou Xiaoding, "周小鼎關於香港中華書局分廠黨總支工作黨談話紀錄" (Discussion by Zhou Xiaoding on the work by the party general branch in Zhonghua Book Printing Company), January 11 and 13, 1941, *GDGM*, 44:73–125; citation from 101–3; Zhu Yamin, 252–67. Zhu's discussion on the strike in early 1938 was very brief.

notes during the printing process. Attentive to labor activities in the colony, Butters blamed the war-induced dislocation for workers' grievances and viewed the strike as legitimate with economic motivations:

> There had been unrest for several months, the root cause of which was a feeling of insecurity among the workers, many of whom had left their families in Shanghai, and who felt themselves strangers in the Colony, where their future was obscure. Two trivial incidents brought matters to a head. The management declared a lockout—with pay, and dismissed sixty-nine men whom it regarded as ringleaders. When the works were opened the other workers returned and, adopting an equally novel technique, seven hundred in one department commenced a combined sit-down and hunger strike.

Butters offered arbitration, but management rejected it.[93] What he did not mention here is that news of the strike spread throughout the colony, eliciting great sympathy among locals who sent food and supplies to the workers. According to Chinese sources, the strike even attracted the attention of a journalist from the London *Times*. This increased public pressure to force the company back to the negotiation table.[94] Butters, whom the company invited now to arbitrate, defended the legitimacy of the workers' representatives and argued against punishing them as ringleaders. The company agreed to rehire all sixty-nine labor activists, except the two who were fired for quarreling during work. The strike ended in the workers' favor but, as Butters perceptively observed, planted "the seeds of further trouble."[95]

The third and final wave of industrial conflict at Chung Hwa erupted in late 1939, this time initiated by the company after careful preparation. On August 7, simultaneously as the company announced large-scale dismissals, several hundred police descended on four company dormitories at Hung Hom,

---

93. Butters, 119.

94. See Zhu Yamin, 262–63; my search of the *Times* shows no report on Chung Hwa—it was probably too small an event to appear in the paper.

95. Butters, 119; Zhou Xiaoding, *GDGM*, 44:104–9; Zhu Yamin, 260–64. There was a slight difference between the account by Zhou and Zhu, regarding the two fighting workers; Zhu's memoir indicates only one was fired. I took Zhou's account, because his report was made soon after the event and it seems more logical that the company should punish both workers for fighting in the workshop.

Kowloon, Sung Wong Toi, and To Kwa Wan.[96] The company declared that the job of printing Chinese currency was completed and dismissed most workers with a severance package of two months' pay. In addition to the police, Hong Kong's colonial state gave more assistance to the employer. An order from the Secretariat for Chinese Affairs instructed workers from Shanghai—the majority of the 1,200 dismissed workers—to leave Hong Kong by the end of August. The workers viewed this sudden turn of events as retaliation for their successful collective bargaining in the previous year. They refused to accept conditions set forth by the company and demanded their jobs back. As the conflict entered a stalemate, workers survived on donations sent by social groups in Hong Kong, Shanghai, Southeast Asia, France, and the Philippines. The company engaged Du Yuesheng, the Green Gang leader from Shanghai, who had taken refuge in Hong Kong, for mediation. In mid-December, the colonial government arrested thirteen workers for making "insulting speeches to the King." Pressure and intimidation from those in power and those with money, as well as financial difficulties in sustaining the basic needs of 1,200 people, forced workers to accept the layoff conditions brokered by Du Yuesheng. They left in February 1940 with a severance package of six months' pay, thus ending the seven-month industrial conflict, the longest of all collective labor actions before the war reached Hong Kong.[97]

Although the incident at Chung Hwa mostly involved workers from Shanghai, it became a Hong Kong event not just because it took place in the colony and gained wide publicity and sympathy among the locals. It became a Hong Kong affair also because of the direct involvement of the colonial government, which alternately aided workers and supported the company. This seemingly contradictory attitude revealed the divergent approaches taken by different offices and, more accurately, by officers at different levels in the colonial establishment. Butters, who had recently assumed the position of labour officer,

---

96. The company's announcement was also posted in major local newspapers, see "中華書局港廠啟事" (Announcement by the Hong Kong branch of Zhonghua shuju), and "中華書局港廠員工公鑒" (Hong Kong branch of Zhonghua shuju to all employees), *WKYP*, August 8, 1939, 4.

97. Zhou Yi (2009), 111; Zhu Yamin, 264–67. Zhu led a support team when workers' representatives went to negotiate with Du Yuesheng. He vividly recalled how he avoided confrontation with the police by ordering his team to sit down when the police arrived, ready for action.

showed his sympathy to the workers in his report and in his mediation of the disputes at Chung Hwa. Although he only briefly mentioned the event in his report, worker appreciation for his fairness was so apparent that when negotiation results were announced, they shouted, among other things, "Respect Labour Office's arbitration!" Probably because of his demonstrated sympathy, Butters was not engaged to mediate the last conflict at Chung Hwa in 1939. His superior, the secretary for Chinese affairs, stepped in and sided with the employer. That official reversal was in line with the time-honored principles of governance in colonial Hong Kong: anyone who disturbed the "good order" of the colony would have to be punished and banished.

How much the colonial state knew about the internal workings of labor activism at Chung Hwa between 1938 and 1939 is an open question, for there is no British document available on the incident except Butters's report.[98] But official vigilance against labor activism and civic activism for national salvation came out in the open in 1938 when the colonial state enacted the Emergency Regulations Ordinance. In late January, the colonial regime again outlawed the four-month-old Hong Kong Seamen's Union, citing no reason but the Emergency Regulations Ordinance.[99] Its target was well chosen. Seamen in Hong Kong had always been in the vanguard of labor activism, and proved so once again in the anti-Japanese boycotts. There were Communists in the Seamen's Union; their identity might not have been known, but vigorous labor activities suggested effective organization. In the Chung Hwa Book Company, indeed, there were some fresh underground Communists among young labor activists. The twenty-one-year-old Zhu Yamin from Shanghai, for example, had grown indignant about the unfair treatment of workers in the factory. Having learned about the founding of the Hong Kong Printing Workers' Union, Zhu eagerly joined its preparatory committee, mobilized two fellow workers to join the union, and maintained Chung Hwa workers' connection with it. His activism caught the attention of the Communists, who recruited

---

98. Hong Kong in 1934 had already established the Special Branch for the purpose of political surveillance, though nothing about this incident surfaced in any official document. According to one former operator in the Special Branch in Hong Kong, it only became truly vigorous in 1946. See Lo Ah, 5.

99. Zhou Yi (2009), 94.

him into the party in spring 1938.[100] Zhu became one of thirty-five Communists among the 1,800 workers at Chung Hwa and assumed responsibility for the party's organizational work.[101]

The Communists were only one among several political forces in Chung Hwa, all of which tried to exert their influence on workers. The Guomindang had no known member among the workers. Only three workers joined its youth organization, the Youth Corp of Three Principles of the People.[102] The company itself sponsored "native place associations" and encouraged friction among them. These native place associations had no role in the three waves of strikes at Chung Hwa. The most popular organization among workers was the Printing Workers' Union, whose membership increased from 900 to more than 1,100 after the first two waves of successful collective action. The Chung Hwa workers accounted for a third of the membership in Hong Kong Printing Workers' Union and formed a separate branch.[103] The thirty-five Communists, most of whom had become labor activists in Hong Kong before becoming party members, were passionate about "collective actions" but, according to a Communist internal report, not so eager about recruiting party members among fellow workers.[104] Their action as Communists in organizing labor strikes came only after the first wave of collective actions at Chung Hwa. But their passion for "mass work"— that is, their struggle to improve employment conditions for workers—helped bring about a better deal in the last strike.

---

100. Zhu Yamin, I, 258–60. Zhu's original name was Zhu Fu (朱復), the name that appeared in Wu Youheng's internal reports on labor and youth movement in Hong Kong and in the memoir by Zhou Xiaoding, a fellow worker and Communist in Chung Hwa.

101. Various sources give different numbers of workers: 1,400 (Zhu), 1,500 (Butters), and 1,800 (Zhou). I use Zhou's figure because he gave a detailed estimate of each section with specific number of workers, including temporary hires.

102. Zhou Xiaoding, *GDGM*, 44:75–76, 84, 90.

103. Zhou Xiaoding, *GDGM*, 44:101; "唐克邓衍基黄一甦关于香港反汪工友回国服务团的报告" (Report by Tang Ke, Deng Yan, Huang Yisu on the anti-Wang [Jingwei] workers' Return-to-homeland Service Group from Hong Kong), *GDGM*, 44:47–72, citation from 48.

104. Zhou Xiaoding, *GDGM*, 44:97.

They proved to be the most committed and effective leadership for workers among all contending forces.

Across the great divide, local and global crises moved the colonial state and working Chinese in Hong Kong to action. The question of colonial labor, recognized in London as indispensable for the survival of British Empire, became the contact point bringing the two together. In response to London's decision to take on the problem of colonial labor as a state responsibility, British Hong Kong departed from its past ad hoc approach to labor problems and expanded the administrative establishment with an additional labour office. The first labour officer, Henry R. Butters, enforced the metropolitan policy of state intervention in labor affairs on the ground, undertaking an unprecedented survey to obtain first-hand data about labor conditions in Hong Kong, and stepping into industrial conflicts to achieve constructive solutions. He had drafted a trade board bill, which became law after a second reading at the Legislative Council in June 1940.[105] But his draft trade union bill fell into a void. The Legislative Council never put it on its working agenda.[106] As a progressive in the colonial establishment, Butters envisioned the advent of British-style industrial relations in Hong Kong, the betterment of working conditions and living standards for Chinese workers through legally sanctioned collective actions, and an organized labor force without ties to the politics of China. His vision loudly echoed that of the labour opposition in London. It had to wait a decade to be tested on the ground.

On the other side of the divide, working Chinese became mobilized once again as their country faced the new crisis of foreign invasion. Labor unions

---

105. *Hong Kong Government Gazette* 1940 (Supplement), no. 261; *Hong Kong Hansard* 1940, 73–74, 87. The Hansard shows no further reading of the bill, and the published Trade Boards Ordinance indicates that it became law on June 21, 1940, the second day after the bill's second reading. It was extraordinary that the bill was passed with only two readings in the Legislative Council. One may assume, from the records in *Hansard*, that there was little controversy over the bill. Butters had already become the colony's acting financial secretary after one year in the post of labour officer, and the colony, now fully in the shadow of the advancing Japanese invasion, had to focus on its defense.

106. Miners.

sprang back to life and collective actions to address economic grievances revived once they became legal in Hong Kong again. Although the strikes at Chung Hwa Book Company entered British records through the Butters report, it was merely one among many episodes of labor activism. Chinese labor activism went hand in hand with civic activism for national salvation. Unlike the General Strike-Boycott a decade before, the resurgent anti-imperialist nationalism was aimed not at the British but at Japanese military expansion. In seeking the best national representation for their voice, the most active among working Chinese in Hong Kong embraced China's political opposition—the Communists. Although this choice did not immediately affect the overall configuration of organized labor, it started a ground-level shift as young labor activists became members of the political opposition and gave new vitality to the party and the labor movement in Hong Kong.

Under the threat of Japanese invasion, working Chinese and British authorities were both preoccupied with the looming crisis while their hearts and minds turned in different directions: toward the Chinese nation for the former and toward the British Empire for the latter. Nonetheless, the cooperation between the colonial state and mobilized Chinese labor during Butters's short tenure raised questions about the future. How far would the colonial establishment in Hong Kong be willing to go to enforce labor-related reforms? What changes would working Chinese desire? Citywide civic activism for China's national salvation throughout the 1930s and alternative state approaches—between constructive mediation and high-handed coercion—to the industrial conflict at Chung Hwa hinted at a highly uncertain future. As the two sides on the great divide started to grapple with these questions, both faced a more urgent problem: by October 1938 the Japanese Imperial Army arrived at Hong Kong's door.

2

In the Battlefield

Hong Kong's safety under the British flag came under direct threat in October 1938 when greater Guangzhou fell into Japanese hands. Chinese refugees had already started pouring into Hong Kong months before Guangzhou fell. By November the daily influx had reached 10,000. From Guangzhou, the Japanese army made sure that its presence was noted; jet fighters flew over the British-ruled New Territories several times and caused border incidents.[1] Preparations for war now involved all residents in Hong Kong. To thwart imminent air raids, colony-wide blackout drills began in 1938 and intensified in the spring of 1939 when urban Hong Kong was divided into twenty-two air raid districts for better organization.[2] The government urged noncombatants to leave and started to evacuate foreign women and children in August 1939. As a result, "all steamers sailing next week have their berths fully booked, and there are long waiting lists. People have been taking money out of the banks all through the day," the Hong Kong correspondent for the *Times* observed.[3] A month later, ocean liner tickets had become exorbitant and difficult to get, "even if one is willing to pay first-class price for a third-class berth."[4]

---

1. *Times* (London), July 26, 1938, 11; July 29, 1938, 13; November 26, 1938, 11.

2. See, for example, "昨晚筲箕灣區開始防空訓練，上中下各區不日舉行" (Air-raid drills began at Shaukeiwan last night; drills in Upper, Middle, and Lower districts soon to begin), *WKYP*, March 16, 1939, 2:1; "防空行動組織化，港九二十二個分區工作概況" (Air-drills organized in twenty-two districts of Hong Kong and Kowloon), *WKYP*, March 31, 1939, 2:1; "本月下旬防空大演習" (Big air-raid drill late next month), *WKYP*, April 10, 1939.

3. *Times*, August 25, 1939, 11; August 26, 1939, 9.

4. Song Qingling to Grace Granich, September 3, 1939, in Song Qingling Jijinhui and Zhongguo Fulihui (eds.), 150–56; citation from 151.

During the three years after the fall of greater Guangzhou, the mood in Hong Kong's European community swung from opportunistic complacency to a panicked urge to flee. Occasional Japanese attacks across the border and the diplomatic apologies that followed added to the sense of uncertainty. But tension dissipated between incidents. This gave rise to wishful thinking: Japan dared not attack Hong Kong because the British were invincible. Despite the border incidents, "the pleasure of life appeared to suffer little interruption … the British had made their usual comfortable provision for all their sports, from golf and cricket to yachting and surfriding."[5] European women slated for evacuation avoided it by making trips to Guangzhou on evacuation day or enlisting in medical and government services to stay on as "essential personnel." Some already sent to Australia tried to return. Except for a few clear-headed residents who saw the war as inevitable, most European expatriates and Chinese residents and refugees did not expect the attack to come so soon, and the colony to fall so rapidly.

Opportunism and racist attitudes clouded official defense preparations. Until the end of 1940, the widely held view in official circles was that Hong Kong was not defendable. But British Prime Minister Winston Churchill, who desperately needed U.S. aid for Britain's war efforts, turned this passive attitude around. He made Hong Kong an example of resistance to convince the U.S. government of Britain's commitment to fight in the Pacific theater.[6] Preparations for defending Hong Kong against a Japanese invasion progressed erratically. Early on, sixty air raid shelters were built on the island. However inadequate for 1.6 million people, the rock and concrete structures seemed to ensure the durable quality of defense plans.[7] In November 1938, Major-General A. E. Grasett arrived to become commander of the Hong Kong garrison. He believed the Asiatic Japanese Army was vastly inferior in training, equipment, and leadership to his battalions. They might easily defeat other Asians, like the third-rate Chinese, but not the British.[8] In preparation for a possible siege, the government obtained large stores of food—canned beef, rice, soybeans, and groundnut oil. But a month before Grasett's arrival, the

---

5. Selwyn-Clarke, 57, 63.
6. Snow (2003), 40–41.
7. Xie, 12.
8. Lindsay, 3.

military stopped fortifying major installations that defended Kowloon against attack from the northern New Territories, a mini–Maginot Line called the Gin Drinkers' Line. In June 1940, the government started to requisition commercial buildings and private vehicles for emergency use. These war preparations—from storage of foodstuffs to blackout drills and various medical and transportation programs—indicated an emerging official consensus by 1940 that Hong Kong "could not be held but must be defended."[9]

Sino-British Cooperation When Hong Kong Fell

The Japanese attack on Hong Kong was coordinated with the attack on Pearl Harbor. It came so suddenly that it literally woke up many Hong Kong residents early on the morning of December 8, 1941. The first air raids targeted the few British fighter planes at the Kai Tak airport, and ended with the destruction of all thirteen planes and one cargo carrier. Never having experienced real war before, some residents thought it was "a really authentic air raid drill!" Others who had witnessed the Japanese invasion on the mainland realized at once that the war had finally arrived.[10] The battle for Kowloon lasted only four days. The Gin Drinkers' Line fell easily, and Kowloon's defense force, formed largely of Indians and new recruits from Canada, quickly retreated to the island of Hong Kong.[11] Yet the British refused to surrender, and after December 13 the Japanese relentlessly bombed the crowded city. Principal targets—the Naval Dockyard at Wanchai, the electric power station on the eastern side of the island, and oil tanks on North Point—were hit. Nor were residential buildings and hospitals spared. After five days of bombing, the Japanese force crossed the harbor and landed on the island. A week later, on Christmas Day, Governor Mark Young finally surrendered. He signed the peace agreement by candlelight in Kowloon's Peninsula Hotel, now headquarters of the invading army. Despite official assumptions that the colony could withstand months of siege and Churchill's repeated exhortation that Hong Kong gallantly defend the empire, it fell in only eighteen days.

---

9. Snow (2003), 40; Xie, 10–11, 192.

10. Tang Hai, 7; Sa, 1.

11. Xie, 62–80.

Realization that the combined forces of arrogance, wishful thinking, and poor preparation had caused the rapid fall of Hong Kong only came in retrospect. At the time, contemporaries were angered by the so-called fifth columnists who provided intelligence to the enemy and even raised Japanese flags before the fall of Kowloon. They were equally amazed that the defense held out for just days instead of months. Only with the advantage of hindsight did broad undercurrents of racist thinking become discernible in defense planning. Racism blinded Grasett to the many holes in Hong Kong's defense strategy and encouraged him to underestimate the enemy's ability and careful preparation. It also discouraged the British from seeking Chinese support and encouraged them to reject Chinese offers of help, which might have sustained the resistance longer.[12]

Not until attack became imminent did the British seek Chinese aid. In late October 1941, the British army and police sent representatives to Liao Chengzhi (1908–1983), who once headed the semi-open Eighth Route Army Liaison Office in Hong Kong. Internal Communist documents show that the British came with an "urgent" request, asking Communist guerrilla forces to destroy the airport on neighboring Hainan Island to prevent its use in an attack on Hong Kong. According to three telegrams sent from Liao Chengzhi to Yan'an, the two sides met five more times to iron out details of delivering explosives and training Chinese technicians. They discussed arming Chinese guerrilla forces in Hainan and in Guangdong province. The very last meeting on December 7 ended with British authorities agreeing to two Communist requests. The Communists obtained permission to open a shadow company as an unofficial office in Hong Kong, and the British agreed to deliver a sizable quantity of weapons to Guangzhou Bay for guerrilla forces operating in Hainan and the East River area of Guangdong. The Communists agreed to send ten people to learn to use explosives.[13] But Japan's attack began within

---

12. The complacency of Hong Kong's official thinking, tinted by racism, had been observed by visiting Chinese, such as journalist Tang Hai, who left a record of Hong Kong's fall soon after he returned to the mainland. In English-language scholarship, no book so far has surpassed the vivid presentation of the racialistic thinking that prevailed in Hong Kong's European community and in its colonial state's preparation for defense than the work by Philip Snow. See Snow (2003), esp. chapter I.

13. "廖承志致毛澤東周恩來電" (Telegram by Liao Chengzhi to Mao Zedong and Zhou Enlai), October 25, 1941; "廖承志致毛主席周恩來電" (Telegram by

hours, before these plans could be carried out. After the fall of Kowloon, the British once more approached the Communists, this time contacting Liao Chengzhi directly to discuss using Guangdong's Communist-led East River guerrilla forces for the defense of Hong Kong. The Communists again raised the question of needed ammunitions. The governor's representative promised to forward the request to a higher authority, but no further communication followed. For the moment, British connections to the more active and committed resistance forces nearby had stopped halfway.[14]

If ideological difference made the British pause in reaching out for Communist military support, cooperation with the Guomindang and Chinese government officials did not go much further. In 1941, Admiral Chen Ce (*Ct. Chan Chak*) represented the Guomindang and the Chinese government as special military envoy in Hong Kong (ZhuGang tepai junshi daibiao) and director of the Guomindang General Branch in Hong Kong and Macau. He had been in the colony since 1938 when he arrived for amputation of his badly infected left leg. In December 1941 he began to cooperate closely with British authorities and came in frequent contact with them over military and security

---

Liao Chengzhi to Chairman Mao and Zhou Enlai), November 14, 1941, in *GDGM*, 38:163–64, 165–66; Liao Chengzhi, "與遠東英軍談判合作抗日給中共中央的電報" (Telegram to the CCP Central Committee regarding negotiation for cooperation with British army to resist Japan in the Far East), October 25, 1941; November 14, 1941; December 7, 1941, in *Liao Chengzhi Wenji* Bianji bangongshi (ed.), I:105–10. Also see Zeng Sheng, 209, in which Zeng Sheng indicates that the negotiations produced agreement only at the last minute because the two sides could not agree on the conditions set by the British, that they send officers to supervise the use of weapons, and that Chinese guerrilla force was barred from entering the New Territories and Kowloon. Zeng did not directly participate in the negotiations and recalled the event many decades later, whereas Liao's telegrams were intended for internal circulation within the party and sent immediately after the negotiation, so I consider the latter to be more reliable evidence. Indeed, the East River guerrillas led by Zeng did not enter territories under British jurisdiction until after the fall of Hong Kong.

14. Xia Yan (1985), 465. Xia Yan, a well-known writer, was then serving the Communist newspaper *Huangshang bao*. His memoirs indicate that the meeting took place on either December 12 or 13 and was arranged by James Bertram, a New Zealand journalist who came to the colony to assist its defense. Xia went with Liao and Qiao Guanhua to meet the British official who served as Governor Mark Young's representative.

matters. Two days before the Japanese attack on Hong Kong, a British delegation, including the head of the Information Bureau David MacDougall, head
of British Army Intelligence Major Charles Boxer, Secretary for Chinese Affairs R. A. C. North, and a police representative visited Admiral Chen to indicate their eagerness to seek Chinese help. At this critical moment of imminent Japanese invasion, Hong Kong faced a reported uprising of the Triads,
and the British badly needed Chen's intervention.[15] Chen immediately mobilized the Triad and Green Gang bosses and formed the A.B.C.D. Chinese
Corps Hong Kong with these "loyal and righteous men." Chen's personal secretary, Xu Heng, went with the gang bosses to make rounds in every district
on the island of Hong Kong and talk to all neighborhood Triad bands, promising every cooperating member HK$5 and two loaves of bread a day. Operat-
ing costs totaled about HK$200,000 by December 21 and continued to in-
crease by HK$30,000 a day. Payment came from China, with promise of
British repayment after the war.[16]

Peacekeeping operations directed by Admiral Chen and assisted by the Triads saved the colony from implosion. Yet for the colonial state, arming an alien
and potentially subversive force to thwart external invasion had frightening
implications it dared not entertain. After the Japanese landing in Hong Kong
on December 18, Chen offered to send an additional 1,000 A.B.C.D. Chinese
Corps Hong Kong members to join in the city's defense. The British paused.
Only on the eve of surrender, at midnight of December 24, were twenty chests
of grenades and seventy-five pistols delivered to Triad headquarters, the Loyal
and Righteous Charity Hall, where Admiral Chen had set up his commanding
post. Just as he was about to order his members to rush to the front, Chen was
once again instructed to wait.[17] "We lost the opportunity to attack and destroy
the enemy," he lamented later, "because the British hesitated."[18]

Unreserved trust between the British and Chinese arrived only at the end.
Without knowing that the British governor had decided to surrender but see-

---

15. Xu Heng, 15; Chen Ce, 167; Snow (2003), 60. Neither Xu nor Chen mentioned the plan by the Triads, but Snow cited police documents and other English-
language sources to detail the information on the British side.

16. Xu Heng, 18; Chen Ce, 173; also see Snow (2003), 60, for the British promise
of repayment after the war.

17. Chen Ce, 172, 75.

18. Chen Ce, 172–73.

ing the inevitable outcome clearly, Chen announced that he would rather die breaking the siege than surrender. The British provided five torpedoes, and several dozen officers and soldiers joined the escaping Chinese force. This time Chinese and British aided each other in a dramatic retreat.[19] On their way through the New Territories, they encountered a militia affiliated with the East River guerrillas, who provided a boat, food, and a guide. In four days the escape party reached safety in the city of Huizhou in northeastern Guangdong Province.[20]

From Grassroots Activism to Armed Resistance

For three years before their encounter with Chen's escape party, the East River guerrillas had been a resistance force already known to Chinese authorities and locals. They were active in the counties of Huiyang and Bao'an along the lower stream of the East River, an area of approximately 800 square miles just north and northeast of the British-ruled New Territories. By the time

19. Chen's report gives a vague figure of "more than 70" British officers and soldiers who followed him in the successful escape, three of them died during the breakthrough; others record sixty-two British (Snow [2003]) or seventy-two Chinese and British (Xie). See Chen Ce, 178, 182; Xie, 156; Lo Koon-cheung, based on secondary sources, indicates that a total sixty-seven "Chinese and foreigners" were able to make the escape. Lo, 116.

20. The guerrilla force was led by Leung Wing-yuen, who once served under Chen Ce but was now affiliated with the East River guerrillas. See Chen Ce, 178. David Mercer MacDougall, who escaped with Chen Ce, appeared to be quite vague about those who helped the escape party along the way out of Hong Kong and thought they were just locals hiding in the hills. See MacDougall, 23. Citing a report by Major Ronald Homes on July 12, 1944, Philip Snow shows that Leung was an ex-bandit affiliated with the Communist-led guerrillas rather than a fully committed Communist. He broke with the East River guerrillas in October 1942 and came into conflict with them. Snow (2003), 375, n.143. Internal correspondence of the CCP provides direct evidence for the critical role of the East River guerrillas in aiding Chen Ce and his party's escape, see Lin Ping, "林平致中央並恩來電" (Telegram from Lin Ping to the Central Committee and Enlai), April 20, 1943, in GDGM, 38:253–57. Telegram indicates Chen Ce and "more than fifty" were the first group that the East River guerrillas had "rescued and escorted" in their operations after the fall of Hong Kong. Citation from 257.

Hong Kong fell in December 1941, this resistance force had already outgrown a phase of early inexperience and extreme adversity. Two months later, a small British group led by Lindsay Ride (1898–1977), former dean of medicine at the University of Hong Kong, escaped from a prisoner of war camp and received help from the East River guerrillas in crossing the difficult terrain. Their effectiveness made an immediate impression. "They were," Ride commented, "the most active, reliable, efficient and anti-Japanese of all the Chinese organizations, and their control extended right through the Japanese-occupied areas, even through the New Territories and into Kowloon."[21]

The emergence of the East River guerrillas—who became the East River Column in 1943—was as much a Communist Party initiative as a local response to widespread anarchy after Chinese troops retreated from greater Guangdong, and to the brutality and destruction unleashed by Japanese invasion and occupation. As soon as Japanese forces landed at Daya Bay (Bias Bay) in early October 1938 and began their assault on greater Guangzhou, the leading Communists in Hong Kong held a secret meeting at Hung Hom across Victoria Harbour. In a small apartment, Liao Chengzhi relayed a party directive to Wu Youheng, now party secretary of the Hong Kong City branch, and Zeng Sheng, an underground Communist leading the Seamen's Union in Hong Kong. The party headquarters in northwestern China urged them to develop guerrilla resistance against the anticipated Japanese occupation of greater Guangzhou. Both young men competed for the assignment. Discussion among them and the party headquarters concluded that Wu's responsibility for more than 600 party members in the colony should keep him in Hong Kong, while Zeng Sheng, as a native of the area, was better suited for the task of leading the East River guerrillas.[22]

In late October, more than 120 young workers and students left Hong Kong still in peace and safety. They traveled in small groups or alone to Pingshan, Zeng Sheng's hometown in Huiyang County, some thirty miles north of the British colony. The Huiyang Youth Society, a regional youth association in Hong Kong, played a critical role in mobilizing at least half of these young people to join Zeng Sheng. Two leaders of the CCP's City Branch in Hong

---

21. Lindsay Ride, "Spheres of Military Influences in Kwantung," dated around mid-1942, cited in Chan Sui-jeung, 56. For biographical information, see Ebury.

22. Zeng, 93–94; He Lang, 9–10.

Kong, Liu Xuan and Zhou Boming, came to help train the young volunteers. The majority turned out to be unfit for battle, so they were sent to work among villagers as "people's motivators."[23] About thirty stayed and formed the initial guerrilla force. They approached Chinese government troops still in the region to seek official recognition and military supplies. From a brigade commander of the 151st Division, Zeng's small guerrilla force received ten rifles on loan and were designated the People's Resisting-Japan Guerrilla Brigade in Hui[yang]-Bao[an].[24] In 1939, the guerillas became the New Brigade under the Third Guerrilla Column in China's Fourth War Zone. Although receiving no supplies or ammunition from the Fourth War Zone, the New Brigade was officially commended for its "prompt restoration of order, best fighting capability against the enemy, best and accurate intelligence, and model behavior in discipline."[25]

This initial rapport between the Communist-led guerrilla force and government troops deteriorated before long. The government attempted to integrate and control these most active and committed resisters. Once that failed, it launched a campaign to annihilate them. Through spring 1940, government troops ambushed Zeng's guerrillas and forced them out of the East River area. When the guerrillas received a Communist Party directive to return and rebuild their base, their strength had dwindled from more than seven hundred to one hundred.

The government troops' about-face toward Zeng's guerrillas was a small episode in the larger picture of rising conflict between the Guomindang and the Chinese Communist Party. The two parties temporarily put aside their political differences when the government agreed to form a second United Front in 1937 to fight the Japanese invasion. Anxious that Communist-led guerrilla forces were establishing bases in Japanese-occupied eastern China, the Guomindang government blockaded the Communist center at Yan'an in 1939, using crack military units to prevent shipments of medicine and industrial goods from entering the area. This pressured Communist-led guerrilla forces, especially south of the Yangtze River, to adjust their organization and tactics. In May 1940, Zeng's troops merged with another guerrilla force led by

---

23. Zeng, 97–98.
24. Zeng, 100, 103–4.
25. Zeng, 124, 128–29, 139.

Wang Zuoyao, which had been active in the neighboring Dongguan area to the southwest of the East River. They openly declared themselves to be a Communist-led resistance force and named it the Guangdong People's Resisting-Japan Guerrilla Force.[26] For the remaining years of the war, this local resistance force fought on two fronts: fending off incessant attacks by Chinese government troops and collaborating Chinese troops under Japanese command on one front, and waging guerrilla warfare against the Japanese army on the other. Amazingly, it thrived despite military disadvantages and perennial shortages of everything from food to ammunition and medicine. From merely 120 in its earliest days, the East River Column was more than 3,500 strong by late 1943 when it formally adopted that name.[27]

The fortunes of the East River guerrillas during their first three years of existence did not wax and wane due to Chinese government toleration or repression alone. Inexperience caused mistakes and setbacks, yet they survived on determination, patriotic enthusiasm, and local support. Formed by volunteers and led by people with no military experience, this small force had no time for training before its first battlefield engagement. When the guerrilla force formed in 1938, the CCP sent a few seasoned soldiers to provide basic military training to the new recruits—workers, students, and farmers from Hong Kong and Guangdong province. Zheng Jin (a.k.a. Zheng Tianbao), who had fought against warlord armies during the Northern Expedition in the 1920s, and Lu Weiliang, a Red Army veteran of the Long March, came from the New Fourth Army to serve as military advisers.[28] They taught the fresh volunteers basic military skills and remained with the guerrilla force. Financially, the East River guerrillas survived on overseas donations from Chinese in Southeast Asia and North America. The China Defence League, headquartered in Hong Kong and led by Mme. Song Qingling, forwarded funds from overseas donations, as well as medicine, clothing, and bedding, to the guerrilla fighters.[29] Outside aid, however critical to supporting day-to-day operations, was not all that sustained the East River Column volunteers.

---

26. Zeng, 104, 124, 127–28, 142–49, 153–57, 168.
27. Zeng, 318–23.
28. Zeng, 107, 125–26.
29. Zeng, 132–33.

Looking in from outside, Lindsay Ride, a conservative member of Hong Kong's British establishment before the war, thought Communist indoctrination was the force that goaded people toward armed resistance. As he went through the New Territories during his escape from the POW camp, Ride noted the presence of Communist leadership in the guerrilla force. In particular, he found that the "political pep talk ... played an important role in establishing support and in instilling Communist ideology among the Chinese peasants."[30] But Lieutenant Donald Kerr, a U.S. pilot in the 14th Air Force whom the East River guerrillas rescued after his fighter jet was shot down near Kai Tak airport, had a different opinion. From Tan Tian (Francis, 1916–1985), his young interpreter during his month-long journey with the guerrillas, Kerr learned that "exemplary action" (*shiji xingdong*) of Communist leadership was key to motivating the guerrillas and mass support.[31] These opposite views, either too condescending or elliptic, were inadequate to comprehend why the East River guerrillas remained the only "flicker of active resistance"[32] after well-equipped British troops dropped weapons and surrendered to the invading enemy.

Without broad social support and the vital energy generated by national salvation activism, the East River guerrillas could never have come into existence. Nor was the "political pep talk" enough to sustain them through extraordinary adversity. Well before the guerrilla force took shape, the groundwork for armed resistance had been laid out, not by party directives from above but by national salvation activists from below. Zeng Sheng, the initial organizer and principal commander of this force, is a telling case. His personal development demonstrates the close link between the National Salvation Movement and armed resistance, between vigorous grassroots voluntarism and Communist leadership, and between Hong Kong's labor activism and wartime resistance.

Just two years before his small army took shape at Pingshan, Zeng was a student at Sun Yat-sen University in Guangzhou. He arrived in Hong Kong to

---

30. Ride, 41.

31. Tan Tian; Tan's encounter and conversation with Kerr is confirmed by Kerr's memoir, recently published in Hong Kong. See Kerr, 144, n.101, and particularly chapter 18, 249–69.

32. Snow (2003), 77.

escape repression on the mainland and in hopes of "finding the party." Working as a bellboy on the *Empress of Japan*, Zeng made the ship his new field of
activism. He made fast friends with a few seamen, who turned out to be Communists back in the 1920s but had lost organizational connection after the
party's total destruction in 1934. Working from the ground up and making
use of native place bonds among Chinese seamen from Huiyang or Pingshan
in Guangdong province, Zeng formed a self-help group on the ship. This led
to the revival of the Music Society for Leisurely Entertainment (Yuxian Yueshe), a group popular among ocean-going seamen who performed Cantonese
opera to dispel the boredom of long voyages.

Zeng's activities among seamen on that particular ocean liner soon acquired
a political edge and gained greater appeal in Hong Kong. When war broke out
on the mainland, seamen on the *Empress of Japan* began to perform national
salvation songs and plays to passengers and raised funds for resistance.[33] The
revival of the Music Society for Leisurely Entertainment on the *Empress of Japan*
became contagious. By 1937 so many seamen on other ships had revived the
Music Society that it led to the formation of a colony-wide association. An
initial membership of more than 17,000 rose to 30,000 a year later. In August
1937, the Music Society joined up with more than sixty groups to form the
Hong Kong Seamen's Union. When it was banned four months later by the
colonial government, Zeng had been a member of the Chinese Communist
Party for more than a year and was directing the Organization Department of
the party's Hong Kong Seamen's Work Committee.[34]

Working among Chinese seamen made Zeng Sheng more attentive to the
centripetal force of native place connections. After completing his academic
study during a political respite in Guangzhou and earning a bachelor's degree
from Sun Yat-sen University in 1937, Zeng sold his family land for HK$500
and returned to Hong Kong to found a Haihua School (Haihua xuexiao) for
seamen's children. A Huiyang native, he joined the Huiyang Youth Society
already in existence in Hong Kong. His leadership in the Seamen's Union facilitated a close link between the union and the Youth Society, thereby merging youth activism and labor activism. All three organizations—the Haihua
School, the Huiyang Youth Society, and Seamen's Union—provided the ma-

---

33. Zeng, 59–62, 63, 76–77.
34. Zeng, 70–72, 78.

jority of the first 120 volunteers to Zeng's guerrilla force.[35] In late 1938, other native place associations in the colony and elsewhere in overseas Chinese communities formed Return to Homeland Service Corps and went to greater Guangzhou and Hainan Island to provide logistical and medical assistance to the Communist-led armed resistance.[36]

In addition to native-place associations, many civic organizations served as conduits for the transition of national salvation activists to armed resisters at this time when lines of local difference disappeared in the national struggle for survival. Cai Guoliang (*Ct.* Tsoi Kwok Leung, 1912–1952), a mid-level leader of the East River guerrillas well known to most European escapees from Japanese POW camps during the occupation, came to armed resistance through one of the grassroots youth groups.[37] The son of a fishermen's family in Xiamen (Amoy), Fujian province, Cai was a recent migrant to Hong Kong when the Xiamen-based Taohua Datong Canned Food Factory opened a branch in the colony and hired him as a foreman. Then named Cai Shunfa (Abiding the Law), Cai organized self-help and literacy groups in the factory. Fellow workers respected his leadership and appreciated his care for their well-being. Outside the workplace, Cai joined the Society for Cultivating Virtue through Learning (Xuede lizhishe), one of the ten most active youth groups in the colony, newly started by the sons and daughters of seamen, hawkers, and vegetable growers living in Kowloon City.[38]

Cai's popularity among the workers came to the attention of Zhou Boming, a fellow worker and a leader in Hong Kong's recently revived Communist organization. Their first conversation about current affairs brought the young men closer. In less than two months, Cai asked to join the CCP and became a member. When Zeng Sheng's armed resistance began in the East River area, Cai, taking the new name Guoliang (Nation's Pillar), mobilized seventeen fellow factory workers to join the East River guerrillas. His two younger sisters, Cai Bingru and Cai Zhongmin, were workers at Datong

---

35. Zeng, 86–89.

36. Dongjiang zongduishi bianxiezu (ed.), 24.

37. Ride, 39. Ride spells Cai's name as Tsoi Kwok Leung, closer to the Cantonese pronunciation.

38. Society for Cultivating Virtue through Learning then had around eighty members. According to a CCP internal report, there were four to five underground Communists among its members. See *GDGM*, 44:219.

Canned Food and activists in women's organizations. They followed their brother and joined the guerrilla force: Bingru became a nurse, and Zhongmin coordinated intelligence transmission.[39]

The transition from city life to rural guerrilla warfare had not been easy for most urban youth, who made up the bulk of the early volunteers. The personal initiative and determination required for such a transition has been viewed as necessary and often recalled in summary terms. However, detailed recollections come from an extraordinary young woman. Cai Songying (1926–), daughter of a post office clerk (unrelated to Cai Guoliang), was already a national salvation activist while still a pupil in primary school. She led an Ants Troupe of Children, formed by her schoolmates and friends, who performed at schools and for civic organizations in the city of Hong Kong. They even brought national salvation songs and plays to nearby rural areas. Some students in the Ants Troupe became "little teachers" and volunteered at a night school in Kowloon for illiterate newspaper or shoeshine boys. Family circumstances forced Cai Songying to end her education after primary school, and she began to earn a living in a gas lamp factory. After work, she joined a reading group whose members met regularly to discuss the war on the mainland. In early 1940, fourteen-year-old Songying left Hong Kong without telling her family and joined the fourth Service Troupe to the Homeland organized by the Student Relief Society. When she returned home after seven months of service, she agreed to her family's wishes that she return to the normal track of life for a girl, and she was allowed to attend middle school. Then Hong Kong fell. Songying left home again, despite her mother's opposition. She connected with the East River guerrilla force through the network of national salvation groups and became, at age seventeen, a member of the Hong Kong–Kowloon Independent Brigade. Like many other women members of the East River guerrillas, she was not assigned to combat missions but to work for "people's mobilization" through civic activities promoting local education.

Even though she grew up with few material comforts, Cai Songying found the challenge that came with her work as a people's motivator beyond imagination. She summarized the most common, yet overwhelming challenges as "three barriers" to her work: language, mobility in the local manner through rough terrain, and night travel. Situated between Hong Kong and southern

---

39. Zhou Bomiing, 24–27.

Guangdong, the vast New Territories had a complex linguistic map, with a population broadly divided between Cantonese-speaking and Hakka-speaking groups. A Cantonese speaker, young Songying quickly acquired the Hakka dialect. The tougher part was walking barefoot all the time as the villagers did: whether working in the field, climbing thorny hill tracks, or collecting shellfish on stony beaches. Knowing this was the way to be accepted by the villagers, Cai Songying persevered no matter how initially painful, as her feet were cut and bloodied by sharp grasses, thorns, and shells. She learned to walk over hilly passes in darkness. For the three years and eight months under Japanese occupation, the nights she spent in villages—a great comfort and luxury—added up to less than a month. To avoid the danger of betrayal or the implication of friendly villagers, she routinely camped in the hills with only a blanket, in the open or inside a rock crevice. On one night, she found a safe spot and lay down exhausted, taking what she thought was a rock as her pillow. She woke up the next morning with astonishment, as the "little rock" turned out to be a human skull![40]

With motivated and informed youth leaders like Zeng Sheng and Cai Guoliang, the East River guerrillas emerged from the popular movement for national salvation to establish a base of armed resistance. From there, committed and determined people's motivators like Cai Songying, many in their late teens and early twenties, connected the East River guerrillas to ordinary villagers. They did not simply "propagate" resistance or give "political pep talks." Their words and deeds made ordinary, illiterate villagers understand the difference between the East River guerrillas and the bandits marauding in rural Hong Kong, where colonial officials had rarely set foot. They brought new organizations to the villagers; they helped them form self-defense militias, Children's Corps, and Women's Corps; and they taught literacy classes at the night schools that began to spring up in rural areas. Sometimes they became much-needed doctors in places where medical services were a luxury, providing first aid and medicine. In 1942, when the New Territories suffered from drought and famine, people's motivators helped villages open up new fields while guerrilla forces shipped in food, including piglets, from the greater Guangdong area, and "loaned" supplies to villagers for later return.[41] After

---

40. "Cai Songying," in Zhang Huizhen and Kong Qiangsheng, 1–19.
41. Cai Hua, 97–101; Zhang Wanhua and Dai Zongxian, 2:104–5.

Hong Kong had dramatically changed from a colony under British rule to a Japanese occupied territory, people's motivators proved to be a critical force on the civilian front, merging rural improvement with war resistance.

"People's Guerrilla"

Militarily and politically, Japanese occupation of Hong Kong integrated the British colony into the wide China battlefield, designated by the Allies as the China theater with Chiang Kai-shek as commander-in-chief. For the East River guerrillas, the occupation broadened their theater of operation, as territories formally under British jurisdiction now became part of the ongoing Sino-Japanese War. When the British surrendered, the East River guerrilla headquarters immediately dispatched several dozens of their best fighters, divided in two units. One entered the Sai Kung peninsula and the eastern half of the New Territories, while the other made the western New Territories its zone of operation, an area stretching from Lowu to Yuen Long, Tsuen Wan, and Shatin.[42] In February 1942, this new force was designated the Hong Kong–Kowloon People's Anti-Japanese Guerrillas—later known as Hong Kong–Kowloon Independent Brigade—with Cai Guoliang as commander. By 1944 the brigade had grown to more than 800 strong. It firmly controlled the rural New Territories, and its intelligence network penetrated well into urban Hong Kong.[43] Its Pistol Company, a special task force, carried out raids on the Japanese army and surprise attacks to eliminate collaborators with known criminal records. Its Marine Company, started by a few seamen from the East River base and joined by hundreds of local fishermen, shipped large quantities of supplies and provided protection from pirates to local fishermen. Its Downtown Company carried out clandestine missions inside the occupied cities of Hong Kong and Kowloon to wage psychological warfare, gather intelligence, and occasionally carry out acts of sabotage.[44]

The Hong Kong–Kowloon Independent Brigade of the East River Column made its base in rural Sai Kung in the eastern half of the New Territories,

---

42. Dongjiang Zongduishi bianxiezu (ed.), 57; Chen Daming, 26.
43. Zeng, 349.
44. GangJiu duli daduishi bianxiezu (ed.), 177–79.

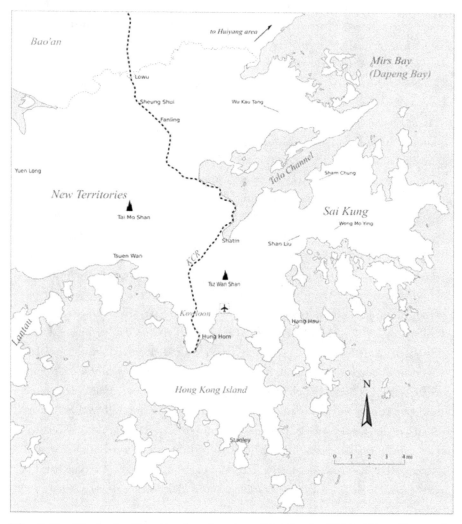

Map 3. New Territories. Coastlines based on Army Map Service (U.S.), "Hong Kong and New Territory," 1945.

turning underdevelopment in this area to its strategic advantage. Extending eastward from the mountain ranges on Kowloon, Sai Kung is surrounded by the sea to the north, east, and south. Going to the East River guerrilla base on the mainland from Sai Kung required a relatively easy water crossing at Mirs Bay. The area was sparsely populated, with a farming population in the villages and a fishing population, the so-called Danjia (*Ct.* Tanka), living on boats. Underdeveloped infrastructure overturned the Japanese army's technological advantages. Quick mobilization of large armies into the area was nearly impossible, for only one motor vehicle road connected urban Kowloon to Hang Hau southwest to Sai Kung. Across the rest of Sai Kung, roads were narrow, meandering trails through the mountains. It was a terrain suitable for the guerrillas, if they could gain local support.

Support from the locals was won by some twenty young men and women, people's motivators like Cai Songying, working throughout the over one hundred villages in Sai Kung and elsewhere in the New Territories.[45] In large measure, arrival of the guerrillas became a stabilizing force for ordinary villagers in a world ruled by chaos and terror. Since the fall of greater Guangdong in 1938, the rural New Territories had seen an increasing number of bandits and pirates. Some were old hands at the trade; others were new recruits from defeated Chinese troops. Amid widespread fear after the government collapsed, a few ordinary villagers also took up the predatory business. He Zhuozhong (1919–2005), a youth in Tsuen Wan, then a rural area in the New Territories northwest of urban Kowloon, was nudged by acquaintances to join their band and "take the chance and make a fortune" (*chenji facai*). He refused and was teased for being a coward.[46] When Hong Kong fell in 1941, more than a dozen large bands of bandits suddenly sprang up in rural New Territories, while smaller bands, like the one formed by He Zhuozhong's acquaintances, were "as numerous as the hair on a piece of cow hide."[47] Some bandits flew Japanese flags to scare away villagers and make looting easy. Others tor-

45. Zhan Wanhua and Dai Zongxian, "回憶西貢區的民運工作," in *HGGJDD*, 2:101.

46. He Zhuozhong, 46.

47. Xu Yueqing, "懷念敬愛的父親" (Remembering my beloved father), in Xu Yueqing (ed.), 184–92, citation from 185. "Bandits were as numerous as the hair on a piece of cow hide" became a common expression at the time and used in several memoirs. See also Zeng, 214.

tured villagers during raids. Soon after Japanese occupation began, He Zhuozhong recalled, bandits arrived at his village in Tsuen Wan and tried to force open a store owned by a rich merchant. When that failed, they poured gasoline on the door and lit it on fire. Instantly, the north wind in winter spread the fire from one store to another, and the only street in Tsuen Wan was reduced to ruins overnight.[48]

Villagers in the New Territories initially viewed the newly arrived East River guerrillas as yet another army of bandits. But the guerrillas quickly proved that they were not just disciplined troops but troops for the people. When they first arrived at Wu Kau Tang, the guerrillas encountered a nearly abandoned village. Fear of this army of "bandits" had sent nearly everyone to the hills. Before running away, they had hidden everything and locked every house. The guerrilla fighters could not even find drinking water. Seeing the guerrilla leader go over a broken wall into her yard, an old woman, who had been left behind, fell on her knees and begged him not to take away her only hen, whose eggs provided the "cash" she had for buying basic necessities such as salt and cooking oil. Deeply saddened by what he heard, the guerrilla leader took out HK$1.50, the only money he had, and offered it to the old woman. His soldiers fixed the broken wall in her yard. That small labor, a common practice for the guerrillas, won the trust of the whole village.[49] Wu Kau Tang embraced the guerrillas' cause heart and soul. The village hosted the founding ceremony of the Hong Kong–Kowloon Independent Brigade, and later housed the Brigade's wireless station.

At another village, Shan Liu, where a guerrilla unit camped, the quiet and astute village leader came to the conclusion that they were different from other troops. He had watched the guerrillas for days after their arrival and became convinced they were not simply disciplined and diligent in their daily training. He also sensed an "optimistic spirit" in their drills and songs that no other troops had. The view of this local leader affected those in his village; word traveled quickly to other places and drew in a desperate merchant pleading for help. Xu Guansheng, a fish wholesaler and well-known local leader, came to Shan Liu after fleeing from bandits three times, once during a meal. By running away, Xu saved his family, but his village and household were emptied of

---

48. He Zhuozhong, 50.
49. Chen Daming, 59–60.

everything, including salt. At Shan Liu, Xu found his own nephew among the guerillas and was doubly assured. The guerrilla leader treated Xu cordially and discussed their plan of eradicating the bandits and leading the resistance. The encounter made Xu a staunch supporter of the East River guerrillas. At their suggestion, he pretended to openly collaborate with the Japanese. Covertly, he mobilized fellow merchants to procure grain for the guerrillas, risked his life to store their supplies in his spacious home, and housed their intelligence agents.[50]

More than protecting the local peace and serving as a force of stability, small teams of East River guerrillas helped social transformation in this isolated region. Convinced that the guerrillas worked for their interests, locals extended their support without reservation. To avoid Japanese patrols, guerrilla supplies often had to be shipped under cover of night. Transporting supplies to storage areas deep in the mountains could not have been achieved without the help of locals, particularly women, who in Hakka custom always performed most of the farm labor. "They came at any time upon request. They did it day or night … no matter how far it goes over mountains or rivers. They simply put the load on their shoulder pole and set off right away."[51] Desire to aid the guerrillas under the exigency of war nudged locals to break long-held taboos against going out after dark. They invented ways of transmitting intelligence. Women hid notes in their hair or in gift boxes and made it safely through enemy checkpoints. They used coffins to ship grain for the guerrillas.[52] Young teenagers organized into a Children's Corps became eager and reliable messengers and frequently engaged in reconnaissance.

In helping local society survive the brutality of war and chaos, the East River guerrillas had a leveling social impact by opening participation in the resistance to an underprivileged group, the Danjia. Traditionally marginalized, Danjia lived on fishing boats and were not allowed to live onshore in

---

50. Xu Yueqing, 187–89; Zheng Minyou, "觀生叔助我搞情報" (Uncle Guansheng helped me obtain intelligence), in Xu Yueqing (ed.), 172–73; Chen Daming, 59.

51. Zhang and Dai, "回憶西貢區的民運工作" (Recollections on people's mobilization in Sai Kung), in *HGGJDD*, 2:108.

52. Cai Zhongmin, "西貢人民對港九大隊的支持" (People of Sai Kung Gave Support to the Hong Kong–Kowloon Brigade), *HGGJDD*, 2:95–98.

South China.[53] When East River guerrillas entered the rural New Territories, occasional help from these boat people in transporting troops, escapees, and supplies soon developed into a constant need. In spring 1942, the brigade announced its intention "to abolish old customs and taboos against fishermen" and appealed to them to join the guerrilla force. The people's motivators helped fishermen and fisherwomen organize women's associations, friends of the guerrillas, and sisterhoods. In turn, fishing communities in the New Territories found guerrilla patrols on the coast truly helpful in protecting them from pirates, who had raided their boats like the bandits raided farming villages. The guerrillas helped these communities found the Mutual Help Fishing Cooperative, a method widely used in CCP-controlled areas in North China that invigorated production. Fish catch increased when fishermen worked together and were provided protection by the guerrillas. They could sell the surplus and buy vital necessities at a time when the occupation forces rationed rice at a very low level of 6.4 Chinese ounces a day for each adult.[54]

The popularity of the guerrillas gained them loyal support and helped them expand. Within half a year, more than fifty young fishermen joined the guerrillas; some families sent all their sons. One extraordinary case was Yuan Rongjiao. This fisherwoman became a widow in her thirties and lost two daughters to adoption, because raising them alone became impossible after her husband's death. She became one of the most determined supporters of the guerrillas. When the Marine Company was formed within the Hong Kong–Kowloon Independent Brigade, she sent her eldest son, then only thirteen, to enlist and told him to "perform loyalty to the nation," an expression that she probably learned from the people's motivator and took to heart. She herself became a regular courier for the guerrillas, carrying messages and transport-

53. The word *Dan* 蜑 in ancient usage means "southern barbarians" as the word first appeared in 《說文解字》, a dictionary composed by Xu Shen (circa 100 CE) in the Eastern Han dynasty. Not all versions of the dictionary, such as the one edited by Duan Yucai, include the word. The boat people, particularly those in Hong Kong, have attracted attention from scholars in the English-language world. See Eugene N. Anderson, "The Boat People of South China," in E. N. Anderson (1972), 1–9. In a study published in the mid-1960s, Anderson provided an estimate of 3 million boat people living in South China. See E. N. Anderson (1970), citation from 1.

54. Xu Yueqing (ed.), 81–82; Xiao Chun, "開展漁民工作的回憶" (Recollections on the work among fishermen), in *HGGJDD*, 1:122–26.

ing troops or supplies. She made her fishing boat one of the tax collection points, where fishermen receiving protection from the guerrillas sent 3–5 percent of their catch. Tax in kind provided a major source of income for the Hong Kong–Kowloon Brigade, sustaining guerrilla warfare after the fall of Hong Kong stopped overseas aid completely.[55]

The guerrillas and locals thus became interdependent; their mutual support was vital for the survival of both. When the Japanese army exerted more control in 1943 and carried out wipeout operations in rural Hong Kong, villagers' voluntary protection proved critical for guerrillas, who moved about alone or in small groups. At Sham Chung, a village strategically located between the eastern and western halves of the New Territories, the brigade set up a major collection station for transit tax, using the spacious house of Li Huaqing, a wealthy local leader, to accommodate the station's staff. When the Japanese army came to search for guerrillas in August 1942, housemaster Li insisted on his ignorance of the guerrillas, while a woman servant shielded a young staff member at the station as "her son."[56] At Wong Mo Ying, villagers sent a third of their young adults to join the guerrillas and opened the village church for the founding ceremony of the Hong Kong–Kowloon People's Guerrilla. In late 1944, villagers helped a group of people's motivators to escape when the Japanese army suddenly arrived on a tip from a local informer. The Japanese tortured the villagers to force them to confess. Half a dozen were hanged above fire. One had his back broken by a wooden pole pushed down by two soldiers. Another died from burns. Yet no villager revealed the whereabouts of the guerrillas.[57]

A Way Out of the "World Without Tomorrow"

Like the rural New Territories, after its change of masters urban Hong Kong descended into a hellish world of looting, raping, and wanton killing. As

---

55. Chen Zhixian, "大鵬灣的海燕" (A seagull at Dapeng [Mirs] Bay), in Xu Yueqing (ed.), 83–85; Xu Yueqing (ed.), 151–54; GangJiu duli daduishi bianxiezu (ed.), chapter 13.

56. Zhang Fa, "懷念何娘" (Remembering Mother He), in Xu Yueqing (ed.), 179–83.

57. Zhang Wanhua and Dai Zongxian, 106, indicate that a meeting of several people's motivators was held that night in a nearby village; all escaped.

it erupted, the chaos appeared distinctively different from that in other Chinese cities on the mainland. Local ruffians inflicted the first round of terror on defenseless residents, beginning in Kowloon even before the British abandoned it.[58] But the island of Hong Kong, the center of British rule, remained orderly during its defense, thanks to Admiral Chen Ce's aid in restraining the sworn brotherhoods on his leash. Still, rape and looting spread throughout the fallen colony like wildfire as soon as Chen escaped to the mainland after British surrender. Ruffians demanded "protection money" from panicking pedestrians and residents. "Torn pillows littered Shanghai Street in Kowloon," thrown away by looters searching for money or other valuables after they had broken into apartments and homes. Journalist Sa Kongliao (1907–1988) and his friends took refuge in a school but had to pay protection money to ruffians who "began door-to-door collection of it in every district of Hong Kong." One day in late January 1942 when Sa Kongliao was walking alone, a few men cornered him. One pointed a gun at one side of his head and the second held a dagger to the other side, demanding money. Without a penny in his pocket, he offered them his padded silk gown instead. Surprisingly, after thoroughly searching him from head to toe, the men let him go and let him keep his gown. "They were probably looting to survive, and there's still goodness in their hearts," Sa laughed the episode off as he walked away.[59] He was lucky. Knowing that people hid money in the seams of their clothing, ruffians robbing a passerby would throw him the clothes of their previous victim and take everything he had on, including underwear. Out of desperation, some people outwitted bandits by taping precious money to the soles of their feet.[60]

---

58. Snow (2003), 55–57. Tao Xisheng (1899–1988), a well-known writer who served the Guomindang-led government as its leading publicist and ghostwriter for Chiang Kai-shek's 《中國之命運》 (China's Destiny), was living in Kowloon for a brief period between his departure from the collaboration regime under Wang Jingwei in Nanjing and his return to Chongqing. He wrote about his and his family's experiences in a short memoir, which provides a vivid description of these chaotic days in urban Kowloon when the terror of local ruffians reigned. See Tao Xisheng, "重抵國門" (Returning to homeland), in Ye Dewei (ed.), 317–38. For Tao's role as a ghostwriter for Jiang, see Chen Boda, 1–2. Chen cited "official publications in Chongqing" that indicated Tao to be the "copy-editor" of Chiang's China's Destiny, a euphemism for ghostwriting.

59. Sa, 91–92, 141.

60. Xia Yan (1980), 189–202; Xia Yan wrote the recollection after arriving in the rear area in 1942, citation from 189–90.

Local women suffered the worst terror as victims of the occupation army. Machine guns and bullets were far less threatening than rape, women reasoned, because instant death would be a relief. But the "sound of heavy boots of enemy soldiers" would send nervous women rushing to any hiding corner. Threat of rape, which often meant gang rape by enemy soldiers, compelled locals to invent a "passive way of defense." For days, loud clashes from beating gongs, wash basins, and kerosene tins would burst out from one neighborhood to another, lasting for hours on end. It started in one household, was taken up by neighbors, and immediately spread to the whole district. When such noise suddenly rose during a midnight quiescence, it "made one feel unspeakable horror," wrote one journalist who spent a few weeks in newly fallen Hong Kong. Eventually, the unending din of metal became so embarrassing to the occupation army that it sent in military police to disperse marauding soldiers.[61]

Ironically, the occupation force stopped the first round of looting, raping, and extortion in Kowloon and Hong Kong, wishing to demonstrate its benevolence in the occupied city. Local ruffians were rounded up and shot on the spot. But the initial stern show of punishment aimed at lawless elements among the Chinese was replaced by the "most savage chaos" when the invading army declared a three-day "holiday." Japanese soldiers sacked Hong Kong and looted everywhere; some were seen "sporting half-a-dozen Rolex watches, right up to the elbow" while one sentry on the Peak even wore a lady's mink coat.[62] The army itself organized the plundering, shipping 84 percent of the rice in storage to other war zones. The population of Hong Kong survived on whatever food was at hand during those final days of 1941 because rice shops and markets remained shut.[63] "Should this continue for another two months," a journalist cited the locals, "cannibalism will be the only way to go in Hong Kong."[64]

---

61. Tang Hai, 100–103; Tao Xisheng, 332.

62. Snow (2003), 81.

63. For market closing during the beginning of the occupation, see Tao Xisheng, 322; for the three-day "holiday" of looting and raping by Japanese soldiers and organized plundering by the Japanese army, see Snow (2003), 81, 86–87.

64. The Chinese journalist Tang Hai noted, out of 950,000 piculs of rice in storage, the Japanese army shipped out 800,000 piculs (close to 107,000,000 pounds). See Tang Hai, 103. Philip Snow notes that the Japanese army shipped away 107,000

Even after the Japanese Gunseichō (Military Government Office) reined in the killing and molesting of Europeans by its own soldiers, savage assaults on the local Chinese population continued. Li Shufen (*Ct. Li Shufan*), a well-known doctor and conservative member of the Legislative Council, was approached by Japanese officers immediately after the end of fighting, demanding that he help find women for the Imperial Army. To protect his fifteen-year-old daughter, Li bandaged her from head to toe and put her in his hospital ward before managing to smuggle her out of Hong Kong.[65] He treated rape victims "ranging from the early teens to the sixties ... with their teeth bashed in, their noses broken, their bodies showing bayonet prods; wives so heavy with child that the assault had brought on miscarriage; and young, tender girls whose minds had been affected by the pain and horror of multiple rape." Many rapes went unreported and victims were untreated, for the Chinese viewed it with unspeakable shame and disgrace. At 10,000 reported rape victims, Li noted, the number was a significant underestimate.[66]

As the widespread disorder finally gave way to "normalcy" when 1942 began, the occupation force issued an order to all Chinese without residence or employment to leave. Many took the opportunity to go to the mainland. Within a month, a quarter of a million people left. The population kept shrinking at an average speed of 23,000 a month during the remaining years of occupation. In spring 1943, the authorities stepped up its population reduction measures to round up those without a residence permit, especially the destitute and beggars, and threw 10,000 of them into a refugee camp in North Point in preparation for forceful deportation. Each day about 1,000 were put on junks and sent to uninhabited islands south of Hong Kong or simply left on the junks to drift away and die in the sea.[67] By August 1945, when the war

---

pounds of the 127,000 pounds of rice the British had stockpiled for the siege, which sounds like a very small amount for a whole population, then at 1,800,000 by some estimates. The whole amount of 127,000 pounds would not sustain the colony for even a day. See Snow (2003), 86–87.

65. Li Shufen (Li Shu-fan) (1964), 145. I have not been able to locate the episode in the Chinese version of the book, *Xianggang waike yisheng* (Li Shufen [1965]).

66. Li Shufan, 111.

67. Cai Rongfang (Tsai Jung-fang), 265. Chen Junbao, then curator of the Fung Ping Shan Library at the University of Hong Kong, also recorded the arrest of the poor by the Japanese military in mid- to late 1943. See Chen Junbao, 2:80, 381.

ended, only 500,000 to 600,000 lived in Hong Kong after wanton killing, mass migration, deportation, and starvation.[68]

With trade at a standstill and transportation becoming increasingly difficult, the problem of food supply in Hong Kong persisted even as the population shrank drastically. Rice ration at 6.4 Chinese ounces became part of the "normalcy" at the beginning of 1942.[69] This amount of rice, in average quality, could make only one meal for a Chinese adult, whose usual intake of protein was limited. But the rationed rice, bought at local shops with coupons, turned out to be crushed rice "full of bits of glass, broken porcelain, and cockroaches."[70] Nonetheless, there were still people with money going to Chinese or Western-style restaurants, at least for much of 1942 and some months in 1943. For the ordinary majority, a few spoonfuls of thin rice porridge became a regular meal. Many turned to crushed peanut waste after oil extraction, sweet potato leaves, and tree bark to supplement their meager rations. There were exceptions among the working Chinese. Workers in Japanese-operated industrial establishments and public service received a full cattie (sixteen Chinese ounces) of rice ration a day. In the much-reduced industrial sector, the best maintained was shipbuilding and ship repair, which was taken over by the Japanese to serve the military. They appointed their own top-level administrators, but left department-level management to the locals.[71] That was no small income in those days of mass starvation, as the central concern for everyone was survival, and "for most this meant rice."[72]

Hong Kong under the Japanese occupation became "a world without tomorrow,"[73] a world that forced different people to make different choices. The

---

68. Endacott and Birch, 139, 141–42.

69. Initially the occupation force allowed 4 ounces of rice ration per person in late January 1942, but soon increased it to 6.4 Chinese ounces (equivalent to about 240 grams, or 1.2 cups). See Liu and Zhou, 60–61.

70. "Lady May Ride," in Sally Blyth and Ian Wotherspoon (eds.), 13.

71. "Mai Suilin," in Zhang and Kong (eds.), 123–31; citation from 124, 125. The extra amount of rice ration for works from Japanese-operated establishments is inferred from Mai's recollection that, while employed at Hitachi Shipyard (renamed from Hong Kong & Whampoa Shipyard), he took other jobs to work as a cement worker in a public park at Kowloon to earn that one cattie of rice. Other recollections of wartime employment at privately owned shops or factories never indicate such was the case, and sometimes mention the problem of starvation under the 6.4-ounce regime.

72. Endacott and Birch, 142.

73. Guan Lixiong, 66.

once powerful Chinese elite in the previous colonial establishment, who were accustomed to collaboration with conquerors, found the Japanese to be far more discriminatory, racist, and arrogant than the British.[74] Most of those who remained chose to "hold breath and keep silent" no matter what happened.[75] Yet a small number of extraordinary people, who had been too young to join the National Salvation Movement or too well shielded by family comfort before the war, sought alternatives to meek submission. Liu Jieyun (1926–), a teenager from a Christian family in Kowloon, quit school to earn a living at the Chung Hwa Book Company when her family's comfortable life was destroyed by the war. She saw fellow Chinese endure brutality inflicted by the invaders. At work, Japanese guards slapped her and made her feel humiliated and frightened. Increasingly she found "national anguish and family grief" (*guochou jiahen*) unbearable. Her elder sister, who operated the elevator in a hospital and made many friends, agreed to help connect the sixteen-year-old Jieyun with an underground resister. Ten months into the occupation, Liu Jieyun was sworn in as a member of the clandestine Downtown Unit of the Hong Kong–Kowloon Independent Brigade.[76]

Started by a dozen or so guerrilla fighters sent in from their base in the East River area and commanded by a young woman, Fang Lan (Kong Xiufang, 1922–1998), the Downtown Unit operated in what its members called a "battlefield without gunshot."[77] Although her given name meant "orchid," a delicate and elegant flower, Fang Lan was a seasoned activist and guerrilla fighter. She had been a student activist during Hong Kong's National Salvation Movement in the late 1930s and one of the earliest volunteers to join the East River guerrillas. Most under her command in the Downtown Unit were new volunteers, like Liu Jieyun. They worked on intelligence gathering, on helping Allied prisoners escape from POW camps, and on psychological warfare. The unit appealed to young and old residents in Hong Kong. By the end of the war, the team had grown to more than 300 strong, including workers, janitors, bank clerks, housewives, teachers, and even Chinese employees of the Japanese Military Police.[78]

---

74. Lethbridge (1969), citation from 85, 107.

75. Liu and Zhou, book title.

76. Liu Jieyun (2012a).

77. Liang, 115–16.

78. *HGGJDD* includes at least fourteen recollections by/about these underground guerrilla fighters; see 2:11–17, 2:35–41, 2:44–85.

Once again, the network from the grassroots National Salvation Movement provided critical channels for a few guerrilla leaders to mobilize more Hong Kong Chinese into the resistance. In 1942, the first year of Japanese occupation, the East River guerrilla headquarters dispatched a former worker from Kowloon, Lin Guanrong, back to the colony to organize the underground resistance. Lin found a job at the Kowloon Dockyard and reconnected with half a dozen young workers who had been members of the Self-Strengthening Society, a national salvation activist group in the 1930s. Lin formed a reading group among the workers who already "had a determination to join the resistance." They became Friends of the Guerrillas and helped obtain and forward intelligence about the movement and repair of Japanese warships and about railroad transportation of war matériel. By the end of the occupation, more than twenty young workers in the Kowloon Dockyard had become formal members of the guerrilla force.[79]

Operating within enemy-controlled facilities demanded courage as well as forbearance and self-control, especially for those bearing "family grief" from the Japanese invasion. Zheng Bin, a teenage janitor working at the district headquarters of the Japanese Military Police, had lost his mother and two younger sisters to the Japanese bombing of Guangzhou. Through a coworker, he connected with an underground resister working at the Dairy Farm and, "after a period of test and assessment," was admitted to the guerrilla team and given the assignment of collecting intelligence. To gain the trust of the Japanese military police in the office, Zheng Bin eagerly offered additional services besides his normal job and ran personal errands for them. Despite limited education with only two years of primary school, he quickly learned to speak and read Japanese as the occupation force promoted the language. He reached such fluency that he was often mistaken on the phone for speaking in his native tongue. To establish a contact point for underground resisters, he rented a room near the headquarters. More than once, Zheng Bin was tempted by opportunities for sabotage at the many meetings held at the Military Police Headquarters; he wanted to place a bomb there to avenge the death of his family members. But his superior at the Dairy Farm, who was only four or five years older and treated him like a brother, dissuaded him. He was convinced

---

79. Huang Dengming, "紅磡區的抗日游擊戰士" (The guerrilla fighters in Hung Hom), in *HGGJDD*, 2:66–70.

to do nothing risky for personal revenge and to keep working for the resistance and the greater good at his valuable post.[80]

Just as desire to avenge the death of his loved ones motivated Zheng Bin, love for family members brought less likely volunteers into resistance. One such case was Fang Lan's mother, who became an extraordinary supporter of the Downtown Unit's covert operation in her advanced age. She had quietly aided her daughter's national salvation activities before the war. She took care of students her daughter brought home for meetings and even pawned her clothes to buy food for them. Three days after the fall of Hong Kong, her daughter returned from the guerrilla base to lead the clandestine operation. The old woman provided cover for her daughter when Japanese military police and their collaborators were everywhere searching for resisters. She went with Fang Lan around Hong Kong "without asking a word." In 1943, she volunteered to become a courier with the guerrillas. A year later, she was caught in a body search when boarding the ferry. Torture failed to pry open her mouth. In June 1944, at age sixty-two, Fang's mother was brought to the execution ground with another underground resister, Zhang Yongxian (1926–1944), an eighteen-year-old girl from an affluent Hong Kong family. Zhang was betrayed by her handwriting in the message about Japanese battleship movements that the old woman carried.[81] Grief turned members of the Fang family who had not been involved in the resistance into Friends of the Guerrillas, lending active support to the Downtown Company's operation.[82]

Despite ever-present grave danger, members of the underground resistance discovered a meaning greater than self-protection through their work. He Zhuozhong, the twenty-two-year-old youth from Tsuen Wan who refused to join his neighbors' looting gang, chose a different path to survival.[83] The son of a family in destitute poverty that sold him at age four, He grew up in a family headed by his opium-addicted foster father. He had less than three years of education before starting to work as a manual laborer on odd jobs at

80. Zheng Bin, "往事回顧" (Recollections of things past), in *HGGJDD*, 2:58–65.

81. Liu Jing, "碧血繁花相映紅" (Martyr's spirit shines like brilliant flowers) in Xu Yueqing (ed.), 139–47; Chen Daming, 141. Chen, a student activist–turned-resister, was the political advisor of Hong Kong–Kowloon Independent Brigade.

82. Ji Wen, "地下火" (Fire underground), in *HGGJDD*, 2:40.

83. Unless otherwise noted, the narrative about He Zhuozhong is based on his handwritten memoirs.

age twelve. Treated as a human beast, he was paid little and worked far beyond his physical capacity. As a coolie for a local candy workshop, he cooked for the master's family and workers, purchased raw materials, helped make candy, and made deliveries to candy stores around Kowloon and Hong Kong with only four hours of sleep each night. Exhausted from excessive work, he often sleep-walked while carrying more than 100 pounds of candy in two baskets dangling from a shoulder pole. Only when his head hit a building column or, worse, when he bumped into a pedestrian, would he wake up to an aching head or angry shouts from the offended person. "I felt no self-respect," was all He could say about his first twenty years of life.

When the occupation began, He, then in his early twenties, became a janitor at the District Office of Tsuen Wan, which was controlled by several local bullies. He felt angry yet helpless when he saw the military police torture fellow Chinese and sexually assault women, while the bullies managing the District Office tortured outside passersby for fun and embezzled a third of the rice ration for the district's population. A chance encounter with a well-connected interpreter opened a job for him at the office of the Fishery Syndicate, formed by the occupation army. Assigned to collect taxes from fishermen, He "kept one eye shut" when he knew that fishermen showed him false accounts, so that they were able to keep a bit more from their catch. Now with a much higher salary but still single, He opened his wallet and gave out hundreds of dollars whenever friends or acquaintances asked for help with food, medicine, or funerals.

He Zhuozhong's generosity attracted the attention of an underground resister among his coworkers. He had been seeking ways to join the resistance since war broke out in 1937 but "found no lead toward it." When the underground resister approached him, He Zhuozhong eagerly responded. Even though the resister and his superior warned about the danger of the underground resistance, He would not change his mind. He was convinced to remain at the Fishery Syndicate and collect enemy intelligence, instead of going to the East River base and joining the fight as he had requested. After the spring of 1943 when He joined the East River guerrillas, each day he "used a piece of thin paper and wrote in tiny, tiny words about the enemy situation, and gave it to Li Wenhui, my leader, who forwarded it to the guerrilla troops."[84] Among

---

84. He Zhuozhong, 77.

his coworkers, He recruited more than twenty into the underground resistance. Occasionally, though, his recruitment attempts ended with an outburst of laughter and great joy, because his recruit turned out to be an underground resister already. After carrying out many dangerous missions, He Zhuozhong survived the war in dignity, fighting the brutality and humiliation inflicted by the occupation forces through what he viewed as an honorable alternative to the shameful predation on their fellow countrymen by some of his neighbors.

A Local Force of National and International Importance

Weak in armament and outnumbered by the enemy, the East River guerrillas could not transform the strategic and military maps of South China. The force grew out of the local needs of self-protection and resistance. In this lawless time, guerilla operations against marauding bandits garnered widespread popular support in the New Territories. Surprise attacks on small units of Japanese troops and executions of collaborators with criminal records destabilized Japanese rule while kindling hope among local Chinese. Japanese wipeout operations against guerrilla resistance in the rural New Territories and colony-wide hunts for individual resisters, such as Fan Lang, demonstrated their profound fear of Chinese determination, as embodied by the East River guerrillas and their local supporters, to resist foreign conquest.

Despite its local character, the national and international importance of the East River guerrillas was thrown into high relief when Hong Kong fell and, later, when the Allies launched a counteroffensive. With the British defeated and Chinese government troops in retreat, no one else in South China could save the roughly 800 political, social, and cultural elites from the mainland trapped in the occupied colony.[85] Elites captured by the Japanese army could be forced to collaborate and thus become enemy pawns or, should they refuse, be jailed or executed. Anticipating Hong Kong's fall as soon as the Japanese army launched its attack, Chongqing began airlifting out family members of highest-ranking Chinese officials, who had taken refuge in Hong Kong. Communist leadership, on the other hand, immediately ordered its un-

---

85. This is probably a more conservative estimate, for some of the evacuees indicate in their memoirs that the total number rescued was around 1,000.

derground organization to mount a massive rescue operation to locate, transport, and escort nongovernmental elites and political dissidents out of Hong Kong. The party also transmitted 200,000 *yuan* to the East River guerrillas and its underground network as payment for permits to exit occupied Hong Kong and for transportation and lodging costs along escape routes.[86]

Within urban Hong Kong and Kowloon, finding several hundred Chinese among nearly two million people amid the chaos was a daunting task. Adding to the difficulty was the fact that these people had gone on the move as soon as the siege of Hong Kong began. They sought safety from enemy shelling, from harassment by local ruffians and, after the city finally fell, from an occupation army wanting their "cooperation." Some had moved more than five or six times before their rescuers finally found them. Rescue missions fell on a few Hong Kong Communists, who enlisted aid from hotel workers or in trading firms that sojourners frequented. Chen Wenhan (1911–1953), a vehicle driver and labor activist, was among the core rescue team members. His familiarity with the roads in urban Hong Kong expedited the safe travel of evacuees, who were guided from residences to hotels, trading firms, and coffee houses that served as relay stops on the way out of the city.[87]

Weeks ahead of these operations, the East River guerrillas started eliminating marauding bandits beyond the cities and in broad rural areas of the New Territories to secure safe passage for evacuees. One preparatory team was led by Zeng Hongwen, a former Triad boss who supported Sun Yat-sen's revolutionary cause before becoming a Communist in 1938. Zeng took a local approach to his mission and more or less peacefully cleared a path through to Tai Mo Shan (Big Hat Mountain)—so named for the mist atop its peak. "Big Brother Zeng," as locals called him, used his prestige as a local leader to call a meeting of more than 400 bandit representatives. He appealed to them in their familiar language of righteousness, urging these able-bodied men to use their strength to fight the invading Japanese instead of harassing fellow Chinese. Several days later, Zeng ordered the execution of a few much-hated col-

86. "Preface," in Huang Qiuyun et al., 1–4, citation from 1 and 3; Zeng, 215, 224.

87. Liang Guang, "緊急營救號令" (An urgent order to rescue) in He Xiaolin and Guo Ji (eds.), 5–7; Pan Zhu, "虎口救精英" (Rescuing the elites from tiger's mouth) in Huang Qiuyun et al., 29–36; Huang Shimin, "緊急抢救的日日夜夜" (Day and night working on the rescue mission), in Huang Qiuyun et al., 37–40.

laborators. Local people applauded what "Big Brother Zeng" had done for them and came forward to volunteer information. Deterred by the better-organized guerrilla force, the majority of bandits cleared out of the area. Those who remained were quickly eliminated.[88] Zeng's operation secured passage through the western half of the rural New Territories. A second team, led by Huang Guanfang, a worker in Hong Kong before he joined the guerrillas, marched into Sai Kung in the eastern half of the New Territories. Huang also used persuasion and punishment to clear this region, pestered by more than twenty bands of predatory bandits. Blackie Liu (Liu Heizai, a.k.a. Liu Jinjin), a former rural teacher who became a crack shot and a local hero, was particularly efficient in his path-clearing mission in Sai Kung. With his small "collaborator eliminating squad," he executed a few of the most hated local collaborators. The path they cleared went as far as Kowloon City, where the guerrillas secured the cooperation of a few Chinese openly working for the occupation army.[89]

Just as many had feared, the occupation army started looking for particular Chinese elites from the mainland within days of Hong Kong's fall. At movie theaters, an announcement accompanied every show in the form of slides projected on the screen. It was an "invitation" to the Imperial Army's headquarters at the Peninsula Hotel for five cultural leaders, including world-renowned Peking opera singer Mei Lanfang and film directors Cai Chusheng and Situ Huimin. In alarm and fear, nearly two dozen writers, directors, and movie actors made a hurried exit from Hong Kong on January 5, 1942.[90] Paying exorbitant fees, they left Hong Kong for Macau in small fishing boats on the first part of their journey. To avoid being caught without the Japanese-issued "good person identification" required on every overland passage, they navigated westward along the coast, again in small fishing boats, and finally walked overland through western Guangdong to safety in Guangxi.[91]

---

88. Zeng Hongwen, "在茫茫的大帽山上" (Through the misty Tai Mo Shan), in Huang Qiuyun et al., 105–11.

89. Huang Guanfang, "戰鬥在九龍交通線上" (Clearing the passage through Kowloon), in Huang Qiuyun et al., 65–73, esp. 65–69.

90. Situ Huimin, "一九四二年從香港撤出的經過" (Making exit from Hong Kong in 1942), in Huang Qiuyun et al., 333–56. Situ had sixteen people under his charge when they escaped Hong Kong, Xia Yan counted twenty-one. The difference might result from mixing with others in Situ's group when they took the boat.

91. Xia (1980).

Despite the successful escape of this first group of refugees, the route they took never became popular. The treacherous sea passage between Hong Kong and Macau on small fishing boats, the difficulty dodging Japanese patrols on land and at sea, and high transportation costs made it impractical for anyone physically or financially impaired. Most Chinese used paths cleared and guarded by the East River guerrillas, even though getting out of occupied Hong Kong posed significant challenges to evacuees and rescue teams.

Miraculously, a Japanese decision made possible the mass exodus of China's many national elites still trapped in Hong Kong. To relieve the food and fuel shortage, the occupation army ordered the Chinese to leave Hong Kong in early 1942. Three Communist leaders who became known locally had to be evacuated first: Liao Chengzhi, the public face of the Communist Eighth Route Army in Hong Kong; Qiao Guanhua, journalist and future minister of foreign affairs of the People's Republic of China; and Lian Guan, who had served in the semi-open Eighth Route Army Liaison Office. Disguised by hats and glasses, they joined a large crowd of refugees and walked northward through urban Kowloon. A courier escort from the East River guerrillas walked with them all the way to Sai Kung in the eastern New Territories. From there they crossed Mirs Bay at midnight to avoid enemy patrols, then walked another ten miles or so to reach the guerrilla base in Pingshan on January 3, 1942.[92] All three leaders remained in Guangdong for most of the remaining war years, either serving at a relay station for rescue missions or coordinating guerrilla warfare.

The escape route taken by Liao Chengzhi, Qiao Guanhua, and Lian Guan was relatively easy because most of the passage could be made by boat along the coast and across the bay. Several elderly Guomindang leaders, such as Liao's mother, sixty-two-year-old He Xiangning, and fifty-five-year-old Liu Yazi, made the journey largely in boats operated by guerrilla supporters among the fishing population.[93] The other route overland across Tai Mo

---

92. Huang Guanfang, 70–72; Lian Guan, "黨中央的重大決策: 香港淪陷後我黨營救著名民主人士和文化人脫險的回憶之一" (An important decision by the Party Central Committee: Our Party helped to rescue famous democratic activists and cultural leaders after the fall of Hong Kong, Recollection I), in Lian Guan tongzhi jinian wenji bianxiezu (ed.), 290–94; Zeng, 219–20.

93. Jiang Shui, "護送何香凝廖承志母子倆的經過" (Recollection on escorting He Xiangning and Liao Chengzhi to safety), in HGGJDD, 1:62–66.

Mountain and Yuen Long on the western side of the New Territories was physically more demanding.[94] Evacuees were usually arranged in small groups for an inconspicuous exit. One of the earliest evacuated groups numbered more than twenty. Well-known left-wing writers such as Mao Dun, Liao Mosha, and Zou Taofen, and their families set out on January 10, 1942. They went with some local youths selected by the Communists to accompany them out of Hong Kong and speak for them at checkpoints. In addition, small squads from the Hong Kong–Kowloon Brigade placed guards along the trail to ensure their safe passage. After the successful passage of this first group, guerrillas escorted more groups to safety via these escape routes every day or two through February.[95] The size of the groups gradually dwindled from more than twenty people to fewer than ten as the mission approached completion.

Left-wing writers and political leaders were not the only ones who bene-fited from the East River guerrillas' efficient rescue operation after the fall of Hong Kong. Family members of important Guomindang leaders and often large quantities of their property, negotiated the difficult terrain with help from the guerrillas. The wife of General Yu Hanmou went through the easier eastern route with hundreds of cases of luggage. Ma Chaojun, mayor of Nan-jing and Guomindang's labor leader, had the Hong Kong–Kowloon Brigade escort his wife and sister-in-law to safety via the eastern route.[96] Famous movie star Hu Die (Butterfly) escaped from Hong Kong with so much luggage that it caused considerable aggravation.[97] No matter what the trouble, the guerril-las did what they could for any fellow Chinese in duress, making extra efforts to send these dignitaries and their belongings to safety.

The Hong Kong–Kowloon Brigade's rescue operations extended to the British and other Allies in and outside POW camps. For this purpose, the brigade formed a special International Work Unit at the beginning of 1942. This small unit had only two English-speaking members and was led by Huang Zuomei (Raymond Wong Chok-mui, 1916–1955). A very popular civil servant who was elected chair of the Hong Kong Chinese Civil Servants

94. GangJiu duli daduishi bianxiezu (ed.), chapter I, esp. 19–20.

95. Li Jianxiang, "九龍樞紐站" (The transit station in Kowloon), in Huang Qiuyun et al., 41–50.

96. Li Jianxiang, 58–62.

97. Huang Guanfang, "電影明星胡蝶九龍遭劫記" (Hu Die the movie star was robbed at Kowloon), in *HGGJDD*, I:67–71.

Association for five years, Huang also became an activist during the National Salvation Movement. By the time he was assigned to lead the International Work Unit at the beginning of 1942, Huang, like Zeng Sheng and Wu Youheng, was a fresh member of six months in the underground Communist Party.[98]

Tasked with contacting and rescuing Allied personnel in occupied Hong Kong, the International Work Unit started operation by delivering messages from those who had reached safety to their family members still trapped in Hong Kong. It made rescue attempts, yet messengers sent by the East River guerrillas to contact POWs sometimes failed because of enemy vigilance. One unfortunate guerrilla, carrying a note from Lindsay Ride to others still held prisoner shortly after Ride's successful escape, was shot and killed as he approached the POW camp.[99] Most frustrating, however, was British distrust toward the Chinese and the messages from Chinese guerrillas, as members of the work unit repeatedly noted. Members contacted various people, ranging from ordinary Europeans or Eurasians to former high officials, such as Medical Director Selwyn Selwyn-Clarke (1893–1976). None replied positively to their offer of help.[100] The majority of POWs never tried to escape, argued one postwar British Army officer, Oliver Lindsay, because of their fear of reprisal against the remaining prisoners, the danger of being caught and executed, and their deteriorating physical strength from malnutrition in the prison camps.[101] Lindsay Ride echoed the British distrust that the International Work Unit had noted. POWs in the camp, Ride believed, "did not know whether safety

---

98. Lin Zhan, one of the two members of the unit, noted that there was one more member, Lu Ling, who had worked for the unit only briefly at the beginning. Lin Zhan, "港九大隊國際工作小組" (The International Work Unit of Hong Kong–Kowloon Brigade), in *HGGJDD*, 1:72–77, esp. 73.

99. Ride, 127.

100. Lin Zhan, 74. A few British escaped after Ride, including Police Superintendent W. P. Thompson and Mrs. Gwen Priestwood. See Priestwood (1943). Thompson was referred to in Priestwood's memoirs as Anthony Bathurst, though both Ride and Israel Epstein, the Polish-born, nationless journalist who also made a daring escape with four others on the same day as Thompson, confirm that Thompson was the one who escaped with Gwen Priestwood. See Ride, 58, 123; Epstein, 144–45. Epstein was approached by Thompson about escaping together, which Epstein decided to decline.

101. Lindsay, 187–89.

lay ten or fifty miles away, nor did they know whether the Chinese through whose territory they would have to pass were pro-Allies or pro-Japanese."[102]

Without the support and assistance of the East River guerrillas, no international rescue operation could have taken a single step within or beyond urban Hong Kong. For helping the POWs escape, Lindsay Ride initiated the British Army Aid Group (BAAG) and set up its headquarters in Huizhou, eighty miles northeast of urban Hong Kong. It sent a few agents, all Chinese, to make contact with the prisoners in Japanese camps. "Almost all of this activity was assisted by the Chinese Communist guerrilla forces," Ride admitted, simply because "there was no overland route into or out of Hong Kong other than through Communist territory, and no one, either Chinese or foreigner, could pass in or out without their agreement or assistance."[103] Thus, the BAAG set up its only forward post, Post Y, at the East River guerrillas' mobile headquarters near Long Harbour.[104]

In return for limited trust from the BAAG, the East River Column made its utmost effort. Leader of the International Work Unit Huang Zuomei involved his own family members in the cause and suffered heartbreaking loss for it. In late 1942, in response to a request by the recently formed BAAG, Huang Zuomei set up a relay station inside a sundry goods store at Shamshuipo. The East River guerrillas sent two operatives, and Huang enlisted his father and his younger sister to serve as shop owner and clerk. The store transmitted intelligence, funds, instructions, and documents from BAAG as directed by Colonel Lindsay Ride.[105] The Huangs paid a dear price for this international cooperation. In summer 1943, Huang's father, sister, and younger brother were arrested when the Japanese army caught BAAG's only contact at this relay station.[106] The old man and the young woman were released the same day, but the teenage boy was held in jail for two weeks, probably as a warning to the Huangs. He was confined in a "communal cell" holding about

---

102. Ride, 52.

103. Ride, 96.

104. Ride, 216.

105. Lin Zhan, 72–77; Ride, 61–62.

106. Lin Zhan, 76. Lin, however, did not specify if the arrested BAAG agent gave up information about the relaying station, though recollection by Huang Zuocai, the younger brother of Huang Zuomei, indicates that the Japanese plainclothes detectives came to search for one of the East River operatives who managed the relaying station.

forty prisoners, mostly Chinese, from there he also saw Selwyn-Clarke, who
was in terrible shape after savage torture by the Japanese and was held in a
smaller cell divided by iron bars.[107] Prevented by the imperative of underground operations, the guerrillas had to refrain from making contact with the
Huangs after the exposure of the relay station. The family barely survived.
When the guerrilla base eventually sent for them, Huang's father had already
died from starvation.[108]

The East River guerrillas' spirit of generosity and unreserved commit-
ment saved more than one hundred Allied personnel who escaped from
POW camps and went through the difficult terrain of the New Territories.
Huang Zuomei cited "an incomplete figure" of eighty-nine "international
friends," including twenty British, eight Americans, fifty-four Indians, three
Danish, two Norwegians, one Russian, and one Filipino.[109] The BAAG cited
assistance from the East River guerrillas to "33 escapers belonging to the
British and Allied services; to over 400 Indians, 140 of whom were in the
forces and whose escapes were wholly engineered by it, and to nearly 40
American evaders."[110]

When Allied air raids reached the western shores of the Pacific, counterattacks on Japanese military targets became totally impossible without the help
of accurate intelligence on the ground from the East River guerrillas. By then,
the national government in Chongqing had effectively lost all its operatives in
Hong Kong after the Japanese army uncovered its only secret unit, the Hong
Kong Station of the Central Statistics Bureau, in April 1943. More than forty
members, from director to ordinary operatives, were arrested. The incident,
viewed by the bureau as its greatest loss, virtually ended the Chinese government's directed operations against the Japanese in Hong Kong.[111] Allied forces

---

107. See also Selwyn-Clarke, 84.

108. Huang Zuocai, 3–4.

109. Huang Zuomei, "東江縱隊營救國際友人統計" (An estimate of the num-
ber of international friends rescued by East River Column), *Huashang Bao*, February
19, 1946.

110. Ride, 305.

111. Eight of the arrested were given death sentences and decapitated. Twenty-one
died from torture, and two more died after being released. The bureau reestablished
its cells later, though the focus of its operation turned to collecting information
about Communist activities in the area. Its ineffectiveness made Wu Tiecheng, who
directed the operation, fume: "Why could the Chinese Communists keep their oper-

had already dispatched their own agents, who could not get close to the principal target, the Kai Tak airport in Kowloon. They turned to the East River Column for help when their own agents failed to acquire any information. Blackie Liu and Wu Zhan, a leader from the headquarters of the Hong Kong–Kowloon Brigade, dressed up as businessmen to survey external airport conditions. For the internal survey, local Chinese came to their aid when some allowed their teenage sons to assume the task. With measuring tapes in their pockets, the boys pretended to play hide and seek in the airport and obtained detailed information in three scouting "games." When a draft map detailing the four-level structure of the airport was forwarded to the Allies, its representative was "utterly astonished" because a job that engaged trained agents for months without result was accomplished in days by the guerrillas.[112]

Air raids on the Kai Tak airport eventually brought a U.S. Air Force serviceman into immediate personal contact with East River guerrillas. On February 11, 1944, the P-40 fighter flown by Lieutenant Donald Kerr of the 14th U.S. Air Force was shot down near the Kai Tak airport in a bombing raid. Kerr managed to parachute out and maneuver away from the airport. Japanese soldiers ran out to catch him. After he landed by the main road on Tsz Wan Shan (known to Europeans as the Lion Rock), one local woman, possibly out of ignorance, pointed him in the wrong direction, toward the Japanese-controlled airport. In his desperation, a "Small Boy," as Kerr called him in his memoir, came to his rescue. Li Shi (1929–2009), a young member of the Hong Kong–Kowloon Brigade, was on his way to send a message to the guerrillas. Realizing that this was "a soldier of the Allies," he gestured for Kerr to follow him and ran toward the winding paths over the mountains. As Kerr hid behind a boulder covered with weeds, Li left to alert a people's motivator in a nearby village before continuing on his mission to deliver intelligence.[113]

---

ation continuously, while our comrades have achieved nothing?" See Liu Weikai, 477–500, citation from 494.

112. Wu Zhan 吳展, "調查日寇香港啟德機場" (An investigation of the Kai Tak airport under Japanese occupation), in *HGGJDD*, 1:92–96.

113. Kerr, citation from 178–81. Kerr's handwritten memoir was compiled by Andrew H. Kerr, David C. Kerr, and Kathleen Ibeng Kerr, with Chinese translation by Li Haiming and Han Bangkai. In English-languages sources, Kerr's rescue by East River guerrillas has been mentioned in Ride, which cites source from one of the BAAG members who met Kerr in Huizhou after his nearly two months' long ordeal in Kowloon and the New Territories. In Chinese languages, several short memoirs by

For eighteen days, the Japanese army mobilized 2,000 soldiers to comb through the mountains searching for the American pilot. Kerr had to move from one hiding place to another, guided by locals who followed the guerrillas' instructions. The guerrillas, as Kerr gradually found out later, paid villagers to feed him and warned one, who intended to turn the pilot in to the Japanese army for a reward, that he would be "answerable" for Kerr's safety.[114] Unknown to Kerr, the Downtown Unit of the brigade waged psychological warfare in urban Hong Kong to divert Japanese attention from Kowloon, where Kerr was in hiding. They posted leaflets everywhere, announcing the formation of the East River Column. When Kerr finally departed Kowloon by sea to safety, two ships of the brigade's Marine Company launched attacks on Japanese targets in the opposite direction.[115] Only after lying low for several more days, until the occupation troops withdrew their search, could East River guerrillas escort Kerr out of the Kowloon area to their headquarters at Pingshan.[116]

In the following month, trekking on foot for a while, then carried in a chair by guerrilla fighters because of an infection in his wounded leg, Kerr was often amazed by the dedication and resourcefulness of the guerrillas. He chatted frequently with Francis, his young interpreter, who learned English in a church school and loved Hollywood movies. In a rare moment when they had a conversation about the guerrillas, Francis "came out with a mind-dwelling observation" when asked "what sort of uniform they might wear or how they identified themselves," to which Francis answered:

> How do you know the guerrilla? We have very little, we are not like regular army with many guns, all alike; we have no clothes all alike—even some have no shoes, some have shoes of straw, can get no amount of anything. But still the Japanese fear us and we have lived in the middle of them two years.

---

individual guerrilla fighters involved in the rescue have been published since the 1980s, some of which I cite later. The rendition in BAAG contains much vagueness that can only be corrected by cross-reading with Kerr's memoir, written during his hiding in occupied rural Hong Kong and soon after his arrival in the rear area.

114. Kerr, 241–42, 250–51, 253–54.

115. Li Zhaohua, "掩護克爾中尉脫險記" (A recollection of rescuing Lieutenant Kerr), in *HGGJDD*, I:78–81; Tan Tian, "和克爾中尉隱蔽在一起的日子裡" (The days spent with Lieutenant Kerr in hiding), in *HGGJDD*, I:82–85.

116. Kerr, 260–69.

Kerr was fully convinced:

That was it, alright [*sic*]. These guys made the best of what they had and kept on
the job when some other peoples might have said the fight was hopeless and
waited for rescue. And even with their material lacks they all seemed to be determined and confident that they'd eventually win.[117]

The guerrillas won in the end. The confidence Francis expressed only gave a
small hint of a profound social change in Hong Kong wrought by the war of
resistance. In this Japanese-conquered territory, where the far better equipped
British army had been defeated, the poorly armed Chinese workers and villagers rallied around Communist leadership and continued resistance. Resistance
was waged, as Francis so succinctly put it, with "very little" in terms of armament, medical supplies, and every kind of basic necessities. Yet they had no
shortage of determination, confidence, and popular support because they were
fighting in their own country for their own survival. The resistance in occupied Hong Kong was by ordinary Chinese who formerly counted little in the
official mind during the century-long British rule. Through resistance, the war
became a turning point in which the vast bottom of Hong Kong society mobilized and was transformed.

The occupation did not produce the new order desired by the Japanese invaders, nor even ephemeral support for the Japanese "liberator" as seen in
Southeast Asia. But a new order did emerge in this former British colony. It
was a moment when the vitality of change, which once resided in urban Hong
Kong, shifted to the rural backwater. In urban Hong Kong, where the occupation force had a firm grip, the old social structure continued. Chinese elites of
the prewar colonial establishment chose to continue their trodden path of
collaboration that was, as sociologist Henry J. Lethbridge convincingly
demonstrates, out of imperatives of managing the conquered society and defending "their entrenched positions and interests."[118] No such record of collective submission can be found in rural Hong Kong or among the working
Chinese. In popular resistance, rural Hong Kong was transformed into a base

---

117. Kerr, 262.
118. Lethbridge (1969), citation from 109.

of activism, with its force extending and penetrating into urban Hong Kong. The younger generation of national salvation activists made rural Hong Kong their base of armed resistance when the established order in the colony crumbled in urban Hong Kong. The East River guerrillas, though not strong enough to launch frontal attacks on the invading army, brought protection from violence and lawless banditry to rural Hong Kong and won support from the rural elders. As they fought against a common enemy, rural Hong Kong saw the leveling of cultural and social barriers that once separated the Cantonese from the Hakka, or landed people from underprivileged boat people.

Armed resistance gave new meaning and opened a new vision to those whose lives never mattered in prewar British Hong Kong. Fighting for the survival of one's own country—not just saving one's own skin—dignified the resisters. It turned them from mere sojourners into activists. In lending vital help to national elites and international allies, the ordinary workers and villagers of Hong Kong crossed the great divide, reaching out to the other side to give humanitarian help at the risk of their own lives. Their heroic deeds made them equal to whoever they helped. No indoctrination could be more effective and immediate in validating the national and international significance of their efforts and sacrifices than these voluntary actions. Awareness of their contribution to the victory remained in the minds of these ordinary Chinese well beyond the moment of triumph. At the war's end, many demobilized guerrilla fighters returned to civilian life and resumed their work in factories, as bus drivers, tramway conductors, mechanics, janitors, hotel boys, domestic servants, and restaurant servers. Labor movement in postwar Hong Kong would no longer be the same again.

3

Restoration

The Japanese takeover of Hong Kong and other parts of British Asia did more than change the political map in the region. From colonial Burma to the Straits Settlements, Indonesia, and the Philippines, local nationalists organized voluntary armies to support Japanese attacks and provide assistance critical to Japan's rapid conquests in the Pacific and Southeast Asia.[1] Although "liberation" excitement quickly evaporated as Tokyo dragged its feet to fulfill promises of national independence to these former European colonies and, instead, subjugated them once more, the idea of seeking national sovereignty captured the hearts of millions in Asia. The Japanese occupation ironically accelerated the pace of decolonization and postwar independence in British Asia.

In the name of national liberation, Japanese conquest of former European colonies forced the question of decolonization onto the table of world leaders. To thwart the Axis challenge, the Allies needed to wrest back the anticolonial agenda and make it a component of their war aims. U.S. President Franklin D. Roosevelt had persistently advocated for decolonization. He did so not out of idealistic sentiments but from realistic concerns about possible implosion within the British Empire. In India, Britain's most important "possession" in Asia, the Congress Party led by Mahatma Gandhi refused to cooperate with the war effort and fight on the British side. A revolt in British Asia would inflict irreparable loss on America's European allies and weaken their fight against Nazi Germany. Before the United States formally entered the war, Roosevelt traveled to the north Atlantic in August 1941 for his first meeting with British Prime Minister Winston Churchill, with the goal of achieving a public declaration of war goals. Their historic meeting off Newfoundland

---

1. Lebra, passim.

resulted in the Atlantic Charter, jointly signed by the two leaders. The charter's third clause, in particular, restated Woodrow Wilson's noble but unfulfilled principle of self-determination formulated a quarter of a century earlier.[2] In signing the Atlantic Charter, Roosevelt and Churchill pledged to "respect the right of all peoples to choose the form of government under which they will live" and declared their "wish to see sovereign rights and self government restored to those who have been forcibly deprived of them."

Although chiefly for propaganda and of little practical value in creating postwar world order,[3] the Atlantic Charter nevertheless positioned leading Western powers on top of a tall ethical pedestal for worldwide display. It made decolonization a leading moral issue and made resistance to decolonization ideologically problematic. Fourteen months after the fall of Hong Kong, in February 1943, the United States and Great Britain renounced their extraterritorial rights in China after more than a decade of resistance.[4] On the question of Hong Kong, however, Chinese attempts to reclaim the territory encountered greater obstacles.[5] Realpolitik calculations again defeated noble principles when the balance of power shifted on European battlefields and on the Chinese mainland.

No Chinese Hong Kong Yet

Less than two years after the Atlantic Charter was signed, discussion in London about Hong Kong's future turned from abandonment to reoccupa-

---

2. See Manela for four case studies of responses and interactions with President Wilson at the Paris Peace Conference by nationalist activists in China, Egypt, India, and Korea.

3. I take the term *propaganda* from Wilson, esp. chapter 9; citation from 149. A recent work on the chief negotiator on the U.S. side, Undersecretary of State Sumner Welles, uses a different term that indicates the similar nature of the charter as "essentially a proclamation rather than a formal … treaty." See O'Sullivan, esp. chapter 3; citation from 51. As both works show, negotiations regarding the charter focused not quite on decolonization but on access to world markets and raw materials after the war.

4. In 1930, ten countries relinquished their extraterritoriality in China: the Soviet Union, Germany, Austria, Poland, Finland, Greece, Czechoslovakia, Persia, Mexico, and Bolivia. See H. L.

5. Koo, 5:27–35.

tion. This change of direction materialized in the responsible colonial and diplomatic offices and other branches of government. Leading members of the British business community in China made critical contributions to the process as well. In contrast, the Chinese relied mostly on international goodwill and, in particular, informal consultation with national leaders and high officials. Not surprisingly, these different approaches reflected different choices. As each government assessed the Hong Kong question in relation to other national priorities, the fallen British colony began to be pushed toward a future in the opposite direction to the principles of the Atlantic Charter.

For a brief moment in 1942 when Britain's defenses at home and in Asia were at their weakest, London was ready to give up Hong Kong for good. The Foreign Office assessed Hong Kong and Malaya as "nonessentials" that should be let go for Britain to "maintain the really important things."[6] As the representative of Britain's overseas "possessions," the Colonial Office immediately fought back. Led by the energetic Assistant Undersecretary Gerard Edward Gent (1895–1948), the Colonial Office argued forcefully for retaining Hong Kong. It created a Hong Kong Planning Unit to articulate the rationale of reoccupation to place Hong Kong once again under the British flag.[7] This "Hong Kong for Britain" policy was secured through a personnel change at the Foreign Office in 1944. Its Far Eastern Department, formerly headed by anticolonialist Ashley Clarke, came under the helm of J. C. Sterndale-Bennett, who rejected his predecessor's view of Hong Kong's future. One of the British undercover organizations overseas, the Strategic Operations Executive (SOE), added a powerful voice in emphasizing the strategic importance of a British Hong Kong to counter a resurgent China. In 1944, the SOE hatched a series of schemes, ranging from a propaganda war in which smuggled British flags created a pro-British appearance in Hong Kong, to the "good work of bribery and corruption" on Japanese expulsion and Allied reentry into Hong Kong.[8] The final decision of the British government became public on November 8, 1944, when Deputy Prime Minister Clement Attlee declared in the House of Commons that Hong Kong would be retained as a part of the British Empire.[9]

---

6. Lee and Petter, 124.

7. Tsang (1997a), 39–42.

8. Snow (2003), 191, 237–39. Although none of the SOE schemes were put into practice, all had received serious attention at the Foreign Office and even the Cabinet.

9. "British Empire (Hong Kong)," *Hansard Parliamentary Debates: House of Commons*, November 8, 1944, 5th Series, vol. 404, cc1352–3.

In contrast to Britain's determined and energetic fight, Chinese efforts to regain Hong Kong were timid at every turn. The wartime Chinese government relied largely on U.S. goodwill to achieve its international objectives. Despite loud official statements about taking back Hong Kong, it made no concrete plans as it pleaded to the United States for help. In early 1943, the Chinese government sent Mme. Song Meiling, the wife of Chiang Kai-shek, to Washington to informally approach President Roosevelt about getting Hong Kong back after the war. Knowing of the British reluctance, Roosevelt found a middle ground. He conveyed his idea in conversation with T. V. Soong, China's foreign minister, who had been in Washington for three years as Chiang Kai-shek's personal representative. In Roosevelt's scheme, Britain and China would make "a magnanimous gesture" regarding Hong Kong. "Without anyone knowing it two simultaneous declarations [will have] to be made in due time, the one about handing over [Hong Kong back to China] and the other about [making Hong Kong] the free port."[10] With assurance from the United States, the Chinese Foreign Ministry charged the task of planning Hong Kong's recovery to its European Department. It produced a proposal by September 1944, recommending negotiation with Britain on Chinese recovery of Hong Kong and the leased New Territories. No specific plan of implementation followed.[11]

China's failure to work out an effective plan to recover Hong Kong did not grow from individual incapacity alone.[12] Fundamentally, it stemmed from a systemic problem: the government placed its priorities elsewhere. Since 1939, Chiang Kai-shek's government had made eliminating its political enemy, the Communists, its central task. Its best troops were positioned in the northwest to blockade Yan'an. Government inattentiveness and inadequate preparation on other fronts led to dismal defeat during Japan's Ichigo Offensive in 1944. For years, U.S. diplomatic reports about official corruption and nepotism had

---

10. "Memorandum on Dr. Soong's Conversation with the President, March 31st, 1943," T. V. Soong Papers, Box 32, Hoover Institution, cited in Liu Xiaoyuan, 138.

11. Tsang (1997a), 34–37.

12. This is the view by Steve Tsang (1997a), who blames an irresponsible head of the European Department for failure to work out a plan to recover Hong Kong. The behavior of an individual on an important position, as I view it, was only the symptom of a failing system of the Nationalist-led government.

eroded Chongqing's reputation in Washington. The fiasco of the Ichigo Offensive critically undermined U.S. confidence in Chiang's government.

Hong Kong fell through the cracks in China's crumbling political edifice. The official attitude softened toward recovering the former British colony, and the British took note. In late November 1944, Foreign Minister T. V. Soong, recently returned from the United States, signaled its new position on Hong Kong in "a long talk" with John Keswick, a *taipan* (head of a commercial firm) of Jardine, Matheson & Co. in Hong Kong and Shanghai. Keswick was simultaneously head of the SOE's China branch and a political liaison officer at the British embassy in Chongqing for Lord Mountbatten's Southeast Asia Command.[13] T. V. Soong reportedly said that "China definitely wishes to get Hong Kong back but my own view is that we should not exert any pressure on the British to this end." He trusted "common sense" on the part of Britain and reminded Keswick of the lease on the New Territories: Hong Kong would be unsustainable should China revoke the lease on this vital hinterland. "China needs do no more than show her interest in the Colony," he declared, "and the processes of good sense will work upon the British Government."[14] Even though the British had already made up their minds on Hong Kong regardless of what the Chinese said or did, T. V. Soong's quiet talk ensured that no open protest from Chinese government would be forthcoming. China's retreat from its adamant position on recovering Hong Kong was further confirmed by David M. MacDougall, who traveled to Chongqing in April 1945. Ironically, all the British individuals MacDougall met had taken Attlee's statement about keeping Hong Kong within the empire "with a pinch of salt." In contrast, "the Chinese seem a good deal more reconciled to not getting possession of Hong Kong the day after tomorrow than they were in 1942."[15]

As Allied victory came within reach, British preparation for retaking Hong Kong sped up. London paid particular attention to the views of British *taipan* in the colony. In fact, the China Association (Yingshang Zhonghua xiehui,

---

13. T. V. Soong had lost Chiang Kai-shek's favor over their disagreement on the Stilwell Affair and was called back. See Kuo and Hsiao-ting.

14. "Extract of letter from Mr. G. Wallinger, Chungking, dated 13th November, 1944 addressed to Mr. to J. C. Sterndale Bennett, Foreign Office," CO 129/592/8, "Future Policy in Hong Kong," 175–76. For Keswick's position in the SOE, see Snow (2003), 191.

15. D. M. MacDougall to Gent, April 18, 1945, CO 129/592/8, 141–42.

literally, Association of British Merchants in China), the organization of British business leaders, actively lobbied the Colonial Office since early 1943 when, in the nadir of the war, Hong Kong was still deemed nonessential to Britain's defense of the empire.[16] During December 1944, the Colonial Office approached the China Association, seeking two business representatives "for confidential consultation with this office on matters affecting business interests in Hong Kong after the war."[17] In willing response, G. Warren Swire (1883–1949), senior director of John Swire and Sons, and Arthur Morse (1892–1967), chief general manager of the Hong Kong and Shanghai Bank, offered to serve as liaisons with the Colonial Office "in a personal and confidential capacity." Monthly meetings between the two *taipans* and G. E. J. Gent, J. J. Paskin, N. L. Mayle, David M. MacDougall, and Alice Ruston, who formed the Far Eastern Planning Unit, began in February 1945.[18] For these "informal and confidential" discussions, they agreed that "no note of it should be recorded." Significantly, their discussion on Hong Kong's reoccupation took place within a new context of the U.S. retreat from anticolonialism. At their first meeting in late February, Gent assured Swire and Morse "in some detail" that Britain already had "the agreement ... with the Americans that policy in recovered British territory should be formulated by H. M. G. and that this was assumed to mean that it would be carried out by British Civil Affairs Officers."[19] As the United States embarked on global dominance, no "great odds" but only small bumps lay in Britain's path toward retaking Hong Kong.[20]

---

16. "Secret," letter from British embassy in Chongqing to J. C. Sterndale Bennett of Foreign Office, February 21, 1945, CO 129/592/8. This letter mentioned that Li Shu-fan had suggested to Keswick at the end of 1943 that "British control should be retained for a certain period after the war" (Wallinger's letter to Ashely Clarke on December 31, 1943).

17. Minute by A. Ruston, January 29, 1945, CO 129/592/8, 3; also see N. L. Mayle to E. A. Armstrong (War Cabinet Offices), January 9, 1945, CO 129/592/8, 179–80.

18. Minute by Paskin, January 8, 1945; memo by A. Ruston, January 29, 1945, CO 129/592/8, 2, 3.

19. Minute by Ruston, February 27, 1945, CO 129/592/8, 5–6.

20. Steve Tsang (1997a), 42–44, has given detailed discussion on how the British worked "against great odds" to achieve ground-level reoccupation.

Even though official secrecy leaves much in the dark, available documents reveal the influence of leading British businessmen on official thinking about the postwar restoration of British rule in Hong Kong. In a two-page, twelve-point "note" titled "Hong Kong," G. Warren Swire articulated the reasons "Hong Kong must remain British." He highlighted the importance of Hong Kong as "a trade base and symbol of our Far Eastern interest," "a transshipment port," the only service center with "modern shipbuilding or repair facilities between Singapore … and Japan," "an important centre for British insurance," and "an oasis of law and order." Of course, Swire was aware of rising sentiments in Asia and around the world against European colonial rule. He echoed a growing sensitivity in official circles toward "natives" and justified restoring British rule in Hong Kong as serving the interests of Chinese merchants and Chinese who "have invested large amounts in property in Hong Kong."[21]

Swire's argument provided useful ammunition for British officials to counter America's last serious attempt to support Chinese claims to Hong Kong. In spring 1945, Patrick Hurley came to London as Roosevelt's personal representative to confer with Churchill and Foreign Secretary Anthony Eden on the situation in China and the plans for a postwar Asia. Anticipating Hurley's support for returning Hong Kong to China, Gent in the Colonial Office drafted a seven-point memo that took much from Swire's twelve-point note. In Gent's presentation, Britain, via Hong Kong's governance, emerged as the benevolent guardian of regional order in East Asia. The colony was not merely "a free port for the service of all trade and commerce in the Far East" but a safe haven for all in times of disturbance and revolution. Echoing Swire, Gent stressed Britain's right over Hong Kong because "the direction of the British Government" helped transform "a desolate island" into "one of the great sea ports of the world." He argued that "British Law and order" allowed Hong Kong to play "a special role" in times of revolution: that it "has been a centre of settled and orderly conditions for the benefit of all countries having relations with China." Britain's benevolent role in Hong Kong, he concluded, "may have no less a value in post war years."[22] The Foreign Office added an aura of national mission to the assessment. "We have a heavy responsibility in

---

21. "Hong Kong," by G. W. S., CO 129/592/8.
22. G. E. J. Gent to Sterndale Bennett, March 29, 1945, CO 129/592/8, 154–55.

respect of Hongkong towards all nations interested in the stability and welfare of the Far East," H. Brideaux-Brune argued, with fresh emphasis on the global importance of British rule in Hong Kong. "The position of Hongkong as a great centre of population and a focus of shipping, commercial, and other activities, give it a special role in the furtherance of these objects. ... We therefore regard it as a *national duty* not only to recover the Colony but to restore it to its state of order and prosperity."[23]

Consensus in London favoring Britain's recovery of Hong Kong as a "national duty" but not an issue for diplomatic negotiation inflamed Churchill's fight against U.S. pressure. Meeting with Hurley, Churchill bargained hard to keep U.S. troops in the southeast theater to stabilize British control, and opposed U.S. plans to divert resources to China, where the situation was deteriorating. Churchill raged as soon as the question of decolonizing British Hong Kong was raised. An old-school imperialist who believed in the greatness of the British Empire, he simply derided U.S. support of China as "the great American illusion." He made it clear that he would "fight for Hongkong to the finish." Hurley realistically reminded Churchill that he had reaffirmed the principles of the Atlantic Charter in a recent speech to Parliament and, if Britain refused to give up Hong Kong, Russia might make a claim in North China. He failed to convince the prime minister, who simply snapped back: "Britain is not bound by the principles of the Atlantic Charter at all." In his famously dramatic language, Churchill declared that "Hongkong will be eliminated from the British Empire only over my dead body."[24]

London was soon freed from U.S. opposition to a British Hong Kong when U.S. anticolonialism beat a dramatic retreat at war's end. As Hurley completed his spring mission to London, President Roosevelt died suddenly on April 12, 1945. International responsibilities of the world's only superpower overwhelmed Harry Truman, who assumed the presidency with far less experience, a limited vision of world affairs, and little sympathy with China's anticolonial nationalism. British reoccupation of Hong Kong began to glide through an easy passage. In the United States, as British diplomats noted, official mood

---

23. "Hong Kong," by H. Brideaux-Brune, March 31, 1945, CO 129/592/8, 150–51; emphasis added.

24. Patrick Hurley to the secretary of state, April 14, 1945, *FRUS, 1945, The Far East: China*, 8:329–32.

and popular sentiment began to diverge. Anticolonialism in U.S. public opinion was still prevalent in mass media. They found in the *Chicago Daily* that "a considerable segment of opinion" wished to see the British win Chinese goodwill "by relinquishing control of that great Chinese city [Hong Kong] to the Chinese people." The *New York Times*, too, "does not believe that the present [British] position [of retaking it] can continue indefinitely." However, reports from Washington indicated that the Truman administration "feels less strongly about changing the status of Hong Kong and other Imperial possessions than President Roosevelt is alleged to have done. *America's acquisitive mood towards the Pacific has in any case undercut much of the earlier criticism.*"[25]

As the great powers jettisoned the principles of the Atlantic Charter in spite of global opinion, China faced enormous odds in its attempt to prevent British reoccupation of Hong Kong. The Chinese and British governments argued about the arrangements of ceremony accepting Japanese surrender in Hong Kong. Through feeble diplomatic gestures, the Chinese government insisted on China's right to accept the surrender because Hong Kong was part of the China theater where Chiang Kai-shek was supreme commander. The Chinese position was severely undercut by Chiang's military priorities of competing with the Communists for territory and defeating them in the battlefield. Even though at least 60,000 government troops, including the New First Corps led by General Sun Liren (1900–1990) and the Thirteenth Corps led by General Shi Jue (1908–1986), were within 300 miles of Hong Kong well before the Japanese surrender, no order was ever issued to them for retaking Hong Kong.[26]

---

25. "Extract from Telegram from Washington to Foreign Office dated 26th August, 1945," CO 129/592/8, 78; emphasis added.

26. The 60,000 troops appeared to be an underestimate, as cited in Tsang, (1997a), 45–46. By August 11, 1945, the Thirteenth Corps, well equipped with U.S. supplies, had defeated Japanese forces and taken Wuzhou on the border of Guangxi and Guangdong after a relatively easy battle. See Shi Jue, 3, 192–93. The Thirteenth Corps eventually used civilian boats to reach Guangzhou after Japanese surrender and passed through Hong Kong in its transition northeast to fight the Communists. The New First Corps under General Sun, according to his biographer, had already been relocated to Guangzhou in June 1945. See Zheng Jinyu, photo caption on 156. In addition, the government had moved its Sixty-Third Corps and Sixty-Fifth Corps from southern Jiangxi into northern Guangdong to fight the Communist-led East River guerrillas in late July 1945. It would have taken at most three or four days for

In contrast to Chinese government inaction, London matched its imperial resolve with swift, well-coordinated diplomatic and military maneuvers. In spring 1944, while U.S. opposition to British reoccupation of Hong Kong remained strong, the Southeast Asia Command under Lord Louis Mountbatten moved its headquarters from Delhi to Kandy in British Ceylon. This relocation, as U.S. General Joseph W. Stilwell remarked in his diary, shifted British priority toward the Pacific to "horn in at Hong Kong again."[27] In August 1945, newly elected Labour Prime Minister Clement Attlee took another step along the path begun by Churchill's blunt refusal to discuss the Hong Kong question. He simply informed President Truman that Japanese forces in Hong Kong would surrender to a British commander.[28] Sensing imminent Japanese surrender, London issued an order to the commander-in-chief of the British Pacific Fleet to prepare a naval task force for retaking Hong Kong. U.S. permission—as the British Pacific Fleet operated under the vast U.S. Pacific Fleet Command—came promptly, one day before the Japanese surrender. Within two hours of Hirohito's announcement, the British naval squadron left Sydney. Once diplomatic matters were sorted out with Washington, a reinforced naval expedition force departed on August 27 from the Philippines for Hong Kong under the code name Operation Ethelred. Commanded by Rear-Admiral Cecil Harcourt, the British fleet consisted of two aircraft carriers, four destroyers, and two cruisers with one auxiliary anti-aircraft ship, eight submarines, a submarine depot vessel, and six minesweepers.[29] Simultaneously, a twenty-five-person team of the Hong Kong Planning Unit of the Colonial Office, led by David MacDougall, flew from London to Ceylon to await

---

these troops to march south to Hong Kong. See Zeng Sheng, 432, for the movement of the two corps.

27. Stilwell, 332. Stilwell was the first deputy commander of the South East Asia Command and responsible for the China-Burma-India theater, next in the chain of command under Mountbatten. The British refused to join the Burma campaign of 1944, which Stilwell led in person and marched with foot soldiers through Burmese jungles. The refusal provoked Stilwell's suspicion of British intentions to preserve their force for end-of-the-war recovery of the lost empire. Also see Tuchman, chapter 17, on the conflicting strategic goals regarding the Burma campaign between Britain and the United States.

28. Fedorowich, citation from 38, 40.

29. Snow (2003), 242, 258.

orders. The team reached Hong Kong in early September, a week after the military administration reoccupied the territory.[30]

While Harcourt's mighty fleet raced toward Hong Kong, London made yet another move to preempt a military takeover by Chinese forces in the vicinity. London had one loyal servant on the ground in Hong Kong, prewar Colonial Secretary Franklin Gimson, who was the highest-ranking official among the internees at Stanley Camp. Gimson tried but failed to claim authority as the king's representative in the camp, but he maintained some communication with the Colonial Office during his imprisonment. By dealing with insurgent inmates, he attained a cooperative relationship with the camp's Japanese authorities. Through the British ambassador in China, London sent an order to Gimson on August 10. It was carried by BAAG, passed through BAAG relay points built on the East River Column's underground network, and reached Gimson twelve days later. Even before receiving these instructions, and with the acquiescence of the Japanese commandant, Gimson had declared the resumption of British rule on August 18.[31] Gimson's interim civilian administration transferred power to the British military administration when it was proclaimed on September 1.

What was in the hearts and minds of the ordinary Chinese in Hong Kong as the British raced to reoccupy Hong Kong by sea, land, and air? No doubt the predominant majority did not know that Chinese government troops had been in the area for weeks but halted their advance within a few days' march away from Hong Kong. Well before diplomatic and military maneuvers at the commanding heights brought British forces back to Hong Kong, Chinese resistance to the Japanese invasion had transformed Hong Kong inside out. Ordinary Chinese loudly and lavishly displayed their feelings when Rear-Admiral Harcourt's British fleet entered Victoria Harbour on August 30, 1945. "Chinese crackers were heard instead of rifle shots; Union Jacks were displayed that had been concealed throughout the occupation," an official history of the British military administration noted. "But on every junk and on nearly every house there flew the flag of China."[32] Once again, Kowloon became "the scene of much excitement and jubilation" when British officials met the Japanese in

---

30. Fedorowich.

31. Snow (2003), 202–3, 249–50; Ride, 285–86, 299; Endacott and Birch, 229.

32. Donnison, 202.

the Peninsula Hotel to arrange the takeover. "Packets and packets of firecrackers, hurled indiscriminately into streets from the upper floors of the houses in all districts, greeted the Japanese on their trek to camps. The Chinese flag is being prominently displayed from all buildings."[33]

Voices Against British Reoccupation

With resolution sustained by military force, Britain beat China in the race to recover Hong Kong. Restoring British rule in the reoccupied colony, however, was a different matter. The Pacific War and the Japanese conquest had decisively transformed existing relationships between European colonial powers and their Asian subjects. To retake Hong Kong with force was merely a symbolic step, for restoring colonial rule could not be achieved by might alone. Well before British reoccupation began, its legitimacy was questioned around the world.

Colonial rule in Hong Kong surely had core supporters from the prewar establishment, despite the increasingly apparent incongruity of colonialism in Asia. Li Shufen, the Edinburgh-trained medical doctor and unofficial member of the Legislative Council before the war, witnessed the horror of Japanese occupation firsthand and fled to the mainland after spending more than a year in occupied Hong Kong. He made his way to China's war capital and then to London and Washington in 1944. In Chongqing in late 1943, Li raised the issue of Hong Kong with John Keswick and urged the British to consider retaining control of Hong Kong "for a certain period after the war."[34] In London, he offered his opinion to the Colonial Office in a letter to Gent, in which he argued the benefit of British recovery of Hong Kong. Anticipating civil war in China, Li Shufen believed that retaining British rule "for a period of time" would be "a possible and wise policy." He voiced opposition to constitutional

---

33. "Meeting with Japanese," *South China Morning Post*, September 4, 1945, 4. The display of Chinese flags throughout Hong Kong in these days appeared to be a prominent scene noted by everyone and especially by the *South China Morning Post*. Stuart Braga cited one report on September 3, 1945, which notes: "Plenty of Chinese flags up yesterday but very few British." See Braga, 437.

34. From British Embassy, Chongqing, to J. C. Sterndale Bennett of F. O. on February 21, 1945, CO 129/592/8, 75–76.

reform, because it would open elections to the Chinese who, in his view, "could not be relied upon to vote favourably if given the franchise" simply because they "are not British subjects."[35] An outsider, Li Shufen probably did not know that official circles in London had already decided on retaking Hong Kong. Although eager to see the return of the British, his repeated emphasis on restoring British rule for "a period of time" without permanence betrayed his wariness about a world moving irreversibly toward decolonization and self-determination.

In contrast, some longtime European and U.S. observers of British rule in Hong Kong argued for the need to heed the rising tide of decolonization, despite disagreements on what approach should be taken. Some recognized a definite need for reform; others believed that the time to return Hong Kong to China had come. Among articulate center-conservatives was John V. Braga (1908–1981), the eighth son of Hong Kong's first Portuguese legislator, José Pedro Braga (1871–1944), whose twenty-two-page memorandum made its way into official files. The Colonial Office noted that Braga was a well-known Hong Kong resident of "Anglo-Portuguese descent." Locally, he was known as a "connoisseur of old Italian violins" and worked for China Light and Power Company as an assistant secretary after the war.[36] Giving his long memo the title "Anti-British Feeling in China," Braga detailed his frustration with what he called "British incivility" that he and particularly his Chinese friends and acquaintances experienced in Hong Kong. The memo reached the Foreign Office through a British member of Parliament, then circulated to the Colonial Office in mid-February 1946, when discussions about transitioning from the British military administration to a civilian government were under way. Braga was not for handing Hong Kong back to China. Nonetheless, he considered reforming the uncivil daily practices of ordinary British by promoting respectful behavior as desirable for improving British–Chinese relations and therefore possible in keeping the colony safely within the fold.

---

35. Li Shufan to G. E. J. Gent, March 7, 1944, FO 371/41657, "Future of Hong Kong," 5–7.

36. Braga's position at China Light and Power is confirmed by two publications in 1948 and 1958–1960; each provides a short paragraph for most of the entries. See *Hong Kong's Who's Who & Residents Register 1947/4*; Luzzatto and Remedios (eds.), 35.

Racial prejudice and racist behavior stood out in Braga's vivid narrative of British Hong Kong, which detailed several instances he witnessed at a bank, a shipping company's booking office, and in elevators of luxurious hotels where only wealthy, propertied, and hence "respectable" Chinese could go. In each case, Braga was shocked by the intentional neglect, outright contempt, and personal insults that "respectable" Chinese received. He heard "a beautifully dressed Chinese lady" blurt out "imperialism!" after waiting patiently at a bank counter and watching the bank's "British official [who] ... promptly jumped up from his desk" to attend an Englishwoman, a British military officer, a Dane, and a Swiss—all had come after her. Another incident involved "an elderly American-born Chinese lady" who went to a "well-known shipping company," hoping to book a first-class passage. She was shouted away by an English manager because she came in "just a few minutes before lunch hour." In yet another incident, "an annoyed Englishman knock[ed] off the hat of a Chinese for not taking off his hat in a lift into which a European lady had entered." Referring to an occasion when Braga was at work, a "Mr. X" "loudly reprimanded one of his senior [Chinese] clerks before a junior" and Braga. When Braga suggested that such embarrassment be avoided, Mr. X replied:

Oh no, Braga, you're wrong. Letting these yellow-skinned Chinese feel themselves on a level with us white men—not on your life! You pander to these wretches and you'll soon find they have no respect for you, and they get out of hand. They don't understand. They take kindness for weakness. Chinese are almost as bad as Indians. Give them an inch and they'll take an ell. Yes, rough handling is the only way to manage the Oriental, the only way to keep him in place and make him retain his respect for you.

A sensible observer, Braga pointed out that British colonial conquest was the root cause of persistent racism in Hong Kong. He indicated that "the British first comers to the Colony after it was ceded to Britain" assumed the attitude "of a conquering people towards a subject race." As a longtime European resident in Hong Kong, Braga found that this conqueror's attitude "was characteristic of very many British people in the Colony before the war." He recommended several measures to correct it, such as setting up a department of propaganda, producing a pamphlet to guide English people in everyday dealings with Chinese of different classes, appealing to the heads of British banks and companies to select staff who would treat the Chinese with respect, and opening up the exclusively European Hong Kong Club to Chinese.[37]

That Braga should have held such a deep grudge against racist practices by the British while still desiring continued British rule must be explained in the context of the peculiar social standing of the Portuguese in colonial Hong Kong. Viewed as "not really Europeans" yet well above the local Chinese population in the "rigid and unyielding class system based on race, occupation, and location," the Portuguese took advantage of the British rule, became a "clerk class" in the colony's major firms, and secured a comfortable life in Hong Kong.[38] They endured their subordination with melancholy acceptance, suppressed their discontent, and sometimes paid a personal price when a few of them attempted, unsuccessfully, to trespass the imposed social limit. In private, Braga wrote at the war's end that "the days of the European in Hong Kong are numbered and in the matter of a few years the Chinese will have everything."[39] Although his memo to the British authorities rendered the thought more subtly, this awareness could not have been his own but shared, readily or grudgingly, by the European expatriate community as it saw the Chinese national flags throughout Hong Kong at the war's end.

Braga's memo received attention in both the Foreign Office and the Colonial Office, probably because it arrived at a moment when London was looking beyond military reoccupation and Braga's recommendations concurred with the official line of desirable action. Officials at the Foreign Office read it "with interest" and were "following up with the idea of a pamphlet for British subjects going to China."[40] In late spring 1946, just before the civilian administration under Sir Mark Young resumed its operation, the memo was sent to Hong Kong for review and comments. There, it was discussed by Colonial Secretary David MacDougall, Secretary for Chinese Affairs R. R. Todd, and Mark Young. Interestingly, MacDougall and Todd "disagree[d] with a great deal of what Mr. Braga says." In the typically rambling, noncommittal official

37. John V. Braga, "Anti-British Feeling in China," citations from 20, 23, 25, 32–34, CO 129/595/1.

38. Coates, 4–8.

39. John Braga to James Braga, March 27, 1946; cited in Braga, 447.

40. G. V. Kitson (Foreign Office) to N. L. Mayle (Colonial Office), April 5, 1946, CO 129/595/1, 14.

language rendered by Sir Mark, the two secretaries "accepted the fact that the possibility of taking any action which may help to improve relations between Chinese and British people should be constantly kept in view."[41] Sir Mark himself endorsed Braga's idea of a British counteroffensive in the propaganda war and considered a propaganda pamphlet "an excellent idea" and was "in favour" of "creation of a department of propaganda." He saw no need, however, for an immediate reform of the European-only Hong Kong Club.[42]

This small episode of internal exchange contradicts a commonly held image of Governor Young, sustained by his famed progressivism in promoting the constitutional reform in Hong Kong and overseeing the repeal of the racist Peak Ordinance. He might also have shared with Braga a more "liberal" concern for eliminating British racist expressions and behavior than other prewar expats in Hong Kong and in China. But the episode reveals his preference of keeping most of the existing institutions in the racial hierarchy intact. The reforms Young and Braga favored were superficial and skirted the fundamental cause—colonial rule.

While those within or near the official circles chose to avoid the question of colonialism, those outside these circles and the privileged realm confronted it directly. In their dissenting voices, a new attitude emerged and drew from on-the-ground observations of the revolutionary transformation of China through the war. "Post-war China is different from Boxer China, different from 1936 China ... it passionately desires to be treated by the other nations as a real equal and partner," one British missionary wrote from central China in Hunan province, where he spent years living among the Chinese.[43] Although he had no way to reach his parliamentary representative from China, his observations and opinions were quoted at length by his sister, Mrs. Margret Riley of West York, in a three-page letter that eventually reached the Foreign Office. Because of his close contact with ordinary Chinese who were "mostly Christian, of all ranks of society," he came to the conclusion that British re-

---

41. Mark Young to T. I. K Lloyd, July 9, 1946, CO 129/595/1, 7–9; citation from 7.

42. Mark Young to T. I. K. Lloyd, July 9, 1946, CO 129/595/1, 8.

43. Mrs. Riley to J. Belcher, M.P., n.d., CO 129/593/1, 25–27. Responses by Foreign Office and Colonial Office officials show that Mrs. Riley's was an enclosure of Belcher's letter dated November 29, 1946. See Belcher to Foreign Office, November 28, 1946, CO 129/593/1, 24.

occupation of Hong Kong and Kowloon "are making the very worst of impressions." In the context of the rising national pride among the Chinese and "from the point of view of our own interests," the missionary argued, the British move became "crass foolishness."[44]

Although "practically isolated from European contacts," this missionary was well informed about ongoing world affairs. He knew that, after the British restored colonial rule in Hong Kong, two events had caused widespread protest: the construction of an airfield at Pingshan in the New Territories, and the killing of a Chinese hawker by a Portuguese man in Hong Kong's police force. Referring to the rising demand for respect among Chinese and the anticolonial principle proclaimed in the Atlantic Charter, he insisted that British retention of Hong Kong "can be justly criticised here." He rejected Britain's official argument about the ongoing civil war in China as an excuse to retain Hong Kong and Kowloon. Having these ceded territories back, he said, "is very much on the Chinese mind." A better approach would be "a plain statement from H. M. Govt. of intention to hand [Hong Kong] back within the next decade … progressively."[45] Incidentally, this suggestion echoed an approach Roosevelt had recommended to China and Britain during the war. Mrs. Riley strongly agreed with her brother: "It seems so utterly unfair that an ally who has fought and suffered so greatly should be treated so spuriously." Keeping the colony, she concluded, caused "a blow to our prestige."[46]

Two longtime observers of China agreed. Oxford-educated New Zealand journalist James M. Bertram (1910–1993) had ardently supported China's resistance against Japanese invasion since his arrival there just before total war broke out. Bertram established his international reputation with cutting-edge reporting on China, first on the Xi'an Incident in 1936 and then a long reportage on the Eighth Route Army as he moved with its fighting units on the North China front. While reporting on the war in China, Bertram passed through Hong Kong often and, with his wide connections, helped Mme. Song Qingling's China Defence League in expanding its international network. He joined the defense of Hong Kong, served as a gunner, and was thrown into a

---

44. Mrs. Riley to Belcher, citation from 26.
45. Mrs. Riley to Belcher, 25.
46. Mrs. Margret M. Riley to Mr. Belcher, M.P., CO 129/593/1, 27.

POW camp after Hong Kong fell.[47] Bertram was freed after nearly four years in captivity. British officials considered him a "likely" candidate for the New Zealand External Service, whose "views in any case are considered to carry some weight with the New Zealand Government." They took note of his report on Hong Kong in March 1946. Like Mrs. Riley's missionary brother, Bertram admitted that "a British Colony might serve as a model of liberal democracy, to anyone acquainted with the oppressive atmosphere of Chinese politics today."[48] But colonial restoration should not be the path taken. Even though the Chinese government focused its attention on the civil war in the north, while Britain succeeded in reoccupying Hong Kong in the south, "the issue of Hong Kong ... is far from dead." He stated his "own private view" as such:

> Hong Kong will have to go back to China; and the sooner this is made clear to all concerned, the better. The great moment for such a gesture was of course the end of the War with Japan; that moment was lost, and not merely lost but poisoned by diplomatic bickerings that will not be forgotten overnight. There was a good case to be made for at least temporary retention of the Colony to secure private British interests—though even that case was not made—but in my view the public interest that might have been served by a spontaneous act of generosity by the British Government to a proved comrade-in-arms would have far outweighed it.[49] [underscoring in original]

What gave Bertram's discussion on Hong Kong and Sino-British relations unusual force was his penetrating critique of Britain's record of decolonization. The experiences of India, he pointed out, had demonstrated Britain's reluctance to surrender its empire: "It is sometimes a habit of British Governments to postpone the making of decisions until the last possible moment."

---

47. Bertram is probably best known for reporting on the Eighth Route Army, *North China Front* (1939), which was immediately translated into Chinese and published in Shanghai in 1939. After settling down in his home country after the war, he took up a position at the University of Auckland teaching English literature and continued to write about China. See Bertram (1993).

48. "Extract from the Report dated 7th March, 1946, made by Mr. James Bertram," CO 129/593/1, 40–41, citation from 40.

49. "Extract from the Report dated 7th March, 1946, made by Mr. James Bertram," 41.

The resulting consequences were particularly harmful to the colony concerned because "the decisions thus made, under the pressure of events whose shadow has long been visible, are not always the happiest or wisest."[50] True to his reputation as a cutting-edge reporter, Bertram's prediction soon became reality when colossal tragedy erupted during the partition of India in 1947.

In contrast to Bertram, who argued through empathy with his intended audience, Polish-born Jewish journalist Israel Epstein (1915–2005) dispatched a forthright and passionate anticolonial critique. Having arrived in China at age two, when his parents fled from the advancing German army, Epstein had made a living as a journalist since his youth and developed a deep sympathy toward the common people in China. Like Bertram, he had worked for Mme. Song Qingling's China Defence League in Hong Kong. He also became a POW after the colony fell but made a daring escape with four other campmates. Wartime observations and reporting from both Guomindang Chongqing and Communist Yan'an moved Epstein further to the left. Just before the war ended, he left China with his British wife, Elsie Fairfax Cholmeley, and arrived in the United States. He reconnected with many of his wartime journalist friends in New York City, wrote about China's monumental struggle for change, and published widely in U.S. and Canadian newspapers. With activist Cholmeley, Epstein joined the Committee for a Democratic Far Eastern Public Policy, which included many notable liberals in political, cultural, and film circles.[51] At this moment of his journalist activism in the United States, the Colonial Office took note of Epstein's article "Hongkong: Past and Present." In it Epstein took Manhattan as an analogy for Hong Kong and made a case about it from the U.S. perspective. What would Americans feel, he asked, if Manhattan were occupied "by a foreign power which clung stubbornly to it"?

Epstein took a further step in criticizing British policy by highlighting the social ills created and sustained by the political system in the colony. He found in British Hong Kong "a reasonable facsimile of modern administration" but "its citizens have no political rights and do not vote." Most objectionable to him was the sharp and deep social divide, with "the great Hongkong and

---

50. "Extract from the Report dated 7th March, 1946, made by Mr. James Bertram," 41.

51. Epstein, esp. chapters 10 and 13, and 224–29.

Shanghai Bank Building, the palatial Hongkong, Gloucester, and Peninsula hotels and the mansions of Chinese millionaires which present an opulent and modern façade." In "the incredible slums of the western area" where "the crowding and tuberculosis rate are among the worst in the world," "'cockloft,' 'cubicles' and 'bed-space' are the commonest terms in Hongkong's housing vocabulary." Epstein recognized that the colony was where Sun Yat-sen learned Western "progressive thought" while China's liberal Democratic League found a base. But he disagreed with Bertram in assessing Hong Kong's value to China's political development. In reality, it provided what he considered an economic haven to "rich Chinese" and warlords who "warehoused their goods." He saw Hong Kong's growth as "a result of its stability relative to the instability of China in her repeatedly impeded revolution, to which the imperialism that created Hongkong contributed so much." Yet the survival of the colony, he indicated, depended so much on the hinterland that "a united, stable China," when it became reality, could easily "cut Hongkong out altogether as an entrepot." Therefore, Epstein concluded with an aphorism that was repeated by many others, including China-born Eurasian writer Han Suyin and Australian journalist Richard Hughes in later decades, "colonialism in Hongkong is living on borrowed time."[52]

Arguments for decolonizing Hong Kong, made by people as diverse as a British missionary, a famous liberal New Zealand journalist, and a Jewish reporter firmly committed to socialism, did not affect British policy. London was already quite aware of the problems highlighted by these astute and eloquent observers. The challenge Britain faced, then, was what policy could best serve colonial restoration in Hong Kong while dulling the edge of domestic and international criticism.

Reversal of British Promise for Constitutional Reform

To criticisms against turning the clock back in Hong Kong, Mark Young (1886–1974), the returning governor of Hong Kong whose tenure had been

---

52. I. Epstein, "Hongkong: Past and Present," CO 129/593/1, "Unofficial Views," 43–46. The phrase was much popularized by Richard Hughes, author of *Hong Kong: Borrowed Place, Borrowed Time*, who learned the phrase from Han Suyin, who attributed it to a former Shanghai businessman.

interrupted by the Japanese occupation, responded to only the one by Braga. Although in agreement with Braga's recommendation for strengthening British propaganda, Governor Young assigned correcting day-to-day British behavior in the colony an extremely low position on his list of priorities.[53] Young must have viewed abolishing the Chinese-discriminating Peak Ordinance after the war to be an adequate accomplishment in ending racism in Hong Kong. However important a symbol the Peak Ordinance was, eliminating it did not change the fact that the Peak continued to remain a forbidden territory reserved only for Europeans and the rich and powerful. To Young, systemic reform of discriminatory prewar practices in the colonial establishment was unnecessary. He continued to endorse recommendations placing British in superior positions in the colony's bureaucratic apparatus, an issue we shall encounter when discussing the Labour Department.

What preoccupied Governor Young during his brief return to the colony between May 1946 and July 1947 was constitutional reform in postwar Hong Kong. On May 1, 1946, when he resumed office, Young announced the reform in his public speech as the intention of the British government: "His Majesty's government has under consideration the means by which in Hongkong, as elsewhere in the Colonial Empire, the inhabitants of the Territory can be given a fuller and more responsible share in the management of their own affairs." This "fuller and more responsible share" meant "a Municipal Council constituted on a fully representative basis."[54] In October 1946, the so-called Young Plan was submitted to the Colonial Office, recommending a municipal council with a majority of twenty directly elected members out of a total of thirty seats. In addition, the Legislative Council was to be slightly restructured by increasing unofficial members. In July 1947, London announced approval of the Young Plan.[55]

Set against the tide of anticolonialism in the postwar years, the Young Plan was intended not to reverse but to reinforce the course of colonial restoration in Hong Kong. Young envisioned the reform as a critical step toward keeping Hong Kong inside the empire by gradually involving the Chinese in a British-

53. Mark Young to T. I. K. Lloyd at Colonial Office, July 9, 1946, CO 129/595, 7.

54. "Governor's Speech, 1st May, 1946," CO 129/595/4, "Arrival of Governor in Hong Kong: Resumption of Duty," 19–21; citation from 21.

55. Tsang (1988), 33–34, 46.

led system and enabling their self-government. His plan disenfranchised the overwhelming majority of local Chinese through property qualifications and residence requirements, which differentiated between Chinese who were not British subjects (a six-year residence out of the past ten years to qualify for voting rights) and those who were British subjects (only a one-year residence after age twenty-three to qualify for voting rights). This scheme was remote from the principle of "one person, one vote" characteristic of participatory democracy. The proposed municipal council with greater power would depart from prewar colonial practices in certain regards. It could nominate two members to the Legislative Council and appoint municipal officers. Most radically, it would be free from external financial and political control, without reserving special power for the governor.[56] The proposed reforms, however limited, aroused great fear in unofficial members of the Executive and Legislative Councils, who foresaw their vested interests in Hong Kong's economy and political institutions eroded by rearrangement of the governing structure. Fortunately for them, the appointment of Alexander Grantham (1899–1978) as the colony's twenty-second governor added decisive weight to their resistance.

Grantham was no stranger to colonial Hong Kong. He had learned the "Hong Kong way" during the thirteen years between 1922 and 1935. Arriving in Hong Kong as a cadet and then working as a junior official in the administration gave him a deep understanding of its strictly hierarchical world, in which junior staff had to treat *taipan*s and department directors in government with "utmost deference." "When we were leaving their presence," noted Grantham, "we always had to walk out backwards in front of them." As a young man, Grantham had laughed at the operation of Hong Kong's colonial government, calling it "ponderous, cumbersome in the extreme."[57] Accepting appointment as Bermuda's colonial secretary in 1935 opened a fast track to his promotion. He served on that bucolic and peaceful island for three years and then was posted to Jamaica when labor unrest swept the British West Indies. During the war, he was sent to Nigeria, an appointment he did not particularly like because West Africa's climate was believed to be harmful to Europeans. But it was a necessary step toward his much-desired promotion to the governorship of Fuji with the concurrent position of high commissioner of the

---

56. Tsang (1988), 34–35.
57. Grantham (1968), 6.

Fig. 3. Governor Alexander Grantham. Courtesy of Information Services Department, Hong Kong Government (SAR).

western Pacific. This ascendance in the British colonial administrative hierarchy started as a "gamble," as Grantham put it half-jokingly in retrospect.[58] It
reaped a handsome reward. He became one of only three Far Eastern cadets
(among eighty-five trained between 1862 and 1941) to rise to this position of
distinction.[59]

Although both Young and Grantham had served in British colonies in the
West Indies and West Africa, Grantham took a different view of the constitutional reform in Hong Kong that Young advocated. Based on his observation
and experience with Chinese society, Grantham believed Young misunder-
stood Hong Kong. Young saw opening positions to local Chinese as a way
toward self-government under British tutelage, and thus keeping Hong Kong
within the empire. Grantham considered Young's rationale an illusion because
"Hong Kong can never be independent. Either it remains a British colony, or
it is re-absorbed into China as a part of the province of Kwangtung [Guang-
dong]."[60] Geographical proximity to the mainland was not the only reason for
his rejection of the Young Plan. Momentarily, Grantham saw the need to
emphasize the Chinese inability to participate in Hong Kong's political process, however limited that might be. He argued that the Chinese, who made up
more than 97 percent of Hong Kong's residents, were "generally speaking,
politically apathetic."[61] Later, he sang this litany to London again and again.
Others repeated his line, too, without thinking twice that it was uttered not
from Grantham's conviction or knowledge about Hong Kong, but from the
political imperative of sustaining a system that had outlived its time.

In fact, Grantham deeply understood the political potential of working
Chinese in Hong Kong. He had witnessed political crises in two colonies—
Hong Kong in the 1920s and early 1930s and Jamaica in the late 1930s. These
experiences powerfully shaped his outlook when he returned as Hong Kong's
governor. In both Hong Kong and Jamaica, labor made up the predominant
part of the population and brought great challenges to colonial rule during
those years. When 200,000 Chinese laborers walked out of Hong Kong in

---

58. Grantham (1965), 19, chapters 2–5; Grantham (1968), 8.

59. The other two are Francis Henry May (1912–1918), the twelfth governor
(1912–1918), and Cecil Clementi (1925–1930), the seventeenth governor (1925–
1930). See Lethbridge (1978a), citation from 31.

60. Grantham (1965), 111.

61. Grantham (1965), 111–12.

1925 to protest the British killing of Chinese demonstrators on the mainland, not only did the economy decline sharply but everyday tranquility in Hong Kong's European community vanished. Then fresh to colonial administration, Grantham tried to make light of the 1925–1926 General Strike-Boycott. What concerned him most, he said, was that his wedding at the end of 1925 not be postponed by the unrest. He was married on schedule. "As a junior I was not concerned with the politics of the matter," he admitted, "and was only inconvenienced to the extent of having to do duty as a special constable and trying to cope with my own cooking and other household chores, since all our servants had left." In his first decade in Hong Kong, Grantham appeared to be more attentive to advancing his career, using his two home leaves to read for the bar and attend a year-long course at the Imperial Defence College. He noted the severity of anti-Japanese protests by Hong Kong Chinese in 1931, however. The clash between Chinese protesters and police and garrison troops ended with more than 400 deaths among the protesters.[62]

Transfer and promotion in the West Indies brought Grantham into the thicket of widespread labor disturbances in 1938. Jamaica, he noted, "had had strikes and riots on a serious scale." Instead of admitting that the cause was mismanagement by European firms paying locals below-subsistence wages, he saw the trouble stemming from explosive population growth "outstripping the means of supporting it." As Jamaica's new colonial secretary, the second senior official below the governor, Grantham's duties ranged from attending the Legislative Council to overseeing the government budget. Because he "never worked so hard before or since," he and his wife had to reduce "social evenings" to twice a week. Nonetheless, he gained insights in colonial administration during that extraordinary time by observing the performance of Governor Arthur Richards, a model governor in Grantham's view: "Firm, sympathetic to the under-privileged, and progressive in his political outlook, he was neither a reactionary nor a sentimentalist."[63] These qualities, centered on paternalistic benevolence, became Grantham's own when he assumed the governorship of Hong Kong at yet another "troublous time."

Sad scenes wrought by the war, relieved only by a few positive changes, were waiting for Grantham in Hong Kong. In July 1947, he landed at the Kai Tak

---

62. Grantham (1965), 15, 18, Grantham (1968), 8.
63. Grantham (1965), 32, 36–37.

airport and made the ferry crossing to Hong Kong Island. The depressed economy was visible everywhere he turned. Nearly a year had passed since the Japanese surrendered, yet Victoria Harbour, once noisy and crowded with ships from all over the world, was "all silent" with only a few battered freighters. He noted that about 70 percent of European-style residences and 20 percent of the tenements were still dilapidated. He also noticed "a greater mixing of the races," and a "decline in social snobbishness." The *taipan* and senior government officials no longer viewed themselves as "demi-gods." To him, these were important signs of social progress.[64]

An old Hong Kong hand, Grantham knew whose voice carried weight in the colony. Its primary character as an entrepôt, in his judgment, made trade "vital to the people of Hong Kong."[65] Recovery from the sad state evident in Victoria Harbour would require intensive labor input; skillful management from the top, in his view, was critical. Arthur Morse, the chief manager of the Hong Kong and Shanghai Bank, whose arguments shaped London's justification for reoccupying Hong Kong at the end of the war, topped Grantham's list of people indispensable to Hong Kong's revival. Morse was so keen about British restoration in Hong Kong that he placed £5 million at the disposal of the Hong Kong Planning Unit without government guarantee. He was appointed an unofficial member of the colony's Executive Council as soon as he returned in 1946.[66] The other person high on Grantham's list was Man Kam Lo (Luo Wenjin), the most eloquent and articulate non-European member of the Legislative Council. A British-educated lawyer and a Eurasian, M. K., as he was referred to, was the most outspoken critic against racial discrimination in the colony's establishment. Yet politically he was "conservative and elitist to the core."[67] Grantham considered him as having "a first class brain, great moral courage and a capacity for digging down into details without getting lost in them." When chairing meetings of the Legislative Council, Governor Grantham "could hardly wait for the previous speaker to finish and to hear

64. Grantham (1965), 99, 103, 104; Hong Kong Government, *Annual Report of Hong Kong*, 1947.

65. Grantham (1959), 120. This was Grantham's speech to the Royal Central Asian Society on November 10, 1958.

66. Grantham (1968), 10; Grantham (1965); King.

67. Pepper (2008), 96.

'M. K.'" and always found him "invariably right to the point."[68] Indeed, M. K. Lo turned out to be the most stringent and important opponent to the Young Plan on constitutional reforms.

Grantham himself was not in favor of the Young Plan in general and op- posed one issue in particular: its limit to the power of the governor. At a briefing in the Colonial Office before his departure for Hong Kong, Grantham had voiced his opposition to a Municipal Council with no external control. Citing the case of Jamaica, he argued the need for the governor "in certain circumstances to reassume certain or all of the functions of the Municipal Council." He appeared to have convinced the Colonial Office to accept his view of the power of the governor.[69] Young had retired just as London en- dorsed his plan, so implementing the reforms fell on Grantham. In what po- litical scientist Suzanne Pepper defined as "new beginnings, old solutions," bureaucratic procrastination under the Grantham administration became the first offensive against the Young Plan. Legislation to implement the plan took two years to complete. Once it was sent to the Legislative Council, unof- ficial members, led by M. K., rose to their feet to detail their oppositions, and vetoed it.[70]

As Grantham applied the brakes to reform, he was aided by the rapidly changing political situation in China and corresponding positions in London. On the mainland, Chinese Communists began to turn the tide of the civil war, winning battle after battle in their rapid southward advance. Grantham's argu- ment that direct elections opened ways to "Communist infiltration" thus eas- ily won the attention in the Colonial Office. Meanwhile, constitutional reform still had its advocates among Hong Kong's small but vocal professional and business circles, who tried to continue the campaign. They formed two civic organizations, the Hong Kong Reform Club with mixed expatriate and Chinese

---

68. Grantham (1965), 110.

69. Minutes by Goldsworthy, July 28, 1947, and August 1, 1947, CO 129/609/2, Future Policy: Constitution—Municipal Council, 2, 3; also see "Extract from letter received from T. M. Hazlerigg dated 24.11.1947, to Mr. Roberts-Wray," 6, in which Hazlerigg alerted the Colonial Office about the infiltration of 2,000 "ragtag and bobtail—office boys, lift operators, door keepers, and the like" into the Chinese Chamber of Commerce, a nominating body for the proposed Municipal Council.

70. Pepper (2008), 96; "Minutes of the Legislative Council, June 22, 1949," *Hong Kong Hansard* 1949, 184–205, esp. 188–205.

membership, and the Hong Kong Chinese Reform Association, primarily Chinese. But their voice became timid in 1949. The chairman of the Hong Kong Chinese Reform Association suggested in May that constitutional reform was not for "self-government" but to begin cultivating the capacity for "home rule."[71] By then the Colonial Office no longer supported changing Hong Kong's political structure. Preoccupied by the Malayan Emergency, which erupted a year earlier and continued at full force, and fearful of a possible domino effect in Southeast Asia caused by the Communist victory in China, London focused on face-saving measures, back-stepping from its promised constitutional reforms in Hong Kong. In 1952, London finally put the reform to sleep for good.[72]

Communist Retreat from South China

Simultaneously as the British braved the headwind of anticolonialism and focused their energy to reoccupy the lost colony, the Communists were readjusting their national strategy and turning attention to tasks far away from Hong Kong. It is ironic that, just as constitutional reform in Hong Kong under the British flag died a slow and inconspicuous death from fear of "Communist infiltration," the once-active resistance force under Communist leadership evacuated itself from Hong Kong and South China. Although coincidental, these moves left the reoccupied colony more firmly in British hands.

The war ended in a brief moment of celebration for the Communist-led East River guerrillas, though the excitement of victory over the Japanese invaders quickly diminished after Chinese government troops began relentless attacks. In the wake of the Japanese surrender, the East River Column enlisted more than 3,000 new local recruits, bringing its total force up to 14,000 strong.[73] Expansion turned out to be temporary. Already in July 1945, the government ordered the Sixty-Third and the Sixty-Fifth Corps in south Jiangxi to march down to north Guangdong. By late July, these troops had

---

71. S. Y. Wong [Huang Xinyan], "Reform Platform," *Hong Kong Standard*, May 18, 1949, cited in Pepper (2008), 97.

72. Tsang (1988), 165.

73. Zeng, 434.

swept into base areas established by the East River Column in north and central Guangdong. A major battle near Shaoguan at the beginning of August inflicted heavy casualties on the Communist guerrillas and caused more than 120 deaths among the locals. The East River Column faced an overwhelmingly strong enemy deploying eleven divisions. To survive, the column divided its troops and retreated from many of its bases.[74] In an all-Guangdong campaign in October, the Chinese government aimed for eliminating all Communist troops in three months.[75] By the time the U.S.-mediated Chongqing negotiations started in September 1945, Guangdong was already one of eight major sites in an emerging national civil war.

The ordeals of the East River Column in South China mirrored the national experiences of the Communist forces during and after the war. With widespread popular support yet no guaranteed supplies of weaponry or provisions, the Communist forces were at a material disadvantage vis-à-vis the government troops, which were supplied by a flood of U.S. arms and equipment. However disappointed with the Guomindang-led government, the United States still found it a closer ideological ally than the Chinese Communists. When the Japanese invasion suddenly ended, the U.S. Marines and Air Force helped ship-lift and airlift Chiang's troops from the western hinterland to the north, east, and along the coast. U.S. support gave the Guomindang government a decisive edge in the escalating civil war. Reoccupying Beijing was a case in point. In early October 1945, government troops easily captured the city even though it was within a largely Communist-controlled area. "Chinese Communists are no match for Central Govt troops acting with American assistance," the U.S. military attaché observed; "their area of influence has been shrinking and center of their power withdrawing to north."[76]

The Communists found U.S. partiality especially alarming, because they initially hoped for a political solution to their differences with the Guomindang through U.S. mediation. They had not forgotten the bitter lessons of 1927 when Chiang Kai-shek turned against the Communists and massacred thousands of them. They remembered the tragedy of the New Fourth Army

---

74. Zeng, 432–33.

75. Zeng, 437.

76. "The Chargé of China (Robertson) to the Secretary of State," October 14, 1945, in *FRUS 1945, the Far East, China*, 7:579–80.

when government troops ambushed it in 1941. In the continued U.S. aid to government troops, the Communists began to recognize echoes of ongoing events in Europe. In early 1945, the left-wing Greek People's Liberation Army put down arms after signing a cease-fire agreement with British-led Allied forces in the wake of a month-long military conflict. Subsequently, the Greek government, supported by Britain and controlled by former collaborators and right-wing groups, systematically persecuted former resisters.[77] The Chinese Communists understood that international forces played a vital role in this modern Greek tragedy. They named it "Scobie's Danger" (*Sikebi weixian*) after the British commander in Greece, Lieutenant General Ronald Scobie.[78] They held no illusions when Chiang Kai-shek, pressured by the United States for a political settlement in postwar China, telegrammed Yan'an repeatedly in August 1945 inviting Communist leaders to meet for negotiation.

In fact, top-level negotiations between the CCP and the Guomindang had been under way since early 1945, with no success in bridging their differences. Mediated by Patrick Hurley, U.S. ambassador to China, the two sides were unwilling to compromise on two sticky issues: the Communist troops and the form of government in Communist-controlled areas. With Hurley, the Communists initially worked out a five-point proposal, including unifying all armed forces after Japanese surrender, forming a coalition government, and legalizing all political parties.[79] The Guomindang-led government in Chongqing flatly rejected the proposal by demanding immediate incorporation of Communist forces into the national army before considering other issues.[80] Top-level talks broke down after March 1 when Chiang, in a public statement, refused to relinquish the Guomindang's "power of ultimate decision."[81] Meanwhile, Hurley rejected a recommendation by the U.S. chargé to provide a small

---

77. Mazower, epilogue, esp. 368–75. As Mazower notes, there were still thousands of former resisters and leftists in Greek jails due to the turn of events in 1944 and 1945.

78. "Zhonggong zhongyang guanyu Riben touxianghou wo dang renwu de jueding (The decision on our party's future tasks after Japan's surrender)," August 11, 1945, in Zhongyang danganguan (ed.), 15:228–31; citation from 230.

79. "The Five-point Draft Agreement, November 10, 1944," Department of State (1967), 74. Hereafter cited as *USRC*.

80. "The Three-Point Plan," in *USRC*, 75.

81. "The Generalissimo's Statement of March 1, 1945," in *USRC*, 83.

amount of war matériel to the Communist forces, believing it would undercut "the established policy of the United States to prevent the collapse of the National Government and to sustain Chiang Kai-shek as president of the Government."[82] CCP–Guomindang talks resumed in July and eventually culminated in a forty-three-day visit to Chongqing by Mao Zedong and his delegation. Even so, all that had really been achieved was a reaffirmation of Guomindang confidence in U.S. support and deepening mistrust among the Communists.

Awareness of Scobie's Danger, their own material weakness, and their need of armed self-defense shaped the Communist approach to the Chongqing negotiations. In the historic month of Japanese surrender and the subsequent talks, decisions made by the Central Committee of the CCP were militarily conservative. The choice resulted from the Communist failure to achieve a short-term goal, which turned out to be overly ambitious. On August 11, 1945, the Central Committee issued a "Decision on Our Party's Tasks after Japan's Surrender," anticipating a short-term expansion and a long-term war. It viewed the foreseeable future in "two phases." The first was to "force the [Japanese] enemy and its puppet troops to surrender to us … expand vigorously the liberated areas, and occupy as many big or small cities and transportation arteries as possible." More important was an anticipated second phase: "the Guomindang is most likely to launch a large-scale offensive against us. Our party must mobilize troops to confront a civil war."[83] The short-term task of expanding Communist areas failed. In mid-September, as talks in Chongqing continued, the Communist Central Committee shifted its "national strategy" in response to a reported Soviet army withdrawal from Manchuria. The Central Committee understood the strategic importance of the northeast, and was determined to "get [it] into our hands." To that end, the Central Committee decided to concentrate its armed forces and adopted a "national strategy" of "advance in the north, defense in the south."[84] Coordi-

---

82. "Ambassador Hurley's Recommendation against American Aid to the Chinese Communists," in *USRC*, 87.

83. "中共中央關於日本投降後我黨任務的決定" (Decision by the party Central Committee on our task after Japanese surrender), *ZGZYWJXJ*, vol. 15, citation from 228, 229.

84. "中央關於確定向北推進向南防禦的戰略方針致中共赴渝談判代表團電" (Telegram to CCP negotiation delegation to Chongqing regarding the decision

nating instructions were issued to party organizations in south and central China as soon as the decision was agreed on by the Communist delegation in Chongqing.[85]

At the war capital, the Communists reached a conciliatory deal with the government and signed with it a twelve-point memorandum that ended negotiations on October 10, 1945. Titled "Summary of Conversations between Representatives of the National Government and of the Chinese Communist Party," the document was far from a final agreement. Two problems that fundamentally divided them remained. The question of local governments in Communist-controlled areas was left undecided. The issue of military reorganization was settled for the time being by reducing and relocating Communist troops away from the government heartland. The Communists agreed to "take prompt action to demobilize their anti-Japanese troops" in seven provinces (Guangdong, Zhejiang, southern Jiangsu, southern and central Anhui, Hunan, Hubei and southern Henan). Once reorganized, the Communist troops would withdraw to areas north of Longhai Railway, to northern Jiangsu, and northern Anhui.[86] These provinces were economically more devel-

---

by the Central Committee on the strategy of offense in the north and defense in the south), September 17, 1945, in *ZGZYWJXJ*, 15:278–80; "軍委關於爭奪東北的戰略方針與具體部署的指示" (Specific instructions on deployment by the Military Committee to pursue the strategy of taking the northeast), September 28, 1945, in *ZGZYWJXJ*, 15:299–301.

85.   "中共赴渝談判代表團關於向北推進向南防禦的戰略部署等給中央的復電" (Reply telegram from the negotiation delegation to Chongqing to the Central Committee regarding the strategy of offense in the north and defense in the south), September 19, 1945, in *ZGZYWJXJ*, 15:280; "中央關於統一分散堅持的部署給廣東區黨委的指示" (Central Committee directive to the Guangdong Regional Branch regarding continuing the work through coordinated separation of troops), September 19, 1945, in *ZGZYWJXJ*, 15:281; "中央關於撤退江南部隊向北進軍問題給華中局的指示" (Central Committee directive to Central China Bureau on withdrawing troops from areas south of the Yangtze River to march northward), in *ZGZYWJXJ*, 15:286–87, "中央關於必須控制江北給華中局的指示" (Central Committee directive to Central China Bureau on firmly control areas north of the Yangtze River), September 26, 1945, in *ZGZYWJXJ*, 15:298.

86. "Summary of Conversations Between Representatives of the National Government and of the Chinese Communist Party," initially issued by the Chinese Ministry of Information on October 11, 1945, and reprinted as Annex 49 in *USRC*, 577–81; citation from 579.

oped and in close proximity to the national capital; removing the Communist presence resulted in a temporary gain for the Nationalist government.

However superficial a gesture of reconciliation, the general agreement reached at Chongqing led to the removal of the East River Column from South China. Executing the Chongqing agreement brought commanders of the East River Column and government troops in Guangdong face to face across the negotiation table in Guangzhou, while U.S. officers mediated and assisted during months of arduous negotiation. At one point, a commander of the East River Column was nearly killed by an "accidentally" derailed train. He had intended to board the train from Guangzhou to Hong Kong to ready his troops for relocation. Fortunately, failure to get a ticket saved his life. On another occasion, the East River Column delegation had to borrow the U.S. representatives' wireless station after government special agents disabled their device.[87] Even after the memo of agreement for the evacuation was reached in late May 1946, all East River Column branches remained extremely vigilant as they marched to rendezvous for assembly, as several units were ambushed by government troops along the way. When three U.S. warships arrived at Mirs Bay on June 26, 1946, to transport these troops, some demobilized guerrilla fighters came forward and insisted on being taken north as well. The generous U.S. officers agreed to take as many on board as their ships could carry. Thus, the total evacuated to the north increased to 2,583 from the originally agreed on number of 2,400.[88] Once they reached the city of Yantai on the Shandong peninsula, these relocated guerrillas formally enlisted in the People's Liberation Army, as the Communist troops were now called.[89]

Evacuation of the East River Column marked a new phase in Communist activities in South China and Hong Kong. During the transitional period between Japanese surrender and British reoccupation, the East River Column

---

87. Zeng, 461–62.

88. Zeng, 478.

89. The evacuated East River Column did not join the ongoing battles in Manchuria but remained in north China to receive further training. In 1947, these experienced former guerrilla fighters assumed the core leadership in a reorganized Guangdong and Guangxi Column of the People's Liberation Army, which incorporated thousands of surrendered soldiers from the government troops. Three years later, they returned to Guangdong, fighting in the battle for South China in late 1949. See Zeng, 491–94.

liberated and controlled the New Territories beyond urban Hong Kong and Kowloon. Instructed by the Central Committee of the Communist Party, the Guangdong branch dispatched Tan Tiandu (1893–1999), one of the party's oldest members who was then an administrator of the district of Dongguan and Bao'an under guerrilla control, to negotiate the status of Communists in postwar Hong Kong with a representative from the British military adminis-tration. Their talks began in early September, just as the military administra-tion began governing Hong Kong, and concluded in late October. Huang Zuomei, soon to be appointed director of the Communist Xinhua News Agency in Hong Kong, assisted with translation during the early phase of negotiation.[90] This direct contact between the Communists and the British in Hong Kong paralleled ongoing Chongqing negotiations between the govern-ment and the CCP. It enabled the Communists to secure some advantages in postwar Hong Kong.[91]

The East River guerrillas' wartime assistance to the Allies and their solid control of the New Territories presented the Communists with useful leverage in negotiation. The British agreed to allow the Communists "semi-legal" sta-tus and maintain their "semi-open" offices in the colony.[92] In addition, Tan sought British permission for Communist-funded newspapers and journals and operation of a wireless station in Hong Kong. He requested British guar-antees for the safety of Communist noncombatants and wounded guerrillas, relief for local Chinese in the New Territories, and a pledge not to enter Communist-controlled areas without permission. To demonstrate their com-mitment to not interfere with British rule in the area, on September 28 the

---

90. Tan Tiandu, citation from 60. Although the reference of "representative of the Hong Kong Governor" indicates some confusion in Tan, a non-English speaker, over the nature of the British governance at the time, what he left in this memoir was an important record of the first contact between the Communist organization and the British authorities at the moment of transition. While no record can be found on the British side on these talks, actual practice in Communist activities in subsequent years proves the integrity of Tan's record. The importance of this mutual understand-ing, kept by both sides as an internal secret, is shown in the fact that Tan did not disclose it until 1997, when Hong Kong was reintegrated into China.

91. Tan Tiandu, 60–63.

92. The term used by Tan was "semi-open" (半公開), though it is better trans-lated as "semi-legal" within the Hong Kong context, with an emphasis on legality.

East River Column issued a "Statement of Evacuating from Hong Kong, Kowloon and the New Territories by Hong Kong–Kowloon Independent Brigade of the East River Column," publicly announcing its plan to evacuate from the area within a week.[93] In early October, the British representative agreed to most of the conditions laid out by the Communists, including "freedom of travel, residence, and employment in Hong Kong and Kowloon" for Communist personnel.[94] These arrangements, as practiced in postwar Hong Kong, defined the basic latitude for Communist activities and lasted until 1997.

The British–CCP accommodation was mutual. An acute shortage of personnel and police during the transitional months of reoccupation forced the British to use the East River guerrillas as a local security force. Fully aware of their reliability and popularity among the local Chinese people, the British representative in talks with both Tan Tiandu and guerrilla leaders requested a delay in departure of the Hong Kong–Kowloon Independent Brigade. The two sides agreed to keep some brigade personnel in the New Territories for another three or four months, and military representatives met at Kowloon's Peninsula Hotel to hammer out specific arrangements. In October 1945, demobilized guerrilla fighters from the Hong Kong–Kowloon Independent Brigade formed four self-defense militia groups, ranging from twenty to thirty members each. The British military administration provided each militia member with a rifle, a uniform, and a monthly stipend of HK$60. As it turned out, their services were needed, not just for the three to four months initially anticipated, but for nearly a year until the early fall of 1946.[95]

Of course, arrangements on the ground grew out of pragmatic needs. CCP-British accommodations in postwar Hong Kong were not an abrupt departure from the past. In the second half of the 1930s, as Japanese invasion escalated on the mainland, British authorities had acquiesced to the operation of a Hong

---

93. "東江縱隊港九獨立大隊撤退港九新界宣言" (Statement of Evacuating from Hong Kong, Kowloon and the New Territories by the Hong Kong–Kowloon Independent Brigade of the East River Column), September 28, 1945, reprinted in Gangjiu Duli Daduishi bianxiezu (ed.), 190–91.

94. "廣東區黨委致中央電" (Telegram from Guangdong Regional Branch to the Central Committee), October 2, 1945, in GDGM, 38:527–28; "林平致中央電" (Lin Ping to Central Committee), October 9, 1945, in GDGM, 38:529–30.

95. Tan Tiandu, 65; GangJiu duili daduishi bianxiezu (ed.), 184–85.

Kong liaison office of the Communist Eighth Route Army, even though they placed it under close watch of the Special Branch. Postwar arrangements went a half step further than prewar practices, not because the British trusted the Chinese Communists more than before but because they desperately needed to regain control of reoccupied Hong Kong. During 1945–1946, the Communists appeared less threatening than the Guomindang to restored British rule in Hong Kong. This differential approach to China's two major political parties, as the following discussion will show, reversed when their relative power on the mainland rebalanced in the late 1940s.

The new Communist strategy of "advance in the north, defense in the south" necessitated the readjustment of local organizations in South China, including Hong Kong. In late 1945, the Communist Central Committee ordered guerrilla forces in Guangdong to relocate northward to border areas near Hunan Province. Forces in control of small cities also had to "withdraw and retreat into the countryside for guerilla warfare." They were advised to "waste no arduous efforts on taking over the major cities such as Hong Kong and Kowloon, Shantou, and Guangzhou; such action should wait until the military force is ready to do so."[96] By moving away from major cities, Communists in every location tried to preserve their strength for long-term struggle in the civil war on the mainland. To assure the British that the CCP in the foreseeable future would focus only on fighting its political rival in China, the party again explicated its intention regarding Hong Kong at the end of 1946. In a conversation between Mao Zedong and British intelligence officer Colonel Gordon Harmon in early December 1946, Mao was reported to have said that he was "not interested in Hongkong, and will certainly not allow it to be a bone of contention between your country and mine" as long as "your officials do not maltreat Chinese subjects in Hongkong."[97] As it turned out, no interference in Hong Kong affairs and no mistreatment of Chinese in Hong Kong proved to be the basic principles the future Commu-

---

96. "中央關於創立湘粵邊根據地等給廣東區黨委的指示" (Central Committee directive to Guangdong Regional Branch on establishing a Hunan-Guangdong border base), August 11, 1945, *ZGZYWJXJ*, 15:225–27.

97. J. R. Boyce (Acting Consul in Beiping) to British Embassy in Nanjing, December 30, 1946, FO 371/63318. Harmon visited Yan'an between December 4 and December 11, 1946.

nist government continued to insist on until Hong Kong's reintegration into China.

Communist organizations in Hong Kong went through readjustments between late 1945 and 1947 to comply with "semi-open" accommodation. In August 1945, the CCP Central Committee accepted the recommendation from Yin Linping, then secretary of Guangdong District Committee, to designate personnel for works in Hong Kong. The instruction emphasized a "strict division between the united-front work with middle-upper social classes and the work in the city. ... Therefore the leadership must be divided into two sets, both report directly to the [Guangdong] District Committee."[98] The first was an "open line" with those working on cultivating sympathy and understanding of Communist endeavors in Hong Kong society and therefore known to the police and the public. Lian Guan, who had worked at the Eighth Route Army Liaison Office in the late 1930s, assumed leadership in the "open line" of united front work in Hong Kong. The second line of command remained secret and focused on mass organization activities at the grassroots. Liang Guang, a veteran Communist who remained in Guangdong and directed activities in occupied South China throughout the war, was appointed to lead these underground activities.[99]

In summer 1946, the two offices in Hong Kong finally took shape after months of preparation. The Hong Kong Work Committee (abbreviated as Work Committee, Gongwei) directed open or semi-open activities or activities tolerated by the British. Its members were tasked to openly interact with British authorities and Hong Kong society. The City Committee of Hong Kong (abbreviated as City Committee, Chengwei) operated as an internal branch. Its work included activities in Hong Kong and regions of South China still controlled by the Guomindang-led national government. Directing these parallel committees was the Branch Bureau of Hong Kong headed by Bureau Secretary Fang Fang (d. 1971), which reported to the Nanjing Bureau led by

---

98. "中共中央致尹林平電" (Central Committee to Yin Linping), September 17, 1945, Central Archive; cited in Yuan Xiaolun, 26–27.

99. "林平致中央電" (Linping to Central Committee), September 8, 1945, GDGM, 38:517; "廣東區黨委對廣東長期堅持鬥爭的工作佈置" (Arrangements by Guangdong Regional Branch on long-term persistence in the Guangdong), GDGM, 38:523–24.

Zhou Enlai. In May 1947, a separate Hong Kong Bureau was established, which reported directly to the Central Committee in the northwest.[100]

These adjustments in the chain of command reflected geopolitical shifts in the ongoing civil war between the Communists and the Guomindang-led government. The two parties terminated their negotiations in spring 1947 when the civil war ramped up with greater intensity. The Nanjing Bureau, which commanded Communist organizations in South China, was abolished and the Communist delegation in Nanjing was recalled to Yan'an. The change also highlighted Hong Kong's importance in the overall strategic design of the Communists during these uncertain years. Still far from achieving firm control in the northeast and north China, the Communist Party treated Hong Kong not as a separate entity but as a part of South China still in enemy hands. Differences caused by accommodations to British rule resulted in mixed feelings among Communist leaders. Qiao Guanhuan, a leading international affairs analyst working from Hong Kong in those years and the future minister of foreign affairs, voiced his caution: "Britain took a double policy toward China. On the one hand they worked closely with Chiang Kai-shek. On the other hand they did not refuse us [Communists]."[101] Out of pragmatic needs and taking advantage of British accommodation, the Communists placed Hong Kong within the scheme of their national strategy. "Hong Kong at present can only be the second-line to Beijing and Shanghai," as Zhou Enlai put it explicitly in October 1946, "while Southeast Asia is to be the third-line."[102] This vision emerging at a time of Communist weakness was retained well into the early decades of the People's Republic of China.

---

100. Instructions from the Nanjing Bureau provided specific guidance to each committee. See "中共中央南京局對港澳工作指示" (Directive from the Nanjing Bureau of the CCP Central Committee for works in Hong Kong and Macau), in *ZGZYNJJ*, 63–64; the Hong Kong Bureau was to be renamed the South China Bureau in February 1949, receiving orders directly from the Central Committee. Fang Fang was named to be its secretary. See *GDZZSZL*, 1:370–71, 387–88. Also see "An Outline," in *ZGZYNJJ*, 1–13.

101. Zhang Hanzhi, 351–52.

102. "周恩來關於對港工作意見致延安轉方方尹林平並工委電" (Telegram Regarding the Work in Hong Kong from Zhou Enlai to Fang Fang, Yin Linping and the Work Committee via Yan'an), October 29, 1946, *ZGZYNJJ*, 178.

During the transitional phase of the civil war, rebalance of power on the mainland caused significant flux in the Communist organization in Hong Kong. Two party branches—one for local Communists in Hong Kong and the other for sojourners or political refugees passing through—remained strictly separate. More than 1,000 political and cultural leaders, either Communists or with pro-Communist attitudes, passed through Hong Kong between 1947 and 1948. They included members of the Guomindang left, famous writers, and future leaders in the Communist government, such as Qiao Guanhua and Zhang Hanfu. These people took up temporary residency in Hong Kong and had rather superficial effects on local social movements while holding temporary posts in the local party organization. Following the instruction that "the lower level [activists] should absolutely refrain from making contact within the party network,"[103] activists working in trade unions no longer had direct contact with those working in the press or cultural circles. This tradition was retained well beyond 1949 until Hong Kong's reintegration into China in 1997.[104]

Like many other former European colonies in Asia, Hong Kong became a testing ground of moral principle for the great powers at the end of World War II. British reoccupation disregarded worldwide opposition to colonialism and recapitulated the grand failure of the Wilsonian principle, this time in the failure of the Atlantic Charter. Just as the Wilsonian principle of self-determination retreated at the negotiation table in Versailles in the face of joint pressure from imperialist powers, the Atlantic Charter's vision disappeared in Britain's struggle to maintain its imperial interests and in the United States's race to dominate the postwar world. Hong Kong did not decolonize as the Chinese and many others around the world desired. Eventually, British reoccupation made Hong Kong a "colonial dinosaur" in the modern age of decolonization.

Ultimately, restoration of British rule in Hong Kong succeeded because of China's weakness and internal division. Eager to fight its internal political

---

103. "中共中央南京局對港指示" (Directive to Hong Kong from the Nanjing Bureau of CCP), June 2, 1946, *ZGZYNJJ*, 63–64.

104. Interview with Lo Hoising, summer 2008, recorded.

enemy and obtain U.S. aid for that purpose, the Guomindang-led Chinese government was pathetically weak-kneed on the Hong Kong question. Its nearby troops remained idle while the British grasped this symbol of national honor. The Communists had a military presence in Hong Kong as China's political opposition. One can speculate that the Communists did not want to take over Hong Kong for the Guomindang-led government in South China, which would have only weakened their position in the north. But this can be easily disputed. In reality, the combined strength of the East River Column and the guerrillas in Hainan was inadequate to confront either the regular troops of Chinese government or determined British takeover. Nonetheless, on the eve of its ascendance to national power, CCP pronouncements began to sound more like those of "legitimate" national governments as they ranked different priorities. And Hong Kong ranked very low.

Great uncertainty still obscured the path of British restoration of colonial rule in Hong Kong. The greatest uncertainty came not from claims or competition from any government power but from the multitude of Chinese national flags that flew on "every junk and on nearly every house" when the British fleet entered Hong Kong's waters. "The Chinese felt it was their victory first, rather than anybody else's," as one British instantly noted at war's end.[105] The vibrant social changes that had taken place when British colonial rule was leveled during the war and during Chinese resistance against Japanese occupation would not disappear overnight. During postwar reconstruction, this transformed society and its reinstated overlords had to meet at a crossroads.

---

105. Laufer, 8. Laufer arrived in Hong Kong in 1938, made friends with Chinese, and "felt at home among Chinese."

4

At the Crossroads

Hong Kong was "a dead city" when David M. MacDougall (1904–1991) returned to the colony in September 1946. An assistant colonial secretary in prewar Hong Kong, MacDougall was one of several dozen British officers who escaped to the mainland with Admiral Chen Ce after Hong Kong fell. In the remaining years of the war, he was appointed to join, and then head the Hong Kong Planning Unit in the Colonial Office, which made preparations to reoccupy Hong Kong. Returning to the colony with a military rank of brigadier, MacDougall became Hong Kong's de facto administrator in the eight-month military administration led by Rear-Admiral Harcourt, who gave him free rein in running civil affairs.[1]

Like many other war-trampled areas in the world, Hong Kong was on the brink of disaster. The infrastructure had collapsed, and "the urban area was ... virtually overrun with rats." Garbage and refuse piled up in huge heaps on main thoroughfares, in back streets, and in alleyways, polluting the water system and threatening the city with outbreaks of infectious diseases.[2] Public transportation was virtually nonexistent, as nearly all equipment and trucks had been looted and shipped to Japan. The nineteen-mile tramway serving the Island of Hong Kong was down to only 15 cars out of the 112 before the war, and its maintenance facilities were stripped of tools and machinery. All buses and stocks of spare parts had been confiscated and shipped to Japan or else-

---

1. MacDougall, 50; Snow (2012). Snow notes that MacDougall was "at the heart of the pre-war British elite in the colony" but eschewed the colonial pomp and declined to wear a uniform or a sword.

2. "British Military Administration Report," May 1, 1946, CO 129/595/9, 19, 31.

where in its empire.[3] Throughout Hong Kong, housing damage was estimated at around 15 percent, but European-style buildings had suffered more. About 60 percent were uninhabitable due to the combined effects of neglect, looting, bombing, and fire.[4] Only the roads were spared destruction because the Japanese army maintained them for military purposes.

Under MacDougall's eight-month directorship, the military administration skipped normal bureaucratic procedure and worked hard and fast to stabilize the colony. Trade, the main sector of Hong Kong's economy, revived quickly. Commerce surpassed prewar levels by more than 20 percent the year after the war ended. This boom generated "a mushroom growth" of trading firms, a trend that continued for the rest of the decade.[5] In contrast, the colony's budding light industry, particularly cotton textiles, light metalwares, and rubber shoes, nearly all Chinese-owned, trekked a rough road to recovery. War damage, scarce raw materials, and foreign competition—chiefly from Japan—confronted Hong Kong's wobbling industries and affected the lives of tens of thousands of workers.

Paradoxically, the overwhelming task of bringing Hong Kong back to normalcy also presented a golden opportunity to the reinstated British to fulfill prewar promises of labor reform and demonstrate their virtue as Hong Kong's rightful masters. Economic reconstruction depended on a productive labor force. Amid the recovery and boom, social activism was revived with new energy and new leadership. Although elite-centered activism for constitutional reform gradually declined under the careful and skillful management of Governor Grantham, grassroots labor activism charged forward with surprising vigor and resolve. During the years between the spring of 1946 and early 1950, rarely a month passed without collective labor action in the colony.

Chinese workers had long perceived themselves as living a life "like cattle and horses."[6] Underpaid and toiling for excessive working hours, they understood keenly the material deprivation that degraded them in this humiliation. Workers in postwar Hong Kong came to see the need of "protecting our live-

---

3. *HKAR* 1946, 90.

4. *HKAR* 1946, 28. This estimate was later raised to 70 percent. Also see Grantham (1965), 103.

5. *HKAR* 1946, 24, 26; *HKAR* 1947, 33–35; *HKAR* 1948, 36.

6. Smith.

lihood and interest" through their own "strength," said a woman worker when she voiced the desire to be free from the pain of excessive physical exertion through the long workday and mistreatment in the factory.[7] Now spurred by radically changed economic conditions and lagging wages, working Chinese became more determined to seek a life of dignity with a new strength nurtured by the National Salvation Movement and wartime resistance. Eager to bring the colony's economy back on track, the colonial state encouraged this new development, thus opening a vital space to the longest wave of labor movement the colony had ever seen.

First Wave of Postwar Strikes

As Hong Kong struggled to rise from the ruins of war, material shortages defined the terms of everyday life for most people. For nearly everyone, food was a primary concern in the immediate months after reoccupation. The military administration skirted the United Nations' regional quota by sending out individuals and groups to neighboring areas to make purchases. Rice shipped in from South China, Thailand, and elsewhere prevented mass starvation, but the supply was far from adequate. The ration system devised under the military administration lasted into the early 1950s. At its worst in May 1946, the daily rice ration fell to five ounces plus an additional four ounces of flour per person. The rice shortage went hand in hand with shortages of nearly every kind of basic necessity. Sugar, condensed milk, and peanut oil, indispensable to Chinese cooking, had to be rationed.[8] Prices soared in markets where nonrationed commodities were available for sale. The cost of basic goods was much inflated after the war, according to official reports (see Table 3).

This 500–1,200 percent price hike in daily necessities might not be a terrible problem for the rich. But even average Europeans, who were generally far better off than the majority of Chinese, found that the comfortable life they were accustomed to belonged to yesteryear, as "it costs at least three times as

---

7. Zhen, "我們要用自己的力量爭取我們的權利" (We must use our own strength to attain our rights), in Gangjiu funü zhigong zonghui (ed.), no. 1 (June 21, 1948), 8.

8. *HKAR* 1946, 53.

Table 3. Comparison of price in basic goods before and after war
(1 catty = 0.5 kilogram)

	1939	1946 (end)
Rice (third grade), per catty	$0.07	$0.84
Fresh fish, per catty	$0.28	$1.65
Salt fish, per catty	$0.24	$1.95
Beef, per catty	$0.35	$2.45
Pork, per catty	$0.54	$3.25
Oil, per catty	$0.24	$2.30
Firewood	$0.10 (5.6 catties)	$0.10 (1 catty)

Source: Hong Kong Government, *Annual Report of Hong Kong 1946*, 11.

much to maintain a standard of living considerably lower than that normal in 1941."[9] To working Chinese, who literally lived hand to mouth with most of their income spent on food and rent, rapid inflation threw a tightening rope around their necks.

Both European and Chinese employers were anxious to resume business and move forward, yet they approached problems of inflation and labor costs differently. European industrial investment concentrated on shipbuilding, ship repair, warehouses, public utilities, public transportation, and public services. These well-established companies dominated Hong Kong's international trade and urban infrastructure, and their business was in high demand once recovery began. Many of these companies had an urgent need for skilled and unskilled workers, both in acute shortage. European employers made use of a temporary "rehabilitation allowance" system devised by the military administration, which paid workers a flat rate of HK$1.00 a day in addition to basic wages.[10]

In contrast, Chinese factories and workshops paid piece rates and produced crafts, performed services, or operated light industries of many kinds. Most employees in light industries were in three lines of production: cotton yarn and textiles, metalwares, and rubber shoes. Recovery of the European companies was secure, guaranteed by Hong Kong's trade-oriented economy and the needs of urban life. Recovery of Chinese-owned factories and workshops, on

9. *HKAR* 1946, 13.

10. Labour Office (Hong Kong), *Labour Office Report (Covering the Period 1st May 1946 to 31st March 1947)*, 3; Donnison, 314.

the other hand, started on shaky ground. In early 1946, the Chinese newspaper *Kung Sheung Daily News* noted that the war had damaged 85 percent of Hong Kong's industrial infrastructure. Of more than 400 prewar factories, some were totally destroyed and others had lost a third of their factory equipment. The report estimated that only 10,000 factory workers had returned to work, a mere fraction of the prewar total of 300,000.[11] Chinese factories also struggled with the labor shortage, but they took what the labour commissioner scornfully called an "opportunistic" approach. Not adopting the rehabilitation allowance as European companies did, Chinese paid much higher wages to skilled workers, often four or five times higher than wages at European companies.[12] Unlike the stable employment at European concerns, work at Chinese factories was not always available or guaranteed.

Disparity in wage standards and skyrocketing food prices triggered the first wave of postwar labor strikes, initiated by workers at Hong Kong's three largest dockyards: the Kowloon Dock owned by Jardine, Matheson & Company, the Taikoo Dock owned by Butterfield & Swire (Hong Kong) Company, and the Naval Dockyard operated by the Royal Navy. Of the 8,000–9,000 mechanics in the colony, these three dockyards alone employed nearly 5,000 of them. Because more than 3,000 mechanics were still unemployed, skilled workers at the three dockyards amounted to nearly all employed mechanics at the beginning of 1946.[13] All were running at full capacity and overtime repairing dock facilities damaged by the war and performing maintenance work on ships coming into port. Toward the end of 1945, grievances fermented among workers at the three dockyards, partly because in October their employers refused to increase the rehabilitation allowance from HK$1 to HK$1.5 as recommended by the military administration. The real sticking point was

---

11. Special report, "本港四百余家工廠復工極感困難" (Recovery is very difficult for the more than 400 factories in this port), *Kung Sheung Daily News*, February 13, 1946, 4.

12. *Hong Kong Annual Report of the Commissioner of Labour, 1st April 1947 to 31st March 1948*, 11. Beginning the financial year of 1951 (from April 1st 1950 to 31st March 1951), the title of the annual report by the Labour Department changed to *Annual Departmental Report of the Commissioner of Labour* followed by specific fiscal year. Hereafter cited as *LDAR* for reports published in years after 1947.

13. "機工勞資的糾紛" (Industrial dispute over mechanics' demands), *Sing Tao Jih Bao*, January 26, 1946, 3.

the workers' demand for an eight-hour workday, rather than the nine-hour workday then in effect, with the same daily wage. The dockyard owners insisted on recalculating the new daily wage based on the old hourly wage from the nine-hour day, which would result in decreasing the daily wage once an eight-hour day was implemented.[14]

Dockyard workers were no longer the same. During the Japanese occupation, activists had turned major dockyards into bases of underground resistance. Former resistance fighters with ideas and initiative soon realized the need for collective action and became labor leaders acknowledged by their fellow workers. In mid-January 1946, organized workers from all three dockyards met to form an alliance in preparation for negotiations. Workers at the Naval Dockyard elected three representatives on January 15. One of them, Mai Yaoquan (Mak Eu-chuen), was a guerilla fighter in the East River Column.[15] Workers at the Kowloon Dockyard also elected a wartime resister, Huang Dengming, as their negotiator.[16] With these resisters in leadership, workers adopted the tactic of a brief work stoppage by holding a meeting during the workday. It was not yet a strike, but they made a point, and their voices were heard. At a time when Hong Kong's overall recovery had reached only 30–40 percent of its prewar level, a work stoppage spreading across the colony could easily derail the still-shaky economy.

---

14. "機工勞資談判" (Mechanics negotiation with employers), *Sing Tao Jih Bao*, January 18, 1946, 3; "機工昨日會議, 否決資方提案" (Mechanics held meeting yesterday, refusing proposal by employers), *Sing Tao Jih Bao*, January 21, 1946, 3. Huang Yeheng, the secretary for the Workers' Union of Naval Dockyard between September 1949 and 2009, indicates in his memoirs that "the owners had planned to reduce workers' daily rate from HK$2 to HK$1.5." This appears to be a vague and inaccurate estimate. He likely got this impression from conversation with union workers, because he had not started working for the union at that point. See Huang Yeheng, 6. Zhou Yi (2009) presents a more detailed description of the negotiation process that can be verified by contemporary newspapers, 111–13.

15. Huang Yeheng, 6. In addition to Mai Yaoquan, Mai Haien, and Wu Yaguangn, there were two more elected representatives. For Mai Yaoquan as an underground resister in the Hong Kong–Kowloon Independent Brigade, see Pan Jiangwei.

16. Zhou Yi (2009), 111. For Huang's resistance activities, see Huang Dengming, "Hong Hum qu de kangRi youji zhanshi," in *HGGJDD*, 2:66–70, and He Jiari, "Chuanchang dixia douzheng," in *HGGJDD*, 2:71–75.

Recognizing the workers' legitimate demands for living wages and the efficacy of their protest, the Labour Office urged the European companies to reconsider their response. The office invited the owners for a long discussion that ended on January 25.[17] Government insistence worked. European dockyard owners agreed to keep the same daily rate when workday was shortened to eight hours, plus retroactive payment of wages lost due to the Japanese occupation.[18] This collective action victory at the dockyards marked the first step toward a standard eight-hour workday at European companies, as the conditions announced in the agreement were soon adopted by all public utilities.

Implementing this agreement turned out to be a real test of the dockyard owners' public pledge as well as the strength of labor solidarity. Within a few weeks, workers at the Taikoo Dockyard were restless again. The immediate cause was a day's delay in the payment of wages, from February 15 to February 16. This made workers desperate as they counted on timely pay to buy food and basic necessities. Wage reductions for manual laborers and apprentices deepened grievances. At their meeting, workers unanimously approved a slowdown beginning on February 21.[19] A Labour Office investigation into the dispute concluded in favor of the workers. Four days after the work stoppage, the company was compelled to announce publicly that it would abide by its January pledge, resume the $2 minimal daily wage plus standard rehabilitation allowance, and implement an eight-hour workday. This relatively quick and favorable settlement gave the dockyard workers confidence in their power. "We reached this agreement because we united," their representative said; "we came to understand that only when we bring together our strength could we protect the fruits of our victory."[20]

---

17. "機工勞資的糾紛" (Industrial dispute over mechanics problem), *Sing Tao Jih Bao*, January 26, 1946, 3.

18. "機工改善待遇圓滿解決, 實現八小時制度並補發戰前欠薪" (Satisfactory conclusion of mechanics' demand for improvement of employment condition; eight-hour day and compensation of unpaid prewar wage will be enforced), *Sing Tao Jih Bao*, January 27, 1946, 3.

19. "山雨欲來風滿樓, 太古船塢工人醞釀罷工" (Wind blowing hard through the pavilion as mountain rain approaches, workers at Taikoo Dock agitating for strike), *Sing Tao Jih Bao*, February 22, 1946, 3.

20. Qiu Zhen, "工廠新聞" (News from factories), *Huashang bao*, March 9, 1946, 2.

Industrial relations at the Royal Naval Dockyard, the largest employer in the colony owned and administered by Britain's Naval Office, were a more complex matter. As a government establishment, the Naval Dockyard used the British government in London as a shield and continued past practices. Both workers and the Labour Office confronted an impenetrable wall of resistance to the agreed-on basic wage for an eight-hour workday. On February 25, workers sent Mai Yaoquan, Mai Haien, and Wu Yaguang to urge the dockyard to fulfill its January promise. These representatives presented four specific demands. The dockyard representative only promised to "consider" making retroactive pay for 1941, which workers did not receive because of the British surrender. He promised to forward their other demands to the naval commandant for deliberation. Unable to move officials through reason, on March 3 workers announced their intention to "take action."[21] Ten days after this warning, the workers went on strike. With no power over the military, the Labour Office could do nothing but watch the event unfold.[22]

The strike at the Naval Dockyard became the first all-inclusive, large-scale collective action in postwar Hong Kong initiated from the shop floor. Decisively, it departed from the prewar practice of exclusive strikes by skilled workers led by the Chinese Mechanics Union. This time, the workers themselves initiated the action, and their collective bargaining included everyone from skilled mechanics to coolies and women workers performing unskilled tasks. On March 13, 8,000 Chinese workers, including unskilled laborers and skilled mechanics, began a sit-down. In silence, they "stood at their work position. At the end of the work day, they followed one another to leave the dockyard and workshops in an unusually orderly manner." The discipline dignified workers. It impressed even European employees in the dockyard and

---

21. "海軍船塢工人要求改善待遇，舉派代表提四點要求" (Labor at Naval Dockyard demand improvement of employment conditions, sent representatives with four demands), *Sing Tao Jih Bao*, February 26, 1946, 3; "船塢勞資協定廠方仍未履行，短期內再無明示工方採自由行動" (Employers still have not enforced labor-employer agreement; labor will take action if no clear intention in short term), *Sing Tao Jih Bao*, March 4, 1946, 3.

22. "八千船塢工人怠工，資方要先復工然後談判，工方堅持絕不中途妥協" (8,000 workers slowed down; employer demanded resuming work before negotiation; labor insist no compromise midway), *Sing Tao Jih Bao*, March 14, 1946, 3.

Fig. 4. Workers taking lunch at a curbside, Wanchai, circa 1946. Courtesy of HKFTU.

159

Fig. 5. A cubic, 1940s. Courtesy of HKFTU.

the police; they began to speak about the workers "with deep sympathy."[23] One week later, on March 20, the Naval Dockyard made partial concessions on an adjusted pay scale comparable to that at other companies in the colony. Yet on workers' other demands, such as a victory bonus (which other government employees had received), raising foremen's wages, and a guarantee of no lay-offs without a disciplinary violation, the management once again gave a vague promise to report to higher authorities in London.[24] Workers at the Naval Dockyard agreed to resume work the next day. But the unsolved issues sowed the seeds of future conflict.

Not all industrial negotiations achieved a compromise as quickly as those in the dockyards, and the wide gap in pay scales between Chinese and non-Chinese employees created more grievances. At the Hong Kong Electric Company, a leading European firm, Chinese workers and staff had been making their case against substandard pay since March 1946. Their earnings, according to a newspaper report, were "so meager that they could not even sustain their living at the subsistence level."[25] The Chinese workers began collective bargaining with the company, which had reneged on its promise of a 38 percent pay raise. The workers demanded paid holidays, paid sick leave, and retirement gratuities in addition to the pay raise. The company refused to raise wages based on 1946 rates, insisting instead on calculating raises from wages in 1941. This counteroffer would have reduced Chinese employees' pay.[26] Not on the workers' agenda was racist treatment of Chinese and non-Chinese employees, which was brought to light in newspaper reports about this industrial dispute. Besides a monthly HK$65 rehabilitation allowance for every employee, all Chinese—regardless of their position as staff or workers—were paid a monthly wage between HK$48 and HK$58, with only one exception at HK$140 a month. In contrast, non-Chinese "common staff," including Portu-

---

23. 本报讯, "海军船坞停工工友秩序良好深获同情" (Striking workers' orderly behavior at Naval Dockyard won sympathy), *Huashang bao*, March 14, 1946, 2.

24. "海坞工潮完全解决" (Complete solution achieved for industrial dispute at Naval Dockyard), *Huashang bao*, March 21, 1946, 2.

25. Hong Kong News, "Diandeng gongren yaoqiu gaishan shenghuo" (Workers at electricity industry demand treatment improvement), *Huashang bao*, April 23, 1946, 2.

26. Special report, "請求改善待遇談判決裂; 電燈工人昨起罷工" (Request for improved treatment but negotiation broke down; electricity workers went to strike yesterday), *Huashang bao*, May 18, 1946, 2.

guese and Indians, received salaries ranging between HK$200 and HK$400. The company's decision on May 10 to provide an additional allowance of HK$70 to non-Chinese employees further widened the already glaring wage gap between these two groups. The income of non-Chinese employees now became five to eight times higher than that of Chinese doing comparable jobs.[27]

The more than 500 Chinese mechanics and office staff decided on direct action after repeated failures in negotiating with the Hong Kong Electric Company. Now united around the Association for Progress in Unity by the Chinese Employees at the Electric Company (Diandeng gongsi Huayuan xiejinhui) with former underground resisters in leadership, they went on strike one week after the company announced the additional allowance for non-Chinese employees. Like the workers at the Naval Dockyard, Chinese workers and staff at the Electric Company exited the power station in a responsible manner. They put all facilities and equipment in good order, signed off work at 2 pm, and walked out. They knew the strike would affect life in the colony and they wished to "reach a reasonable solution through absolutely civil behavior." Darkness descended on most of Hong Kong Island when night fell. Only a few key areas, such as Central, Mid-Levels, Wanchai, and Happy Valley were lit by electricity from a single generator operated by the remaining non-Chinese staff at the Electric Company. The price of candles soared to at least $2 each, equivalent to a skilled worker's basic daily wage. In the sudden disappearance of the recurrent "ding-ding" sound on Hong Kong's major thoroughfare as electric tram cars stopped running, the strike made its loudest statement.[28]

In its quiet way, the Hong Kong Electric Company strike generated very different responses. *China Mail*, one of the major English language newspapers and a mouthpiece for the European community, had never cared about any Chinese affair in the colony. Now it began screaming. With the strike headlined, *China Mail* accused it of being "more a political than economic one" and warned that Kowloon could be affected the next day.[29] In response to this

---

27. "工會代表談罷工苦衷" (Representative discloses the bitter reasons for choosing strike), *Huashang bao*, May 18, 1946, 2.

28. Special report, *Huashang bao*, May 18, 1946, 2.

29. "Power House Strike," *China Mail*, May 18, 1946, 1.

groundless accusation, the Association for Progress in Unity by Chinese Employees at the Electric Company held a news conference. Its lead representative stressed again that the choice to strike was made "under the enormous pressure of the living cost." More than twenty labor unions sent their representatives to this high-profile public event to show support. All pledged donations on behalf of their unions.[30] Workers across the harbor at the Kowloon Dockyard and the China Light and Power Company, which provided electricity for Kowloon, launched a "one dollar donation" movement for the powerhouse strike. Tramway conductors and drivers took out a portion of their weekly wage. Telephone workers donated rice.[31] While European expatriates were disturbed by what they saw as political subversion, sympathy poured in from industrial workers who shared the electrical workers' grievances and understood their needs.

The widely publicized powerhouse strike now forced the traditional labor leaders of the Chinese Mechanics Union (CMU) to make a public stand. For decades, this labor organization for skilled workers kept a venerable status with the official recognition as the representative of all Chinese workers in Hong Kong. Having taken a passive attitude toward labor strikes in the colony to this point, it began to realize that continued silence would hurt its status.[32] An emergency directors' meeting was called to discuss the powerhouse strike, with journalists in attendance. One of the three CMU chairmen, Han Wen-hui (Ct. Hon Man-wai), had been recently appointed to Hong Kong's Labour Advisory Board. Following CMU's established tradition of walking the official line, Han criticized electrical workers for taking action without the en-

---

30. Special report, "港電燈公司罷工代表聲明絕無任何政治背景, 罷工迫於生活不達目的不止" (Representative of striking workers at Hong Kong Electric Co. clarifies that they have no political background; strike was forced by the pressure of life and will not stop until goal is reached), *Huashang bao*, May 19, 1946, 1.

31. "聲援港方罷工要求, 九龍電燈公司華員提請加薪" (Support the demands of striking workers at Hong Kong Electricity, Kowloon electricity workers request pay raise), *Huashang bao*, May 19, 1946, 1; "Gefang gongyou relie shengyuan" (Warm support from workers from all directions), *Huashang bao*, May 19, 1946, 2.

32. In all official documents and publications, the name of this union has been rendered as Chinese Engineers Institute, which reflected its declared intent when the union was first founded. I opt for the translation by Ming Chan, which better reflects the nature of the union. Ming K. Chan (1975), 166–72.

dorsement of his union. He demanded that the journalists attending the meeting make their reports following an approved script. His arrogance backfired. Other directors rejected Han's view on the spot and criticized him for practicing "news censorship." To his dismay, the board voted to support the powerhouse strike.[33]

Disruption of the power supply and a major transportation system forced the colony to listen to the workers' grievances. Widespread echoes reverberated among working Chinese, and strong pressure was brought to bear on the colonial state. Workers in other industries began to speak up about stagnant wages lagging far behind skyrocketing living costs. Chinese employees at two European businesses, the China Light and Power Company and the Yaumatei Ferry Company, demanded "improvements in employment conditions." Similar action was taken by Chinese employees at two government agencies, the Water Works Department and the Fire Brigade.[34] Most significantly, colonywide labor solidarity emerged at a meeting of representatives from more than twenty labor unions, held at the office of the Fraternity of Tramway Employees (Dianche cun'aihui). They unanimously voted on making "A Statement to People of All Circles in Hong Kong and Kowloon," which criticized company owners for the present stalemate in industrial negotiations. A quick and fair solution to strikers' problems, they argued, should "generate great benefit for the company" as well. As a result of the meeting, a delegation was elected among representatives from five industrial lines and service—postal service, tramway, the Telephone Company, the Naval Dockyard, and motor drivers—to address the Labour Office. Major H. F. G. Chauvin, deputy labour officer, met with the delegation and expressed sympathy for the strikers but voiced

---

33. Special report, "華人機器會昨開緊急會議決議聲援罷工工友" (Chinese Mechanics Union held an emergency meeting yesterday and decided to support striking workers), *Huashang bao*, May 20, 1946, I.

34. Special report, "水務局華員代表議定八項要求今日提出" (Representatives from Chinese employees at Water Department decided on eight-demands and sent it out today), *Huashang bao*, May 20, 1946, I; "消防局隊員請改善待遇" (Firefighters request for improvement on conditions of employment), *Huashang bao*, May 21, 1946, 2; "九龍電燈公司工人今向資方提出要求" (Workers at Kowloon electricity company presented demands to the company today), *Huashang bao*, May 21, 1946, 2; " 小輪員工請改善待遇" (Employees at small ferry request improvements on employment conditions), *Huashang bao*, May 24, 1946, 2.

doubts about a quick solution.[35] His mediation, however, helped end the strike two weeks later.

The agreement that ended the Hong Kong Electric Company strike on June 1, 1946, made the most comprehensive improvement in employment conditions of all the strikes in that year. Although the company won its bargain in pay increase of 38 percent based on the 1941 wage scale, it agreed to raise the pay for both skilled and unskilled workers. The company guaranteed overtime wages, an annual raise of HK$2 a month, sick leave, eighteen annual holidays, a retirement gratuity, and funeral expenses while in service.[36] No dramatic change took place to narrow the wide disparity in pay between Chinese and non-Chinese employees. Skilled Chinese workers now earned between HK$51 and HK$80, still at the bottom of the company's hierarchy. But improvements in other benefits gained by powerhouse workers and staff soon became the model for workers in other industries seeking "improvement in employment conditions."

Despite limited change in employment conditions, collective labor actions during the first half of 1946 revealed new tendencies that characterized the resurgent labor movement in postwar Hong Kong. Above all, inclusive collective action had become the new norm, organized along industrial lines and bargaining on behalf of both skilled and unskilled workers. New leadership among organized workers began to emerge, with wartime resisters at the core, while the CMU became marginalized. From the very beginning, postwar labor activism demonstrated a democratic spirit as workers initiated collective actions on the shop floor. From this new kind of labor activism, cross-colony labor solidarity emerged among workers from different industries. Short of drastic actions such as sympathy strikes, industrial unions were quick to lend support to fellow workers on strike. If coordination and mutual support among workers of different industries was not new, the resurgent labor move-

35. Special report, "港九工團舉行座談會檢討電工罷工事件" (Labor unions in Hong Kong and Kowloon held a meeting to discuss electricity workers' strike), *Huashang bao*, May 24, 1946, 1; "港九工團代表昨謁勞工司" (Representatives of labor unions in Hong Kong and Kowloon made visit to see Labour Commissioner), *Huashang bao*, May 25, 1946, 1.

36. Special report, "電燈工潮昨已解決；全部復工電燈全亮" (Strike of electricity workers ended yesterday; all returned to work and all lights are lit), *Huashang bao*, June 1, 1946, 2.

ment brought forth new participants and new leadership who exuded an impressive spirit of discipline, civility, and confidence that drew directly from their recent triumph over extraordinary adversity through the war.

Old Hands Lose Their Grip

With a dynamic interaction of factory floor initiative and popularly chosen leaders who led successful collective bargaining, postwar labor activism presented a powerful challenge to the established authority of the CMU. Founded in 1909, the Hong Kong CMU initially took the form of a study group, with the incongruous name Chinese Institute for the Study of Mechanics (Zhongguo yanji shushu, literally, Chinese Studio for the Study of Mechanics).[37] To call a union of mechanics a "studio" betrayed the harsh political reality and the timidity of its founders. Fearful of arousing official opposition, yet in need of self-protection and self-improvement, the mechanics made education an agenda of their union. They opened training classes for members and classes for members' children and published a newsletter. By all accounts, this guild adopted an apolitical orientation from its inception.

The CMU became the leader among skilled workers in 1920, when "mechanics in thirteen trades" answered the union's call and participated in an eighteen-day strike in Hong Kong.[38] About 6,000 skilled workers from twenty-six factories and workshops joined the strike, left the colony, and returned to Guangzhou. The more political National Union of Chinese Mechanics, then an active participant in Sun Yat-sen's anti-imperialist movement, lent financial support to the Hong Kong mechanics on strike. The strikers demanded a 40 percent pay raise, which was resisted by employers. But the CMU managed to negotiate a 30 percent raise and ended the strike amicably. During the remaining years of the 1920s, the CMU eschewed politicization even as other Chinese workers moved in that direction. Their choice was very

---

37. If not otherwise noted, description of the CMU is taken from Chow.

38. The thirteen trades are as follows: engineering mechanics, draftsmen, foundry workers, blacksmiths, operators of lathe and other machines, welders, riveters, electric welders, motor drivers (including tram cars, automobile, and locomotive), coppersmiths, electricians, special carpenters (especially in shipbuilding and repair), and plumbers. See Zhou Yi (2009), 133.

much appreciated by the colonial state. Whenever the CMU bargained to raise the pay of skilled workers in prewar years, the colonial state often helped it succeed.

The postwar colonial state again officially endorsed CMU leadership in labor affairs for Hong Kong's changed working population. As soon as the Labour Office resumed operation in late 1945, it reestablished the Labour Advisory Board. First formed in the late 1920s, the postwar board was still composed of "representatives of several of the larger European firms and of the Services under the chairmanship of the Labour Officer." But it now included Chinese representation. Han Wenhui, then vice chairman of the CMU and owner of M. W. Hong & Company, a machine shop, was appointed by the colonial state to be one of three labor representatives.[39] No one on the board was a worker.[40]

Just as British authorities coopted Han Wenhui as a symbolic inclusion of labor in policy consultation, his influence and the influence of the union he controlled were waning. Chinese workers in postwar Hong Kong were no longer merely laborers who would do anything to secure a bowl of rice for themselves and their families. Their self-perception had undergone a profound transformation during the war. Some remained in Hong Kong and endured unspeakable hardships; some fled the colony and spent the war on the mainland. While the most passive had watched British rule collapse within three weeks under the Japanese attack, the more courageous had joined the resistance led by the East River Column and, through their actions, realized that they were indispensable to ground-level Allied operations. They took pride in contributing to China's victory. They grew more confident of their right to a decent life after the war and believed they could achieve it.

With this new mindset and new leadership, labor activism resurged between 1946 and 1947. Its challenge to the officially endorsed authority of the CMU became more acute from the second half of 1946 onward as labor dis-

---

39. For Han Wenhui, see P. C. Lee, 109; *LDAR* 1946–47, 15–16.

40. It took the colonial state nearly a decade to adjust its Labour Advisory Board to this reality. Han Wenhui remained on the board after the civilian government took over in May 1946 as one of three "representatives" for Hong Kong labor, until the fiscal year of 1953–1954, when Ip King, chairman of the CMU, replaced him on the board. The CMU stopped having a representative on the Labour Advisory Board in 1954–1955. See *LDAR* 1947–48, 6; *LDAR* 1953–54, 9; *LDAR* 1954–55, 8.

putes occurred in nearly all major and minor industries and trades. Without participation or consent from the CMU, workers with or without their own industry's union initiated collective action themselves. In 1946, workers in public transportation, the film industry, electric power, furniture, harbor ferries, printing, restaurants, and tea houses demanded pay raises and an eight-hour workday. Seamen raised their voices to oppose resumption of the contractor system, which had given middlemen significant power in defining the terms of their employment. Dockyard labor unions joined the uphill battle against the contractor system. The year 1947 started with a strike by Peak Tramway workers, followed by cotton weavers, dairy farm workers, workers at the British-American Tobacco Company, bus companies, electric bulb factories, and taxi companies.[41] By July 1947, at least twenty industrial disputes had taken place; some ended with workers' demands met, some failed to change existing working and pay conditions, and a few had no conclusion in sight.[42] These collective actions contrasted sharply with patterns established in the past. Now collective bargaining included all workers—skilled and unskilled, men and women. Hong Kong's labor movement was breaking new ground where the CMU had never gone before.

Taking its usual approach of quietly working with the powerful, the CMU had been seeking pay raises for mechanics in thirteen trades.[43] It made its case based on the living costs for one worker plus two family members at HK$229.50 a month, including food, rent, clothing, medicine, utilities, and education for one child. In 1946, the highest income from government service or non-Chinese business enterprises for this upper echelon of Chinese workers

---

41. These labor actions are reported in local newspapers. My summary is based on surveying *Huashang bao*, which followed labor activism closely and often made detailed reports during these months.

42. The number of labor disputes is based on Zhou Yi (2009), 156–57, who lists more than fifty industrial disputes based on a survey of three local newspapers, *Kung Sheung Daily News*, *Huashang bao*, and *Sing Tao Jih Bao*, as well as the *Yearbook of Hong Kong 1948* published by *Wah Kiu Yat Po*.

43. "機工加薪要求昨遞呈勞工司" (Demands for raising wages for mechanics had been sent to Labour Commissioner yesterday), *Sing Tao Jih Bao*, February 12, 1947, 6; Special report, "討論改良善後津貼，各工團今開大會" (Labor unions hold meeting today to discuss adjustment of rehabilitation allowance), *Huashang bao*, March 2, 1947, 4.

was HK$150, rehabilitation allowance included. The CMU had tried to negotiate pay raises with European employers, and failed. It turned to the Labour Office and submitted a formal petition for mediation on February 11, 1947, proposing a 150 percent pay raise.[44] Labour Commissioner Brian C. K. Hawkins responded in writing two weeks later. The Labour Office could do nothing, Hawkins explained, because employers, including government departments that hired Chinese mechanics, were unable to permanently change basic wages when living costs remained unpredictable. Moreover, Hawkins echoed the views of European employers, who evaluated the technical level of available mechanics at only 25–33 percent of that seen in prewar times.[45] Unsatisfied, the CMU sent two more petitions in April and July with additional data. Both were rejected by the Labour Office. After the third appeal, Hawkins questioned the CMU chairmen on whether their union could represent mechanics in the thirteen trades, because workers in various industries had already formed their own unions along industrial lines.[46]

How Europeans quantified and compared changes in Chinese mechanics' ability is not clear. Only one thing becomes increasingly obvious: the CMU was losing trust from above and below. Not only were workers turning to new unions, the Labour Office was more attentive to collective actions led by the new unions while overlooking CMU initiatives. Motorized vehicle drivers, for

---

44. Li and Ren, 174.

45. "機工加薪昨遭挫折, 勞工司覆函機工會謂資方認為難解決" (Effort to raise wage for mechanics failed yesterday; labour commissioner wrote to CMU and said employers believed it cannot find solution), *Sing Tao Jih Bao*, March 2, 1947. 6; "勞工司函覆華機會婉拒機工加薪要求" (Labour commissioner replied to CMU gently refused demand for wage raise by mechanics), *Sing Tao Jih Bao*, March 4, 1947, 7; Special report, "港九工團工廠代表所提改善津貼四建議蘇雲也表示同情; 華機請求提高基本工金雇主指為不合時宜" (Major Chauvin sympathizes with the four recommendations for adjustment of allowance by the labor unions in Hong Kong and Kowloon; employers consider it improper to raise basic wage as appealed by the Chinese Mechanics Union), *Huashang bao*, March 4, 1947, 4. Pauline Chow, in her study of the CMU states that an agreement reached by the CMU and employers in January 1946 had brought the daily wage of mechanics from HK$3 to HK$5.6; see Chow, 121. The news report in March 1947, however, indicates that the basic daily wage for mechanics remained at HK$2, and the CMU was seeking 150 percent raise to bring it to HK$5 per day.

46. Li and Ren, 175.

instance, were among the "mechanics in thirteen trades" traditionally represented by the CMU. They struck out on their own and joined the Motor
Drivers General Union, founded in 1920 and revived by dedicated leaders
after the war. The Motor Drivers General Union worked diligently to improve
employment conditions and defend workers involved in accidents beyond individual control.[47] Eager to encourage development of industrial unions in the
colony, the Labour Office supported the Motor Drivers General Union in
negotiations with two major bus companies in 1946, which concluded successfully with a contract that satisfied workers.[48] In mid-1947, after CMU appeals
to the Labour Office had repeatedly failed, taxi drivers represented by the
Motor Drivers General Union made eight demands to their employer, the
Kowloon Taxi Company. Without a strike, they won a monthly basic wage of
HK$150 plus a rehabilitation allowance, an eight-hour workday, and overtime
pay. The company even volunteered bonus pay to reward exceptional earnings.[49] Unions organized on an industrial basis once again proved capable of
achieving victory without the CMU.

The change was not missed by the colonial state. At the first negotiation
meeting between the CMU and European companies, arranged by the Labour
Office, Hawkins questioned whether the CMU represented all mechanics in
the colony.[50] After the second round of negotiation broke down, the Labour
Office wrote to the CMU on August 15, complaining once more that the
union represented only "certain mechanics." Hawkins argued that, under present circumstances, the best way forward was to include other unions in the
negotiation.[51] What the old guards of the CMU did, however, was to distance

---

47. "一年來的工作" (The work in the past year), Motuoche yanjiu zonggonghui, 2–3; Fang Wen, "入會有什麼好?" (What's the benefit of joining the union?),
Motuoche yanjiu zonggonghui, 9.

48. The complete version of the contract is printed in Motuoche yanjiu zonggonghui, 17–18.

49. Special report, "九龍的士司機工友要求改善待遇成功" (Taxi drivers of
Kowloon Taxi succeeded in making demands of improvements on employment treatment), Huashang bao, June 9, 1947, 4.

50. "香港機器工人罷工風潮調查報告書" (Investigative report on the strike by
mechanics in Hong Kong), Bureau of Asia & the Pacific 亞太司, #11-01-19-04-03-011.

51. "勞司發表聲明" (Statement by the Labour Commissioner), Sing Tao Jih Bao,
August 15, 1947, 4; "華民司勞工司接見本報記者, 發表對工潮意見" (Reporter of

the union further from the new, inclusive industrial labor activism. One such effort was a manipulated election in spring 1946 that ousted left-wing chair Ouyang Shaofeng and brought pro-Guomindang members to power. Later that year, the CMU expelled Ouyang and other left-wing labor leaders, including Mai Yaoquan, Huang Dengming, Ye Guang, He Jiari, and Huo De for "violation of the Union bylaws."[52] Eliminating these activists and former resisters, however, did not help the CMU regain the trust of British authorities. Nor did it help its leadership among Chinese workers, which fell into a deeper crisis in 1947.

Attempting to salvage its prestige, the CMU made a drastic decision to call an all-colony mechanics strike with direct support of the Guomindang-led government. From Hong Kong, the CMU sent a report to the Guangdong Mechanics Union, which forwarded it to the Guangdong provincial government, Guangzhou municipal government, and the Guomindang. These authorities dispatched Li Boyuan, a director of the Guangdong Mechanics Union, to Hong Kong to "make connection and provide comfort," a euphemism for sending monetary support.[53] Despite party-state backing from the mainland, the CMU faced serious troubles on the ground. Tension soared in the first meeting between CMU leadership and labor representatives from dockyards, public utility companies, transportation, and major hotels where employed mechanics joined unions organized along industrial lines. When Han Wenhui, now an unofficial justice of the peace, declared in a meeting on August 13 that the collective action was not intended as a "general strike" but as a phased strike starting with mechanics at the three major dockyards, he was "unanimously opposed by all in attendance." Han had no choice but to retract his proposal.[54]

---

this newspaper received by the secretary for Chinese affairs and labour commissioner who gave comments on the strike), *Sing Tao Jih Bao*, August 17, 1947, 4.

52. Li and Ren, 187–88.

53. Li and Ren, 179. The phrase implies that Guangdong government authorities provided monetary support.

54. Special report, "加薪談判昨無結果, 機工執行決議, 罷工委員會組成" (Negotiation for pay increase had no result yesterday; mechanics decided to enforce their resolution and formed a strike committee), *Huashang bao*, August 14, 1947, 4; "昨晚各代表報告: 工友支持罷工" (Representatives made reports last night: workers support strike), *Huashang bao*, August 14, 1947, 4.

Support from the new labor unions proved to be critical in sustaining the Mechanics Strike of 1947. On August 16, 7,600 workers from eight companies walked out on their jobs. The three major dockyards provided the most supporters, with 6,400 (84 percent of all strikers) joining the strike on the first day. Mechanics from the Kowloon-Canton Rail (KCR), the Green Island Cement Factory, the Water Works Department, and the Bailey's Shipyard made up the rest, each contributing as many as 350 strikers or as few as 30 to 40 participants. Over the course of the strike, which lasted twenty-seven days, the total number of participants reached 11,000.[55] Newly formed industrial unions coordinated to make it a disciplined collective action. Not wanting to bring chaos to the city, workers at European-owned public utility companies initially chose to not participate. Even without them, the scale of the strike far exceeded the 2,000 members claimed by the CMU. This convinced the Labour Office of the CMU's influence, so it stepped in to mediate. But negotiations quickly came to a standstill when differences over pay raises appeared too great. Employers were only willing to increase pay by 30 percent, while the CMU bargained for a 120 percent raise in basic wages.[56] Three weeks into the Mechanics Strike, negotiations had gone nowhere.

Were it not for the collective actions of the industrial unions at this critical juncture, the strike probably would have ended in total failure. On September 3, employees of the five major public utilities companies—Hong Kong Electric, China Light & Power, Hong Kong Telephone, Tramways, and the Gas Company—announced their readiness for collective action to seek "improvement in employment conditions." Through their own unions, they presented demands to employers two days later, which included 100 percent pay raises, annual bonuses, paid sick leave, and retirement gratuities.[57] Postal workers,

---

55. Zhou Yi (2009), 136–38. Also see *LDAR* 1947–48.

56. For employers represented by the three major dockyards, see Special report, "昨機工勞資談判, 資方願提高底薪" (At negotiation yesterday with CMU, employers willing to raise basic wages), *Huashang bao*, August 21, 1947, 4; Special report, "機工勞資逾顯僵局; 工友領薪被收回牌仔" (Stalemate at the Chinese Mechanics Union's negotiation with employers; workers' work ID was taken back when wage was paid), *Huashang bao*, August 30, 1947, 4. The report mentioned the new term for pay raise at HK$4.40 as demanded by the union.

57. Although the 100 percent pay raise sounded huge, in reality it meant to raise a daily wage that was far below the subsistence level. The example for such may be

who had been asking for a living wage since 1946 but had "refrained from making a move in consideration of public interest," now joined the others, demanding from the government a 100 percent pay raise, paid sick leave for workers injured on duty, annual bonuses, and overtime.[58] Chinese labor unions at government facilities took to collective action as well. Chinese employees in nine government departments (including hospital, sanitation, shipping inspection, and fishing unions) demanded pay raises among other changes of working conditions. Together with the Union of Workers in Foreign-Style Services, formed by employees serving in restaurants, hotels, and domestic servants in European and wealthy households, they organized a Delegation of Employees Seeking Improvement of Employment Conditions at Civic Services and Government Departments (Minzheng jiguan ji zhengfu gongtuan yaoqiu gaishan daiyu zhigong daibiaohui) to coordinate collective action.[59] Skilled and unskilled workers at the China Bus, at the Dairy Farm, and in other industries and businesses made union resolutions and pressed employers with similar demands. "Improvement in employment conditions" (gaishan daiyu) became a rallying cry written on banners held high by industrial unions. The colony was experiencing what a newspaper described as "wave after wave of labor actions."[60]

Sensing that this widespread labor unrest could balloon into a general strike, the Labour Office pressed both sides harder for reconciliation.[61] On

---

gleaned from the demands by workers at public utilities companies: "Current pay below $1.99 to be increased by $1.5; wage at $1.5–1.99 to be increased by $2.5; wage at $2–2.9 to be increased by$2.5; wages above $3 to be increased by $3." See "七大重要部門工友要求改善待遇步驟相繼決定" (Workers at seven vital enterprises have made decisions one after another on taking actions to seek improvements of treatment), Huashang bao, September 4, 1947: 4. Also see "四電煤氣郵政海軍船塢政府機關職工對改善待遇要求緊鑼密鼓" (Workers at four public utilities, gas, postal service, Naval Dockyard, government offices are urgently preparing for making demands on improving treatment), Huashang bao, September 3, 1947, 4.

58. Huashang bao, September 8, 1947, 4.

59. "港府華人職工今晚開代表會商討要求加薪" (Chinese employees in government service will hold meeting tonight to discuss action for pay raise), Huashang bao, September 9, 1947, 4.

60. "工潮後浪推前浪" (New waves of labor actions push the previous ones forward), Huashang bao, September 8, 1947, 4.

61. "機工談判今午重開" (Negotiations led by the Chinese Mechanics Union restart noon today), Huashang bao, September 4, 1947, 4.

September 11, the negotiation team of three chairmen of the CMU suddenly announced victory and ordered strikers back to work. The agreement they produced, however, sharply reduced the union's initial demand for a 150 percent wage increase to 50 percent. The concession was not a total surprise. An earlier CMU proposal of a 60 percent raise tied to an increased rehabilitation allowance had been rejected by the employers.[62] The real blow in the final agreement was its exclusion of contract workers, who in companies like the Taikoo Dockyard, made up the majority of strikers. When the three CMU chairmen presented the agreement at the Taikoo and Kowloon Dockyards, workers exploded. "The Chinese Mechanics Union betrayed our representatives," some shouted with great anger; "and our representatives betrayed us workers!"[63] In the end, the CMU's partiality to a select segment of labor alienated about 30 percent of the strikers.[64]

In contrast to the CMU's lopsided deal, collective actions taken by labor unions on industrial bases were making strides to improve employment conditions. At the Hong Kong Electric Company, unionized workers agreed not to take further action when the company responded immediately, though not satisfactorily, to their demands. The recently arrived new governor, Sir Alexander Grantham, met with postal workers in person and promised pay raises for all government service employees, with priority given to postal workers.[65]

---

62. Special report, "昨華機提讓步條件, 資方拒絕予以考慮" (CMU conceded yesterday, employers refused to consider), *Huashang bao*, August 26, 1947, 4.

63. "華機復工有波折" (Trouble with the end of the Chinese Mechanics Union strike), *Huashang bao*, September 12, 1947, 1; "資方允加薪百分之五十; 華機昨下令復工" (Employers agreed to pay raise of 50 percent; yesterday CMU ordered return to work), *Huashang bao*, September 12, 1947, 4; "昨晚太古船塢工友窮詰華機會主席" (Workers from Taikoo Dockyard demanded explanation from the chairman of CMU), *Huashang bao*, September 13, 1947, 1. By the agreement, less than 1,000 among the more than 3,000 who joined the strike were to benefit.

64. Li and Ren, 178–79. This is probably a conservative estimate because Li Boyuan, the coauthor, was the agent sent by the party-state on the mainland to Hong Kong to support the CMU-led strike when it started. Communist internal documents made it clear that the strike was a Guomindang-led action. See "Luo to Zhou Enlai," September 18, 1947, and "Luo to Zhou," October 5, 1947, *XGFJWJ*, 54–55, 56.

65. "五大公共事業工友決暫候資方答覆" (Workers at five major public utilities services decided to wait for answers from employers), *Huashang bao*, September 13, 1947, 1; "港督昨對工友宣示, 公務員將普遍提高薪金" (Governor met postal

The Royal Naval Dockyard conceded to workers' demands for a pay raise for contract workers.[66] In late September, workers in the public electric and gas utilities, as well as tramway workers, reached agreements with their employers. Workers who had been successful in collective bargaining made donations to telephone workers still on strike.[67] By early October, the lingering dispute at the Telephone Company finally ended with an agreement favorable to workers.[68] In news reports and union publications, 1947 became "the year of great labor movements."

This extraordinary year witnessed decisive changes as labor leadership slipped out of the old hands. The bitter end of the Mechanics Strike hurt contract workers, who constituted the majority of dockyard workers and were leading participants in the strike. It also damaged the status and appeal of the CMU. In 1947, when the CMU led the strike, its membership rose from 2,000 to 6,000.[69] By limiting its representation to the labor aristocracy, however, the union lost its position as one of the two largest organized trade unions within two years. Membership in the unions of seamen, motor drivers, and textile workers surpassed it in the early 1950s.[70] Even though the official Labour Advisory Board continued to include one member from the CMU leadership, the union stopped playing an important role in labor action after 1947. In its place, more vigorous, democratically oriented industrial unions flourished in postwar Hong Kong with confidence and high hopes.

---

workers and promised pay raise for public servants), *Huashang bao*, September 14, 1947, 4.

66. "傳海軍船塢內定非機工照樣加薪" (Naval Dockyard reportedly made internal decision to raise wages for non-mechanics), *Huashang bao*, September 16, 1947, 4; "海塢非機科工友以後口頭答覆加薪" (Non-mechanics at Naval Dockyard have got verbal promise of pay raise), *Huashang bao*, September 18, 1947, 4.

67. *Huashang bao*, September 25, 1947, 4.

68. "電話勞資也獲協議; 五大工團籌備聯歡" (Agreement also reached at Telephone Company; five major labor unions are preparing for joint celebration), *Huashang bao*, October 5, 1947, 4.

69. Chow. Also see *LDAR*, which began to include statistics of labor unions and shows that the CMU was one of the two largest trade unions, with a membership of 6,200 in 1948–1949. Its size had a slight increase over the next five years, reaching 6,700 by 1952–1953. But it disappeared from the statistics by the Labour Department after that.

70. Table of unions with more than 5,000 members, in *LDAR*.

Restoring the Status Quo in the Labour Department

Vigorous resurgence of labor activism in the first two years after the war made the reconstituted and upgraded Labour Department a busy office. Resuming operation as soon as the British military administration was established in Hong Kong, the office was separated from the Secretariat for Chinese Affairs and reorganized as an independent department under the civilian government in June 1946. A year later, in September, the title of labour officer was officially upgraded to commissioner of labour and the office expanded to a full-fledged department. Its importance was demonstrated in its ranking among the thirty departments that made up Hong Kong's government. Within the "Social Services" cluster, the Labour Office (renamed department in 1949) ranked just below the Secretariat for Chinese Affairs and was followed by the Medical Department, Sanitary Department, and Public Works Department.[71]

The Labour Department's quick elevation in Hong Kong's administrative structure concurred with London's renewed attention to the labor question. In a 1946 circular to the colonies from the Colonial Office, G. H. Hall, secretary of state for the colonies between August 1945 and September 1946, reemphasized a point made by his predecessor in 1938: Labour Offices should be made "actually or potentially ... the most important" among all departments in colonial governments. Moreover, British colonies were now urged "to build up a balanced Labour Department." It must be staffed, above all, by "persons with experience of labor problems from the employees' standpoint." Experience in personnel management, education comparable to an administration cadet, and labor-related specialties such as factory inspection and labor exchange were sought-after qualifications.[72]

In forming its new Labour Department, Hong Kong was in close communication with the Colonial Office. While following London's general guidelines, it made a subtle, yet decisive twist. Henry R. Butters, the first labour officer in Hong Kong, had spent war years in the POW camp at Stanley under the Japanese occupation. He retired in 1949 after a brief service in Nyasaland in Africa and as assistant secretary in the Finance Department of the

---

71. *HKAR* 1946, 103; *HKAR* 1947, 13; *HKAR* 1949, 15.
72. G. H. Hall, "Circular," August 24, 1946, CO 129/615/1, 58–60.

Colonial Office.[73] The newly appointed head of the Labour Office was Brian Charles Keith Hawkins. Unlike Butters, Hawkins did not have the same extensive on-the-ground interactions with working Chinese in the colony but worked mostly in the office of the Secretariat for Chinese Affairs. He came to Hong Kong as a cadet in 1924, two years after Butters. By the mid-1930s, Hawkins had become one of the two chief assistant secretaries for Chinese affairs. Hawkins replaced Butters as labour officer in March 1940 and remained in the post until war reached Hong Kong.[74] He was considered as a possible successor to R. A. C. North as secretary for Chinese affairs at the British reoccupation of Hong Kong.[75] Apparently, Hawkins's appointment to head this important department in Hong Kong was not intended to promote radical reform in labor relations but to keep power in the hands of those "with experience" in colonial governance.

Hawkins proved to be a staunch and skillful defender of the old regime when facing more reform-minded Colonial Office advisers. In early 1946, the Colonial Office dispatched Eleanor Hinder to Hong Kong to discuss establishing the new Labour Department. Before the war, Hinder had acquired substantial experiences in industrial China as chief of Industrial and Social Division of the Shanghai Municipal Council from January 1933 to August 1942, responsible for supervising the daily operation of inspecting and improving labor conditions. This decade-long experience had brought her in touch with the enormous problems in China's most industrialized city, where the pattern of long hours, unsafe working conditions, and housing congestion had loud echoes in Hong Kong. In no less measures, the Shanghai experience had made Hinder keenly aware of Chinese national aspiration and taught her the importance of Chinese involvement in solving industrial problems.[76] It was

73. Miners; Colonial Office, *The Colonial Office List 1948*, 415.

74. *Hong Kong Government Gazette*, November 22, 1940, 1616. During the period between Butters's transfer at the end of 1939 and March 1940, the secretary for Chinese affairs, Roland Arthur Charles North, was temporarily appointed labour officer. See *Hong Kong Government Gazette*, December 8, 1939, 1273. Also see Colonial Secretary's Office (Hong Kong), 12.

75. Snow (2003), 255–56.

76. In *Life and Labour in Shanghai* (1944), Hinder outlines the policy of the Municipal Council and summarizes the work of the Industrial and Social Division and unsolved problems in industrial establishments in the International Settlement. For her view

Fig. 6. Brian C. K. Hawkins, labour commissioner. Courtesy of Information Services Department, Hong King Government (SAR).

no surprise that she should have voiced such concerns when meeting with Hawkins to discuss substantive personnel changes in the new Labour Department. Hawkins, however, disagreed with her critical points. In a five-page memo laced with subtexts of racial and class bias, Hawkins countered, point by point, most of Hinder's recommendations for structural reform.

Hawkins centered his opposition on the issue of appointing Chinese to positions of higher responsibility. He disagreed with Hinder's recommendation to recruit a Chinese labour officer, with significant responsibilities just one level below the commissioner. Instead, he proposed to create "a post of Deputy Commissioner of Labour to be filled by a senior and experienced Administrative Officer who is prepared to make Labour Department his career." Recruiting a Chinese labour officer should "hasten slowly" "because of the importance of *securing the right type of man* for the job." Hawkins also disclosed that one of the two proposed labour officer posts had, in fact, already been filled by Major H. F. G. Chauvin. An intelligence officer under the Strategic Operations Executive before the war, Chauvin was responsible for setting up the first serious British intelligence network in the Hong Kong region.[77] Hawkins argued that Chauvin had Cantonese language ability, which was "essential" in "dealing with the Chinese." He rejected Hinder's recommendation for "a Senior Chinese female inspector" as well. Instead, he proposed to recruit Mrs. Marjorie Allison, who had served in the colony's education department before quitting after marriage. Hawkins recommended her to be the lady assistant "in direct control of the female inspectorate" as well as "problems connected with women workers."[78]

In Hawkins's counterproposal, the Colonial Office emphasis on recruiting staff with demonstrated knowledge of labor problems "from the employees' standpoint" disappeared and was replaced, repeatedly, by the word *European* when specific candidacies were recommended. To convince the Colonial Office, Hawkins went to London in late 1946 and won his argument by warning about "the dangers of political control of the Trade Unions" from the main-

---

on Chinese national aspiration and Chinese involvement in her division's interaction with industrial establishments in Shanghai, see esp. 20 and 26.

77. Ozorio, citation from 166.

78. B. C. K. Hawkins, "Comments on recommendation made by Miss E. Hinder for the future development of labour administration in Hong Kong, dated 15.2.46," CO 129/615/1, 77–81.

land.[79] Governor Mark Young, who had made the symbolic gesture of eliminating racial discrimination by repealing Hong Kong's notorious racist Peak
Ordinance, fully endorsed Hawkins's proposal.[80] Following well-established
tradition of leaving decision making to the "men on the spot" in managing the
empire, the Colonial Office went along with the colony's proposal.

Due to significant shortage of available European personnel, Hong Kong
did accept a qualified Colonial Office appointee with labor expertise. Internal
discussion on this appointment in London was interesting, as it revealed a
tension between defending the colonial establishment and reforming industrial relations. Kenneth A. Baker, who had been president of the UK Fire Bri-
gades Union before taking a temporary position at Mauritius as trade union
adviser in late 1944, was singled out by some in the office as "the best" among
all candidates for Hong Kong. Baker had taken the job of developing trade
unions in Mauritius seriously. Yet he clashed with Sir Henry Charles Donald
Cleveland Mackenzie-Kennedy, the governor of Mauritius. Condemning
Baker for his "uncertainty in distinguishing between his loyalty to trade
unionism and his duties as a civil servant," Mackenzie-Kennedy refused to
make Baker's appointment permanent.[81] For this reason, some officials within
the Colonial Office felt reluctant about sending Baker to Hong Kong "where
the Trade Union movement is no doubt far from being settled in its organisation and relations with the Government." Yet Baker's labor union credentials
won him the Hong Kong post. He joined the Labour Department in 1947 and
became the labour officer next in rank to Major Chauvin.

During 1946 and 1947, new appointees at the Labour Department worked
hard to mediate industrial disputes and participate in public events organized
by labor unions. They won trust and respect from labor leaders and workers
with their willingness to reach out. Chauvin, who followed a long tradition of
Western practice in China by adopting a Chinese name, Su Yun (*Ct.* So Wan),
made an appreciated gesture to deliver a public speech in Cantonese at the

79. Minutes by A. Ruston, December 30, 1946, CO 129/615/1, 4.

80. Mark Young to Arthur Creech Jones, November 8, 1946, CO 129/615/1,
72–75.

81. For a succinct discussion of the making of the Peak District Ordinance in
1902, see Peter Wesley-Smith, esp. 98–101; Secretary of State to Mark Young,
March 4, 1947, CO 129/615/1, 43–44; minutes by Colonial Office staff, CO
129/615/1, 12–14.

colony's first postwar celebration of International Workers' Day. "Although the workers could not fully understand what So Wan said [because of his inadequate Cantonese]," a reporter noted, "his sympathy and encouragement to the laboring class touched the hearts of all in the audience."[82] In mediating the industrial dispute at the China Bus Company in 1946, Chauvin sided with the workers' union in negotiating their employment contract and later intervened on their behalf when the company failed to fulfill its agreement. In a review of that dispute, the Motor Drivers General Union expressed its appreciation for Chauvin's "fairness, firmness and transparency" (*gongzheng yanming*).[83]

As the "most important" department in the postwar colonial state, the Labour Department's efforts in building healthy industrial relations, and hence a quick economic recovery, were critical to the success of British reoccupation of Hong Kong. Shortage of skilled and unskilled workers in the first year after the war placed employers in a disadvantage at the negotiation table. This partially explains why Labour Department officers often sided with the workers in industrial disputes.

Change in the labor market at the end of 1947 reversed the balance between workers and employers in negotiations. By the end of that year, a steady influx of returnees, as well as civil war refugees, brought the total population in Hong Kong to 1.8 million, 200,000 more than its prewar peak in 1941.[84] The labour commissioner's annual report noted that "employment has clearly been more difficult to obtain," partly due to a large lay-off of workers from the Naval Dockyard after completing major repairs on damaged facilities.[85] Sea-

---

82. "五個勞動節紀念會, 工友熱烈慶祝" (Workers enthusiastically celebrate the International Labor Day in five rallies), *Huashang bao*, May 3, 1946, 2.

83. Deng He, "港九巴士職工要求改善待遇的前前後後" (A chronicle of efforts to improve employment conditions by bus company employees), Motuoche yanjiu zonggonghui, *Resumption Newsletter*, February 20, 1947, 8.

84. *HKAR* 1946, 9; *HKAR* 1947, 9.

85. *LDAR* 1947–48, 9. The annual report by the labour commissioner only mentioned 500 workers being laid off, yet the local newspaper, *Huashang bao*, which followed the whole event closely, indicated more than half of 9,000 workers employed by the Naval Dock had been laid off by mid-February 1948, with 2,000 more scheduled to be laid off soon. See also "四千工友已被裁; 還有二千將失業; 海軍船塢工方昨披露裁員真相" (4,000 workers had been laid off; another 2,000 will lose their jobs; workers at Naval Dock disclosed yesterday the truth of the lay-off), *Huashang bao*, February 16, 1948, 4.

men and shipfitters resumed their fight against the resurgent contractor system and lay-offs without compensation or legitimate excuse.[86] The Labour Department devoted "a considerable amount of the work" to mediation. Between spring 1947 and 1948, it settled 276 minor industrial disputes and mediated 25 major ones, some involving "many meetings and protracted negotiations." The department considered its relations with labor unions "generally satisfactory" because "the advice of the Commissioner of Labour and the staff of the office is frequently sought and accepted."[87] Many recently formed or revived labor unions, especially those in opposition to Guomindang-controlled unions, would agree.

New Leadership in Organized Labor

Despite their economic struggle, or perhaps because of it, organized labor acquired a centrality in Hong Kong's public life as the colony navigated through the first year of peace. Newly organized labor unions began to take leading roles in public events that attracted colony-wide participation. One such event celebrated the successful conclusion of the Political Consultative Conference in China, another was International Workers' Day in 1946. The first celebration involved more than thirty mass organizations across a broad social spectrum, with a public rally attracting more than 3,000 participants. Recognizing the importance of organized labor, participants elected a presidium, which included labor representatives from the Telephone Company, the Tramway, the Hong Kong Electric Company, Naval Dockyard, Seamen's Union, postal workers, motor drivers, painters, and carpenters. Ouyang Shaofeng, leader of the Tramway Workers' Union, known for his eloquence and international experience in Southeast Asia, chaired the event.[88] Hong Kong's public celebration of the first May Day as International Workers' Day coincided with the resumption of civilian government in the colony. Five ral-

---

86. See various reports on *Huashang bao* in February and March 1948.

87. *LDAR* 1947–48, 10, 28.

88. Special report, "民主的怒潮在洶湧：工團熱烈慶祝政協成功" (The torrent of democracy gushes forward—labor organizations passionately celebrate the success of the Political Consultation Conference), *Huashang bao*, March 25, 1946, 2.

lies, each attracting at least 1,000 people, took place across the colony. The newly formed industrial unions held the largest rally, with more than 3,000 representatives, where Chauvin gave his speech in Cantonese that expressed "sympathy and encouragement" to his intended audience.[89]

The ascendance of organized labor on Hong Kong's public stage was not entirely new. But its spirit and its leadership carried energy renewed and strengthened by prewar activism and wartime resistance. While the urgency to achieve a living wage invigorated grassroots participation, experienced and dedicated leadership helped the revival or formation of some of the best-organized nonestablishment unions. The Motor Drivers General Union, which won victory in collective bargaining when the CMU failed, was a case in point. Its prewar leader, Li Xifen (*Ct.* Lai Sek-fan), came back from the mainland "within days" after the end of the war and "went hither and thither to seek workers' opinions about the revival of the union." Li offered his own apartment to house the union office and save costs, while union chairman Yang Ji (d. 1947) contributed his personal savings to buy out the apartment's other renter. With everything in short supply after the war, union activists made registration forms and receipts for union dues out of used paper from foreign banks. They turned wood planks from a disassembled bed into "desks," worked late into the night by candlelight, and sat on straw mats on the floor when meetings were held. The Motor Drivers General Union, which initially formed in 1920 and contributed substantially during the National Salvation Movement in the 1930s, successfully registered with the Secretariat for Chinese Affairs in November 1945. The union expanded rapidly. By early 1947, its membership grew to 4,000 strong.[90]

Another major union that quickly regained vitality at the war's end was the Hong Kong Seamen's Union, which we encountered in chapters 1 and 2. Because of its left-wing positions, the union had suffered a concerted political repression unmatched by any other prewar union. Formed in the early 1920s, union-led seamen had organized the fifty-six-day strike in 1922 and instantly

---

89. "五個勞動節紀念會, 工友熱烈慶祝" (Workers celebrated enthusiastically in five rallies for the Labor Day), *Huashang bao*, May 3, 1946, 4.

90. Li Huaxuan, "一年來的工作" (The work over the past year), Motuoche yanjiu zonggonghui, February 1947, 2; "光輝的八十年" (Glorious eighty-years), *Qiche jiaotong yunshuye zonggonghui chengli bashi zhounian jinian tekan 1920–2000*, 43–59, citation from 43.

became targets of colonial surveillance. Hong Kong outlawed the Seamen's Union that year and again in 1927 after its brief revival.[91] But seamen's activism never died. Maintaining a pro-Communist stance developed during the National Salvation Movement, the postwar Seamen's Union rejected agents sent by the Guomindang through democratic election.[92] Its popularity among seamen increased as the union led successful collective actions to improve employment conditions and, in particular, to end the much-hated contractor system. In 1948, the left-wing Hong Kong Seamen's Union successfully registered with the Labour Department and boasted a membership of more than 3,500. By 1950, its membership had reached 15,719, and it began to seriously challenge the Guomindang-controlled Hong Kong branch of the Chinese Seamen's Union, which still claimed 21,033 members. Two years later, membership in the left-wing Hong Kong Seamen's Union increased to 19,526, while the right-wing Hong Kong branch of the Chinese Seamen's Union dwindled to 8,471.[93]

Emergent postwar industrial unions also drew energy from grassroots initiatives in prewar activism and wartime resistance. For decades, the colony's largest industry, shipbuilding and repair, had been the territory of the pro-Guomindang CMU. Before the war, national salvation had motivated young workers to form activist groups, such as the Ringing Bell Society (Lingsheng she) at the Naval Dockyard and the Association for Cultivating New Spirit among Employees at the Kowloon Dockyard (Jiulong Chuanwu zhigong peixinshe). When Hong Kong fell, some of these activists joined the East River guerrillas.[94] Others, such as Huang Dengming, whom we met in the previous

91. See, for example, the correspondence between London and Hong Kong as well as the secret report from Messrs. Butterfield and Swire in CO 129/583/14; Liu Nai, "香港海員工會成立經過" (A brief account of the formation of Hong Kong Seamen's Union), Xianggang haiyuan gonghui, resumption issue, September 20, 1946, 7; Jian, "重放光明的海員燈塔" (A beacon for the seamen has been reignited), in Xianggang haiyuan gonghui, resumption issue, September 20, 1946, 8; Zhou Yi (2009), 40, 51, 92–94.

92. Li Fa, "認識現實改善環境走向光明" (To understand the reality, to improve our environment, and to march toward a brighter future), Xianggang haiyuan gonghui, no. 2, November 20, 1946, 3–4.

93. LDAR 1947–48, table 6; LDAR 1950–51, table 10; LDAR 1952–53, table 10.

94. Huang Yeheng, 2–3; Zhou Yi correspondence to author, August 11, 2013. Zhou, who was a youth activist in postwar Hong Kong, frequented these labor meet-

section on postwar labor strikes, continued to work at the Kowloon Dockyard under Japanese occupation and became an underground resister in the Hong Kong–Kowloon Independent Brigade of the East River Column. They sabotaged Japanese war efforts whenever and wherever they could. They went around the colony posting anti-Japanese handbills under the cover of night; they added sand to machines to cause malfunctions; they slowed down work in the dockyard where artillery shells were manufactured.[95] When the war ended, prewar activists and wartime resisters became the moving force on the shop floor to initiate collective action.

These seasoned resisters, still young when the war ended, led the postwar labor movement away from the influence of the guild-like CMU. Their leadership united workers and gave them courage when they confronted threat during collective actions. In March 1946, the Association for Progress in Unity by Chinese Employees at the Naval Dockyard in Hong Kong (Xianggang haijun chuanwu Huayuan xiejinhui) organized an all-dockyard sit-down to force the company to fulfill its promise of a pay raise for both skilled and unskilled workers. Refusing workers' demands, the Naval Dockyard deployed British marines to lock the workers out. Yet this show of force failed to scare workers emboldened by wartime resistance. With prewar members of the Ringing Bell Society in core leadership positions, and older labor activists from the 1920s offering wise counsel, the 9,000 strikers demonstrated remarkable solidarity. All returned to work once the union's conditions for negotiation were accepted. All put down their tools when the union ordered a work stoppage in response to the dockyard's refusal to negotiate in good faith. Labor discipline and determination left the Naval Dockyard no other choice but to concede to the workers' major demands in their first postwar collective action. As a result, the Association for Progress in Unity led by these young men became the most popular labor organization at the Naval Dockyard and held its inaugural celebration in late April 1946. With Chauvin of the Labour

---

ings and continued to report on workers' activities in Hong Kong after he joined the *Wenhui bao* in 1950.

95. Huang Dengming, "紅磡區的抗日游擊戰士" (The guerrilla fighters in Hung Hom District), in *HGGJDD*, 2:66–70; He Jiari, "船廠地下鬥爭" (Underground resistance at the dockyard), in *HGGJDD*, 2:71–75; Gongren jizhe, "敵佔區的香港工人怎樣反抗日寇統治" (How Hong Kong workers under Japanese occupation resisted the enemy), *Huashang bao*, March 16, 1946, 3.

Office, the naval commandant, and representatives from other labor unions across the colony attending the event, the association elected Mai Yaoquan as chair.[96] Similarly, Kowloon Dockyard workers left the CMU when they formed their own Labor Union of Kowloon Dockyard (Jiuwu laogong lianhe-hui) with an elected leader.[97]

Collective action resurged not just among male workers in well-established industries. For the first time in history, women workers began to unionize during those promising years. Since the 1930s, textile and metalwares had developed into the largest lines among emerging light industries, ranking just under shipbuilding and repair. In these lines of production, women workers made up the majority of the labor force. In rubber wares and match mills, women workers were also the dominant workforce.[98] These were labor-intensive industries, where basic training took less than a month to complete. As Butters noted in 1938, female workers on these unskilled jobs were mostly illiterate and paid much less than were male workers. Just as they did in prewar times, women in metalware production in postwar Hong Kong still received the lowest wages of all industries, earning less than HK$1 a day. In their mostly substandard work environment, basic safety protection was often absent. Losing a finger to the widely used power presses was common.[99] Some cotton spinning mills provided neither uniforms nor protective gear, except for aprons. At the end of the workday, workers' black hair looked white as they

---

96. Special report, "Haijun chuanwu gongren zuoyi fugong" (Workers at Naval Dock returned to work yesterday), *Huashang bao*, March 17, 1946, 2; Huang Yeheng, 10–11.

97. Huang Dengming, the underground resister active in Kowloon Dock during the Japanese occupation, had already left Hong Kong to join the Communist guerrilla force in the ongoing civil war. His comrade-in-arms in labor activism, Huo De 霍德, was elected chairman of the new union. See Zhou Yi (2009), 140.

98. Metalwares refer to an assortment of production lines of household hardware, light bulbs, torchlights, oil lamps, and wristwatch tapes. For the relative size of various industries, see "Appendix D," in *LDAR* 1946.

99. Chen Yin, Feng Shutang, and Liu Guangrong, "解放戰爭時期香港五金行業的女工組織和鬥爭回顧" (Recollections on women's organizations in the metal works industry in Hong Kong and their struggle during the war of liberation), *XGFYZL*, 184.

emerged from their workshops.[100] In some factories with outdated equipment, loose shuttles frequently bounced off machines and injured weavers.[101] Women workers thus viewed workplace safety and a living wage as their most urgent concerns.

Labor unions were not totally absent in labor-intensive industries with predominantly female labor forces, though existing unions often failed to promote and defend the interests of the majority of workers. In the textile industry, for example, a Hong Kong–Kowloon General Union of Textile Industry (Xianggang Jiulong fangzhi zonggonghui) under Guomindang influence existed before the war. Skilled workers, often male, dominated the union and controlled the recruitment of new workers. They "regularly set up several tables for mahjong" and "turned the union office into a mahjong parlor," where money could be scooped into the pockets of a few. The union's leader was a member of the Guomindang and adopted a pro-employer approach. When the factory resumed operation after the war, he offered a copy of a prewar contract to the company, giving it decisive leverage against workers' demands for pay raise amid inflation.[102] Instead of promoting the workers' interests, the leader of the old union brought them harm.

Fortuitously, women workers' desire for an alternative union became possible in the changed postwar reality. Better leaders appeared within their own ranks, and the newly formed Labour Department wanted a counterbalance to the Guomindang-influenced labor unions. Demobilized resisters who had worked as people's motivators in the East River Column had returned to civilian life and become ordinary workers. They now turned skills learned in resistance mobilization to labor mobilization. Stepping up on a bench, a soapbox, or a street corner, former people's motivators appealed to fellow workers about women workers' need for their own union. To uplift spirits, they organized fellow workers into singing groups and literacy classes to provide basic social

---

100. Zhou Yuhua and Lu Xiuhua, "解放戰爭時期香港九龍南洋紗廠的兩次罷工" (Two strikes at the Nanyang Cotton Mill in Kowloon during the war of liberation), *XGFYZL*, 212.

101. Ou Lihua and Liang Shaochu, "解放戰爭時期的港九婦女紡織總工會及其活動" (Activities at Hong Kong–Kowloon General Labor Union of Women Cotton Workers during the civil war), *XGFYZL*, 179.

102. Ou and Liang, 177–78.

skills as well as after-work recreation. The Labour Department endorsed their efforts in organizing a separate union as a way of taking workers away from the Guomindang influence—more accurately, Chinese government influence—that threatened the existence of British Hong Kong. When the new Hong Kong–Kowloon Female Knitters Union was formed on June 21, 1947, the Labour Department sent an officer to its celebration meeting. Li Yimei, a former resister in the East River Column who led the new union's public relations department, made an eloquent speech that excited the audience and impressed the labour officer.[103]

The emergence of rival unions within one industry inevitably led to conflict. This was particularly intense between the new Female Knitters General Union and the old Hong Kong–Kowloon General Union of Textile Industry. To protect its turf, the old pro-Guomindang union used Triad thugs to intimidate the leaders of its new competitor. Labor activists had to remain vigilant against physical attacks. Sentries were posted in neighborhoods where activists held meetings, so that participants could dodge ambush by taking alternative exits when thugs were lurking in the area. For self-defense, every female labor activist carried a whistle to blow for help when confronting physical attack.[104] However intimidating, these threats and attacks paled in the opinions of former guerrilla fighters, who had confronted far greater challenges during the war. With self-confidence and ability, as well as initial encouragement from the Labour Department, they sowed seeds of activism among fellow workers. In 1948, the new Hong Kong–Kowloon Female Knitters Union was still a medium-sized union with 850 members, while the Guomindang-controlled Hong Kong Spinning and Weaving Workers General Union claimed a mem-

---

103. Ou and Liang, 178–80. Their memoir gave a wrong year of 1946. For correct date, see Special report, "女織工會昨日成立" (Female Knitters Union was established yesterday), *Huashang bao*, June 22, 1947, 4.

104. Ou and Liang, 178–79. Their memoir lists six labor activists and organizers who had been demobilized from the East River Column: Ou Lihua, Liang Shaochu, Zhang Yue, Li Yimei, Li Yiwen, and He Yubing. The activities of the last one can be cross-referenced in Zhang Wanhua, "回憶西貢區的民運工作" (Recollections of the works in people's mobilization), in *HGGJDD*, 2:101. Most women guerrilla fighters in the East River Column worked mainly in two assignments: as nurses and as people's motivators.

bership of 2,182. Three years later, their numbers reversed. Guided by energetic leaders, membership in the new union soared to 1,891, while the old
union declined to only 188 members.[105]

Not all new unions led by demobilized wartime resisters grew through
confrontations with old unions. In the metalwares industry, a recently formed
union benefited from the experiences of underground resistance and an inno-
vative use of a local tradition of sisterhood. One of its founders was Liu Jieyun,
whom we met in chapter 2. Barely twenty years old at the war's end, Liu was
already an experienced worker and a seasoned underground resister. As a courier for the Hong Kong–Kowloon Independent Brigade, Liu faced death more
than once as she took secret intelligence through enemy checkpoints during
the war.[106] Dodging enemy soldiers taught Liu the tactic of sidetracking, which
she used in organizing her fellow female workers at the Hong Kong branch of
U.S.-owned Eveready Flashlight.

To avoid open conflict with the established pro-Guomindang, pro-employer
union, Liu Jieyun and her fellow workers started a sorority to observe the
Double Seven festival. Ostensibly their sisterhood followed a traditional practice popular among unmarried young women in the Pearl River delta and in
other parts of China. Girls wanting to find an ideal mate formed sisterhoods
and made offerings to Heaven on the seventh day of the seventh month in the
lunar calendar, the day of the annual rendezvous of the weaving maid and her
cowherd lover in the Chinese legend. The Heavenly Queen permitted the famous celestial couple to meet only on this day by crossing the Milky Way over
a bridge made of the spreading wings of sympathetic magpies.[107] Former guerrilla fighters, labor activists, and youth activists from night schools and singing

---

105. *LDAR* 1948–49, table 6; *LDAR* 1950–51, table 10. Although the translation
in this official registration table does not appear to accurately reflect what the Chinese
names intended, I use the ones in the official record in English to keep the language
consistent for English-language readers.

106. Liu Jieyun (2012a). Also see Liu Jieyun, "Zai Zhonghua shuju jingxing duidi
douzheng" (Fighting against the enemy in Zhonghua Printing Company), in
HGGJDD, 2:82–85.

107. The legend of the weaving maid and the cowherd has been popular in folk-
lore throughout China, with some local variations. Practice in South China is discussed in Stockard, 41–44.

groups formed the core of the Double Seven Worshippers. Instead of seeking ideal mates, this postwar sorority turned its energy to improving employment conditions for fellow women workers.

Like the magpies that bridged the vast Milky Way, the "sorority" expanded its membership through one-to-one conversations among fellow workers, small group discussions on the factory floor, and free literacy classes. Within months, the sorority achieved industry-wide participation, and announced the founding of the Hong Kong–Kowloon Sorority in Metalwares Industry in November 1947. Soon the new union successfully registered with the Labour Department. Through a victory in its first negotiation with an employer, winning payment of medical expenses, paid sick leave, and job retention for an injured worker, the reputation of the sorority soared. In spring 1948, when more than forty women workers at the Guangyu Gas Lamp Factory were laid off for redundancy, the sorority organized a collective action in which every worker in the factory participated. They presented an ultimatum to the owner that he chose between retention of the forty workers and resignation of all workers. Facing determined and united workers, the owner agreed to retain the forty workers part-time. At the end of 1948, the sorority was renamed the Hong Kong–Kowloon Metalwares Industry Workers General Union when it became an all-industry labor union, having assimilated an existing union and opened its membership to male workers. With five branches throughout the colony and nearly 1,000 members, the union achieved leading status among organized labor in the industry by 1949.[108]

Colonial Regime Versus Resurgent Labor

At a time when the value of labor became "progressively important" for reviving the colony's trade and industry, the new Labour Department did more than simply make a ceremonious statement in its first annual report in 1947.

---

108. Chen Ying, Feng Shutang, and Liu Guangrong, "解放戰爭時期香港五金行業的女工組織和鬥爭回憶" (Recollections of the struggle of the women workers' organization in the metal wares industry in Hong Kong during the civil war period), XGFYZL, 182–86; Liu Jieyun (2012b). Also see LDAR, 1948–49, table 6, which noted the union with registration no. 115 and membership 736; LDAR 1949–50, 90, table 10, notes the membership of 1,163.

The department positively evaluated and encouraged the emergence of new labor organizations, partly because it preferred "the tendency ... now towards organisation on an industrial rather than a craft basis." It nodded approvingly at this new tendency as it "led to the formation of a number of works unions, some of which are of considerable size."[109] The Labour Department recognized the impact of the war as key to vigorous labor activism. "The labouring classes had during the years of war become increasingly aware of the desirability of organisation and combination in pursuit of common ends," confirmed the department's first postwar annual report. But mixed feelings toward the resurgent labor movement remained. The Labour Department considered two features in the overall labor movement as "regrettable." One was the multiplicity of labor unions, which made some unions "too small to be of real value to their members." The other was "the increasing influence of Chinese party politics" on labor organizations in Hong Kong. In 1947, the Labour Department admitted that entanglement with China's politics was "probably inevitable in present circumstances." But it feared such influence would become "a grave impediment in the way of establishing a healthy, independent trade unionism in the Colony."[110]

In contrast to this mild and equivocal public statement concerning the influence of China's politics on the vibrant development of labor organizations in postwar Hong Kong, internal correspondence spoke in a more candid voice. Between 1945 and 1947, the central concern for colonial officials in Hong Kong was Guomindang influence that publicly opposed British restoration. An internal memo sent to the Colonial Office revealed deep anxiety about the Guomindang's grip on labor unions, noting that its intention was "to weld the Unions under their direct control ... through the Triad Societies." The same memo also suggested that "the best chance for healthy development in Trade Unionism in Hong Kong lies in combating K.M.T. infiltration. This means encouraging the growth of the anti-K.M.T. unions."[111] This corroborated labor

109. *LDAR*, 1946–47, 2, 15.

110. *LDAR* 1946–47, 1, 2.

111. "Summary of Memorandum on Trade Unionism in Hong Kong (Enclosure to No. 75)," CO 129/615/1, 36–38. The noted correspondence no. 75 is not included in the file, nor is the summary of the memo dated. But its text as well as its location in this file of correspondence between Colonial Office in London and the colonial officials in Hong Kong, including Governor Mark Young and Commissioner

activists' recollections of the Labour Department's eager endorsement of their new and separate unions. From the other side of the political divide, failure of the pro-Guomindang CMU to win Labour Department support in 1947 also evidenced a deliberate choice by the colonial state to reduce the influence of the Guomindang-led Chinese government.

Rapidly changing international circumstances in East Asia soon began to reverse Hong Kong's postwar approach to labor unions. In late 1947, the undercurrent of disintegration within the Guomindang government irreversibly turned into an unstoppable torrent. Despite increased U.S. supplies of combat matériel, government troops lost one battle after another in northern China after Communist troops began their counteroffensive in August 1947. Key strategic centers in Manchuria fell in rapid succession from March 1948 onward, until the region came under Communist control that November. As 1949 began, the Communists achieved control of the vast territories in northern and central China. In urban areas, hyperinflation caused by military spending and disastrous government currency manipulation eroded the failing regime's last shred of support among the salaried and propertied population.[112] The final outcome of the civil war on the mainland was not a total surprise to the British and U.S. governments. Western diplomats and foreign journalists with firsthand experience in China had observed and reported on internal corruption in the Guomindang government and predicted its inevitable fall since the early 1940s. But when the prospect of a Communist-led government in Asia became imminent, widespread fear in Western official circles of an emerging Communist bloc creating a domino effect in East and Southeast Asia altered the dynamics of postwar colonial practice. In U.S.-occupied Japan, the prolabor, anti-zaibatsu policy took a "reverse course" as the occupation force released war criminals and returned them to prominent positions while ousting 13,000 alleged Communists from public or private jobs.[113] In British Hong Kong, prolabor practices also underwent subtle but unmistakable changes.

---

of Labour B. C. K. Hawkins all indicate that the memo should have been written and sent during the years of 1946 and 1947.

112. Pepper (1978), xviii–xx, and chapter 4.

113. A well-established case in Japanese history, "reverse course" has been the topic of scholarly studies as well as documentary films. For a succinct summary, see Gordon, 237–38.

The first sign of the Labour Department's changing policy came about in late 1947, when it stepped back from encouraging new left-wing unions. It reversed its practice of encouraging non-Guomindang unions and became vigilant against Communist influence within resurgent labor activism. Communists in Hong Kong quickly took note. One internal report in August 1947 summarized British policy toward the labor movement in Hong Kong as "limited reform." It noted "constant shifts" and partiality in the Labour Department's mediation of industrial disputes and choices between China's two major political parties. The report indicated that the Labour Department sided with labor in early 1946 but switched its support to employers in 1947. Parallel to this shifted position in industrial disputes was a tilt in partisan choice, as the report noted that "the British were more vigilant toward the Guomindang last year [1946]; they went against it by using us. But this year [1947] they became more vigilant toward us and used the Guomindang to go against us."[114]

The reorientation of Hong Kong's labor policy was nowhere more decisive and explicit than in the revision of labor laws. Back in 1938, when Butters first investigated labor conditions in the colony, one of his recommendations was to legalize labor unions. In early 1947 the colonial state made public its intention to follow up on this prewar plan. It generated a widely shared hope among recently mobilized workers that a general union would be part of it.[115] Left-leaning labor unions, whose resurgence had so far received the Labour Department's blessing, formed a preparatory committee in March. Representatives from the five largest and most active unions—the Tramway Workers' Union, Telephone Workers' Union, Motor Drivers General Union, Seamen's Union, and the Fraternity of Chinese Employees in Government Service—made up the committee. A month later, the committee discussed the organization and bylaws of a general union at the Motor Drivers General Union.[116] They were eager to bring industrial unions to the next stage of development. In contrast,

---

114. Anonymous, "Telegram to Xiaolong—Report of work in Hong Kong," *XGFJWJ*, 44–47, citation from 46.

115. Special report, "本港將制定勞工法案並組總工會" (This city will make a labor law and allow general union), *Huashang bao*, February 2, 1947, 4.

116. Special report, "改善津貼未獲解決，工團昨曾交換意見" (No solution attained on raise of allowance; labor unions held discussion yesterday), *Huashang bao*, April 10, 1947, 4.

right-wing unions controlled by the Guomindang showed neither comparable enthusiasm nor development of a coordinating structure for colony-wide activities. Their operation appeared listless until late 1950.

After giving explicit and repeated encouragement to new industrial unions led by wartime resisters, the Labour Department had second thoughts as organized labor came to a threshold of development. Mixed feelings and contradictory attitudes surfaced. Its first annual report endorsed industrial unions as progress but viewed new union leaders as "young and inexperienced."[117] An internally circulated document in early 1948 noted fragmentation in labor organizations, as two or three appeared in one industry. The memo also noted that "some of the unions do not look kindly towards female workers in the same industry." But it regarded "a tendency to split the labour unions in a political manner" as most threatening to the desirable development of the trade union movement after the British model.[118] Nonetheless the labour officer who wrote the memo acknowledged that fragmented labor unions had "appeared in the early stages of British and other countries Trade Unionism," and therefore were just a phase of development toward the desired goal.[119] He hoped that a new ordinance would allow labor union consolidation in any particular industry and give the government power to refuse the registration of any union associated with a political force outside the colony. Before the long-anticipated ordinance was brought to the open, at least some in the Labour Department believed it still possible to shape Chinese labor activism after the "healthy" British model of apolitical growth.

On March 3, 1948, the Trade Unions and Trade Disputes Ordinance in Hong Kong was brought to the Legislative Council for first reading. It dropped a bombshell on the labor unions. Labor leaders discovered in the ordinance alarming details that "conflict with the British law of free association" and "interfere with the practice of labor unions." The new ordinance, they argued, was designed not to aid but to hinder labor union development. In particular, the stipulation that union staff must be workers employed in the trade would result

---

117. *LDAR* 1946–47, 15.

118. Anonymous, "Labour Organisation," HKRS 843-1-52. The three-page assessment is undated, but from its text that mentioned registered guilds by December 1947 and the pending Trade Unions Ordinance, which was passed in March 1948, this report was most likely written in the first two or three months of 1948.

119. Anonymous, "Labour Organisation," HKRS 843-1-52, 3.

in weak union leadership and ineffective union offices. A case in point was the cotton-weaving industry, in which weavers worked and rested on alternative days. To abide by the ordinance meant that no one could consistently attend to union affairs, leading to union dysfunction. Moreover, the age limit of twenty-one or higher for qualified union staff further eliminated available candidates, because woman workers usually got married and bore children by age twenty-one, leaving them little energy to attend to union affairs.[120] But labor's objections came too late. The ordinance was swiftly passed on second and third reading in the Legislative Council on March 10, with no discussion or debate.[121]

Alarmed by the sudden back-stepping of Hong Kong's colonial state, representatives of the thirty-eight most active labor unions gathered in the Luk Kwok Hotel at Wanchai on the evening of March 20 to discuss the impending implementation of the ordinance. The meeting resulted in a collective appeal to the Labour Department signed with each union's seal. In a restrained but indignant tone, they argued that the new ordinance "is not favorable to labor, restrictive to the freedom of labor activities, and in conflict with the spirit of the British constitution." Most significantly, passage of the ordinance "has totally overturned the legal status of labor unions that have been accorded to by the Hong Kong Government."[122] Criticism was only part of this collective appeal. Labor representatives made constructive recommendations as well, particularly revision of the ordinance on six issues:

1. currently registered industrial labor unions must be also recognized and registered under the new ordinance;
2. multiple labor unions within one industry must be allowed and registered;
3. anyone who had served in an industry, regardless of age and current state of employment, must be allowed to join a union in that industry and qualify for staff election;

---

120. "GangJiu nieyu zhigongtuan daibiao zuo yantao zhigonghui fa" (Representatives of more than twenty labor unions discuss the Trade Unions Ordinance yesterday), *Huashang bao*, March 8, 1948, 1.

121. Hong Kong Government, *Hong Kong Hansard* 1948, 29, 37.

122. "工人不滿職工會新例，卅八工團聯請修正；通過組工團聯合會" (Workers unhappy with the new ordinance of trade unions; 38 labor unions collectively appeal for revision; a labor unions' alliance was formed), *Huashang bao*, March 21, 1948, 4.

4. labor unions within the colony should be allowed to contact, help, and communicate with labor unions outside the colony; government could only limit their organizational connection;

5. labor union property was private property for its own use at will, and the government had no right to interfere in such usage; and

6. a labor union had full rights to picket during a strike as long as it did not harm people or the property of others.[123]

Passage of the new Trade Unions and Trade Disputes Ordinance of 1948 finally made labor activists realize that the colonial state had rescinded its promise for a general union. In defiance and in hope of achieving greater solidarity, the new industrial unions resolved to form a Federation of Trade Unions (Gongtuan lianhehui) at the meeting on March 20.[124] On March 24, 1948, the first meeting of the Hong Kong–Kowloon Federation of Trade Unions (GangJiu gonglianhui, or HKFTU) was held at the Motor Drivers General Union. From twenty-five affiliated unions, representatives from nine—the Tramway Workers' Union, Hong Kong Seamen's Union, Telephone Workers' Union, Union of Workers in Foreign-Style Employment, Motor Drivers General Union, Naval Dockyard Chinese Employees Association, Taikoo Dockyard Chinese Employees Association, Carpenters Union, and the Fraternity of Chinese Employees in Government Service—were elected to the board of directors. Zhu Jingwen, chairman of the Tramway Workers' Union, was elected first president of the federation.[125]

---

123. *Huashang bao*, March 21, 1948, 4.

124. *Huashang bao*, March 21, 1948, 4.

125. Special report, "港九工團聯會昨日宣告組成" (The Hong Kong–Kowloon Federation of Labor Unions was formed yesterday), *Huashang bao*, March 25, 1948, 4; Special report, "昨港九工會聯合會通過章程職員就職" (Hong Kong–Kowloon Federation of Labor Unions passed its by-laws and swore in its staff yesterday), *Huashang bao*, April 18, 1948, 4. The report on April 18 lists thirty unions, five more than the twenty-five that initiated the federation in March, though it lists one union of the same name twice. Liang Baolong, who wrote a brief description of the federation, provided information that does not match the contemporary records. He dates the founding of the federation to 1947, when it was just being discussed by labor unions. See Liang Baolong, "香港工會聯合會簡介" (A brief description of Hong Kong Federation of Trade Unions), in Ming K. Chan (ed.), 1986, 127–31.

Fig. 7. Representatives to the first meeting of FTU, 1948. Courtesy of HKFTU.

Guomindang-controlled labor unions formed a similar association some six months later. So far they had done little to confront the colonial state. The civil war on the mainland had totally consumed party strength, leaving no spare energy to revive its organization in Hong Kong. On February 27, 1948, just a few days before the Trade Unions and Trade Disputes Ordinance was scheduled to be read in Legislative Council, sixty-five labor unions under Guomindang influence moved to initiate a Trades Union Council. Seven of these unions formed a preparatory committee to draft council bylaws. On September 9, the Trades Union Council held its inaugural meeting on a much grander scale than the HKFTU. More than 1,000 representatives came from its 102 affiliated unions. Representatives elected nine members from the Inland River Steamship and Motor Vessel Seamen's Association, Hong Kong and Kowloon Café Workers General Union, Hong Kong Branch of Chinese Seamen's Union, Hong Kong and Kowloon Teahouse Workers General Union, Tung-tak Coolies General Union, Hong Kong and Kowloon Spinning and Weaving Workers General Union, Chap-yin Stevedores Union, Rattan Ping-dong Union, and Hong Kong and Kowloon Restaurant and Café Workers General Union.[126]

Particular characteristics differentiated the two union amalgamations. At that moment, the pro-Guomindang Trades Union Council was large, with long-established influence. It encompassed more affiliated unions, though most were small in membership. Only two had more than 5,000 members, one of which was the Hong Kong and Kowloon Restaurant and Café Workers General Union. Largely the Trades Union Council represented craft unions, a tendency that became increasingly pronounced later on. In contrast, the HKFTU built its strength on new industrial unions organized or developed in postwar years. Only twenty-five member unions took part in 1948, and that number did not exceed fifty until 1955, the year when relative membership strength switched between the Trades Union Council and the HKFTU. But industrial unions in the federation were larger from the start, and union leaders were collectively more energetic and dedicated to promoting workers' interests regardless of skilled or unskilled status or gender differences.

Although it initially dabbled with ideas of a general union, the colonial regime in Hong Kong brushed that aside in 1948. It refused to treat either the

---

126. Liang, "Brief history of the Trade Unions Council," 132–37.

HKFTU or the Trades Union Council as such. In June 1948, when mandatory registration of labor unions with the Labour Department began in Hong Kong, neither the HKFTU nor the Trades Union Council was allowed to register as a general labor union. Eventually, both had to register as "societies" when a new Societies Bill came into force in 1949, which restored the compulsory registration of all associations as stipulated in the 1911 Societies Ordinance. Aimed against political influence from the mainland and workers' affinity with their Chinese homeland, the new Societies Bill made the police commissioner the registrar of societies and his subordinate officers assistant registrars, with powers only checked by the governor. Now, the labor movement in Hong Kong had to forge forward in an increasingly hostile political climate.

In the two years following the end of the war, a vibrant labor movement surged forward as waves of collective action swept nearly all industries. Frequent industrial disputes erupted not because a few activists instigated labor unrest. As Hong Kong lay in ruins, war damage and material shortage as well as below-subsistence-level wages made postwar labor conditions even worse than Butters had observed in 1938. Labor's call for "improvement in employment conditions" summarized an urgent need for workers to secure living wages and, above all, to be treated not merely as "cattle and horses" but as human beings. Democratic participation from the factory floor and energetic leadership gave rise to robust labor unions and to hopes for the advent of healthy industrial relationships. Never before had labor activism in Hong Kong seen such a broad-based leadership emerging from the working class and from a very long wave of labor activism. Continuing the tradition of early labor activism in the 1920s, this leadership came of age in the civic activism for national salvation, and grew stronger and matured in a war against foreign invasion. The dynamism of ordinary worker empowerment and new labor leadership reshaped the postwar labor movement. As a democratic spirit prevailed in the more vigorous labor organizations, the traditional, officially endorsed leadership of the CMU became increasingly irrelevant in a labor movement that promoted the interests of all workers, not just those of labor's aristocracy.

These were also years when constructive efforts were made by British officials to bridge the great divide in Hong Kong. In the contact zone of labor affairs, labour officers sent to the front line of industrial conflict used their official power to pressure reluctant employers to come to terms with organized labor. Workers came to appreciate these officers for using their power to promote fairness in industrial relations, even though the concessions they won were only the beginnings of systemic improvement in employment conditions. The extraordinary cooperation between the Labour Department and the newly organized industrial unions stemmed from yet another urgent need to bring a recolonized Hong Kong back to its feet. Indeed, the economy in Hong Kong recovered at a fast clip.

Subcurrents of conflicting interest persisted, and the great divide was never bridged. In this recolonized British territory, the colonial state made the reform of industrial relations serve the hegemonic goals and long-term commercial interests of the reoccupied colony. At the crossroads of the colony's rising labor movement, it chose to diverge from London's labor reform agenda. Instead of safeguarding healthy, embryonic industrial relations with robust labor unions, the colonial state began to undercut their strength. The 1948 Trade Unions and Trade Disputes Ordinance, which so angered organized labor, was only a first step. The age-old tactic of divide and rule, counterbalancing one group of unions against the other, soon evolved into more strident efforts to reverse the direction of prewar reformist intervention.

5

Reversals

As the 1940s drew to an end, China was on the cusp of great changes that had been in the making for decades. The Communist Revolution, which rose as an alternative to the vision of the Guomindang-led government for social transformation, was coming close to victory. The foreseeable power change in China would not just realign the regional order in Asia. It raised questions about how Britain could maintain regional interests accumulated through century-long investment and to what extent they could carry business forward. For both the colonial state and the Chinese in Hong Kong, it was an anxious time as they looked beyond to the future of a British colony within the social and geographic South China.

Contrasting moods swept through Hong Kong in the last two years of the 1940s. Great apprehension consumed some segments within the colony, while irrepressible joy overtook others. For a second time since the Pacific War, the colonial state and the imperial center in London confronted the question of whether to defend the crown colony of Hong Kong or give it up. Despite its strategic vulnerability, grimly evident in the quick defeat of 1941, the British decided on making a determined show of defense by reinforcing Hong Kong's garrisons. This tough posture might have comforted supporters of British rule, but it paled against a new culture emerging among working Chinese and youth activists, who had become a major force in public life and embraced Communist power during the war against the Japanese invasion.

To the defenders of British Hong Kong, the Communist victory on the mainland also raised questions about left-leaning labor activism that, as Governor Grantham noted, went "from strength to strength." Would the Communist power change its mind about Hong Kong, as Mao had said at the end of 1946, and wrest it from British hands? What were the Communists doing in Hong Kong on the eve of their national victory? Might they use organized labor as a Fifth Column to bring down British rule from the inside? These worries quickly came to the fore as London and Hong Kong's Government House began to coordinate measures to counter the Communist victory in 1949. Grave threats to British rule seemed to materialize when a new wave of industrial disputes erupted late that year and gained strong, unmistakable local sympathy. Never before had workers' collective actions appeared so explicitly political and so closely linked to British Hong Kong's political survival, regardless of the participants' true motivations.

London and Hong Kong in Consensus

Although uncertain about long-term policy for Hong Kong, the postwar Labour government in London desired to stay in China as long as possible. Within Whitehall, the Foreign Office and Colonial Office no longer had differences over Hong Kong as they had in 1943; now they joined efforts to confront this second crisis in Britain's Far East outpost. Commitment to fighting a Cold War battle against Communism in Europe and Asia made the two offices close allies in 1949. Ernest Bevin, who had served the Labour government as secretary for foreign affairs since mid-1945, was at the forefront of formulating tough foreign policies, assisted by the staff he had inherited from the Conservative government. Strongly anti-Soviet and anti-Communist and believing in the beneficent role of the empire, Bevin held firm in his mission to maintain Britain's status as a world power.[1] As they confronted the rise of Communist China, the Foreign Office and the Colonial Office cooperated to maintain Britain's position in Hong Kong and worked hard to mobilize a

---

1. This very brief sketch of Bevin's attitude is based on two notable biographies by Bullock and Weiler. The last of a three-volume narrative of Bevin's career, Bullock's book is a very sympathetic portrait. It emphasizes Bevin's "conviction" of his ability and his anti-Communism, but gives slight hints of his ability to handle challenging tasks in dealing with the postwar world. See esp. 632. Weiler assimilates more up-to-date scholarship with documents unavailable when Bullock wrote his massive work. It is a more critical and useful assessment of Bevin's ability as the secretary for foreign affairs, as well as his hawkish foreign policy, which contributed to the Cold War divide in Europe.

"common resistance" among potential allies on the eve of the Communists' national triumph.

Despite Hong Kong's secondary importance to Shanghai in terms of British economic interests in China, the imminent Communist victory on the mainland reframed the colony's position vis-à-vis British Asia. In June 1948, a Communist-led insurgence on the Malay Peninsula shook the rubber production region and jeopardized a significant source of Britain's revenue during times of financial distress. Officially named the Malayan Emergency, this revolt of mostly local Chinese lasted more than a decade. As the Communist victory in China threatened to take away British interest on the mainland, Hong Kong's importance to British Asia stood out. Not only did its entrepôt trade constitute a significant part of British business in Asia. It provided the only major shipbuilding and refitting center within the 2,500-mile sea route between Singapore and Tokyo. Yet the island was strategically indefensible: water, food, and other vital resources came from the New Territories, which was leased from the Chinese government.

In late 1948, the Attlee Cabinet came to the conclusion that "Communist domination of China will only be a matter of time."[2] Further analysis by the Foreign Office pointed toward two internal problems more immediate than the eventual takeover. A twelve-page memo argued that war refugees and organized labor would undermine the security of the colony:

> The colony's major problem is likely to be a steady stream of refugees. If, as may be expected, the Communists continue southward, they may well try to "soften up" Hong Kong by instigating strikes to coincide with their advance. Since labour in public utilities and on the waterfront in Hong Kong is mainly Communist in sympathy, such strikes might temporarily paralyse the colony. Serious clashes between Communist and Kuomintang supporters might also occur.[3]

To size up possible repercussions of a Communist victory on the Asian mainland, the Foreign Office dispatched Undersecretary William Strang on a fact-finding mission in early 1949. On January 12, Strang made his first stop at Alexandra, then Karachi, New Delhi, Calcutta, Rangoon, Singapore, Bata-

---

2. Secret, "Recent Developments in the Civil War in China: Memorandum by the Secretary of State for Foreign Affairs," CAB 129/31/29, December 9, 1948.

3. "Annex: China," CAB 129/31/29, 5.

via (Jakarta), and Bangkok, finally reaching Hong Kong on February 4 for a four-day stop before going on to Shanghai and Tokyo. Some of these stops were longer than others so Strang could converse substantially with important national leaders and British officials in these regions. Among those he met were Commissioner-General Malcolm MacDonald, charged with handling the Malayan Emergency, Indian Prime Minister Jawaharlal Nehru, Burmese Prime Minister Thakin Nu, and General Douglas MacArthur, Supreme Commander for the Allied Powers in occupied Japan.

Strang's meetings and discussions with the Asian, British, and U.S. leaders covered a range of important issues regarding the region and the prospect of Communist victory in China. Of all topics, one consensus was embraced unilaterally: the importance of postwar recovery leading toward economic development, which would require sustained outside financial assistance. Despite strong agreement on postwar reconstruction, outstanding differences set apart these leaders' assessments of Communism and its impact on Asia. Nehru, who had been interested in Marxism but was first and foremost a nationalist, "thought that communism … would in the long run be overlaid and transformed by the national character."[4] MacDonald, on the other hand, appreciated Malay nationalism for supporting his fight against "Chinese Communist banditry." Strang, coming from London, found the idea that ethnic hostility underlay Malay support for Communist suppression a bit too much to entertain. At an official dinner in his honor, he noted that "even here, it was significant that the claws were out between Malays and Chinese."[5] In Siam, Strang again noted ethnic differences interwoven with different attitudes toward Communism, for there was "little Communism among the Siamese themselves" and it was only "through the Chinese community that Communism would come." The British ambassador to Siam warned Strang of "signs that the spread of Communism in China will bring about a new wave of Chinese nationalism among the Chinese Communists in South-East Asia, and that the Chinese in Siam will take this opportunity to get back at the Siamese in revenge for past slights and oppressions."[6]

---

4. Secret, "Report by Sir William Strang," February 27, 1949, 6, CAB 129/33/27.
5. "Report by Sir William Strang," 12.
6. "Report by Sir William Strang," 15.

In the cities of Hong Kong, Guangzhou, and Shanghai along China's southeast coast, Strang heard different, sometimes conflicting perspectives on the present and future. The loudest alarm on the prospect of a unified China came from Governor Grantham in Hong Kong. With shrewd insight, he placed Hong Kong's safety in opposition to China's internal stability and strength. "The chief danger to Hong Kong," he argued, "would be a united China, whether Kuomintang or Communist. So long as China was in turmoil, there was no immediate threat." The key was in hearts and minds. Grantham reminded Strang of the major difference between "the Hong Kong Chinese and the Straits Chinese" in that the "former had much closer links with China and were less consciously or loyally British subjects."[7] In contrast to Grantham, European businessmen at the Hong Kong Chamber of Commerce cared little about Chinese loyalty. They were optimistic when considering business prospects. They assured Strang that "the mass of the Chinese people were individualists" who had "the invincible Chinese determination to carry on private trade, lawful or unlawful" and "the age-long Chinese spirit of compromise." They predicted that a Soviet-Chinese Communist bloc would not last long because of "the obstinate refusal of the Chinese to be dominated by foreigners" (read as "Russians"). Based on such "long-term considerations," they believed that "the chances were good enough for us to stay in China and trade so long as we could."[8] The British consul-general in Guangzhou agreed with this optimistic assessment of Chinese nationalism at odds with Communism and Russian domination. During his visit to Shanghai, Strang learned about the continued operation of British firms in North China, now under Communist control. This also seemed to hint at "possibly straws in the wind." Like his fellow businessmen in Hong Kong, John Keswick of Jardine & Matheson assured Strang that the British community in Shanghai were "traders first and foremost" and would "stay in Shanghai as long as they could and use every resource of skill and experience to maintain British interests and prestige."[9]

---

7. "Report by Sir William Strang," 16.

8. "Report by Sir William Strang," 16.

9. "Report by Sir William Strang," 18. True to Keswick's statement, Jardine, Matheson & Company stayed on after 1949 and continued business through the China Trading Division, while maintaining a cozy relationship with leading statesmen in the People's Republic of China. It had a well-developed network of offices in

Although these speculations point toward a broadly shared uncertainty about British hold over the region, there was a wide gap between Britain's keen desire to keep Hong Kong and its inadequate strength to achieve that goal. Already in 1948, the Foreign Office had concluded that Hong Kong's survival depended on the United States, for it was "the only power which could contribute financial, material and military resources for counter action against the Chinese Communists in China."[10] In meeting with Strang, John Keswick in Shanghai and Sir Alvary Gascoigne, head of the U.K. Liaison Mission in Tokyo, again expressed the view that an Anglo-American united front was indispensable in confronting the Communist takeover in China. To gauge American intentions, Strang made his longest stop in Tokyo, only to be disappointed. His two conversations with MacArthur reconfirmed that U.S. policy in East Asia "had not [been] framed" and that they "were improvising from day to day."[11]

Even without assurance of support from the United States, London needed to demonstrate a determination to keep Hong Kong and redeem the humiliation of 1941. After the People's Liberation Army took Nanjing and Shanghai in late spring 1949, the Attlee Cabinet made public its resolve to defend Hong Kong with military force. On May 5, the Cabinet dispatched reinforcements to Hong Kong "sufficient to secure the Colony against internal unrest or sporadic attacks by guerillas." Minister of Defence A. V. Alexander declared the government's resolve in the House of Commons on the same day.[12] In early June, he went to East Asia to coordinate the defense of Hong Kong.

In addition to the logistics of military mobilization and the timely supply of strategic matériel such as food, fuel, oil, and ammunition, the chief problem discussed during Alexander's tour was not external defense but internal sub-

China when it started on its own again in 1981 under the name Jardine Matheson (China) Ltd., just as other major foreign firms began to return to the mainland. See Adam Williams, "A Changing Relationship," in Keswick (ed.), 254–59.

10. Secret, "Recent Developments in the Civil War in China: Memorandum by the Secretary of State for Foreign Affairs," CAB 129/31/29, December 9, 1948.

11. Secret, "Report by Sir William Strang," February 27, 1949, 6, CAB 129/33/27, 20.

12. Secret, "Hong Kong: Memorandum by the Prime Minister," May 24, 1949, CAB 129/35/9.

version. The British Chamber of Commerce in Shanghai was very concerned that "Hong Kong could be rendered untenable by means of a boycott and internal unrest." To counter the possibility of local unrest coordinated with a Communist takeover, the colonial state in Hong Kong made preparations on several fronts. It planned on compiling a registry of the colony's two million residents in eight months as a preemptive move in creating a mechanism of surveillance. In addition to mobilizing regular armed forces, the commanding officer of the Hong Kong Defence Force assured Alexander that more than 2,000 volunteers in the colony were ready to provide essential services. The commissioner of police, D. W. Mackintosh, also confirmed that he "could at any given moment clamp down if the internal situation became difficult." Even so assured, Alexander had serious reservations about the island's ability to sustain supplies of water, food, and fuel in case of a conflict; he returned to London with "sober confidence in our ability to hold Hong Kong as long as our hands are free elsewhere."[13]

Unfortunately, British hands were busy elsewhere just as a united China was appearing in Asia. Britain's economy had turned down sharply in late 1947. Although tensions in Berlin subsided after the division of Germany became a long-term reality, rising nationalist sentiments in Egypt and unrest in Palestine weakened Britain's most important base in the Suez and thus its vital position with respect to Middle East oil supplies. In Asia, the Malayan Emergency showed no signs of letting up. New rounds of global crises underscored Hong Kong's importance for the continuance of the British Empire. In a joint memorandum, Bevin and Secretary of State for the Colonies Arthur Creech Jones argued that losing Hong Kong to the Communists would start political dominos falling in British Southeast Asia, ending with a fatal blow on Britain: "Apart from our historical obligations toward Malaya and the fact that it is our most important dollar earner, South-East Asia is a provider of food stuffs and raw materials which are essential to the economy of the West as a whole."[14] Britain faced a dilemma of overextension and could not "afford to remain so

---

13. Top Secret, A. V. Alexander, "Visit to Hong Kong, 6th June–9th June, 1949, Memorandum by the Minister of Defence," CAB 129/35/24.

14. Secret, "Hong Kong: Memorandum by the Secretary of State for Foreign Affairs and the Secretary of State for the Colonies," August 10, 1949, CAB 129/36/27.

extended so far from the centre of our own activities and commitments in Europe and the Middle East."[15] At this dire moment when the defense of Hong Kong needed support from its "only capable" ally, the United States, Britain found itself virtually alone.

In fact, U.S. involvement in the British defense of Hong Kong had become impossible in 1949. Constant disagreement between the two countries over approaches to the rise of a Communist China led to what historian Lanxin Xiang calls an "open split."[16] Despite the powerful China lobby and Republican Party rhetoric, which whipped up political and ideological fervor in the United States against Communist power in China, the Truman administration had decided on a "wait and see" policy after the failure of George Marshall's mediation. Based on CIA intelligence that the Communist troops would succeed in taking over Taiwan in late 1950, which coincided with U.S. elections, it planned for formal recognition of the Communist government once the dust settled as Chinese unification would have become a fait accompli.[17]

The decisive U.S. disengagement with the Guomindang-led government on the eve of Communist victory bitterly disappointed the British. The U.S. ambassador, John Leighton Stuart, left China in July 1949, followed by an exodus of consuls from the country throughout late summer. "Without any prior warning, United States policy seems to have taken a sharp turn in the direction of retreat," the Foreign Office gasped.[18] As the People's Liberation Army marched southward, the United States closed its consulates in Guangzhou, Kunming, Chongqing, and Dihua and reduced staff at Nanjing and Shanghai. As if washing their hands of the mainland, Americans asked His Majesty's Government to take charge of their consular properties and other U.S. interests in China. Bevin put up a brave face as he tried to frame U.S. retreat in terms of limited interest. "It is easier for the United States to cut their losses

---

15. Although the view was expressed in a memo by Ernest Bevin and Arthur Creech Jones on August 19, 1949, the tone best summarizes the predicament acutely felt by policy makers throughout these two intense years. See CAB 129/36/27 (old catalog number CP [49] 177), "Hong Kong," 1.

16. Xiang, esp. chapter 6.

17. Tucker (1983), passim.

18. Secret, "China: Memorandum by the Secretary of State for Foreign Affairs," August 23, 1949, CAB 129/36/30, 3.

in China than for the United Kingdom to do so," he said. "Their trading interests are fewer and not so deep-rooted and their communities are smaller." It made sense when measured against each nation's economic strength, because "the total loss of their trading interest means less to the United States than a similar loss means to the United Kingdom in our present economic and financial condition."[19]

Going it alone, Britain's defense of Hong Kong was more of a public gesture than a demonstration of confidence. In mid-1949, Hong Kong maintained a garrison of 6,000 troops; in September, reinforcements swelled it to 30,000 men.[20] But leaders in London and Hong Kong, and particularly leaders in the commonwealth, deeply doubted Hong Kong's defensibility should the People's Liberation Army decide to take it by force. They wanted to seek compromise. The U.K. high commissioner in Australia, for example, argued that "holding Hong Kong by force in the years to come may not be possible, and an attempt to do so may easily lead to a major conflict." Therefore, "we are dubious about the deterrent effect of a reinforced garrison." Instead, he suggested that "more attention to the normal commercial functions of Hong Kong and less to its defence may be found not only to provide the best safeguard for the security of Hong Kong, but also to offer the best chance of establishing a practical working relationship with the Chinese Communists against the day when they are in control of all China."[21] The Canadian prime minister was simply critical. In reply to London's call for comments on the Hong Kong crisis, he considered it to be "wrong in principle to endeavor to maintain British rule by force in a Colony which was geographically part of China."[22] Real relief came

---

19. CAB 129/36/30, 3.

20. The figure appeared to have increased in October to 40,000, see "Defence of Hong Kong," *South China Morning Post and the Hongkong Telegraph*, September 17, 1949, 6, which noted "25,000 new Services personnel" in addition to the existing garrison; Ingrams, 283. Officially commissioned, Ingrams's book drew heavily on government documents. Also see "H.K. Defence to Cost More: Building of Garrison for 40,000 Troops," *South China Morning Post and the Hongkong Telegraph*, October 7, 1949, 12.

21. Secret, "Annex B. Telegram No. 365 from the United Kingdom High Commissioner in Australia," June 1, 1949, "Hong Kong: Memorandum by the Secretary of State for Foreign Affairs and the Secretary of State for the Colonies," August 18, 1949, 5, CAB 129/36/27.

22. Quoted in Secret, "Hong Kong: Memorandum by the Lord Privy Seal," October 11, 1949, CAB 129/37/2, 1.

not from enhancing the colony's defense force, but by decisions made on the Chinese side. On October 14, the People's Liberation Army entered Guangzhou with little resistance. The next day, it took Shenzhen, and then halted its southward advance.[23]

In facing the inevitable future of a unified and potentially strong China, London eventually prioritized economic interest over ideology and thus parted ways from its U.S. ally. Even though staunch anti-Communists Bevin and Creech Jones recommended discussing Hong Kong's future only "with a friendly and democratic and stable Government of a unified China," the Attlee Cabinet struck out the word *democratic* as a condition for negotiations.[24] Two and a half months after the founding of the People's Republic of China, the British Cabinet decided on December 15 to offer de jure recognition of China's new government. Negotiations of establishing formal diplomatic relations dragged on for three months in spring 1950, ending with China's rejection of diplomatic relations on the grounds of British duplicity in retaining relations with Taiwan and refusal to endorse China's membership in the United Nations.[25] Nonetheless, London kept "a foot in the door," with a chargé d'affaires posted in Beijing, until diplomatic relations were formalized by the exchange of ambassadors after Britain withdrew its Taiwan consulate in 1972.

Fortifying the "Berlin of the East"

With intensified vigilance against a unified China, colonial Hong Kong's guardians came to the realization that the greatest problem was neither U.S. noncommitment nor the threat of Communist power on the mainland. Rather, it was the dangerous loyalty of the predominant majority of Chinese residents in Hong Kong to their homeland. The British had never felt bothered by what lay in the hearts of these aliens when China remained weak and divided. Now

---

23. "沙頭角解放了！" (Liberation of Shatoujiao!), *Wenhui bao*, October 16, 1949, 4.

24. Secret, "Hong Kong: Memorandum by the Secretary of State for Foreign Affairs and the Secretary of State for the Colonies," August 19, 1949, CAB 129/36/27, 3; Secret, Cabinet 54 (49), "Conclusions of a Meeting of the Cabinet held at 10 Downing Street, S. W. 1, on Monday 29th August, 1949," 161.

25. Jin Guangyao, 119–31.

they suddenly woke up to its grave implications when the colony came under the shadow of a unified China with popular support. Secretary of State for the Colonies Creech Jones laid bare Britain's precarious hold of Hong Kong in a memorandum in fall 1949, in which he estimated "not more than 10,000 persons, including the Police force and the permanent Government service, would prove willing to commit themselves by giving the Government their active and wholehearted support in the preservation of internal order and the operation of the minimum essential services."[26] These 10,000 loyal British subjects amounted to a mere 0.5 percent of Hong Kong's two million people. The frightening specter of 99.5 percent of Hong Kong's population revolting against British rule was explained metaphorically by the Foreign Office: "the colony could continue its life, but would be living on the edge of a volcano."[27]

To prevent an internal revolt like the one in Malaya and to preempt the domino effect a fallen Hong Kong might have on British Southeast Asia, Foreign Secretary Bevin attempted to rally U.S. support with Cold War rhetoric by calling Hong Kong "Berlin of the East."[28] This gesture of British determination to defend a militarily indefensible colony echoed loudly with Churchill's chivalrous declaration on the eve of the Japanese invasion. To wage the battle against the "enemy" within Hong Kong, the Legislative Council took the charge to build an arsenal to fortify the city. Organized labor, particularly the newly formed industrial unions that had become publicly recognized voices, became its first and principal target. The new Trade Unions and Trade Disputes Ordinance, in force on April 1, 1948, intended to limit, not encourage, union activism, as the left-wing Federation of Trade Unions (FTU) had accurately perceived. Brief comments in the Legislative Council made clear that compulsory registration was the "main object" of this new law for keeping labor unions under institutionalized surveillance.[29] To that end, the 1948

---

26. Secret, "Hong Kong: Memorandum by the Secretary of State for the Colonies," May 23, 1949, CAB 129/35/10, 5.

27. Secret, "Annex: China," 5, in "Recent Development in the Civil War in China: Memorandum by the Secretary of State for Foreign Affairs," December 9, 1948, CAB 129/31/29.

28. "Memorandum of Conversation, by Mr. Jacob D. Beam, Acting Special Assistant in the Office of German and Austria Affairs," top secret, April 4, 1949, in *FRUS 1949*, vol. 7, part 2, 1138–41; citation on 1139.

29. *Hong Kong Hansard* 1948, 30.

ordinance created the post of registrar of trade unions. Appointed by the governor, the registrar was empowered to permit or refuse union registration. Any union that failed to register or was rejected for registration was illegal. The ordinance therefore resolutely retreated from official practice over the previous three years that encouraged developing industrial labor unions despite known Communist influence on them.

Circumscribing labor union development was only the first step toward a systematic resurrection of repressive colonial laws. In April 1949, as the People's Liberation Army crossed the Yangtze River, the Legislative Council took another step to tighten the control of labor unions. It reinstated the Illegal Strikes and Lock-outs Ordinance, which was created in 1927 after the General Strike-Boycott of 1925–1926 paralyzed Hong Kong but was abolished in 1948. The ordinance made a strike illegal if it was "designed or calculated to coerce the Government either directly or by inflicting hardship upon the community." It also prohibited government service and public utility employees from engaging in strikes.[30] Discussions within the Legislative Council indicated that resurrecting the ordinance was intended to confront worldwide trends in industrial disputes with a "political objective." In particular, it would serve as "a measure of protection in case a similar tendency were to manifest itself in this Colony."[31] To save face after embarrassingly reinstating a notorious antilabor ordinance that had been repealed the previous year, the colonial regime added a clause on periodic review.

Beyond old and new ordinances aimed at controlling labor unions, the colonial state cast a wider legal net of surveillance over the unreliable 99.5 percent of the population. Some parts of this surveillance network were already in the law books but needed touch-ups to serve the new purpose. The Deportation of Aliens Ordinance, first formulated as the Deportation Ordinance in 1912 after China's 1911 Revolution, had given the governor the power to deport nonlocal residents. In the 1949 version, this power was extended to the commissioner of police, with the governor's authorization. The Legislative Council defined the ordinance mainly as a preventive measure against criminal

---

30. "Illegal Strikes and Lock-outs Ordinance 1949," in Hong Kong Government, "Historical Laws of Hong Kong Online," http://oelawhk.lib.hku.hk (accessed May 12, 2014).

31. *Hong Kong Hansard* 1949, 144.

elements among Chinese refugees. The new version further simplified legal procedures and made the attorney general and secretary for Chinese affairs advisers to the governor and Executive Council on deportation decisions.[32] Despite stated intentions of safeguarding the colony against undesirable "aliens," in the near future this ordinance functioned as a most effective weapon in eliminating labor leaders.

Resurrection of the notorious Societies Ordinance brought back another powerful tool against Hong Kong's Chinese. It was the oldest and the most interesting of British Hong Kong's colonial laws because revisions over a century recorded the shifting targets of perceived enemies to the colony. First created as Ordinance No. I in 1845 and titled An Ordinance for the suppression of the Triad and other Secret Societies within the Island of Hongkong and its Dependencies, it was revised and renamed Triad and Unlawful Societies Ordinance in 1887 after a major outbreak of anti-imperialist protest, in which the outlawed Triads actively engaged in mobilizing Chinese protesters in Hong Kong. The 1887 ordinance defined punishable activities in more detail, including support by nonmembers of the Triads.[33] The colonial state once again modified the ordinance in 1911 after the anti-Qing revolution broke out and gained support from the Chinese in Hong Kong. Simply titled the Societies Ordinance 1911, it retained all the clauses from previous anti-Triad ordinances and, significantly, required all societies to register with the registrar general.[34] Once again it was revised and simplified in 1920 because the Legislative Council discovered that the 1911 ordinance had "failed to give the increased control ... and sometimes tended to drive unlawful societies underground."[35] The 1920 ordinance was much shorter and more straightforward. It focused on defining "unlawful societies," Triads included, and on means of punishment.[36]

The 1949 Societies Ordinance was intended to eliminate potential popular support from Hong Kong's 99.5 percent unreliable Chinese for a unified

---

32. *Hong Kong Hansard* 1948, 286.

33. "Ordinance No. I, 1845," and "Ordinance No. 2, 1887," "Historical Laws of Hong Kong Online."

34. "Ordinance No. 47, 1911," in "Historical Laws of Hong Kong Online," esp. clauses 10–15 for anti-Triad regulations.

35. *Hong Kong Hansard* 1920, 38.

36. "Ordinance No. 9 of 1920," in "Historical Laws of Hong Kong Online."

China. In particular, it targeted undesirable grassroots organizations, which mushroomed during the National Salvation Movement in the 1930s and thrived again after peace returned. The ordinance empowered the registrar of societies to refuse registration to a society (club and association included) or dissolve it when deemed by him or the governor as "likely to be used for unlawful purposes or for any purpose prejudicial to or incompatible with peace, welfare or good order in the Colony." New in the ordinance was an explicit goal of severing connections between organizations within the colony and those without. A society "affiliated or connected with any organization or group of a political nature established outside the Colony" would be refused registration.[37] Also important was the implicit link between this clause in the Society Ordinance of 1949 and the Trade Unions and Trade Disputes Ordinance of 1948, which also outlawed any union with outside connections. In future application, the law was stretched to outlaw organizations without organizational connection outside Hong Kong but with emotional attachments to China.

Two other kinds of legislation, in population control and emergency power, completed Hong Kong's defense short of military force. The first consisted of two newly created laws. The Immigrants Control Ordinance and Registration of Persons Ordinance may be called "positive controls" that ended the colony's century-long practice of free entry. After the Immigrants Control Ordinance became law on April 1, 1949, everyone not born locally could no longer enter, exit from, or move within the colony without a passport and proper travel documents. Even proper documents would not guarantee entry, as the ordinance barred the physically unfit ("maimed, blind, idiot, lunatic or decrepit") and economically unsustainable as "undesirable immigrants." Most important, those "suspected of being likely to promote sedition or to cause a disturbance of the public tranquility" would be prohibited from entering.[38] Still sensing enemies lurking within, the Legislative Council passed another law four months later, the Registration of Persons Ordinance, compelling the registration of all Hong Kong residents. The measure, as one recent study indicates, followed the practice of resident ID hastily enforced by the Japanese occupa-

---

37. "Societies Ordinance 1949," in "Historical Laws of Hong Kong Online."

38. "Immigrants Control Ordinance, 1949," in "Historical Laws of Hong Kong Online"; see esp. part I, section II.

tion regime in spring 1945.[39] With the exception of the governor, the military and police force, transiting travelers, and children under age twelve, everyone was required to be photographed and fingerprinted and to carry an ID card. Registration created an instant, pervasive tool of surveillance, as it empowered any registration or police officer to search a suspect and his or her domicile.[40] In early October, as the government of the People's Republic of China held its inauguration ceremony in Beijing, British Hong Kong prepared to issue registration forms to all its residents who, after the departure of the Japanese army, were again required to carry ID cards.[41]

The "negative control" mainly involved two ordinances resurrected from the colony's law books and updated for changed times. The first was the Deportation of Aliens Ordinance, discussed already. In September 1949, the Legislative Council established a new Expulsion of Undesirables Ordinance, which allowed such expulsions by "the competent authority." Various categories of undesirables overlapped what had already been specified in the Deportation of Aliens Ordinance.[42] Over time, it proved a redundant product rooted in the deep fear surrounding the Communist victory in China, as "no action has ... ever been taken" under the new ordinance. The Legislative Council finally repealed this dead letter a decade later.[43]

A truly powerful, all-encompassing colonial law in Hong Kong was the Emergency Regulations Ordinance, which conferred almost unlimited power on the governor. In the name of safeguarding "public interest," the governor could control not only people and mass organizations but also information. He had the authority to make laws and use violent force.[44] First established in 1922 during the Seamen's Strike, the ordinance empowered the governor to

---

39. Zheng and Huang, 15, 81–82.

40. "Registration of Persons Ordinance, 1949," in "Historical Laws of Hong Kong Online," esp. sections 9, 12, and 15.

41. Special report, "人口登記開始辦理：首批調查表經發出" (Beginning of resident registration; first questionnaire has been sent out), *Sing Tao Jih Bao*, October 5, 1949, 5.

42. "Expulsion of Undesirables Ordinance 1949," in "Historical Laws of Hong Kong Online."

43. *Hong Kong Hansard* 1961, 245, 257.

44. *Hong Kong Hansard* 1949, Minutes of March 9, 1949, 54; Minutes of March 16, 1949, 80–81.

censor the press and other communications, order arrest and deportation, restrict movements of people and transportation, appropriate personal properties and buildings, and suspend trade on "an occasion of emergency or public danger." The updated ordinance of 1949 passed the Legislative Council in March with much harsher terms, prescribing the death penalty to anyone who violated regulations during an emergency.[45]

With ordinances limiting the activities and connections of labor unions, surveillance of social organizations through compulsory registration, control of population movement with border guards and the police force, and the governor's unlimited power over the press, properties, and facilities under declared emergency, British Hong Kong became a fortress of laws backed up by violent force. Most of these ordinances continued to regulate life in the colony for the rest of the twentieth century. Together, these rules exerted a decisive force that reversed the course of reformist intervention and resurrected a culture of "general criminalization of the Chinese community." In a new twist of language, policing industrial relations became the order of the day.

The Communist Semi-Open Front in the National Gravity Shift

While British Hong Kong armed itself to the teeth to thwart Communist infiltration and takeover, its perceived enemy—the Communists in Hong Kong—had a very different task on their minds. In spring 1949, Chairman Mao Zedong announced a "gravity shift" at the second meeting of the Communist Party's Seventh Central Committee. The shift reversed party strategy in place since 1927, when the anti-Communist purge forced the CCP to move their activities to the countryside. "The period of taking this approach has reached its completion," Mao declared. "From now on ... the party's gravity of work has shifted from the countryside to cities."[46] The speech was made

---

45. "Emergency Regulations Ordinance 1922," and "Emergency Regulations Ordinance 1949," in "Historical Laws of Hong Kong Online." See, in particular, section 3 of the 1949 ordinance; for discussion at the Legislative Council, see *Hong Kong Hansard* 1949, Minutes of August 17, 1949, 234–35; Minutes of August 31, 1949, 242.

46. Mao Zedong, "在中國共產黨第七屆中央委員會第二次全體會議上的報告" (Speech to the second meeting of the 7th Central Committee of the Chinese Communist Party), March 5, 1949, Mao, 1314–29, citation from 1316–17.

about seven months before the People's Republic of China was founded in Beijing, but actual preparation for this shift had begun the previous year as soon as battlefield outcomes began to favor the Communists. The central tasks of the gravity shift turned to peacetime administration, first by forming a national government. Winning the support of non-Communist national leaders, whether openly anti-Guomindang dissidents or not, moved to the fore of the national gravity shift.

Once again, the Communist organization in Hong Kong shouldered a significant share of the CCP's new tasks. The city had become a command center for CCP operations in South China as well as a major transit stop for national dissidents who headed for Communist headquarters in North China. The Hong Kong Bureau, created in 1947 to direct operations in Guangdong and Guangxi provinces, had an operational scope broader than its name might have suggested. Two committees below the Hong Kong Bureau—the Hong Kong Work Committee and the Hong Kong City Committee—were also given status higher than their names implied. Both ranked with seven other regional committees, including the Qiongya Regional Committee, Fujian-Guangdong-Jiangxi Border Region Committee, Guangdong-Jiangxi-Hunan Border Region Committee, Guangdong-Guangxi Border Region Committee, Central Guangdong Provisional Committee, and the Guangdong-Guangxi-Hunan Border Region Committee.[47] Between May 1947, when the bureau was created, and October 1949, four of the eight members of the Hong Kong Bureau were from the mainland.[48] They included future diplomat Zhang Hanfu, seasoned underground operator Pan Hannian, well-known writer Xia Yan, and Qian Ying, a skillful organizer in underground operations and future minister of supervision, who arrived in October 1948 and stayed only six months before being transferred to the north.

The high proportion of nonlocal leaders in Hong Kong's Communist organization partly reflected the colony's unusual function as a safe haven for political dissidents during the years of civil war and intensified repression on the mainland before the Guomindang government fell. These nationally known

---

47. *GDZZSZL*, 2:351.

48. The leadership included Fang Fang (secretary), Yin Linping (deputy secretary), Zhang Hanfu, Liang Guang, Pan Hannian, Xia Yan, Lian Guan, and Qian Ying. *GDZZSZL*, 2:371.

Communists, who usually remained in government-controlled areas, were forced to leave. Political dissidents within and without the Guomindang also fled from the mainland. At the time, particularly active in Hong Kong were two dissident organizations outlawed on the mainland, which provided important support to the task of gravity shift for the Communist power. One was the Revolutionary Committee of Guomindang, initiated by General Li Jishen from Guangxi, which attracted members mainly from the Guomindang Association for Promoting Democracy (Guomindang minzhu cujinhui) and the Association of Comrades for the Three Principles of the People (Sanmin zhuyi tongzhi lianhehui). Unlike the Chinese National Revolutionary Alliance Li had formed in prewar Hong Kong, the postwar Revolutionary Committee of Guomindang achieved national significance. It included left-wing Guomindang leaders such as Song Qingling and He Xiangning. The other major organization was the China Democratic League, formed during the war in Chongqing.[49] With intellectuals and professionals as its members, the Democratic League became an influential advocate for a coalition government and was viewed by the Americans as a third force between the Guomindang and the CCP. In 1947, the Chinese government put the league's top leaders under house arrest for their antiwar activities, forcing many others to flee to Hong Kong and set up headquarters there. With so many political and cultural dissidents gathered in Hong Kong, by one estimate, any party celebrating a major national event in 1948 could easily attract more than 1,000 participants.[50]

Interestingly, the new political front uniting Communists and non-Communist dissidents in postwar Hong Kong reversed the pattern of their prewar partnership. In the 1930s when Communist forces reached their nadir and their organization was nearly annihilated, the *Public Herald* published by the Chinese National Revolutionary Alliance provided a platform for individual Communists to find like-minded activists. This helped eventually rebuild the Communist organization in Hong Kong. In postwar Hong Kong, a Communist newspaper, the *Chinese Commercial Daily* (*Huashang bao*), provided a public forum to carry the voices of non-Communist dissidents.[51] The Revolutionary

---

49. Zhou Shuzhen, 102–4.

50. Zhou Shuzhen, 151.

51. The *Chinese Commercial Daily* was a Communist newspaper with Communist or pro-Communist reporters and staff. First published in 1941, it was legally sponsored

Committee of the Guomindang, for instance, issued its founding statement to the national audience in this newspaper. The *Huashang bao* also provided employment for leading mainland writers who took refuge in Hong Kong. For the gravity shift on the mainland, the office of the *Huashang bao* literally functioned as a coordinating center to help the safe exit of many dissidents from Hong Kong to the mainland when the end of the civil war was in sight. From their office at 204 Hollywood Road, the writers and staff of the *Huashang bao* worked out the logistics for hundreds journeying north in 1948 and early 1949. When more than 650 nationally known political, business, and cultural leaders met in Beijing for the Political Consultative Conference in September 1949, about 350 of them had traveled from Hong Kong, or via Hong Kong from south and southwest China, to Communist-controlled North China.[52]

Of course, assisting national leaders traveling to North China was only part of the newspaper's operations. Yet it illustrates one function of the so-called semi-open activities of the Communists and, above all, their attention to work beyond Hong Kong. In addition, the Communists had briefly published *Zheng bao*, a newspaper issued every three days between November 1945 and November 1948, targeting the Chinese audience on the mainland and in Southeast Asia.[53] In late 1948, the semi-open Hong Kong Work Committee

and financed by Deng Wenzhao, a Chinese manager for the Sino-Belgian Bank. Deng Wenzhao was a cousin of Liao Chengzhi, who in the late 1930s headed the Communist Eighth Route Army Liaison Office in Hong Kong, with British acquiescence. See Deng Guangyin, 28–29; also see Liao Chengzhi to Zhou Enlai, February 14, 1941; August 26, 1941, in Liao Chengzhi wenji bianji bangongshi (ed.), I:94, 96–97.

52. Zhou Shuzhen, 174–75. For the number of participants in the Chinese Political Consultative Conference, see Zhou Enlai, "關於人民政協的幾個問題" (A few issues regarding the People's Consultative Conference), *ZELWX*, 129–43, citation from 134; 楊奇, "憶復刊後的《華商報》" (Recollections of the *Huashang bao* after its resumption), in Zhong Zi (ed.), 185–97, citation from 193.

53. *Zheng bao* 正報, which preceded the *Chinese Commercial Daily* and began publication on November 13, 1945, mainly focused on reporting mainland news. Its one dozen reporters/editors were mainly drawn from East River Column veterans. The paper became a ten-day magazine on July 21, 1946, and finally closed on November 13, 1948. It had some market share in Hong Kong, but mainly circulated in South China and in the Chinese communities in Singapore and Malaya. Average circulation was around 8,000, and occasionally reached 20,000. See 鍾紫, "《正報》記者生活的回憶" (Recollections on the life as journalist in *Zheng bao*, and "香港戰後第一家

had 371 party members who worked in any one of its five branches: newspaper, cultural work, diplomacy, finance/business, and the Xinhua News Agency.[54] But most nonlocal Communists, as well as non-Communist dissidents, eventually left Hong Kong for the mainland. Only the Hong Kong Branch of the Xinhua News Agency, which began issuing daily English-language news in May 1947, remained. Later it developed into the semi-official representative for the People's Republic of China in Hong Kong.[55]

Communists and Organized Labor

The Hong Kong City Committee, also called the Guangdong-Hong Kong City Committee (GangYue chengwei), commanded underground operations in the major cities of South China, including Guangzhou and Hong Kong, as well as Guilin and Liuzhou in Guangxi Province. In late 1947, the City Committee had 1,000 party members working in labor unions and schools in Hong Kong, an unusually large figure that probably resulted from the influx of returnees at the war's end.[56] A year later, its membership dropped to 566, more accurately reflecting the reality of Hong Kong–based organizations. The party's internal report described a three-branch structure in Hong Kong. The largest was the Industrial Branch, with a total of 291 members. About 75 percent of them were workers at "the three major dockyards, tramway, electric companies, telephone, motor vehicles, railroad, printing, textile, rubber industry, metal-wares industry, schools for workers, and young women's schools

---

人民的喉舌《正報》" (*Zheng bao* as the first people's organ in postwar Hong Kong), in Zhong Zi (ed.), 206–13, 215–21. Probably due to its limited circulation, the *Zheng bao* does not appear in Kan Lai-bing and Grace H. L. Chu's standard English reference on newspapers in Hong Kong.

54. For the figure in 1947, see telegram from Luo Mai to Yao, August 27, 1947, *XGFJWJ*; for 1948, see "香港分局致中央并中城部电" (Telegram from Hong Kong Bureau to the Central Committee), August 18, 1948, *XGFJWJ*, 181–85, citation from 183.

55. "香港分局致中央并中城部电" (Hong Kong Branch Bureau to the Central Committee and its City Department, August 18, 1948, *XGFJWJ*, 181–85; the report noted that the *Masses* had a circulation of 3,400, and *Zheng bao* had only 2,000; citation from 181, 183.

56. "Telegram from Luo Mai to Yao," August 27, 1947, *XGFJWJ*, 42–43.

(attended by more than a thousand women workers)." About 100 were "young activists," and 70 percent of them were also workers. The second largest was the Seamen's Branch, with 126 party members who worked on riverine ships, at major hotels, in garrison service, and at the Royal Navy Club. The New Territories had a total of 149 active party members directed by the New Territories Branch. About 40 percent of them were teachers working in twenty-eight primary schools and in eleven mass organizations.[57]

This bird's-eye view measures the size of the Communist organization but tells little about the dynamics between Communist influence and organized labor in Hong Kong, where political parties and political activities were illegal. In this restrictive environment, Communist activities on the secret front could appear opaque to an outsider. Day-to-day tasks appeared overly detailed and localized to individual members, as contact with the party organization followed a "single thread" chain of command from one person to another. They rarely knew their comrades within their own units. Having learned the bitter lessons of betrayal and destruction in the 1920s and early 1930s, the Communists took such caution as necessary for survival in any hostile environment. Written communication was forbidden, so our understanding of the dynamics of partisan leadership and labor activism in postwar Hong Kong might have been extremely limited if not for He Zhuozhong, the young resister with a generous soul from a village in Tsuen Wan, whom we first met in chapter 2, who wrote an account of his experiences as a union leader in his memoir. It was a recollection by a resister-turned–union leader, who had a minimal education and wrote in a simple style. The details revealed in this unadorned, straightforward narrative are often astonishing.[58]

---

57. "Telegram from the City Committee of Hong Kong Bureau to the Central Committee and its City Department," September 1, 1948, *XGFJWJ*, 209–13, citation from 211.

58. He wrote his memoir during the Cultural Revolution when he was in Guangzhou and when his loyalty to the Communist Party, as any reader can infer from the text, was questioned. It was a common phenomenon at the time, when numerous dedicated party members in the underground operation were questioned. Yet for his minimal education and his low-key personality, He's writing shows no sign of exaggeration, only restraint, even though he intended to set his record of work straight and clear his name. According to Zhou Yi (Chau Yick), who personally knows He Zhuozhong, He's memoir incurred great displeasure from his relatives, because he

When the war ended, He Zhuozhong's superior in the single-thread chain of command was relocated to Shandong with the East River Column. The new leader instructed He to remain in Tsuen Wan but gave no specific guidance. Upset that village youth spent most of their time gambling, He decided to organize fellow villagers into a youth choir, a mutual help group, and a women's association. Being the best educated among them, he opened a village school and offered literacy classes for young people. A local elder liked what He did and advised him to rename his Youth Mutual Help Group (Qingnian huzhuhui) the Intelligent Chinese Athletic Group (ZhiHua tiyuhui) to avoid "misunderstanding."[59] All the while He survived on a tiny monthly subsidy of HK$30 from the party organization, but he found joy in working among the youth as they put their energy into uplifting activities.

In July 1947, He happened to become a teacher at the Princess Primary School in Tsuen Wan when a friend left for teacher's training and asked him to substitute.[60] The underground Communist organization encouraged him to accept the invitation. During his two months as a substitute, He's work far exceeded expectations despite his limited education.[61] With that successful beginning, He briefly taught at several other schools, including the School for Salt Workers' Children at Tai O on Lantau Island, the Juemin Primary School at Sheung Shui in the New Territories, and at another primary school on Lantau Island near Tung Chung. Except for the two jobs on Lantau Island, his other teaching posts all came through invitations by friends or acquaintances. For various reasons he stayed an average of only one semester at each school. Local workers and farmers in these faraway places admired this new teacher and appreciated his dedication to giving their children better hopes for the future. At Tai O, fishermen expressed their gratitude by sending He fish and other products, which augmented his inadequate monthly income of HK$120 as a schoolteacher. By then, He was married and had a son. His wife, whom he

---

wrote candidly about their poverty and other problems in the family. Author's interview with Zhou, February 2010.

59. He Zhuozhong, 115. Mutual Help Group was a ground-level peasant organization popular during the War of Resistance in Communist-controlled North China.

60. He Zhuozhong, 112.

61. He Zhuozhong, 120.

met and recruited to the underground resistance during the war, stayed home when two more sons were born in following years.[62]

A conscientious and dedicated teacher, He Zhuozhong faced unusual challenges in his teaching post at Juemin School. He had to accept the position of director of the curriculum after two qualified teachers refused the difficult job. The work required teaching arithmetic up to sixth grade and reforming a rowdy student body attracted to gambling. To bolster his inadequate education, He taught himself mathematics and practiced solving problems before heading to his classroom. He reached out to students and convinced them of the importance of learning. His personal involvement drew students away from gambling to more interesting extracurricular activities such as stage performance, public celebration of national events, and discussion of current affairs. Again, these transformative changes in the students earned approval and admiration from parents. He became popular not just as a teacher but also as a leader of young people in the neighborhood. His unusual activism aroused suspicion of pro-Guomindang elements in Sheung Shui. Probably acting on a tip from another teacher, the Education Department sent an inspector to investigate He's homework assignments. Even though the inspector could not find anything wrong, the school, at the instruction of the Education Department, fired him without giving an explanation. With his name entered on the official blacklist, He could no longer find employment as a teacher. Only for one more semester was he able to teach in remote Tung Chung on Lantau Island. Government inspectors rarely set foot in that village because it was difficult to reach without modern transportation.[63]

In July 1949, He Zhuozhong received CCP instructions to leave his teaching post in Tung Chung and work as secretary at the Trade Union of Paint Workers. He worked for the union until late 1952, when the party again instructed him to leave and take a job at a trading company.[64] The CCP gave He additional responsibility as he worked full-time on a paid job at the Trade

---

62. He Zhuozhong, 120–39.

63. He Zhuozhong, 137–39.

64. Under the Trade Unions and Trade Disputes Ordinance 1948, all other union leaders must be full-time workers within the industry of a particular union; only the union secretary could be full-time union staff.

Union of Paint Workers. He was assigned to coordinate work at eight other unions affiliated with the FTU, including the Postal Workers' Union, Hong Kong and Kowloon Union of Paint and Paint Removal Workers, the Union of Western Style Tailors for Ladies, the Union of Seamstresses, the Shanghai Tailors Union, the Union of Flower Growers, the General Union of Hong Kong Gardeners and its branch at Tsuen Wan, and the Salt Workers Union at Tai O on Lantau Island. In his memoir, He did not specify what he did for these eight unions. But his literacy and attention to detail must have made him a valuable adviser for these unions' daily operations, including keeping account books in accord with the requirements of the Trade Unions and Trade Disputes Ordinance. Particularly challenging were his trips between unions on Hong Kong Island, in Kowloon, and on remote Lantau Island using ferries or buses when available, but often on foot. It took many hours and much energy. He often returned home late and went to bed after midnight, totally exhausted.[65] The Trade Union of Paint Workers provided him a subsistence level salary. He had opportunities to make more money or accept a lighter workload than on Communist Party assignments. But as soon as he was called, He Zhuozhong packed his bag and followed instructions without a second thought.

He Zhouzhong's three-year tenure at the Trade Union of Paint Workers was more substantial than his other postwar work episodes, and his activities among workers offers a window into Hong Kong labor organizations during these transitional years. The Trade Union of Paint Workers was once affiliated with the Guomindang-influenced Trades Union Council (TUC). Some of its seven branches were still under Triad influence. But when union members elected He Pei as representative of its Hung Hom Branch, things started to change. He Pei's efforts to improve general employment conditions impressed workers at other branches. They elected him chairman of the whole union, and also voted to leave the Guomindang-influenced TUC and join the left-wing FTU. Once elevated to top leadership, He Pei had to clear up union accounts that a pro-Guomindang secretary had mismanaged. It was at this juncture that He Zhuozhong was hired to replace another incompetent former secretary.[66]

---

65. He Zhuozhong, 146.
66. He Zhuozhong, 141–42.

He Zhuozhong's work strengthened internal union solidarity. Coming from a very poor family and entering the workforce in his teens, he had an intimate understanding of workers' desire for a better life and for respect and recognition. Just as he did with village youth in Tsuen Wan, He Zhuozhong formed a Chinese opera troupe and started choirs for interested workers. Regular practice and performance enriched workers' lives and nurtured a cooperative spirit. He had come to the union in late 1949, just as the colonial state began to clamp down on mass organizations. That year, thirty-eight youth groups were outlawed for their outspoken pro-Communist China sentiment. One of these, the Autumn Winds Choir (Qiufeng geyongtuan), had a history going back to the prewar National Salvation Movement. When its leader asked for help, He instantly recognized an opportunity to address a long-standing demand by workers. He arranged for a dozen of its members to lead the union's choirs, while the union hired the leader of Autumn Winds Choir to teach a literacy class for workers' children with a small stipend at the monthly rate of HK$5 per pupil. When the union's thirty-first anniversary approached, He coordinated the publication of a commemorative journal with articles written by the workers themselves. This writing and publishing experience was especially rewarding to contributors who had gained literacy only recently through the union's classes. He Zhuozhong could tell that the journal, published for the first time in thirty-one years since the formation of the union, greatly enhanced the workers' self-esteem when they held the journal in hand with irrepressible "joy and pride."[67]

In his modest and quiet way, He Zhuozhong easily won friends even among political rivals. He arrived at the Union of Paint Workers just as the majority of union members voted to join the left-wing FTU. But some union members were unhappy about the decision and still embraced the fallen Guomindang as the legitimate power in China. When the paint workers voted to join the FTU celebration for the founding of the People's Republic of China, He persuaded one pro-Guomindang worker, Chen Rui, to attend the FTU banquet for the occasion. Like many other workers, Chen had considered the Guomindang-led government to be the "proper power" (zhengtong) and resented his union's decision to leave the pro-Guomindang TUC for the left-wing FTU. But participation in the banquet totally reversed his view. Chen Rui was

---

67. He Zhuozhong, 146–48.

captivated by the speech of FTU President Zhang Zhennan; it convinced him
that the FTU had far more competent and down-to-earth leaders than anyone
he knew in the TUC. With his mind changed, Chen became a strong FTU
supporter and worked hard to mobilize other workers' support to it as well.[68]

As union secretary, He Zhuozhong's work of course did not always bring
him the pleasure of singing choirs and the satisfaction of winning over new
members. Conflict, contention, and uncertainty were more common. At one
point, the union's Sai Ying Pun branch, which was notorious for unpaid dues,
fiercely challenged union headquarters. Its first attempt became nearly violent.
Fury soared when the delinquent branch heard that a trustee from a different
branch had complained about its unpaid debt. In response, Sai Ying Pun
branch leaders called up a dozen workers and marched on union headquarters
"with knives, iron rods, iron rulers, and hammers in hand" and broke into the
building. While terrified trustees hid behind locked doors, He stepped forward to confront the attackers. Speaking quietly, he convinced the disgruntled
branch leaders that words were a better way to solve differences. On his advice,
union chair He Pei and others went to the Sai Ying Pun branch in person and
discussed various issues with the leaders. The trustee who complained expressed his regrets. Their conciliatory attitude softened the intransigent Sai
Ying Pun leaders, who apologized for their "violent behavior."[69]

Whether the Sai Ying Pun branch ever paid its back dues remains unknown. But the incident provided a glimpse into the inner dynamics of a labor
union in transition. Union secretaries, unlike other union leaders, were the
only hired employees who attended to union affairs full-time. As the records
of the Trade Union of Paint Workers indicated, adequate education was one
of the basic requirements for a union secretary. Yet organizational abilities and
commitment made a critical difference. With He Zhuozhong, a dedicated
Communist with an intimate understanding of grassroots society and empathy toward disadvantaged workers, the Trade Union of Paint Workers acquired a second life. It parted ways with traditional Triad-style practices and
grew into a democratic industrial union, where discussions and voting pre-

68. He Zhuozhong, 144. In the handwritten memoir, He identified the speaker as
Zhang Nan, which was likely a mistake from dropping the word "Zhen" in the name
"Zhennan."

69. He Zhuozhong, 152–54.

vailed over violence in achieving shared goals and improving conditions for workers. What alternative model of industrial unions could the colonial state desire?

A Dissenting Voice within the Labour Department

Watching attentively, the Labour Department noted that the Communist victory inspired changes in mood among ordinary workers and labor activism in British Hong Kong. "Since the recent victories of the Chinese Red Army, a profound change has taken place in the Trade Union movement in Hong Kong," one labour officer commented. He predicted emphatically that broad, positive changes were on the horizon: "I think it can be said with assurance that a vast section of the organised workers have gained an enormous increase in morale through these victories. Rightly or wrongly the organised workers are in the main identifying themselves with the national liberation movement." Despite clear signs that hundreds of thousands among Hong Kong's Chinese workers cheered the rising Communist power on the mainland, this labour officer found no evidence of political control of labor unions: "I am not convinced that the Chinese Communist Party has a strong overriding control of the leftwing Federation—far from it."[70]

However, when top decision makers in both London and Hong Kong viewed Communist infiltration as a major threat amid weeks of heightened defense alert in Hong Kong, this report fell on deaf ears. Its anonymous author, signed as "Labour Officer," presented the assessment based on ground-level investigation without twisting observable facts. Possibly because it directly opposed the prevailing official view or because its author was of low rank, or both, the report remained within the Labour Department in Hong Kong. It became one of the many documents, including reports and letters of correspondence with Labour Commissioner Brian C. K. Hawkins, preserved in a thick folder titled "Monthly Reports, 03.07.1948–24.04.1952," archived in Hong Kong's Public Records Office. A trove of information gathered from

---

70. "Trade Unions and Industrial Relations in Hong Kong," September 15, 1949, HKRS 843-1-52, "Monthly Reports." The report was signed by "Labour Officer," the voice and views expressed are likely Baker's.

factory floors and written for internal assessment by the colonial state, these reports spoke far more candidly about labor unions than did the officially published annual reports. Kenneth Baker, the new labour officer transferred from Mauritius in 1947 after incurring the governor's disfavor, left his signature on some of these reports. Although many documents were merely signed by "Labour Officer," close reading of this file can reveal links between points repeated in many of the anonymous documents and those in reports signed by Baker, whose honest voice was rarely heard in official circles.

Arriving in Hong Kong in summer 1947, Baker came just in time to observe the major strike led by the Chinese Mechanics Union. Before reaching his own conclusions about that long-established, officially recognized organization, Baker made a comprehensive survey of labor organizations in the colony and, on July 3, 1948, submitted a memo to the colony's political adviser. By then, the Trade Unions and Trade Disputes Ordinance, which proscribed general labor unions, had been in force for three months in Hong Kong. Therefore, the formation of the two labor alliances stood out in Baker's memo. He presented a list of sixteen labor unions affiliated with the left-wing Hong Kong and Kowloon Labour Unions Federation, and a list of fifteen unions affiliated with the right-wing Hong Kong and Kowloon Labour Unions Amalgamated General Union, indicating that both lists contained the names of the "more important trade unions" in Hong Kong. Grouping labor unions as such was not his point, however. Instead, Baker argued that the divide between labor associations "cannot be defined in a narrow political way." Labeling them either pro-Guomindang or pro-Communist, he emphasized attitudes toward the falling regime as demarcations of difference, so that the two "in effect are pro-KMT [GMD] and anti-KMT [GMD]."[71]

Baker's astute observations demonstrated the insight of a labour officer in touch with realities on the ground. By coincidence, it echoed observations by He Zhuozhong—the Communist labor adviser—about his experiences at the Trade Union of Paint Workers as the union voted to choose between the FTU and TUC. As power changed on the mainland, an existing belief in legitimacy, rather than a commitment to ideology, was key in workers' attitudes toward

---

71. "Memo," Ken Baker to Political Adviser, July 3, 1948, HKRS 843-1-52. Baker's translation of the two union amalgamations differed somewhat from standardized ones now in use.

the two union amalgamations. Ultimately, workers chose capable and honest leaders who looked after their interests. Although only in the colony for a year, Baker quickly grasped the heart of the issue and differentiated the superficiality of the name from the reality of substance. The question at the moment, as Baker aptly put it, was the shift of legitimacy away from the Guomindang, which for Hong Kong's Chinese workers had once stood as the legal government of their homeland. This was a distinct problem that confronted not only the Chinese workers in Hong Kong but people from all walks of life in the colony, including the British authorities.

The labour officer reported in depth on other problems he found detrimental to the healthy development of trade unionism in Hong Kong. An immediate problem was the historical burden of craft guilds still pervading in some unions. The "long tradition of craft and trade guilds, whose membership comprised both workers and employers," he observed in 1948, had the purpose "not to look after the class interests of masters or workers ... but mainly to foster the craft and to protect and guard its trade secrets." Such traditions were particularly strong in trades like restaurants, building, and glass blowing, where "the closed shop operates." The coexistence of both old-style guilds and new labor unions, he noted, caused "haphazard development" like what was happening in the dockyards.[72] The Naval Dockyard was a case in point. One of the three major dockyards that employed 9,000 workers at its peak, the Naval Dockyard for a time was the largest employer in postwar Hong Kong. In 1948, ten labor unions and guilds operated simultaneously there. Membership in these organizations ranged from as small as 15 in a craft guild to 2,343 in the largest industrial labor union formed after the war, which was affiliated with the FTU.[73] The labour officer nonetheless believed that frag-

---

72. "Trade Unionism in Hong Kong (1948)," HKRS 843-1-52, 1. The report/assessment was probably made after April 1948, when compulsory registration of labor unions began in Hong Kong, an event mentioned in the text. Kenneth Baker was the most likely author, for the report made similar points on the political division between the labor union groups and the need to develop a labor union policy. Both issues were discussed in a report that can be positively identified as his work, discussed later.

73. Huang Yeheng, 21. Huang had worked for Naval Dockyard Chinese Industrial Employees Association, affiliated with the FTU, between 1949 and 2009. See "Epilogue," in Huang Yeheng, 145.

mentation was caused by the transition from old to new, and therefore it was only a temporary phenomenon much like the early stage of trade union development in Britain. He was confident that with "experience and education," unions organized along industrial lines would prevail in the future.[74]

Just as he had experienced in Mauritius, Baker's sympathy toward Chinese workers soon put him at odds with his boss, Commissioner of Labour Hawkins, whose chief concern was to defend the British position and interests in Hong Kong. Their differences came close to a clash, which is evident in the defensive tone of a five-page correspondence from "Labour Officer" to "Commissioner of Labour" in December 1948. References in the text to the author's eighteen months in Hong Kong and his "booklet on trade unionism which was produced in Mauritius" point to Baker as author. He wrote mainly in response to "the criticism directed against the Department and against myself as Trade Union Officer," which he considered to be "not entirely justified." He therefore "put my views in writing" as asked by the Labour Commissioner, and stated that he would like his correspondence forwarded "to His Excellency," that is, Governor Grantham, "should his Excellency desire to see me on these problems."[75]

No record shows that Baker reached Grantham to discuss the real problems in Hong Kong's labor movement. But the reports he made as labour officer identified several of these problems: the nature of labor unions, organizational links of Hong Kong's labor unions to China's major parties, labor–employer relations, and desirable approaches to develop in Hong Kong "a sound, democratic and prosperous trade union movement linked up with a good system of industrial relations."[76]

The critical issue that put Baker in disagreement with Hawkins and other senior officials was the connection between Hong Kong's labor activism and political power outside the colony, as well as the proper approaches to it within the colony. Confident that labor unions were first and foremost concerned with improving employment conditions, Baker rejected the alarmist view about the political implication of their affiliation with the two union confed-

---

74. "Trade Unionism in Hong Kong (1948)," HKRS 843-1-52, 2.

75. "Labour Officer to Hon. Commissioner of Labour," December 1948, HKRS 843-1-52, I, 4.

76. "Labour Officer to Hon. Commissioner of Labour," 4.

erations. He believed that political party control of labor unions in Hong Kong was not substantial, and "neither the K.M.T. nor the Communists control either the right or left wing federations, although the K.M.T. have been recently endeavouring to do so." Rather than seeing the two labor union federations as arms extending from the political parties, Baker's firsthand experiences convinced him that internal differences and variations remained while "the lack of unity" in the whole labor movement prevailed.[77]

Not surprisingly, Baker's diagnosis of the industrial conflicts in the colony put him in direct confrontation with the "Hong Kong way" centering around the colonial power and business interest, which his boss and the governor had labored to defend and preserve. The numerous industrial disputes he mediated convinced Baker that a well-formed united front of employers had effectively blocked improvement in industrial relations. As a result, employers, not workers, had exacerbated class conflict. "Most of the large employers have united in the Employers' Federation," he noted. Strength on the side of the employers sustained their negative approach to labor unions. They refused to negotiate with union representatives, labeling them "not true representative[s]," which in Baker's view was "an excuse by the employers to prevent discussion." He also realized that he had "not been able to gain the confidence" of the Employers' Federation. But the most damaging effect of strong employer resistance was on labor leaders. Baker noted that he and his fellow labour officers had "a number of bitter experiences" when they tried to persuade employers to negotiate with union representatives, yet in the end it resulted "in the victimization of the [union] representative." On another occasion, the agreement labour officers helped reach "was broken by a large number of the employers." Baker's experiences mediating negotiations convinced him that in Hong Kong, "class divisions are prominent between the workers and the employers."[78]

To moderate class antagonism in Hong Kong, Baker wanted to involve the colonial state in positive intervention from the top down and from the bottom up. The bottom-up approach was "trade union education," which Baker viewed as "one of the main keys to these problems." He noted that Hong Kong Chinese workers were "of a different educational standard," much lower than that in Great Britain. Improved education would help workers understand

---

77. "Labour Officer to Hon. Commissioner of Labour," 2.

78. "Labour Officer to Hon. Commissioner of Labour," 2, 3.

labor regulations, cooperate better with the authorities, and possibly reduce class antagonism as it helped official mediation in industrial conflict. The top-down approach, on the other hand, could be more effective in his view. He recommended creating "permanent negotiating machinery" to bring employers, who repeatedly resisted or skirted labour officers' mediation in labor disputes, into a healthy, British-style industrial relationship. In particular, he mentioned his failure "to get permanent joint machinery" set up at two European-owned firms, the Taikoo Dockyard and the Hong Kong Tramway Company. Key to overcoming such resistance would be actions taken at the very top of the colonial state, and "we have to get negotiation at the top level in Hong Kong before we can descend the scale." Doing so would demonstrate to employers that "Government is certainly concerned with its own industrial relations."[79] In suggesting that the colonial state needed to put more pressure on business owners, Baker implicitly criticized its ongoing practice of siding with employers.

Existing records suggest that, as trade union officer, Baker worked more closely than Chauvin in daily operations with organized labor. He was often mentioned in Chinese newspapers by his transliterated name, Bi Ke. In Hong Kong as in Mauritius, Baker developed a sympathy with workers, which apparently grew from his experiences as a union leader in England and his direct interactions with colonial labor movements. In his modest assessment, Baker considered that neither he nor his colleagues in the department had gained "the complete confidence of the workers." But providing advice and regularly attending meetings, "often on Sundays and during the evenings," had made "most of the trade union leaders now understand me."[80] There was little doubt that he took pride in British labor traditions, his active role in the British labor movement, and his work with labor in Hong Kong from the ground up. Yet his superiors disliked his dissenting voice and viewed him as an undesirable functionary within the colonial establishment when it reversed the course of reform in labor affairs. The winds of the Cold War had reached Asia, heralding a new anti-Communist policy that militated against organized labor in modern industrial unions. In a broad reversal of the political climate and colonial policy, organized labor unions were singled out as subversive forces be-

---

79. "Labour Officer to Hon. Commissioner of Labour," 2, 3.
80. "Labour Officer to Hon. Commissioner of Labour," 1, 4.

cause of their national pride and identification with a unified China. However persuasive Baker's argument was about their embodiment of the future of British-style trade unionism, these unions had to be put down for the sake of British Hong Kong and British Asia.

Bloodshed on Russell Street

In 1949, political conflict on the mainland finally spilled over the southern edge of China into British Hong Kong. From midsummer onward, tidal waves of defeated Guomindang-led soldiers and retreating government officials crossed the border and entered the island city. As the defeated army collapsed like a mountain slide and tumbled into Hong Kong, the sudden influx of hundreds of thousands of soldiers strained local order. The rich complained about wandering soldiers camping in neighborhoods and urinating on sidewalks at night. As the population rapidly grew by half a million people, demand for daily necessities spiked and inflation rose nonstop. Rent soared in urban Hong Kong and in the rural New Territories.

Local culture underwent visible and audible changes as the transfer of political power on the mainland neared. Activists in labor, youth, cultural, and professional circles had become prominent participants in public life in the colony since the late 1930s; they anticipated the moment with growing excitement. Particularly vocal and active were organizations already well known before the war, such as the Youth Association of Taishan Sojourners (Qiao-Gang Taishan qingnianhui), a group that organized volunteers for the East River guerrillas in the early 1940s; the Joy-Sharing Youth Association (Qing-nian tongleshe), a group formed by unemployed young workers and youth claiming 180 members; and the Society for Cultivating Virtue through Learning (Xuede lizhishe), initiated in Kowloon City in 1936 by students from poor families that developed into a singing-reading group of 140 members, including bus operators and workers in printing firms and rubber factories, at the Kai Tak airport, and fishermen on Chueng Chau Island.[81] There was also the

---

81. Anonymous, "香港青年工作報告" (Report on youth work in Hong Kong), *GDGM*, vol. 44, citation from 219–20. This internal Communist Party report notes that some of these, such as the Joy-Sharing Youth Association, had a few Commu-

widely popular Rainbow Choir (Honghong geyongtuan), a singing group of 230 young workers, clerks, and students active in the National Salvation Movement. In postwar years, the Rainbow Choir became the most prominent among more than thirty choirs active in the newly formed Hong Kong–Kowloon Choir Association (GangJiu gexie).[82] They gathered weekly for rehearsals, hiking picnics, readings, or occasional seminars with invited guests who reported on the changing situation on the mainland and in the world.[83]

With left-wing attitudes and a few underground Communists among their members, activities of these youth groups contributed to the rise of a new cultural climate in postwar Hong Kong. In 1947 twelve choirs, including the Rainbow Choir, worked together to perform the Yellow River Cantata, a landmark work produced by Communist composer Xian Xinghai, and it attracted a large audience in Hong Kong.[84] Interestingly, this emergent culture among Hong Kong youth inspired a northward journey. A few hundred members from these youth groups made secret trips north to join Communist guerrilla forces in 1948 and 1949. Instead of returning to Hong Kong for "infiltration," as the colonial regime feared, these Hong Kong activists "infiltrated" the Communist army to work as much-needed cultural cadres when the Communists made the gravity shift to urban areas.[85] Naturally, the

---

nists as well as Guomindang members in leadership. Also see *GHZJ*, 105–42, for short descriptions of thirty-two civic organizations, including the three mentioned here.

82. 李淩, "珍貴的戰鬥精神" (Invaluable fighting spirit), *QCJXQ*, 147; Lu San, "窮且益堅不墜青雲之志" (Poor but strong, holding up spirit as high as the blue sky), in *QCJXQ*, 109–10.

83. Yi Ming 伊明 and Li Hanqi 李漢奇, "年輕的朋友來相會" (Meeting of young friends), *QCJXQ*, 58–74; 文彦, 陳秀, "孺子牛篇—記虹虹歌詠團的幹部" (These dedicated cultivators—the leaders of Rainbow Choir), *QCJXQ*, 75–85; citation from 75.

84. *QCJXQ*, 169.

85. About twenty members from Rainbow Choir left Hong Kong to join the Communist guerrillas in South China at the beginning of 1949, see He Jianping, Shen Minyi, and Lu Guoying, "'虹妈' 指引我們參加游擊隊" (Mother "Rainbow" guided us to the guerrillas), *QCJXQ*, 154–55; photo caption 4 shows twenty-two members of the choir joining the guerrillas in the summer of 1949, n.p.; Liang Shaoda, "'虹虹' 是撫育革命青年的搖籃" (The Rainbow is the cradle that cultivated revolutionary youth), *QCJXQ*, 156–58. Liang was already a party member

founding of the People's Republic of China on October 1, 1949, brought into the light of day a secretly nurtured joy among these youth groups and civic organizations.

On October 2, 1949, the FTU held the first major public celebration of the founding of the People's Republic at the Jinling Restaurant (Jinling jiujia) in western Hong Kong. It was attended by more than 3,000 union members and invited guests. The *Sing Tao Jih Bao*, a politically neutral newspaper, ran an enthusiastic and detailed report of the event. It remarked approvingly on the occasion and noted its arrangements "in greatest splendor" (*jijin huihuang*). "A big arch made of flowers" framed the restaurant entrance, with a portrait of Mao Zedong in the center and two national flags of the new Central People's Government on each side. The celebration began with applause, cheers, and firecrackers, which lasted for a long time. Zhang Zhennan, director of the FTU board of trustees, gave a thirty-minute speech "interrupted by applause more than twenty times." The celebration was far from a one-man show. In the three hours that followed, many guests stood up and made spontaneous speeches, among them union leaders from various industries as well as ordinary workers. From eleven o'clock in the morning until two in the afternoon, the assembly was bathed in great joy. This feeling was captured by the reporter from *Sing Tao Jih Bao*, who cited workers expressing themselves in earthy language: "I am happier than getting a wife," said one; "I am happier than having a son," said another. Some told him that the extraordinary joy excited them so much that they "did not sleep very well in the last few days." One rubber worker, Cai Feng, said she had cried during the past three days and, while recalling her family's bitter past, started to cry again in front of the microphone.

---

when he was demobilized from the East River Column and instructed to join the Rainbow Choir. He worked as a company clerk after the war but left his job in July 1949 to join the Communist guerrillas in the Huiyang area. Members of 僑港台山青年會 (Youth Association of Taishan Sojourners), 青年同樂會 (Joy-Sharing Youth Society), 昂聲聯誼社 (Friendship Society of Bright Voice), 學德勵志社 (Society for Cultivating Virtue through Learning), 秋風歌詠團 (Autumn Winds Choir), 螞蟻歌詠團 (Ants Choir), 萃風聯誼社 (Cuifeng Friendship Society), 蜂蜂歌詠團 (Bees Choir), and 新青劇藝社 (New Youth Drama Society) were among those whose members journeyed north to join the guerrilla forces. The total is over 200, though the real figure could be much larger since vague references were not counted. See *GHZJ*, 116–42.

Their feelings echoed in the words of FTU leader Zhang Zhennan: "A free, prosperous, and peacefully happy China is rising in the east, like the sun," giving hope to hundreds of thousands of struggling overseas Chinese.[86] One week later, after the elaborate process of application to authorities for permission, fifty youth groups were able to hold yet another big celebration at the Astor Theater (Puqing xiyuan) in Kowloon, with more than 3,000 in attendance.[87]

Celebratory emotions enjoyed by left-wing labor unions and youth groups spiked again in early November when two airline companies owned by the disintegrated Guomindang government revolted and pledged loyalty to the new government in Beijing. The China National Aviation Corporation (CNAC) and the Central Air Transport Corporation (CATC) had more than 4,000 employees. On the day of their revolt, twelve aircraft, ten owned by CNAC and two by CATC, took off with fifty-two employees from Hong Kong and landed in Tianjin and Beijing.[88] Labor unions and youth groups in Hong Kong cheered this defection originating in their city. With flags and banners leading the way and participants singing songs, they marched to the offices of these companies, located in the upscale Central district in downtown Hong Kong, and made it another site of joyful celebration for the new People's Republic.[89]

86.本報專訊, "港九工會昨舉行大會, 祝新政府成立; 三千多人參加盛況空前" (Hong Kong–Kowloon labor unions held rally yesterday, celebrating the founding of new government; more than 3,000 participated in an unprecedented scale), *Sing Tao Jih Bao*, October 3, 1949, 5.

87. "四青年團體擴大慶祝會" (Four youth groups expanded rally for celebration), *Wenhui bao*, October 4, 1949, 4; "青年, 婦女, 工商界, 昨分別舉行慶祝會" (Youth, women, and industrial and commercial circles all held celebrant rallies yesterday), *Sing Tao Jih Bao*, October 10, 1949, 7.

88. "四千員工通電歸向人民, 中航央航正式起義, 十二架飛機昨安全飛返祖國" (4,000 employees telegraphed to join the people, CNAC and CATC declared revolt, twelve airplanes flew to homeland safely yesterday), *Wenhui bao*, November 10, 1949, 1; for internal preparation by the staff and management within CNAC and CATC as well as their coordination with Beijing, see Zhongguo minyong hangkongju sixiang zhengzhi gongzuo bangongshi (ed.), esp. 10–28.

89. "工聯三十餘歌舞團獻旗慰問起義員工" (More than thirty dance and singing groups from the FTU presented flags and paid respect to the employees of two aviation companies), *Wenhui bao*, December 10, 1949, 4; "港九三十餘工會慰問

One after another, social organizations in Hong Kong began to make open statements: they raised the five-star red flag or made trips to Shenzhen in support of the new government on the mainland. FTU headquarters in Central took the lead in hoisting the new national flag, followed by its affiliated labor unions, as well as left-wing middle schools and offices of youth groups. Two weeks after the People's Liberation Army (PLA) took Shenzhen across the border, 300 representatives from the FTU, led by Mai Hezhi, crossed the border to Shenzhen to greet the PLA.[90] On November 26, a fundraising committee of the Hong Kong–Kowloon Chinese Sojourners of All Circles to Appreciate the PLA organized a three-day carnival in Hong Kong, starting with a performance by youth groups at Confucius Hall. The chorus, dances, and short plays attracted more than 1,000 on the first day. The audience entered Confucius Hall through an entrance decorated with "huge portraits of Chairman Mao and General Zhu ... and the grand and beautiful national flag."[91] During that month, the Youth Association of Taishan Sojourners and the Rainbow Choir traveled to Shenzhen for a celebration party with the PLA.[92] These repeated border crossings culminated in March 1950, when the Motor Drivers General Union, after a successful fund drive that raised HK$12,500 to purchase an ambulance, a truck, and medical supplies, sent the donation directly to the "people's army" in Shenzhen.[93]

In many ways, public demonstrations of support for a rising Communist China echoed the popular enthusiasm of the National Salvation Movement. Popular sentiment this time was quite different. It was not a demonstration of commiseration and indignity over the loss of Chinese lives and territory but a contagious expression of immense joy at China's rebirth. The shared feeling of pride became even more noticeable when it began to intertwine with collective

起義員工, 舉行遊藝大會" (More than thirty labor unions in Hong Kong and Kowloon visited employees of the two aviation companies and held a carnival), *Wenhui bao*, December 11, 1949, 4.

90. Xianggang gonghui lianhehui (2008), 52.

91. "孔聖堂掌聲震瓦, 青年勞軍遊藝會個個節目都精彩" (Applause shook the Confucius Hall, every performance in the youth carnival for cheering the PLA was spectacular), *Wenhui bao*, November 27, 1949, 4.

92. Editor, "虹虹歌詠團活動大事記" (A chronicle of major activities of the Rainbow Choir), *QCJXQ*, 161–74; citation from 172–73.

93. Xianggang gonghui lianhehui (2008), 53.

Fig. 8. FTU choir celebrating May Day, 1949. Courtesy of HKFTU.

Fig. 9. FTU raising the new National Flag outside its office at Lockhard Road, 1949. Courtesy of HKFTU.

actions by organized workers as industrial disputes erupted. It happened just as predicted by the labour officer who observed that many workers did not simply "derive a heap of satisfaction" from the Communist victory but identified themselves "with the national liberation movement."[94]

One immediate repercussion of the Communist victory for Hong Kong's labor movement, as the labour officer noted, was union realignment. The Guomindang-influenced TUC had been recently weakened by the "change over from right to left wing leadership" in unions such as the Shirt Makers Union, and the full dissociation of the Chinese Seamen's Union.[95] He also predicted that the "enormous increase in morale" among workers "will give opportunity for *legitimate* trade union demands" because these demands had been "arbitrarily turned down" by employers in previous industrial disputes. He urged the commissioner of labour to set up "joint negotiating machinery in Hong Kong" to "avoid large-scale labour disturbances."[96]

In 1949, workers in Hong Kong indeed had "legitimate trade union demands" as their livelihood was pinched between sudden hikes in living expenses and the resistance of well-organized employers. From April to June, the price of rice increased 30 percent, and firewood prices increased 29 percent (see Table 4). Recognizing the extraordinary cost of firewood, vital for cooking and heat in winter, the authorities proposed a ration system in November and implemented it in December.[97] The official annual report remarked on "a

---

94. Labour Officer, "Trade Unions & Industrial Relations in Hong Kong, September 1949," September 15, 1949, 1. Again, the author is most likely Kenneth Baker, not only from the similar points he made about employers but also from the reference to his experiences in Mauritius in one report, made on December 28, 1949, contained in the same folder. The insistence on building British-style trade unionism through consultation is repeated throughout in these reports. See Labour Officer to Commissioner of Labour, Confidential, December 28, 1949, 1.

95. "Trade Unions & Industrial Relations in Hong Kong, September 1949," 2–3.

96. "Trade Unions & Industrial Relations in Hong Kong, September 1949," 4, emphasis added.

97. Special report, "柴薪市價亟謀平抑, 港府即將恢復配售" (The price for firewood is in urgent need to be brought down, Hong Kong Government will soon resume ration system), *Sing Tao Jih Bao*, November 17, 1949, 5; "柴薪決恢復配售, 下月中旬開始, 零售價格每擔約十元" (It has been decided that firewood will be sold at rationed price starting in the middle of next month, price will be around HK$10 per picul), *Sing Tao Jih Bao*, November 30, 1949, 5.

Table 4. Price of basic necessities, 1949 (in HK$)

Goods	April	May	June
Rice (picul)	62.00	82.00	80.00
Cooking oil (picul)	210.00	220.00	230.00
Firewood (picul)	7.00	8.00	9.00
Cotton cloth	40.50	44.50	48.00

Source: Guo Qing, "Xianggang gongren de shenghuo," *Sing Tao Jih Bao*, June 6, 1949, 6.
One picul equals approximately 133 pounds, or 60 kilograms.

considerable rise in food prices" by December. Together with "the very acute housing shortage," the general rise in the cost of living "has affected all classes of the community."[98] Demands for wage increases caused a four-month strike (August 1948 to January 1949) by taxi drivers unionized under the FTU-affiliated Motor Drivers General Union. Drivers from eight taxi companies participated but gained little in the end.[99] Price hikes in daily necessities once again placed wage adjustments at the center of industrial disputes as 1949 drew to an end. But workers' legitimate demands stopped eliciting support from the Labour Department that once aided them through fair-minded mediation.

Facing more determined resistance from employers, organized labor decided to forge forward with a carefully coordinated action. In early December, five public utilities and transportation unions, all among the best organized within the FTU, formed a Committee for Improving Employment Conditions and charged it with investigating workers' views about current wages and living costs. Each union then made separate demands, including a HK$3 daily special allowance, to the Hong Kong Tramways Ltd. (hereafter Tramway Company), Hong Kong Electric Company, Hong Kong Telephone, Hong Kong Gas Company, and China Electric Company. The Dairy Farm Workers' Union and workers at the China Bus Company and the Kowloon Bus Company soon made similar demands. The Postal Workers Union, another strong

98. *HKAR* 1949, 21. The report also shows "average weekly food and fuel cost," the major expenses for low-income classes, had risen from HK$12.67 to HK$13.08 between late 1948 and the first half of 1949, and further to HK$15.14 in the second half of 1949. Citation from 25.

99. See Zhou Yi (2009), 215–27, for detailed descriptions of the strike.

FTU member, demanded a HK$2 daily special allowance because postal workers were better paid than the others.[100] Being the best-organized union within the FTU, the Tramway Union held meetings on November 30 and December 1 with more than 1,000 members in attendance. Workers unanimously voted to negotiate with the company for improvements in five employment areas, including the daily special allowance of HK$3, annual bonuses of one month's wages, a death gratuity of HK$500 during service, increase in drivers' wages to HK$4.05 a day (equivalent to that of skilled workers), and adjustment of apprentices' wages.[101] Initially the company only agreed to increase apprentices' wages while rejecting all other demands. In late December, it agreed to increase the year-end bonus and death compensation, but rejected wage increases for drivers and special allowances across the board.

Despite solid support from union members, who made up nearly all company workers, and their unanimous endorsement of this collective action, the Tramway Union still faced formidable odds. The resurrected Illegal Strikes and Lockouts Ordinance of April 1949 outlawed strikes in all public services. The colonial state had stepped up action to eliminate left-wing organizations as well. In late November, the police notified some of the most active and popular youth groups, including the Rainbow Choir, the Youth Association

---

100. "電車煤氣兩業工友堅持提高生活待遇" (Tramway and gas workers insisted on the need to improve employment conditions), *Wenhui bao*, December 9, 1949, 4; "郵務工友加強組織，四項要求昨已提出" (Postal workers strengthened their organization, presented four demands yesterday), *Wenhui bao*, December 14, 1949, 4; "牛奶工友昨函資方，要求改善待遇" (Dairy workers sent request to employer yesterday, asking for improvement on employment conditions), *Wenhui bao*, December 23, 1949, 4; "三電一郵改善待遇要求大部分條件均被拒絕，各工會分別開會，工友情緒激昂一致表示一定要爭得勝利" (Demands for employment improvements by the three "electricals" [China Power, Tramway, and Telephone, the names in Chinese contained the word "electrical"] and postal workers were mostly turned down; at separate meetings for each union, workers were agitated and determined to make greater efforts to reach their goals), *Wenhui bao*, December 16, 1949, 4. On the formation of Committee for Improving Employment Conditions, see Zhou Yi (2009), 266–67.

101. "生活程度不斷高漲，電車工友要改待遇" (Living costs increased ceaselessly, tramway workers demand improvement on employment conditions), *Wenhui bao*, December 2, 1949, 4; their demands were submitted to the company on December 2, 1949, see *Wenhui bao*, December 9, 1949, 4.

of Zhongshan Sojourners, the Readers Club of Hong Kong Students, the Hong Kong–Kowloon Teachers Welfare Association among Chinese Sojourners, and the Hong Kong–Kowloon Branch of Chinese Scientists, about their loss of registration for violating Section 5 of the Societies Ordinance.[102] Thirty-eight organizations were eventually deregistered.[103] In place of postwar tolerance of social activism, severe limitation to freedom of expression and freedom of association stepped in.

Within this increasingly restrictive environment, the Tramway Union decided on bringing workers' grievances to the public with a slowdown, which outwitted the Illegal Strikes and Lockouts Ordinance. On the morning of Christmas Eve, as soon as the trams began daily service, all conductors stopped selling tickets while tram car drivers moved as slowly as they could, disrupting the operating schedule. "The state of affairs continued over the Christmas holidays," ruefully noted the official *Hong Kong Annual Report 1949;* "the populace ... enjoying it to the full."[104] The slowdown caused major losses to the company, which sent a written warning to the union threatening a lockout. In reply, the union stated its willingness to negotiate. Rejecting that option, the Tramway Company immediately dismissed all conductors and gave a seven-day notice of layoffs to drivers on December 28, 1949. The Tramway Union brought the issue to the Labour Department, pointing out that dismissal by the company was illegal. The labour commissioner, however, sided with the Tramway Company and defended its actions.

When the Labour Department refused to mediate, the Tramway Union had no choice but to take direct action. It set up picket lines around the tramway depot near Russell Street to prevent strikebreakers from entering. While refusing to claim severance wages, tramway workers reported to the union of-

---

102. "被取消註冊五團體擬具上訴書，向港督要求註冊官收回成命" (Five groups lost registration are drafting appeal, seeking Governor's intervention to have the Registrar change order), *Wenhui bao,* November 28, 1949, 4.

103. "崇正校友會，文青聯誼會提出理由上訴港督收回成命批准註冊" (Congzheng alumni association, Cultural Youth Friendship Society presented reasons to the Governor, seeking change of order and be allowed to register), *Wenhui bao,* December 8, 1949, 4; "卅七個被迫害團體慰問火柴燈泡工人" (Thirty-seven oppressed groups visited match and light bulb workers), *Wenhui bao,* December 8, 1949, 4.

104. *HKAR* 1949, 20.

fice daily to receive subsidies in rice and a small amount of cash. Intrigued by
the total absence of severance claims eight days after the dismissal and lockout,
the Tramway Company's deputy general-manager went in person to the union
office, located across the street from the tram depot. He witnessed, reported the
Sing Tao Jih Bao, the "well-disciplined manner in which all the workers formed a
long line to receive the forty kilo of relief rice."[105] Before long, twenty foremen at
the Tramway Company, who initially did not join the protest but were outraged
when the company assigned them to clean latrines, left work and joined the laid-
off workers. The Tramway Union achieved complete solidarity.[106]

Frustrated by the tram stoppage, various social groups and leaders publicly
appealed to both parties for a quick solution. The Chinese Chamber of Commerce repeatedly made public statements stressing the need for compromise. It
indicated that the Tramway Union had expressed its willingness to resume
tram operations while continuing negotiations and blamed a very "stubborn
attitude" (*guzhi*) by the company as the cause of the deadlock. By January 26,
the chamber used much stronger language of "protest" (*kangyi*) and "urged the
government to solve the current industrial dispute quickly."[107] Zhang Zhennan,
president of FTU, made a public statement as soon as the tramway slowdown
began, urging the Tramway Company to "negotiate sincerely" and the colonial
authorities to "handle the matter fairly."[108] After the lockout and worker dismissal, Zhang and several other FTU leaders visited the Labour Department to

---

105. "电车工友公开表示，为使工潮尽早解决，提出四项要求" (Tramway
workers made statement in public with four demands for an early solution of the industrial dispute), *Sing Tao Jih Bao*, January 7, 1950, 6.

106. "电车工潮转机，日内打开僵局" (A turning point in tramway dispute; possible end of stalemate within days), *Sing Tao Jih Bao*, January 8, 1950, 6.

107. "市民咸希望早日恢復行車, 華商會明日討論建議解決" (Citizens all wish
to resume tramway operation; Chinese Chamber of Commerce will discuss solution
tomorrow), *Sing Tao Jih Bao*, January 15, 1950, 5; "電車停後商民大受影響, 華商會再
促開車" (Tramway stoppage disrupts daily business and life greatly; Chinese Chamber of Commerce urges resume operation), *Sing Tao Jih Bao*, January 22, 1950, 5; "華商
總會昨會議決定, 抗議電車停開, 促政府訊予解決工潮" (Meeting of Chamber of
Commerce yesterday, protests to stoppage of tramways and urges government intervene to solve the industrial dispute), *Sing Tao Jih Bao*, January 27, 1950, 5. The Tramway Union's willingness to resume tram operation is in the report of January 22.

108. "張振南談話" (Statement by Zhang Zhennan), *Wenhui bao*, December 24,
1949, 4.

seek official mediation for the dispute. The deputy commissioner received them but threw up his hands. He insisted that both sides of the dispute had valid reasons and that neither the Labour Department nor the FTU could do anything. The labor leaders left in disappointment and disillusionment, believing that the deputy commissioner "merely talked official talk."[109]

The tramway stoppage had caused great inconvenience to more than a quarter of a million local passengers, yet public sympathy went to the tramway workers.[110] Not only did left-wing youth groups support laid-off tramway workers with visits and donations.[111] Workers across the colony collected funds and goods to help them. Some, like the workers in foreign-style service—a collective term for lower-level service staff at Western-style hotels, waiters and waitresses at cafés, and domestic servants for foreign families—started "one-dollar" fund drives that echoed National Salvation Movement practices before the war.[112] By mid-January, donations from individuals and social groups reached more than HK$30,000.[113] By January 22, total donations were close to HK$50,000. By January 28, the *Sing Tao Jih Bao* predicted that donations to Tramway workers would soon exceed HK$100,000.[114]

With public attention turned to the tramway dispute at the beginning of 1950, the Tramway Union headquarters on Russell Street attracted an endless

---

109. "工聯代表昨見勞工司, 請從速調解電車工潮, 勞工司表示不能和工聯理事長直接處理此次糾紛" (Representatives of FTU met Commissioner of Labour yesterday, seeking speedy mediation of tramway dispute; Commissioner of Labour said unable to deal with this dispute directly or together with Director of FTU), *Wenhui bao*, December 30, 1949, 4.

110. *LDAR* 1951–1952 estimated that the tramway served about 260,000 passengers daily. Citation from 56.

111. "港九卅八團體昨晚聯合慰問工友" (Thirty-eight groups in Hong Kong and Kowloon visited workers last night), *Sing Tao Jih Bao*, January 6, 1950, 5.

112. "洋務工人議決, 發動一元運動捐慰電車工友" (Labor in foreign-style employment decided to launch "one-dollar" donation movement to support tramway workers), *Sing Tao Jih Bao*, January 4, 1950, 5.

113. "電車工友函勞工司" (Letter from tramway workers to Commissioner of Labour), *Sing Tao Jih Bao*, January 13, 1950, 6.

114. "電車工友獲贈款幾達五萬元" (Donation for tramway workers reached HK$50,000), *Sing Tao Jih Bao*, January 23, 1950, 5; "援助款項日增, 將突破十萬元, 摩總號召工友努力捐輸" (Donation increases daily and may go above HK$100,000; Motor Drivers General Union urges more effort), *Sing Tao Jih Bao*, January 28, 1950, 6.

stream of representatives from other unions and youth organizations. They brought in donations of food, funds, and encouraging words. Unable to accommodate the visiting crowd in its small office, the union turned the building's flat rooftop into a meeting space. Laid-off workers, who came to report at the union office everyday, made room for the visitors and stood below on the street. They followed and joined the rooftop meetings by listening to the ongoing speeches, which were transmitted through the two loudspeakers outside the office on street level. As always, visits from youth group and labor union supporters ended with singing songs together. One song, titled "United We Are Strong," originated in the Communist area during the War of Resistance and had become popular nationwide. It became a favorite for tramway workers, as they sang it with their supporters on each visit:

> United we are strong
> United we are strong
> The strength is iron, the strength is steel
> It is harder than iron, it is stronger than steel
> Open fire on the fascists
> Bring the end to all undemocratic orders!
> March toward the sun,
> March toward freedom,
> March toward a new China
> Shining with great splendor!

To Hong Kong's colonial regime, the five-star red flags, the songs from the mainland calling for democracy and freedom, and repeated visits to Russell Street by activist groups were not music. Perhaps ideas of democracy and freedom were not for the alien, working Chinese. Governor Alexander Grantham, who viewed a united China as the cardinal threat to continued colonial rule, took undiminished public sympathy as a serious political challenge. An astute administrator, he recognized accurately that the "trouble" at the tramway "stemmed from local causes rather than from outside instigation." It was similar to the many strikes that had occurred since Britain's reoccupation of Hong Kong in 1945, and the "basis for all these strikes ... was primarily economic and concerned with the post-war readjustments of wages and conditions of service."[115] He also noted that influence from Chinese politics "was by no means a negligible factor," particularly in "the slow but steady development of the political aspect owing to the rivalry between the two major trade union confederations." The once influential pro-Guomindang labor unions no longer worried him. Now his concern was the left-wing FTU, which, he noted, had "from the time of its formation, gone from strength to strength" and "controlled nearly all the big utilities." Grantham believed that the FTU unions had set "the target of complete penetration [of the right-wing unions] by March 1950," thus creating a situation of dominance "for the Communist party of China to exploit."[116] These words of judgment appeared in Grantham's secret report to London two months after he ordered police action against the tramway workers. In framing his case, he concluded that the openly pro-PRC Tramway Union, by winning colony-wide sympathy during its impasse with the company, was bringing Communist influence into British Hong Kong and subverting colonial authority.

In that frame of mind, the governor could have seen, in late January's developments, additional evidence of subversion spearheaded by the Tramway Union, even though they followed long traditions in this South China city. On January 25, news reached Hong Kong that workers in Guangzhou were sending 5,000 kilograms of relief rice to the tramway workers, a time-honored practice of relief aid moving both ways between Guangdong and Hong Kong. Three days later, the General Labor Union of Guangzhou sent a letter of support to tramway workers in Hong Kong.[117] On January 26, just one month after the Tramway Company dismissed its work force, the FTU issued an open letter to the public, calling on "residents of all circles" in Hong Kong to

---

115. Secret, "To the Secretary of State for the Colonies from the Governor, Hong Kong," March 31, 1950, FO 371/83261, 79–87, citation from 79.

116. "To the Secretary of State for the Colonies from the Governor, Hong Kong," 79, 80.

117. "廣州工友獻米萬斤，熱烈支援電車工友" (Strongly support tramway workers, workers in Guangzhou sent 5,000 kilos of rice), *Sing Tao Jih Bao*, January 25, 1950, 6; "支援電車工人英勇鬥爭，穗工會籌備會來函慰問" (Guangdong labor unions sent letter to support the heroic struggle by tramway workers), *Dagong bao*, January 30, 1950, 1.

help end the dispute.[118] Adding pressure on the recalcitrant Tramway Company and the colonial state was yet another joint statement by labor unions from five major public utility firms in telephone, gas, tramway, and electric power in Hong Kong and Kowloon. They made a joint appeal to the Tramway Company for a quick solution to the current dispute, restating their desire to secure a living wage and reiterating their readiness to "take action."[119]

Workers and social activists responded with a show of solidarity the day after this joint statement. On the evening of January 28, more than 4,000 workers from public utilities and other industries arrived at the Tramway Union office. Their rally began at 8 p.m. with the arrival of bus workers, who marched down the 100-meter-long Russell Street in a neatly formed column, singing the song "We Are Coming" in unison. In the rain, tramway workers lined up on the street to welcome and applaud their supporters. The rally of these visitors and their hosts—more than 6,000 in total—proceeded in an orderly manner, with public speeches and songs sung by those on the rooftop and those on the street.[120] For the first time, Hong Kong police positioned police cars and armed vehicles at one end of Russell Street. Despite the rain and the enormous crowd, nothing disruptive occurred, and the rally ended peacefully.

Two days later, Hong Kong's thirty-eight progressive youth groups organized a collective show of solidarity with the tramway workers. While still appealing to the governor for reinstatement of their legal status, the youth groups planned their rally of more than 2,000 members with the tramway workers at 8 p.m. on January 30. Arriving at Russell Street, they were surprised to find more than 100 police officers already posted nearby.[121] The

---

118. "督促電車資方，支援電車工友，工聯會發出莊嚴號召" (FTU issued serious statement urging the Tramway Company [for early solution] and support tramway workers), *Dagong bao*, January 27, 1950, 1.

119. "四電一煤昨再度聲明，希望合理解決保障生活要求，否則為生存不惜採取行動" (Public utilities unions again made statement yesterday, urging fair solution to [the demand for] living wage, or otherwise will take action with any price for survival), *Dagong bao*, January 27, 1950, 4.

120. "四千多工人兄弟昨慰問電車工友" (More than 4,000 workers visited tramway workers yesterday), *Dagong bao*, January 29, 1950, 4.

121. Description of this event is based on reports from two major newspapers: "鮮血流在羅素街頭，電車糾紛發生慘案" (Blood spilled on Russell Street; tram-

Fig. 10. Tramway workers' meeting, December 28, 1949. Courtesy of HKFTU.

Fig. 11. Tramway workers listening to the daily report by Tramway Union, January 1950. Courtesy of HKFTU.

presence of the large police force made these young men and women more indignant. They proceeded with the planned rooftop rally, with speeches, songs, and the *yangge* dance from Communist China. As always, sounds of the rooftop rally came to workers standing below on Russell Street through loud-speakers at street level outside the union office. An hour into the rally, a European police officer approached the union office and removed both loudspeakers. Provoked, a worker stepped forward to confront him. As the two argued, the policeman clubbed the worker to the ground and beat him. Other workers rushed forward to help the victim, while taking caution to restrain themselves from using physical force. The police officer easily walked away with the loud-speakers.[122]

By then, more police had arrived in the area, commanded in person by Commissioner of Police D. W. Mackintosh. Workers "linked their arms to form a human chain" to defend their headquarters while singing "United We Are Strong." A reporter of the *Sing Tao Jih Bao* was among the thousands of spectators and noted that "all were deeply touched."[123] As if to evoke their inner strength in the face of police in emergency gear, the workers suddenly raised their voices to sing "The March of Volunteers," a song popular in China during the National Salvation Movement in the 1930s and recently selected as the national anthem of the People's Republic: "Arise, ye who refuse to be slaves! With our flesh and blood, let us build our new Great Wall!" These lines in the lyrics seemed to come not from their throats but from the beating hearts in their chests.[124] They held on for two hours until the police started firing tear gas and charged into the crowd, wielding clubs. "One spectator who did not run fast enough was kicked several times by police in heavy boots," wrote one reporter for *Dagong bao*, who was also an eyewitness on the

---

way dispute led to atrocity), *Dagong bao*, January 31, 1950, 4; "電車工人與警察昨夜發生大衝突, 羅素街上竟演成流血事件" (Tramway workers clashed with police last night; bloody event occurred on Russell Street), *Sing Tao Jih Bao*, January 31, 1950, 1.

122. *Sing Tao Jih Bao*, January 31, 1950, 1.

123. "警隊紛紛出動, 形勢越顯緊張" (Police mobilized, situation is tense), *Sing Tao Jih Bao*, January 31, 1950, 1.

124. "硝煙中夾有槍聲, 麥景陶親臨巡視" (Gunshots amidst smoke; Mackintosh came personally), *Sing Tao Jih Bao*, January 31, 1950, 1.

Fig. 12. Police blockade at Russell Street, January 28, 1950. Courtesy of HKFTU.

Fig. 13. Police arriving at Russell Street, January 30, 1950. Courtesy of HKFTU.

Fig. 14. Police action against tramway workers, January 30, 1950. Courtesy of HKFTU.

run. "Dozens of police armed with clubs chased hundreds of spectators from the intersection of Percival Street and Hennessy Road toward Canal Road East, shouting war cries repeatedly as if they were charging the enemy on a battlefield."[125]

The police action ended around midnight. More than 800 policemen were mobilized, aided by regular army troops.[126] According to the *Sing Tao Jih Bao*, nearly seventy workers were wounded, twenty-seven severely. A different source estimated a higher casualty of more than 100.[127] Had FTU leadership not called for restraint, "the workers would most likely have fought the police to the very end with their own lives."[128] When the chaos finally subsided in the early morning, broken furniture, broken glass, and flowerpots thrown from balconies by angry residents littered Russell Street and nearby areas.[129] Eighteen workers, some of whom were members of the picket team and thus black-listed by the police, were arrested during the confrontation. They "were severely beaten by the police, and many of them still have to receive treatment at hospital," wrote Chen Junbao (1898–1982), professor at the University of Hong Kong. He learned from Zhang Zhennan that "one worker from Kowloon was beaten to the point of having his lower back nearly broken. And those doing the torture at police station were all British, most likely in revenge for the deputy police chief who was wounded at the site."[130] Six of the wounded and hospitalized workers were deported on February 10, 1949. At Russell Street, the police sealed the union office and arrested two Tramway Union leaders, its secretary, Li Wenhai, and a youth leader, Zhou Zhang, who represented the youth groups bringing support and donations to the workers that day. A few days later, the chairman of the Tramway Union, Liu Fa, was also

---

125. "在催淚彈和槍聲中慰問大會繼續舉行" (Supporting rally continues amid tear gas and gunshots), *Dagong bao*, January 31, 1950, 4.

126. "衝突事件經過" (A narrative of the clash), *Kung Sheung Daily News*, February 1, 1950, 3.

127. Zhou Yi (2009), 274.

128. Chen Junbao, 3:10. For his efforts during the war to protect the assets of the University of Hong Kong library, Chen was awarded an O. B. E. by the King in 1947.

129. "相持至十二時許, 工友始遵勸散去" (Stalemate till midnight; being advised workers dispersed), *Sing Tao Jih Bao*, January 31, 1950, 1.

130. Chen Junbao, 3:10.

arrested. They were all sent to Lowu and deported to the mainland at the beginning of February.[131]

The police action against the tramway workers provoked a reaction from the Central People's Government in Beijing for the first time. It was a mild protest in the form of local reports in the official newspaper. On February 3, the *Renmin ribao* (*People's Daily*) featured the event on its front page. One report by the Guangzhou branch of the Xinhua News Agency was titled "British Hong Kong Government Used Brutal Force to Suppress Workers, Causing a Huge Event of Bloodshed." Another reported local reactions under the headline "Mass Organizations in Hong Kong and Kowloon Support Tramway Workers with All Their Energy and Strongly Protest the Brutality of British Police." Three days later, the *Renmin ribao* followed with another report about mass rallies by various organizations on the mainland to denounce the British police action in Hong Kong.[132] The tone of these reports on the event and protesting rallies signaled Beijing's assessment of the crackdown as a local event, rather than an intended show of hostility against the new Central People's Government. Read in another way, this measured reaction highlighted the nature of the tramway conflict not as an action instigated by an "outside force" but as truly an economic struggle caused by workers' grievances, despite their explicit identification with the government in China.

With its leaders gone, the Tramway Union was weaker when negotiations reopened in early February. The Labour Department, which had repeatedly

---

131. Special report, "電車工會主席劉法昨被遞解出境" (Chairman of Tramway Union Liu Fa deported yesterday), *Sing Tao Jih Bao*, February 2, 1950, 5; this report specified two more, Qi Yun and Zhou Zhang, who were deported along with Liu Fa; on February 6, the secretary of the Tramway Union, Li Wenhai, was deported. See "電車工會書記李文海被遞解" (Secretary of Tramway Union Li Wenhai deported), *Sing Tao Jih Bao*, February 7, 1950, 5.

132. Xinhua at Guangzhou, "港英政府暴力鎮壓工人，釀成巨大流血慘案" (British government in Hong Kong used violence to suppress workers, causing huge bloody atrocity), *Renmin ribao*, February 3, 1950; Xinhua at Guangzhou, "港九人民團體全力支持電車工人，嚴重抗議英警暴行" (People in Hong Kong and Kowloon fully support tramway workers, sternly denounce British police brutal action), *Renmin ribao*, Feburary 3, 1950, 1; Xinhua at Beijing, "全國人民憤怒表示，抗議香港政府暴行，支援被害工人兄弟" (People of China voice anger to protest the atrocity of Hong Kong Government and to support the persecuted working brothers), *Renmin ribao*, February 6, 1950, 4.

refused to mediate in January as the FTU requested, now stepped in to "urge the two sides sit down for negotiation."[133] The deal was reached and accepted by both sides on February 9, 1950, with the Tramway Company accepting every demand by the union except the special allowance, pending final arbitration for labor dispute at the Dairy Farm. The company also agreed to re-hire all workers—more than 1,700, including those deported from Hong Kong. When arbitration concluded two months later, however, the special allowance announced was only HK$30 a month, a third of the union's initial demand.[134] On February 10, the police unsealed the Tramway Union's head-quarters. Once again, tramway workers gathered at their union office for the ritual of raising the five-star national flag of the People's Republic of China. Taking a determined stand, workers of other industries, professional youth, and students came to join them. As the Chinese national flag unfurled atop the union office, they sang the national anthem of the People's Republic and other songs they had sung during the month of the standoff.[135] That became the last public demonstration of defiance in this longest wave of Hong Kong's labor movement.

The Bloodshed at Russell Street (Luosujie xue'an), as local newspapers of all political stripes called the police action against the tramway workers, brought

---

133. "勞工處促電車勞資重開談判之門" (Labour Department urged resumption of negotiation between labor and the company), *Sing Tao Jih Bao*, February 5, 1950, 5.

134. "四十八天工潮告一段落, 電車今晨正式復開"(Industrial dispute of forty-eight days comes to halt; tramways resume operation this morning), *Sing Tao Jih Bao*, February 10, 1950, 5; "勞方最大讓步, 今晨電車復通" (Labor made the greatest concession; tramways resume operation this morning), *Wenhui bao*, February 10, 1950, 4; "辛辛苦苦曲曲折折, 牛奶公司仲裁結果, 男工月增津貼卅元" (Through so much trouble and detours, result of arbitration of [industrial dispute] at Dairy Farm ended with HK$30 monthly special allowance for male workers), *Wenhui bao*, March 25, 1950, 4.

135. "當國旗在羅素街升起的時候: 瑣記電車工人收回工會" (When national flag is hoisted at Russell Street: tramway workers took back their union [office], *Wenhui bao*, February 11, 1950, 4; "電車工友收回工會; 昨晨清點損失情形" (Tramway workers get back union; inspection shows much damage), *Wenhui bao*, February 11, 1950, 4.

state intervention in labor affairs in Hong Kong to a new phase. Movement toward this breaking point had begun quietly. The Trade Unions and Trade Disputes Ordinance promulgated by the colonial state in 1948 initiated a series of legislation that fortified the Berlin of the East against the majority of its population, who were deemed disloyal aliens. Official justification framed Hong Kong's repressive legal turn in anti-Communist rhetoric. But internal discussions pointed toward another central concern—protecting British interests in Hong Kong and the region.

It was ironic that colonial state action targeted the industrial unions, which its Labour Department once energetically encouraged. The left-wing FTU built its strength on such industrial unions and benefited from British official encouragement. This irony aside, it is important to note that, fundamentally, these unions gained more strength from the dedication of their leaders, from the genuine needs of workers, and from their democratic practice. As this chapter shows, the Trade Union of Paint Workers and the Tramway Union embraced the principles of democracy and involved all members in major decision making. There were a few Communists in the leadership of these unions. Their function, however, was not to undermine British rule, as was feared in London and Hong Kong's Government House. On the contrary, they focused on developing true industrial unions that worked as collective units to protect and advance workers' interests. Under their leadership, as He Zhuozhong's experiences demonstrated, these new industrial unions led workers away from their Triad-influenced habit of using violence to solve problems. With an emphasis on persuasion and negotiation in dealing with conflicts, these unions were exactly what London had wanted and Hong Kong's first labour officer had envisioned in the 1930s. These unions grew popular among Chinese workers not because their leaders followed old traditions but because they led workers with new ideas and new methods and proved their competence in deeds.

As perceived by the colonial regime, the real problem for industrial unions affiliated with the FTU had nothing to do with union practice, which conformed to a desirable model, but came from their growing popularity among Chinese workers and their loud support for a unified China. Their political choice aligned with the choice of Hong Kong's active youth and created a contagious culture. It invigorated cherished desires of belonging among Hong Kong's non-elite Chinese, who had never envisioned the colony as their home.

Their joyful celebration of China's renewal with the founding of the People's Republic brought back the scene of the numerous Chinese national flags on nearly every rooftop and junk when the British fleet arrived in Hong Kong waters in 1945, though this time in a much grander scale. When the five-star red flags were hoisted at labor union offices, at Chinese Chamber of Commerce, at headquarters of youth groups, and at theaters and restaurants where celebrations were held after October 1, 1949, it was a frightening specter to the colonial regime. By showing their hearts and minds so openly, so loudly and so fervently, organized workers made themselves enemies of the colonial state. For the defense of the colony, repression became imperative, regardless of workers' legitimate grievances in industrial disputes. In large measure, the police action at Russell Street against the protesting workers was intended as a public show for Hong Kong's nearly two million Chinese residents, whom the colonial state had never trusted and now deeply feared. However limited in scope, the resolute use of violence did more than break a law-abiding industrial union. It nipped a rising culture in the bud and, in doing so, generated frightening repercussions in Hong Kong.

6

Rebalance

A familiar tranquility quickly settled over Hong Kong after the police action on Russell Street. Industrial disputes declined sharply in the immediate
aftermath. They almost disappeared during the following year, and industrial
unions never regained their former vigor (see Chart I). At the same time, there
were unmistakable indications that employers had gained the upper hand. The
Tramway Company had received official support during the dispute; in its
annual report for 1950–1951, the Labour Department highlighted the company's three reasons for rejecting the Tramway Union as the workers' representative. The Tramway Company's general manager, G. S. Johnston, was appointed to the Labour Advisory Board when it was "reconstituted" in January
1950 to give "equal representation to employers and workers."[1] Among the
four "Chinese workers' representatives" on the board were business owner
Han Wenhui, who controlled the Chinese Mechanics Union, and two representatives from Trades Union Council (TUC)–affiliated unions. One representative, the chairman of the Motor Drivers General Union, came from the
left-leaning Federation of Trade Unions (FTU), but as the absolute minority,
his vote counted for nothing. Should the three union representatives on the
board unite in objection to decisions by the employers' representatives, they
had no way to succeed. The commissioner of labour, who chaired the board,
and Han Wenhui, known for toeing the official line, invariably sided with the
employers. These two and the four employers' representatives formed a decisive majority that could block any union initiative.

I. *HKAR*, 1950, 21; *LDAR*, 1950–1951, 4, 19. The governor nominated two of the
four representatives in each group of the employers and "workers," and the other two
were elected.

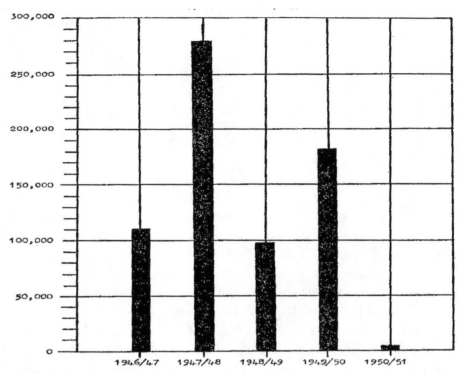

Chart I. Man-days lost in industrial disputes, 1946/47 to 1950/51. *Source: LDAR* 1950–1951, 93.

In addition to restoring and consolidating employer dominance in industrial relations, the colonial state reframed the very nature of the two labor union associations. The Labour Department declared that neither the FTU nor the TUC was formed "on an industrial or occupational basis" but dominated by their "attitude ... towards current Chinese politics."[2] However, it recognized a difference between appearance and substance. The pro-Guomindang TUC was "the most vocal," but its influence was in "a corresponding decline," the annual report by the Labour Department noted, for there was a large discrepancy between its claim of 62,000 members and its actual, fee-paying membership of 33,500. In contrast, the left-leaning FTU had considerable strength, because it had "closely allied" member unions, a "much greater average [membership] per union," and all forty-four member unions paid six to seven times

---

2. *LDAR* 1950–1951, 21.

more in affiliation fees than the TUC-affiliated unions.[3] This caused considerable concern. Furthermore, the Labour Department was disturbed by the observed coordination between FTU-affiliated unions and "certain sections of the vernacular press" whose reports on industrial disputes were "invariably full of vituperation, and sometimes were completely false."[4] Having successfully rolled back the militant activism of the Tramway Union, the colonial state moved to correct the imbalance between the joined forces of organized labor under the FTU and the "press campaign" exuding "vituperation" on the one side and the employers who "received no press publicity" on the other.[5]

In reality, continued state vigilance and renewed repression of the FTU produced notable distress in this active, well-organized union federation. Public sympathy for labor faded after the police action at Russell Street, and the Chinese government in Beijing insisted on restraint. Under these conditions, organized labor in Hong Kong had no alternative but to make major strategic adjustments. Instead of seeking to improve employment conditions through collective action in the workplace, milder approaches ameliorating workers' harsh living conditions by improving union benefits became the central task of FTU-affiliated unions from 1950 onward. Labor organizations, legal on paper, stopped being significant agents in Hong Kong's industrial relations after the Russell Street bloodshed.

This delicate equilibrium between the tamed but deeply discontent working Chinese and the triumphant colonial establishment in Hong Kong might have persisted if no additional force had interfered. Unexpectedly, the Korean War broke out in June 1950, just five months after the Russell Street clash. U.S. entry into the war decisively upset British Hong Kong's precarious tranquility. The Guomindang in Taiwan, recently abandoned by the United States, regained vigor when the United States recognized its strategic value in the Cold War in Asia and resumed its aid and support.[6] The Guomindang reentered Hong Kong and revived its organization there. Situated just outside

---

3. *LDAR* 1953–1954, 38–39.

4. *LDAR* 1951–1952, 25, 26.

5. *LDAR* 1951–1952, 26.

6. For a general discussion on the U.S. support to military build-up and economic revival in Taiwan after Korean War, see Tucker (1994), esp. chapters 3 and 4; for the influence of Korean War on the policies of major powers in the region regarding Hong Kong, see Zhai, esp. chapters 4–6.

Communist China, Hong Kong attracted Western intelligence operations, particularly U.S.-funded cultural offensives against Communism.[7] While other British "possessions" took the path to independence, colonial Hong Kong acquired a new lease on life in the global Cold War. In this new climate, the persistent action by the colonial regime against the perceived threat of organized labor and left-wing voices failed to halt and instead accelerated the colony's slide over the edge of a volcano.

Labor's Retreat from Workplace Activism

As all eyes in Hong Kong turned to the tramway dispute, the police action on Russell Street became a public theater and achieved maximum effect of terrorizing the local population. Meanwhile the colonial state quietly undertook systematic moves to end postwar social activism. The first surgical removal of critical labor leaders started in late December 1949 as the tramway dispute entered its stalemate. Police detained Lou Songping, chairman of the Silk Weavers Union, who had led a militant and successful collective action by silk weavers at the Mayar Silk Company earlier that year.[8] Their eighty-day strike ended victoriously, generating greater popularity for the FTU-affiliated Silk Weavers Union and increasing union membership in Mayar's workforce from 80 percent to 95 percent.[9] The Mayar factory had relocated to Hong Kong from Shanghai in 1937. Its 300 weavers, including Lou, were also from Shanghai and made up half of the silk weaving workforce. Lou's relatively

---

7. For an overview on Hong Kong's special role in U.S.-Britain relations during the Cold War, see Mark. For U.S.-funded, Hong Kong–based cultural offensive against China during the 1950s, see Lu and Xiong (eds.), a collection of interviews with eight people who assumed various important functions; for "denationalization" of education in Hong Kong, see Wong; see Zhang Yang for a case of institutional change in cultural arenas that served the U.S.-led global offensive against Communist China; also see articles by Lu Xun on intelligence and propaganda, by Glen Peterson on Aid Refugee Chinese Intellectuals, by Stacilee Ford on cultural production.

8. "美亞綢廠一片冷清; 勞方執行和平糾察" (All quiet at Mayar; labor enforced picketing peacefully), *Wenhui bao*, May 27, 1949, 4; "美亞綢廠工潮, 前晚工友被打受傷" (Industrial dispute at Mayar; workers beaten the night before), *Wenhui bao*, May 31, 1949, 4.

9. Zhou Yi (2009), 237.

short residency in Hong Kong made him an easy target for deportation. The Silk Weavers Union repeatedly sent appeals to the Labour Department on Lou's behalf and even staged a brief strike at Mayar, but the authorities were unmoved.[10] After ten days of detention, Lou was deported over the border to Shenzhen as 1950 began.[11] An influential leader in the cultural circles, Lu Dong, became the next target of quiet police action. Lu was the founder of the Rainbow Choir and became principal of the Heung To (Xiangdao) Middle School after the war. Under his leadership, teachers and students openly celebrated the founding of the People's Republic and raised the five-star red flag. He was taken from his home by plainclothes police from the Special Branch in the early morning of January 5 and deported just a few hours later.[12]

Despite the arrival of spring in 1950, social activists braced for a political winter. After four middle school teachers and a businessman were deported to the mainland for organizing public celebrations for the People's Republic of China, the colonial state turned to the top leadership of the best-organized labor unions. Ouyang Shaofeng had succeeded Liu Fa as chairman of the Tramway Union and was one of the most eloquent union leaders in postwar Hong Kong; he was arrested on March 9 and deported the next day.[13] In anxiety and fear, the left-wing FTU responded with an announcement that its president, Zhang Zhennan (Ct. Cheung Chun Nam), had just embarked on a

---

10. For the arrest of Lou Songping and subsequent efforts by the FTU-affiliated Silk Weavers Union to get him released through appeals to the Labour Department, see "荃灣絲織工友關心樓頌平" (Weavers at Tsuen Wan are concerned about Lou Songping), *Wenhui bao*, December 26, 1949, 4; "樓頌平被警扣留, 絲織工會發聲明" (Lou Songping detained by police; Weavers Union made a statement), *Wenhui bao*, December 27, 1949, 4; "絲織工友昨日查出, 樓頌平關在監房" (Weavers found yesterday: Lou Songping was jailed), *Wenhui bao*, December 29, 1949, 4; "絲織業總工會為樓頌平被捕將提出嚴重抗議" (Weavers General Union made stern protest regarding the arrest of Lou Songping), *Wenhui bao*, December 30, 1949, 4; "要求釋放樓頌平, 絲織工昨罷工二小時" (Weavers stroke for two hours, demanding Lou Songping's release), *Wenhui bao*, December 31, 1949, 4.

11. Zhou Yi (2009), 291.

12. "香島中學千餘學生為盧動被迫離境事發表告社會人士書" (A public statement by more than a thousand students at Xiangdao Middle School regarding the forced deportation of Lu Dong), *Wenhui bao*, January 7, 1950, 4.

13. "電車職工會主席歐陽少峰被解出境" (Chairman of Tramway Union Ouyang Shaofeng was deported), *Wenhui bao*, March 11, 1950, 4.

mainland tour to investigate workers' welfare and economic production. Zhang remained in Guangzhou, becoming director of the Budget Committee of the Guangdong FTU and later its vice chair. He never returned to his union post in Hong Kong.[14]

In Zhang's absence, another leader who had received high compliments from a labour officer assumed FTU leadership. Mai Yaoquan (*Ct.* Mak Eu-chuen), whom we met in chapter 4, became the first deputy president and director of the board of trustees. As a union organizer at the Naval Dockyard, Mai came to the attention of Kenneth Baker, who praised him for representing "a new growth of leadership" at a time when "the Hong Kong Trade Union movement is really being born." Baker noted that Mai "represent[s] the more militant trade union side," but considered him to be "a better leader than Cheung Chun Nam as far as the workers are concerned," even though "he would be less compromising."[15] Exactly because of his popularity among workers and his forthright style, Mai made the colonial state apprehensive about his ability to reinvigorate labor activism in Hong Kong. On July 7, 1950, police detained him as he started his workday at the Naval Dockyard. Also arrested was Mai Hezhi, chairman of the Kowloon Dock Workers Union, who had led the widely publicized Workers' Delegation to Greet the PLA at Shenzhen in late 1949.[16] Without being shown any warrants for arrest or deportation or any other legal form of due process, the two labor leaders were sent over the Lowu border on the day of their arrest. In the first six months of

---

14. "歐陽少峰又被解出境，港九工人均深感不安⋯ 工聯派張振南返內地考察" (Ouyang Shaofeng deportation made labor in Hong Kong and Kowloon deeply anxious; FTU sent Zhang Zhennan to investigate on the mainland), *Wenhui bao*, March 12, 1950, 4; Zhang's activities after returning to the mainland were mainly in the realm of labor unions, see Guangdong FTU, "廣東總工會重要會議" (Important meetings at Workers General Union of Guangdong), http://gdftu.org.cn; accessed on August 11, 2013.

15. Ken Baker to Commissioner of Labour, "The Hong Kong Federation of Trade Union" (Confidential), December 6, 1949, HKRS 843-1-52, 2.

16. "工人領袖迭遭迫害，麥耀全麥河志昨遭逮捕，警方未宣佈任何理由亦未出示證件" (Labor leaders suffered repression one after another; Mai Yaoquan and Mai Hezhi were arrested yesterday; Police did not state any reason nor presented ID card), *Wenhui bao*, July 7, 1950, 4.

1950, twenty-one activists in youth groups, pro-PRC labor unions, education, and business circles were deported.[17]

In a desperate move to protect its members from impending mass arrest, the FTU sent more than seventy of its leaders and activists away from Hong Kong in December 1950. According to a recent disclosure, this decision was prompted by a private conversation between the police commissioner and a *taipan* of Jardine, Matheson & Company about the upcoming arrest of leftists. The *taipan's* butler, who belonged to an FTU-affiliated labor union, eavesdropped on the conversation between his employer and the commissioner and immediately passed the information on to the FTU.[18] This episode cannot be verified in official documents because most Communist-related files at the Foreign Office and Colonial Office remain closed to this day. It is also difficult to determine if such arrests were truly planned or if the private conversation was merely a ruse to plant misinformation and induce activists to leave the colony voluntarily. Nonetheless, the sudden exodus of so many local leaders revealed profound fear among the most active of Hong Kong's labor unions during the eventful year of 1950.

Sober recognition of British Hong Kong's anti-Communist drive since the end of the civil war and the need to avoid direct confrontation with colonial authorities led to left-wing labor unions' decision of voluntary retreat. Having won victories under greater adversity through vigorous activism, compromise was not easy for ground-level leaders and activists. No documents reveal how the FTU deliberated on voluntary withdrawal. But a parallel case in the semi-open cultural circles illustrates the frustration on the ground. Reluctance and even resistance to Beijing's general guideline of restraint had dominated feelings among journalists and staff in the Hong Kong branch of the Xinhua News Agency. Having obtained permission to operate in the colony after the war, the Hong Kong branch opened in 1947 with initial activities limited to

---

17. "從盧動到麥耀全: 半年來在香港的中國人民被香港英政府拘捕后遞解出港的記錄" (From Lu Dong to Mai Yaoquan: a record of deportation after detention of Hong Kong's Chinese people by British Hong Kong Government), *Wenhui bao*, July 9, 1950, 4; "廣州工人兄弟今日開大會歡迎麥耀全麥河志" (Working brothers in Guangzhou held a welcome rally for Mai Yaoquan and Mai Hezhi), *Wenhui bao*, July 12, 1950, 4.

18. Zhou Yi (2009), 287.

translating and transmitting news from its main branch on the mainland.[19] Verbal instruction from Beijing emphasized that the new Chinese government "will not reclaim Hong Kong, though it does not mean to abandon Hong Kong or withdraw from Hong Kong." The agency was expected to make the colony a base for united front work to win friends for the People's Republic.[20] But the staff at Xinhua, all leftists or Communists, resented colonial rule. They resisted registering for identification cards, as required by British authorities since late 1949, and only did so reluctantly after Beijing insisted that they abide by Hong Kong law.[21] Local repugnance to this conciliatory policy remained dormant but never disappeared. Yet Beijing's nonconfrontational guidelines, combined with resolute colonial repression, pressured both the semi-official Communist establishment in Hong Kong and Communist-influenced organizations such as the FTU to soften their activism.

Under these new circumstances, the FTU stepped away from addressing workplace problems through active collective bargaining and focused instead on workers' welfare outside the workplace. A few months after the Russell Street clash, the FTU's Third Conference of Representatives in April 1950 passed a resolution on "Attending to the hardship of the masses, creating welfare programs for workers" (*guanxin quanzhong jiku, chuangban gongren fuli*).[22] Resulting programs focused on three basic aspects of workers' day-to-day life: medical care, food, and spirit-uplifting activities. In addition, unions continued to offer relief in times of disaster or dismissal.

In their first major welfare effort, the FTU established a clinic. It materialized with help from an unlikely ally, Doctor Li Song (1895–?). Li was well

---

19. Qiao, 181–82.

20. Jin (2005), 30–31.

21. Jin (2005), 40–41. Steve Tsang argues that British authorities from Hong Kong to London were very cautious in handling the procrastination of the Hong Kong branch of Xinhua to register in compliance with the Representation of Foreign Powers (Control) Ordinance to avoid hostility with the Chinese government. Although he treats the Hong Kong branch of Xinhua as if it followed orders from above, the behavior of Xinhua staff clearly demonstrated that friction between Xinhua's branch office in Hong Kong and the British authorities was yet another instance of local initiative that deviated from Beijing's policy. See Tsang, (1997b), citation from 302–3.

22. Xianggang gonghui lianhehui (2013), 24.

known in Hong Kong for his ardent patriotism: he closed his own clinic in 1932 to volunteer his medical services to the Chinese resistance in Shanghai when Japanese marines attacked the city. Socializing with the well-to-do in Hong Kong, Li had always viewed the Guomindang-led government as the legitimate power and "believed that the Communists were killing and looting bandits." In 1948, however, shocking news forced him and his wife to reconsider their opinion. Their daughter, a student at the Jinling Women's University in Nanjing, had joined the Communist guerrilla force after a summer break at home.[23] Their frantic search for information put them in contact with people quite different from "those who cared for fashion and enjoyed good life" in their social circles. These new friends turned out to be "thoughtful and full of initiative," and the encounter altered their views about the Communists and their daughter's choice. Through these new friends, Doctor Li decided to provide free medical service after normal hours at his own clinic for workers sent by the FTU. As workers lined up in the hallway every evening, Li immediately realized that the task went far beyond the capacity of his small clinic.[24]

At Doctor Li Song's suggestion, the FTU opened its first clinic in July 1950 with a loan of HK$3,300 from three affiliated unions. Temporarily, it set up in an office borrowed from the Hong Kong–Kowloon Association for Promoting Workers' Education, until the FTU could relocate it six months later to a third-floor rental on Lockhard Road. The clinic had one chief physician in residence; Li Song and a few other doctors volunteered their services. Every evening after his own clinic closed, Li rushed to the FTU clinic to see patients there. This voluntary work kept him away from home until midnight each day, but it brought him "thorough gratification."[25]

The FTU's first clinic made history in the colony's labor movement as the first such facility sponsored by a labor union association in Hong Kong.[26] It

---

23. Li Song, 153–54.

24. Li Song, 159.

25. Li Song, 161.

26. According to one contemporary source, the pro-Taiwan TUC had one clinic run by one of its unions, which hired a doctor from the mainland. The TUC-sponsored clinic only started in mid-1950s, however, once the FTU clinic became so popular. Author's email correspondence with Zhou Yi (Chau Yick), October 4, 2015. Although no corroborating evidence has been found in my research, the fact that

was a step forward from existing networks of volunteer doctors, which had only been available through better-organized unions such as the Motor Drivers General Union. The clinic made Western medicine a key feature in workers' health care—an option viewed as more effective in the 1950s but too costly to be accessible to ordinary workers in Hong Kong.[27] With only a HK$2 fee and, when needed, an additional HK$1 for an injection, members of FTU-affiliated unions and their families could receive treatment at the clinic. All they needed was a form from their union to qualify for this inexpensive medical care.[28] Widespread needs made the FTU open a second clinic on Canton Road in Yaumatei in July 1951, an X-ray laboratory on the same street in January 1952 with machines and processing equipment donated by Li Song, a midwifery on Cheung Sha Wan Road in Kowloon, another clinic at Tsuen Wan, a Chinese Medicine Clinic in May 1955, and a laboratory with a microscope, also donated by Doctor Li.[29]

Guomindang organizations were revived only after 1950 in the context of the escalating war in Korea makes Zhou's recollection believable. See following discussion on Guomindang activities in Hong Kong.

27. The General Union of Motor Drivers newsletter from 1949 shows that twenty-one doctors, including eleven Chinese medical doctors, two specialists on bodily injuries (which is a branch of Chinese medical practice), three Western medical doctors, two "specialists of throat diseases," one dentist, and two unspecified medical practitioners were the union's voluntary doctors. See "摩托車業職工總會義務醫師一覽" (List of voluntary doctors for Motor Drivers General Union), in 摩托車業職工總會會刊 (一九四九年港九的士工潮特刊) (Motor Drivers General Union Newsletter [Special Issue on taxi drivers' strike in 1949]), September 1, 1949, 15. The Hong Kong Union of Workers in Foreign-Style Services also had similar networks. Its newsletter of 1947 lists thirteen voluntary doctors for its union members, including one Western medical doctor, two eye doctors, one midwife, and specialists in internal medicine or injuries, most likely in the Chinese medical tradition. See Xianggang yangwu gonghui,《香港洋務》, 復會週年紀念特刊, Xianggang yangwu, special issue on the anniversary of resumption of the union), June 1, 1947, 24.

28. 病君, "真真正正為工人福利着想概工聯醫療所" (FTU clinics as a service truly for the wellbeing of workers), Motuocheye zhigong zonghui,《摩托通訊》Motuo tongxun (Motor Newsletter), no. 17 (November 1, 1950), 24.

29. Addresses for these clinics, except the one established in 1955, can be found in GangJiu fangzhiranye zonggonghui (ed.), 2; Xianggang Gonglianhui (2013), 25; Li Song, 164. The official Labour Department report began to note in 1947 that some

How desperately workers and their families needed medical care in postwar Hong Kong was an abstract notion for most doctors who treated well-to-do patients. Only after volunteering his medical services did Doctor Li realize the severity of their problems. At that time, tuberculosis affected a large number of ordinary Chinese workers in Hong Kong. During the first half of the twentieth century, the disease spread quickly in Asia, along with rapid urbanization. For the majority of workers, malnutrition, poor working conditions in badly ventilated cotton mills and workshops, and person-to-person transmission in the crowded living spaces exacerbated the risk.[30] Official records show that in 1949 tuberculosis accounted for 14.6 percent of deaths, while cases of TB meningitis increased threefold in just two years.[31] One of Li's first patients was the president of the FTU, Chen Wenhan, whose tuberculosis had entered an advanced stage. Since his disease required intensive treatment in a fully equipped hospital, Li made arrangements to send Chen to Hong Kong Central Hospital, a small private establishment. But Central Hospital refused to admit this poor worker until Li paid the HK$5,000 treatment cost on Chen's behalf.[32] He Zhuozhong, secretary for the Trade Union of Paint Workers, had also suffered from tuberculosis since his youth. He was diagnosed and cured

---

of the larger business establishments, both European and Chinese, made "medical facilities available for their staff, but usually not for their families." The phrase for "medical facilities" was changed to "medical attention" in a report for 1951–1952. See *LDAR* 1947–1948, 22; *LDAR* 1951–1952, 64. Zhou Yi, who was serving as the Metal Works Labor Union's secretary in 1950, replied to my inquiry about these "large business concerns" that provided "medical attention" to workers in these words: "The Tramway Company did not have a medical facility initially, but workers must go to its designated two doctors. Only a note signed by these doctors, but not any others, could qualify a worker for a sick-leave. The two doctors were brothers, Wu Guo-an [吳國安] and Wu Guo-quan [吳國全]. The workers jokingly called them Wu An-quan [無安全, no security]." Author's email correspondence with Zhou Yi, October 4, 2015.

30. For a general discussion on the high death rate caused by tuberculosis between 1900 and 1950 and the causal relation between overcrowding and the disease, see Jones, 653–82.

31. Ingrams, 220.

32. Li Song, 159. HK$6,000 was the price for an independent Western-style house in Kowloon at the time.

at FTU First Clinic in 1952.[33] Not everyone was so lucky. Many came too late, after advanced disease had caused holes in their lungs, which required expensive treatment in regular hospitals. Without adequate equipment and medicine during the U.S.-led embargo against China, which severely affected Hong Kong, Li introduced a technique at FTU clinics that was used in the Philippines: injecting air into the patient's abdomen to force the holes to close and facilitate healing in the lungs. Using a relatively simple device he invented, Li cured numerous patients during his three decades of voluntary service.[34] The FTU clinics he helped to create eventually became regular medical establishments, attending hundreds of thousands of patients annually today.[35]

Stomach ailments were the second most common disease that brought workers to FTU clinics.[36] Like tuberculosis, stomach ailments were directly associated with working conditions, resulting mostly from irregular mealtimes during work shifts or eating cold leftovers, which the Chinese physique could not tolerate. In 1949 the FTU created a canteen to "reduce the food cost for workers." The initiative inspired its affiliated unions, and by 1950 nine others were operating their own canteens.[37] Textile workers embraced it wholeheartedly because they no longer needed to bring cold leftovers from home to eat in a rush during the brief lunch break. The General Union of Female Knitters operated a canteen on South Wall Road near Kowloon City. It was open to all workers, FTU members or not, and charged only HK$0.60 a meal, about 25 percent less than the bus fare a worker spent each day.[38] The General Union of Textile Workers operated another canteen on Castle Peak

---

33. He Zhuozhong, 155. When He was diagnosed, he was instructed by the party to stop working, while workers in his union sent him medicine and food. Their care and attention "warmed my heart," said He, who nonetheless continued work while being treated.

34. Li Song, 162–63.

35. Xianggang gonghui lianhehui (2013), 25.

36. Li Song, 158.

37. Gonglian mishuchu, "港九工聯第二年工作總結" (Review of the work during the second year of FTU), Xianggang yangwu gonghui, Xianggang yangwu, no. 6 (June 2, 1950), 12–16; citation from 14.

38. GangJiu fangzhiranye zonggonghui (ed.), Fangzhiranye zonggonghui sanzhounian jinian tekan (June 25, 1950), 16.

Road in 1951, serving workers from more than twenty factories in the area.[39] Bus drivers and conductors who could not have meals on a regular schedule particularly appreciated these canteens. When the union branch at Kowloon Bus Company started a canteen by selling stock to union members, more than 75 percent of the workers responded. With over HK$4,000 in its start-up fund, the canteen opened in May 1951 and offered meal delivery service to drivers and conductors. Its menu included two dishes for HK$0.80 for the predominantly male workforce at the Kowloon Bus Company.[40]

Beyond care for workers' physical well-being, FTU's third major initiative aimed at uplifting spirits and enriching lives outside the workplace. Under the rubric *kangle* (well-being and entertainment), FTU-affiliated unions formed a Department of Wellbeing and Entertainment to operate union libraries and organize workers into table tennis teams, sewing groups, and music groups.[41] The practice echoed a well-established tradition from the National Salvation Movement; it generated collective spirit among workers without challenging the colony's political boundaries. One particular *kangle* activity that brought workers the long-term benefits of upward social mobility was adult and children's education. This effort was a collaboration with Bishop Ronald Hall (1895–1975), whose single-minded and tireless work to improve the social lot for the underprivileged had earned him the nickname "Pink or Red Bishop" in Hong Kong's official circles.[42] With Bishop Hall's support, more than twenty labor unions later affiliated with the FTU formed a Hong Kong–Kowloon Association for Promoting Workers' Education in 1947. The colonial state initially endorsed the effort. The Department of Education and the Labour Department dispatched representatives to sit on the association committee and worked with other members from the labor unions.[43]

---

39. 第一屆管理委員會 (First Management Committee), "青山道服務部一年來的工作概況" (An outline of work done in the first year of Service Department at Qingshan Road)," GangJiu fangzhiranye zonggonghui (ed.), *Fangzhiranye zonggonghui wuzhounian jinian tekan* (June 22, 1952), 6.

40. Hun Ming, "事头, 伙计, 客人, 都係我自己" (I am at once manager, employer, and customer), *Motuo tongxun*, no. 20 (August 20, 1951), 14.

41. For example, see Zhong Cheng, "摩分近事" (Recent activities in a branch of Motor Drivers Union), *Motuo tongxun*, no. 18 (April 6, 1951), 2.

42. Chan-Yeung, 115–16, 143, note 22.

43. Zhou Yi (2009), 241–42.

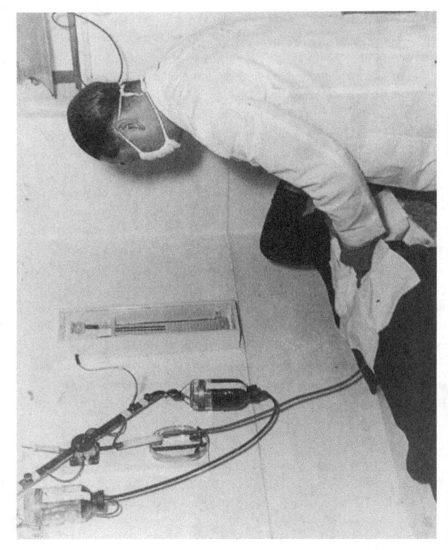

Fig. 15. Doctor Li Song treating a tuberculosis patient at FTU clinic. Courtesy of HKFTU.

Fig. 16. Union-operated canteen sending meal to tramway workers. Courtesy of HKFTU.

Fig. 17. A union-operated canteen. Courtesy of HKFTU.

Fig. 18. A literacy class for women workers. Courtesy of HKFTU.

Assuming a different attitude toward labor activities at the end of the 1940s, the colonial state began to have second thoughts and viewed these union-managed schools as a breeding ground of dangerous thoughts. It withdrew its support for educating socially disadvantaged children. An official decision in fall 1949 to deregister all twelve schools serving workers' children instantly led to colony-wide protests. Even the politically neutral *Sing Tao Jih Bao* criticized the inadequate justification of government closure using the excuse of "unsatisfactory buildings" and urged it to evaluate these schools by teacher quality, equipment, textbooks, and sanitary conditions.[44] Nearly 100,000 ordinary Chinese joined the campaign to defend these schools, while Bishop Hall mediated numerous meetings between the workers and the Department of Education.[45] Public pressure forced the colonial regime to compromise and allow five schools to remain open, but with officially appointed principals.[46] Surveillance by these principals and occasional police raids without warrants kept the schools under close watch and gradually discouraged teachers from expressing pro-China sentiments.[47] In 1959 the colonial state terminated the small annual subsidy to these schools. Nonetheless, determined support from FTU-affiliated unions enabled the schools to survive on donations. Before too long, FTU night schools providing vocational education for union members also mushroomed and became a key feature in FTU's welfare programs.[48]

---

44. "評港當局接受勞校" (On government takeover of the schools for workers' children), *Sing Tao Jih Bao*, June 15, 1949, reprinted in *XGBZJYZL*, 564–65.

45. "勞工教育促進會為勞校事件聲明" (A statement on the closing of schools for workers' children by the Association for Promoting Labor Education), 《華南報》 (*South China Newspaper*), August 19, 1949, reprinted in *XGBZJYZL*, 579–80; Chan-Yeung, 116.

46. "對於教育司談話 勞教會作三項答辯" (Three responses by the Association for Promoting Labor Education to the Department of Education), *Sing Tao Jih Bao*, August 22, 1949, reprinted in *XGBZJYZL*, 581–83; Zhou Yi (2009), 246.

47. "大批軍警昨晨出動, 學校工會突被搜查, 紅磡勞校員生曾遭扣押" (Many police mobilized yesterday morning, searching schools and labor unions; some teachers and students from the school for workers' children at Hong Hum were detained), *Dagong bao*, January 29, 1951, reprinted in *XGBZJYZL*, 593–94.

48. These vocational schools thrived well into the twenty-first century. See, for example, Xianggang Gonglianhui (2008), which lists nearly 2,000 courses ranging

Welfare programs at the FTU became a mainstay of union activities in the post–Russell Street years under the leadership of Chen Wenhan. Chen had been a labor activist before the war and a member of the Communist Party since 1938.[49] We met him briefly in chapter 2 when he assumed a critical role in the rescue operation that lifted hundreds of China's political, social, and cultural leaders out of occupied Hong Kong in 1941–1942. Overwork and malnutrition in postwar years took a heavy toll on this dedicated activist and labor leader. He finally succumbed to tuberculosis and died at the age of forty-two in 1953. His funeral became a moment when the progressive members in the Hong Kong society showed their solidarity with the FTU. Among the more than 1,000 mourners in the union's official funeral procession was Professor Chen Junbao, who walked among other social and cultural leaders. Ten trucks carried wreaths and banners from labor unions and various social circles, followed by twenty cars driven by members of the Motor Drivers General Union, which Chen Wenhan joined as an ordinary member before becoming its elected chairman.[50] As this formal procession of mourners marched slowly, workers displayed in public their appreciation for Chen's leadership in these difficult years. The FTU had dissuaded many of them to participate in the funeral procession, as it feared causing traffic congestion and giving the colonial state another excuse for repression.[51] With no other option, thousands of workers lined the streets to pay final respects to their beloved leader as the funeral procession carried his body and made its slow passage through downtown Hong Kong to his final resting place.

---

from more practical ones in business, management, law, engineering, and computer technology to artistic ones in musical instruments, dance, drama, photography, as well as cooking, horticulture, and gymnastic exercises.

49. Wu Youheng, "吳有恆關於香港市委工作給中央的報告" (Report by Wu Youheng to the Central Committee regarding works at the City Committee of Hong Kong), GDGM, 44:288.

50. "勞績永存萬人悼念, 陳文漢遺體昨安葬" (His accomplishments remain forever; tens of thousands joined the service for Chen Wenhan, whose funeral was held yesterday), Dagong bao, November 28, 1953, 4.

51. Zhou Yi (2009), 293, 298; Xianggang gonghui lianhehui (2013), 274. Chen began to lead the FTU after Mai Yaoquan's arrest and deportation in July 1950.

Fig. 19. Funeral procession for Chen Wenhan, 1953. Courtesy of HKFTU.

Silencing the Left

Surely, turning away from collective workplace actions to welfare programs outside the workplace was a bitter choice forced on the most active unions in a punitive environment. But these programs lent critical support to workers facing additional challenges when Hong Kong entered another economic downturn. The city had been riding a fast track of economic growth until the Korean War derailed its entrepôt trade. London went along with the U.S.-led embargo against China, and Hong Kong was abruptly cut off from its lifeline. Immediately its economy suffered. The official annual report called the embargo "the most serious crisis" economically, noting that "for Hong Kong's business men and industrialists 1951 has been a year of difficulty and depression."[52] Shortage of raw materials and inflated prices continued the next year.[53] Hong Kong's textile industry, in particular, confronted competition from Japanese goods. As a result, "many factories were forced to work almost on a day-to-day basis since ... spells of full employment alternated with periods of stagnation with factory work rolls reduced to a maintenance level."[54]

Unemployment hit the labor market hard during this crisis. The Labour Department estimated that 25,000 to 30,000 workers had lost their jobs in registered factories and workshops by the end of 1951. Among those who still had jobs, 20,000 workers were "by no means fully employed." In addition, an estimated 20,000 "outworkers, cottage-industry employees and miscellaneous workers on the fringe of industry were also affected."[55] This official estimate was appreciably lower than the actual number, because the Labour Department only had data on registered factories and workshops.[56]

The burden of housing expenses never lessened for ordinary Chinese, employed or not, in Hong Kong. The problem was far beyond the ability of labor unions to solve, whose welfare programs could do no more than cushion workers in other small but vital areas. In 1950 Hong Kong had an estimated population of 2.36 million, of which 250,000 had been added during the

---

52. *HKAR* 1951, 7–8.

53. *LDAR* 1951–1952, 10.

54. *LDAR* 1951–1952, 10.

55. *LDAR* 1951–1952, 14.

56. Official reports on industrial establishments leave a huge gap between records and reality, because numerous operations, usually small ones, remained in the dark.

previous year.[57] The inadequate housing supply had come to the attention of the colonial state, which was concerned with attendant social problems. But Hong Kong's political establishment, led by unofficial Chinese members in the Legislative Council, effectively blocked government intervention in the housing market to ameliorate the problem.[58]

Unable to pay the exorbitant rents in postwar Hong Kong, hundreds of thousands chose makeshift, hazardous shelters. Squatting became the poor people's solution to balancing income and expenses. A survey by the Social Welfare Office in late 1950 and early 1951 counted roughly 300,000 squatters living in 47,000 "wooden shacks, scrap-metal hovels or sub-standard stone or brick houses." Although the majority of squatters were recent immigrants from the mainland, an unknown percentage of them were Hong Kong residents.[59] What did not appear in the official survey was that a large proportion of squatters were industrial workers, either employed or recently laid off. Squatter sites were fire hazards. Sheds made of wood and paper burned easily when ignited by tumbled gasoline stoves or broken electric wires. Often such fires gave authorities justification to relocate victims and clear valuable land for development. Invariably, the frequent, large-scale fires turned ongoing social-economic problems into social crises. One squatter fire triggered events that reignited unresolved tensions between pro-mainland labor and Hong Kong's colonial regime.

In the early evening of November 21, 1951, a large fire broke out in Tung Tau Village, a squatter area near Kowloon City where many textile workers lived. The fire spread rapidly in the strong, dry wind of winter. Before it was put out three and a half hours later, the raging blaze had destroyed 3,000 huts

---

The Labour Department did note repeatedly through the 1950s, that at least 100,000 workers engaged in unregistered undertakings below its twenty-person lower registration limit. This situation was not unique in the 1950s but continued into the 1970s. See *LDAR*, for various years in the 1950s. The figure is usually entered in chapter 1, "General Review," in most annual reports. Also see England and Rear, 109–10.

57. See *HKAR* 1950, 10; also see Hambro, table X, which notes 190,000 new immigrants to Hong Kong in 1949 and 130,000 in 1950.

58. Faure (2003), chapter 5; Ure, 87–126.

59. *LDAR* 1950–1951, 11.

Fig. 20. Squatter area, early 1950s. Courtesy of Information Services Department, Hong Kong Government (SAR).

in nine villages, leaving 25,000 homeless.[60] The official annual report defined it as "a serious fire" but cited only 10,000 homeless, less than half of the newspaper estimate.[61] Circulating rumors blamed the fire on either an accident in a cotton workshop or a tumbled gas lamp in a carpentry shop, but FTU-affiliated unions thought otherwise.[62] The General Union of Textile Workers (the recently expanded and renamed Union of Female Knitters) argued that 20 percent of the fire victims were textile workers and their families, among them nearly 100 union activists.[63] The Xinhua News Agency and the FTU saw the fire as a conspiracy by the authorities to drive labor activists out of the Tung Tau area. "They [the authorities] feared the many patriotic workers living together in Tung Tau Village," noted Jin Yaoru, a high-level leader in the Xinhua News Agency. "It would go beyond official control if the workers were mobilized." He believed the fire was a convenient excuse to kick those workers out of the burned-down squatter areas.[64]

Whatever caused it, the Tung Tau fire was a major social disaster. Unfolding events seemed to give force to Jin's speculation. The Social Welfare Office inspected the fire site and within days announced its intention to relocate fire victims.[65] Social organizations, particularly the officially sanctioned *Kaifong* (neighborhood associations), collected individual donations that reached HK$222,409 by mid-December, which the *Kaifongs* decided to distribute to fire

---

60. Special report, "九龍城昨夜空前大火, 九村毀屋三千, 災民逾二萬伍千" (Unprecedented fire last night at Kowloon City; destroyed 3,000 sheds in night villages; victims exceed 25,000), *Sing Tao Jih Bao*, November 22, 1951, 5.

61. *HKAR* 1952, 5.

62. "起火的原因" (Causes of the fire), *Sing Tao Jih Bao*, November 22, 1951, 5.

63. The Fifth Standing Committee, "本會第五年工作報告" (Work report for the fifth year), 港九紡織染業總工會五周年紀念特刊 (Fifth year anniversary special issue of Hong Kong–Kowloon General Union of Textile Workers) (June 22, 1952), 4. The report gave the total number of fire victims at 16,000, a figure also used by left-wing newspapers.

64. Jin Yaoru (2005), 56. I was first made aware of this view in summer 2007, when I interviewed Lo Fu, another Communist intellectual, who was editor-in-chief of the pro-Communist newspaper *Wenhui bao*.

65. "二萬五千人頓苦無家亟待緊急救濟" (Suddenly 25,000 have no home to go to and need urgent relief), *Sing Tao Jih Bao*, November 22, 1951, 5. The Social Welfare Office was set up in 1947 under the Secretary for Chinese Affairs; see *HKAR* 1951, 79.

victims at HK$13.51 per head.[66] Through *Kaifong*, the government distributed 5,000 free meals daily after the fire, and a total of 74,000 meals by December 2 averaging two meals a day to over 3,300 people.[67] Toward the end of November, the chairman of the Urban Council announced publicly that the Tung Tau fire victims would be relocated to a new site at Ngau Tau Kok, some four kilometers east of Tung Tau, without good roads or an adequate water supply.[68]

The large number of FTU members among the fire victims placed leftwing unions at the center of relief work. The FTU sent 5,000 packs of biscuits to the fire victims right after the disaster—as much as its meager funds allowed.[69] While enlisting other support from its grassroots membership, it looked toward the mainland and sought donations from Guangdong, the home province of many members. Workers in FTU-affiliated unions responded enthusiastically by contributing ten metric tons of white rice for distribution among fire victims.[70] When fifteen metric tons of rice from Guangdong reached Kowloon in late January, FTU volunteers distributed it to the fire victims.[71]

Labor activists among the Tung Tau victims began to organize petitions for more official help when various problems appeared one after another. De-

---

66. Special report, "九龍城賑災款廿餘万, 昨決按照人數均派" (Donations for Kowloon City reached more than HK$200,000, which was decided last night to distribute equally on every victim), *Sing Tao Jih Bao*, December 16, 1951, 5; "九龍城賑災緩不濟急" (Relief funds for Kowloon City comes too slow for the emergency), *Sing Tao Jih Bao*, December 28, 1951, 5.

67. Public Relations Office (Government of Hong Kong), "Government's Prompt and Practical Measures to Aid Tung Tau Village Fire Victims," CO 1023/164, 222–27. Citation from 222–23.

68. "Resettlement of Fire Victims," *South China Morning Post*, November 30, 1951, 3. Conditions at Ngau Tau Kok can be gleaned from "Social Welfare Activities in the Limelight," *South China Morning Post*, March 16, 1952, 8.

69. 本報訊, "九龍城災民亟待救濟, 工聯展開急賑工作" (Victims of Kowloon City fire urgently need relief; FTU started on the task), *Wenhui bao*, November 23, 1951, 4.

70. Special report, "九龍城賑災款廿餘万" (Donations for fire victims of Kowloon City reached more than $200,000), *Sing Tao Jih Bao*, December 16, 1952, 5.

71. 本報訊, "祖國贈米三萬斤分發萬餘災胞歡欣領米" (Donation of 15,000 kilo of rice from homeland; victims gladly received distribution), *Wenhui bao*, January 25, 1952.

Fig. 21. FTU relief for Tung Tau Fire victims. Courtesy of HKFTU.

Fig. 22. FTU workers registering Tung Tau Fire victims for relief. Courtesy of HKFTU.

lays slowed the distribution of social donations and repeated police actions destroyed huts rebuilt by fire victims. Leading the Fire Victims Committee was Li Wenxing, a young electrician who had been a wartime resister in the East River Column. FTU-affiliated unions, particularly the Kowloon Branch of the General Union of Spinners, Weavers, and Dyers, which was located near Tung Tau Village, actively supported the committee. Close cooperation between the committee and the union, particularly an open statement in early January 1950 signed by Li and two other victims protesting police actions that destroyed the temporary shelters of fire victims, irritated the authorities. On January 9, 1952, police destroyed the Fire Victims Committee office, arrested Li Wenxing, and deported him to the mainland. A week later they arrested four more people: representative Zhang Sheng, committee treasurer Feng Qin, and two fire victims, Chen Hualong and Liu Fochang. The left-wing *Wenhui bao* reported this important event and published the fire victims' statement of protest.[72] In early morning on January 10, 1952, plainclothes policemen broke into the office of the Kowloon Branch of the General Union of Spinners, Weavers, and Dyers and arrested Director Xian Peilin and Secretary Yao Jian, the two female union leaders who provided active assistance to the Fire Victims Committee. Although Xian and Yao were Hong Kong–born residents, they were quickly deported to the mainland.[73]

The colonial state then turned against cultural circles where left-wing activists openly voiced support to China and the fire victims. On the same day that Xian Peilin and Yao Jian were arrested, police detained well-known writers and playwrights Sima Wensen, Qi Guozhao, Ma Guoliang, and Shen Ji; famous actors Liu Qiong and Shu Shi; actress Di Fan; and director Yang Hua.[74] Three

---

72. "辦事處職員馮欽失蹤後, 災民代表張生被捕" (Staff Feng Qin at the office disappeared, then victims representative Zhang Sheng arrested), *Wenhui bao*, January 18, 1952, 4; 本報訊, "捕人事件造成不安; 災民昨發抗議書" (Incident of arrest caused anxiety; victims issued protest), *Wenhui bao*, January 19, 1952, 4.

73. "九龍城紡織染工會支會主任書記深夜被捕" (Director and secretary of Kowloon City branch of Textile Workers Union arrested late last night), *Wenhui bao*, January 11, 1952, 4; "紡織染工會主任書記被逐出境, 工友續開大會抗議" (Director and secretary of Textile Workers Union deported; workers followed up with a rally to protest), *Wenhui bao*, January 13, 1952, 4; Zhou Yi (2009), 302–3.

74. "香港警察黑夜分頭出動, 電影工作者八人遭逮捕" (In darkness of the night Hong Kong police moved to arrest eight film workers), *Wenhui bao*, January 12,

days later, photographer Jiang Wei and scriptwriter Bai Chen were arrested. All ten were deported to the mainland, as one English-language newspaper reported, "because of their dangerous pressure activities."[75]

The arrest and deportation of widely known celebrities in Hong Kong, mostly mainland-born but recently invited by film companies to work in the colony, sent an unmistakable warning to left-leaning cultural circles as the new year began. Yet the three pro-mainland newspapers—the *Wenhui bao (Wen Wei Po)*, *Dagong bao (Ta Kung Pao)*, and *Xinwan bao (New Evening Post)*—refused to censor negative reports on events in colonial Hong Kong. They carried upbeat news about the mainland while closely following the British authorities' deplorable treatment of fire victims. In the eye of the colonial state, these newspapers defiled Governor Grantham's vision of Hong Kong as "a living example for the Chinese of a free life."[76] Their "obnoxious" reporting upset the governor, and it had to be silenced to keep the colony a safe distance from the "edge of volcano."[77] In spring 1952, the colonial state seized an opportunity to achieve that goal.

On March 1, 1952, a Guangdong People's Relief Mission was scheduled to arrive in Hong Kong. They brought relief funds and goods donated by various mainland social organizations in response to appeals from the FTU and the semi-open Hong Kong Work Committee of the Communist Party. Planning for the mission sped up after Li Wenxing, the fire victims' representative, was deported and arrived in Guangzhou complaining about unresolved problems.[78] To welcome the mission, labor activists, students, and school children, estimated by the *South China Morning Post* at 20,000 to 30,000, gathered near the Kowloon Train Station at Tsimshatsui. The Chinese Chamber of Commerce, official distributor of relief between Hong Kong and the mainland since the days of the National Salvation Movement, formed a ninety-person welcome party with FTU leaders and activists from industrial and commercial circles, film workers, the news media, and representatives of the fire victims. Led by well-known businessman Mo Yinggui (*Ct.* Mok Ying-kuai,

1952, 4. *Wenhui bao* made several more reports on the arrival of these writers and film stars in Guangzhou and their accounts of the deportation process.

75. "Peking Protest," *South China Morning Post*, February 1, 1952, 6; also see Zhou Yi (2009), 304.

76. Grantham (1953).

77. See note 27 in chapter 5.

78. Jin Yaoru (2005), 26; Zhou Yi (2009), 305.

1901–1997) and FTU President Chen Wenhan, the welcome party left Hong Kong on a train at 10 a.m., heading for Lowu.[79] But Hong Kong police stopped the welcome party at Fanling and detached its special coach from the train. Only Mo Yinggui was allowed to proceed to the border. Mo reached Lowu, conveyed the situation to the mission, and returned with his welcome party to Kowloon shortly after 3 p.m.[80] When news of the delay in the relief mission's visit reached the waiting crowd, it began to disperse peacefully and orderly, holding flags and banners and singing songs in a "gay and cheerful" spirit. Then an incident suddenly changed its mood.[81]

What happened was presented quite differently in the colony's English and Chinese newspapers. According to the *South China Sunday Post*, in a "prearranged plan ... some hooligans" attacked a police car, overturned it, and set it on fire, changing a cheerful procession of 20,000 into a "mob." The *Dagong bao* indicated that the clash was provoked by the police. The following report was translated by the U.S. Consulate General in Hong Kong and appeared in its *Review of Hongkong Chinese Press*:

> According to an eyewitness who happened to be at the place at that time, when the masses of people reached the junction of Nathan Road and Jordan Road, a Police car, which was driving from north to south along Nathan Road, ran into the masses and a girl was hit [to the ground] and wounded. Angry shouts broke out from all sides and there was great confusion. Then a large party of armed Police arrived and threw tear gas bombs, which increased the confusion. As a result, several people were wounded.
>
> In the meantime, several smaller clashes also took place on Nathan Road from Austin Road northward to Po Hing Theater. A party of armed Police was stationed at the junction of Austin Road and Nathan Road. It was said that a Policeman later fired at shot [*sic*] into the air at a place near Hsueh Yuan Restaurant, and the confusion was aggravated.[82]

---

79. "港九各界推派代表, 今晨前往羅湖車站迎接, 今晚茶會招待明晚舉行宴會" (Hong Kong–Kowloon all circles sent representatives to go to Lowu station this morning to welcome [the Relief Mission]; tea party tonight and banquet tomorrow), *Dagong bao*, March 1, 1952, 1; "慰問團展期來港" (Relief Mission Postponed Visiting Hong Kong), *Dagong bao*, March 2, 1952, 1.

80. "Mob Violence in Kowloon," *South China Sunday Post*, March 2, 1952, 1.

81. "Mob Violence in Kowloon," *South China Sunday Post*, March 2, 1952, 1.

82. "Big Clash of Police and Masses in Kowloon," *Dagong bao*, March 2, 1952, 1, 4. Translation from the U.S. Consulate General (Hong Kong), *Review of Hongkong Chinese*

More clashes erupted at the junction of Nathan Road and Argyle Street, where an angry crowd attacked police with their wooden clogs. According to the *South China Sunday Post*, two Americans were beaten; one of them received stitches for a cut on his head. When the police finally dispersed the angry crowds after two hours of chaos, forty-two people had been arrested, including some "distributors of Communist pamphlets."[83]

The clash unleashed tensions already fermenting in the colony and inflamed anger and frustration. The *South China Sunday Post* declared the clash to be a premeditated riot by the Communists. But FTU-affiliated unions responded indignantly that police misbehavior had prompted the violence. Two days later, China's state-owned newspaper on the mainland, the *Renmin ribao*, headlined the incident. It published a short editorial the next day: "Protesting the Killing of Our Residents in Hong Kong by British Imperialism."[84] The three pro-mainland newspapers in Hong Kong—the *Dagong bao*, *Wenhui bao*, and *New Evening Post*—immediately reprinted the whole or portions of the *Renmin ribao* editorial on the front page.[85] The Tung Tau fire, which started as a

---

Press, no. 41/52 (March 1–3, 1952), 1. I checked the original and found the translation faithful, except for a few missing words and a grammatical error, which I added in brackets. Zhou Yi (Chau Yick), who was then secretary of the Metal Works Union, was in the crowd walking northward when it dispersed. He witnessed the sudden outburst of anger by workers in the crowd after the police vehicle knocked the girl to the ground. See Zhou Yi (2002), 87–88.

83. "Riots in Kowloon," *South China Sunday Post*, March 2, 1952, 7. The total number of arrests was initially reported at 100, but corrected to 42. Of these, eighteen were released, and the remaining twenty-four either sentenced to prison terms (eighteen) or acquitted (six). See "How Many People Were Arrested during Kowloon Clashes?" *Dagong bao*, March 12, 1952, translated and reprinted in U.S. Consulate General, *Review of Hongkong Chinese Press*, No. 48/52 (March 12, 1952), 1.

84. "英帝國主義在香港製造血腥暴行,　　竟出動大批軍警屠殺我國人民" (British imperialism created bloody atrocity in Hong Kong; large number of military police butchered our people), *Renmin ribao*, March 3, 1952, 1; "抗議英帝國主義捕殺香港的我國居民" (Protest against British imperialism for killing our residents in Hong Kong), *Renmin ribao*, March 4, 1952, 1.

85. "北京人民日報發表評論, 祖國人民支持香港愛國同胞, 英方造成嚴重後果應負全責" (The *People's Daily* in Beijing issued an editorial, people of the motherland support the patriotic compatriots in Hong Kong, British authorities caused serious consequences and must assume complete responsibility), *Dagong bao*, March 4, 1952, 1; "北京人民日報評論九龍事件, 向香港英政府抗議" (The *People's Daily* in

local social disaster, turned into an open confrontation between Hong Kong's left-wing media and the colonial state.

Beyond the visible event on March 1, 1952, and the openly critical voices from left-wing newspapers, behind-the-scene discussions between London and Hong Kong had been under way for more than two years regarding how to handle China's Xinhua News Agency and pro-PRC media in the colony. The initial exchange failed to produce a consensus because London was reluctant to act in a way that could risk Britain's overall interests in China. Governor Grantham first suggested closing down both the Xinhua News Agency's office and Communist newspapers in Hong Kong in spring 1949. But the Foreign Office thought that was "not a good idea" because such an action in Hong Kong "might jeopardise the position of Reuters and the North China Daily News in Shanghai."[86] After crushing the tramway protest in early 1950, Grantham again proposed shutting down the Xinhua News Agency in Hong Kong because of the anticolonial content of its news releases as well as its reports of "violent resolutions passed in cities in China in connection with Hong Kong tramway strike."[87] He suggested using the Representation of Foreign Powers (Control) Ordinance, passed in late 1949, against the Xinhua Agency. But the Colonial Office, in agreement with the Foreign Office, rejected his proposal because it wanted to use Xinhua's Hong Kong office as "a bargaining counter for the grant of reciprocal facilities in China."[88] Furthermore, the Foreign Office showed concerns about "charges of interference with the freedom of the Press" and the potential to "endanger the position of Reuters and the North China Daily News in Shanghai." Nonetheless, it agreed with Grantham on using "a suitable opportunity to pounce on the [Xinhua] Agency and then close it."[89]

Beijing commented on the Kowloon Incident and protested to the British government in Hong Kong), *Wenhui bao*, March 4, 1952, 1. Both papers reprinted the complete version of the editorial from the *People's Daily*.

86. "Minutes: Question of bringing N.C.N.A. under the Ordinance," by P. D. Coates (Foreign Office), March 15, 1950, FO 371/83620, 125–28, citation from 125.

87. Grantham to Secretary of State for the Colonies, February 22, 1950, FO 371/83260, 94–95.

88. H. P. Hall (Colonial Office) to P. D. Coates (Foreign Office), Secret, March 22, 1950, FO 371/83261.

89. P. D. Coates (F.O.), "Minutes," March 15, 1950, FO 371/83260, 127.

For Grantham, the "suitable opportunity to pounce" arrived on March 4, 1952, when the pro-mainland newspapers *Dagong bao, Wenhui bao,* and *New Evening Post* reprinted the editorial from China's state-run *Renmin ribao,* denouncing the police action three days earlier in Hong Kong. Immediately, the attorney-general in Hong Kong brought charges against the newspapers for "publishing seditious publications on March 5 contrary to section 4 (1) (c) of the Sedition Ordinance," an ordinance reinstated in 1949.[90] Three defendants associated with the *Dagong bao*—Fei Yimin, the owner and publisher, Bao Lichu (Richard Bow), the printer, and Li Zongying (Lee Tsung-ying), the editor—were brought to trial first. Court hearings began on April 16 and lasted fifteen days, twice the time initially anticipated. Local English and Chinese newspapers noted that the court was packed full at each hearing.

The colonial state was confident that the trial would easily bring down the pro-mainland newspapers and the case would be closed within the week.[91] What happened was the opposite. The defendants engaged Percy Chen, a Trinidad-born, British-trained lawyer whose father had served under Sun Yat-sen as foreign minister, and Brook A. Bernacchi, a British barrister and well-known advocate for democratic reforms in Hong Kong. Known as a fighter in court, Percy Chen took the lead in the defense.[92] He pointed out procedural "irregularities" wherein the usual magistrate's hearing before the trial was skipped. Through cross-examination, he demonstrated that some witnesses for the crown were "incompetent." More importantly, he showed that the re-published article from China's official newspaper, a key element in the government's sedition case against the *Dagong bao,* appeared on the same panel with

---

90. "Newspapers Accused of Sedition," *South China Morning Post,* March 21, 1952, 1.

91. "Sedition Charge: Statement from Dock by All Defendants Claim of Privilege," *South China Morning Post and the Hongkong Telegraph,* April 30, 1952, 3, 6–7. The foreman of the special jury, the report notes, had been told that the case "would finish in a week," and he was quite frustrated that "it now seemed unlikely that in the next six days the trial would be finished" because he had planned to leave for England on May 8.

92. Percy Chen, 380. This autobiography gives a more detailed discussion before World War II of the author's experiences growing up in Trinidad and training in Britain before he traveled to China, Europe, and Soviet Union. Its discussion on post-1945 years, when he settled in Hong Kong, is very sketchy and completely skips the famous defense in 1952.

a statement from the Delegation of Donors from Guangdong, and a statement on the March First Incident by Colonial Secretary Oliver Lyttleton in London.[93] All were treated by the *Dagong bao* as newsworthy. Percy Chen then presented evidence that other Hong Kong newspapers had printed similar stories. To bring criminal charges against the *Dagong bao*, he argued, was to force the newspaper to "only write things which are favourable to the Government [in Hong Kong]" and "voluntarily censor the material it prints." In defining the limits of what the newspaper could print, "the Crown were seeking to crush the expressions of opinion in writings." In short, Chen concluded, "this case is political in the bigger sense of freedom of speech and freedom to read."[94]

However persuasive the defense, the trial ended on May 5 with the special jury finding the owner and editor of the *Dagong bao* guilty, but discharging the printer as only a paid manager of a printing company. The court ordered suppression of the *Dagong bao* for six months, and fined Fei Yimin and Li Zongying HK$4,000 and HK$3,000, respectively. In announcing the verdicts, Judge Williams called the *Dagong bao* "an influence for evil in the Colony" and "most seditious of the Government of this Colony."[95]

The sentencing did not end the affair. As if to demonstrate the impartiality of the colonial legal system, a full court of three judges stayed the suppression order on May 17, pending a final decision.[96] A month later, on June 28, the full court delivered a twenty-eight-page judgment that dismissed every appeal by the defendants and upheld the initial conviction. But it allowed further hearings from the defense counsels on the six-month suppression order.[97] Surprisingly and almost immediately, as the hearings began in full court, the attorney-

---

93. The *Dagong bao* printed all three reports, in parallel on the first panel, under an overall heading "關於三月一日九龍事件" (About the Kowloon Incident on March 1st), *Dagong bao*, March 5, 1952, 1.

94. "Sedition Charge: Issue of Inaccurate Statement Alleged; Counsel Lays Blame on Government Pro; Defence Opens," *South China Morning Post and the Hongkong Telegraph*, April 29, 1952, 6.

95. "Paper Suspended: Influence for Evil, Says Judge," *South China Morning Post and the Hongkong Telegraph*, May 6, 1952, 5.

96. "Ta Kung Pao Suppression Order Stayed," *South China Sunday Post*, May 18, 1952, 1.

97. "Sedition Appeal Dismissed; Ta Kung Pao Convictions Upheld," *South China Sunday Post-Herald*, June 29, 1952, 3.

general publicly announced on June 30 that he "was instructed not to oppose the variation of the order" and dropped charges against the two other newspapers. The chief justice of the full court announced its decision to vary the initial six-month suppression order to conform to "the period during which the paper has actually been suppressed."[98] In a face-saving explanation, the attorney-general stated that these actions were taken to demonstrate the magnanimity of the crown, for it considered its initial objectives "to vindicate the law on this subject" and "to demonstrate that the Crown could not tolerate ... the publication in this Colony of seditious matter" had been "achieved."[99]

In ending the *Dagong bao* trial with these benevolent words, the British government appeared to emphasize its legitimate and ultimate authority. In reality, this about-face was a hasty exit from an embarrassing situation that had actually damaged colonial authority. During the first round of the trial, when the case was heard in front of the special jury, London and Hong Kong came to realize that things were not going to end as they wished but would expose the contrived nature of "seditious intent." As Hong Kong later admitted in secret correspondence with London, "action in courts leads to long drawn out publicity and enables seditious propaganda to be carried out under privilege."[100] Speaking more candidly in internal correspondence, the British chargé d'affaires in Beijing persistently and repeatedly warned that draconian measures against Hong Kong's pro-China press could be counterproductive because it showed "flagrant denial of the rights and freedoms which we pretend to uphold." In his view, "such action just now might be unduly inflammatory and might only involve the Hong Kong Government in constant and exhausting conflict with the mainland Press, which would, in the long run, prove to be against the best interest of Hong Kong."[101] Indeed, as the hearing continued and the defense produced more and more exculpatory evidence, the trial came to aid not the crown but the pro-mainland press.

What also moderated Grantham's tough line was China's attempt to reach a compromise on the Xinhua News Agency's registration in Hong Kong. Ac-

98. "The Ta Kung Pao: Full Court Varies Suppression Order; Nolle Prosequi in Two Other Cases," *South China Morning Post and the Hongkong Telegraph*, July 1, 1952, 1.

99. "The Ta Kung Pao: Full Court Varies Suppression Order."

100. Secret, O.A.G. (Officer Administrating the Government of Hong Kong) to the Secretary of State for the Colonies, July 23, 1952, FO 371/99362, 180.

101. Secret, Lionel Henry Lamb to FO, April 9, 1952, FO 371/99362, 60.

cording to Jin Yaoru, the top-level leader in the Xinhua News Agency, Premier
Zhou Enlai sent a strong signal to London by notifying the British chargé
d'affaires in Beijing that the Chinese government "is watching closely the trial
of the three newspapers in Hong Kong."[102] British official documents show a
sort of tit-for-tat diplomacy behind the scenes. On May 20, before the full
court's decision on appeal, Percy Chen spoke with the attorney-general and
explained that "it was not the desire" of the Chinese government to issue negative propaganda against British authorities in Hong Kong. But Hong Kong's
prosecution of the Xinhua News Agency, he added, "would be met by retalia-
tory measures." When told that the Information Service in the U.S. Consulate-
General had also registered under the Publications Ordinance, Percy Chen, a
bit surprised, quickly noted that this fact might influence Beijing's decision.[103]
In Grantham's assessment of the meeting, Chen "is certainly acting as adviser
in this matter and his statement usually reflect the probable attitude of the
C.P.G. [Central People's Government]." He retracted his earlier insistence on
deporting the director of Xinhua News Agency in the event it refused to register. He admitted that it was impractical, because the director, Huang Zuomei, "claims British nationality by virtue of birth in Hong Kong." His recommendation therefore fell in line with one advocated by the British chargé
d'affaires: to give the Xinhua News Agency more time and allow it to stay.
Grantham even signaled his willingness to waive the cash bond, a requirement
that had also irritated the U.S. Information Service.[104]

As a result of these quiet communications, the Xinhua News Agency finally
registered in late June. The Foreign Office speculated quite accurately that
Beijing had two major reasons for doing so: it considered Xinhua's overseas
operation to be important, and it felt "there was no discrimination against the
C.P.G."[105] The amicable conclusion of the stalemate over Xinhua's registration
also presented an opportunity of a face-saving exit from the *Dagong bao* trial,
which turned out to undermine the authority of the crown. Within days, the

---

102. Jin Yaoru (1998), 27.

103. Secret, Grantham to the Secretary of State for the Colonies, May 5, 1952, FO
371/99362, 115.

104. Secret, Grantham to the Secretary of State for the Colonies, May 5, 1952,
FO 371/99362, 115.

105. C. H. Johnston, "New China News Agency in Hong Kong," June 26, 1952,
FO 371/99362, 167.

full court announced its decision to reject the *Dagong bao* appeal, yet instantly reversed itself by ending the order of suppression. These decisions were certainly intended to demonstrate a British policy of "cautious firmness."[106] An uneasy balance was achieved where neither side overwhelmed the other. The Foreign Office called it "a small but definite success for a policy of cautious firmness," but also admitted that "unfortunately ... there should be no publicity for its successes."[107] The "obnoxious" Xinhua News Agency and the pro-China newspapers remained. But the Tung Tau fire victims would be relocated whether they liked it or not. Staged as yet another public drama, the trial against pro-China newspapers encouraged anti-Communist sentiment in the colony regardless what the colonial state intended.

Resurgence of Guomindang Operation

In contrast to its heightened vigilance and repression of left-wing labor unions and mass media, the colonial state reversed its attitude toward pro-Guomindang labor unions in early 1950. In a secret report to the Colonial Office two months after the police action at Russell Street, Grantham noted that the right-wing TUC "attempted to build up anew its influence over labour in the Colony" after the war. But "the loss of power and influence of the K.M.T. in China has had the inevitable result of depriving of their strength, part of which was financial, those unions in the Colony which previously depended for support on that party."[108] He applauded the TUC's attempt at "quietly going forward" and hoped it would "lead to a more even balance of influence" vis-à-vis left-wing unions' greater strength.[109] In its weakened state, the Guomindang from Taiwan no longer appeared to be a threat in Hong Kong.

Guomindang operations in Hong Kong had been in steady decline since December 1941, when Admiral Chen Ce made his miraculous escape. As we saw in chapter 2, Chinese resistance against Japanese occupation in greater

---

106. C. H. Johnston, "New China News Agency in Hong Kong,"

107. C. H. Johnston, "New China News Agency in Hong Kong," 168.

108. From the Governor to the Secretary of the State for the Colonies, secret, March 31, 1950, FO 371/83261, 79–87; citation from 79 and 80.

109. From the Governor to the Secretary of the State for the Colonies, March 31, 1950, citation from 87.

Guangdong and Hong Kong was largely a partisan operation sustained by the Communist-led East River guerrillas. In contrast, the Guomindang's intelligence work was limited, short-lived, and inconsequential. Despite its proclaimed intent to recover Hong Kong at the end of the war, the National Government under Chiang Kai-shek left Hong Kong in total neglect. By late 1949, Guomindang operation was in "virtual eclipse ... as a major factor in the political life of Hong Kong."[110]

Hong Kong only reemerged as a useful operational base toward the end of 1950 when the Cold War turned hot within a decisively rebalanced international order in East Asia. Between 1945 and 1950, the Guomindang had no active organizational operations in Hong Kong. Its first two years in Taiwan had been challenging, as the party-state took on multiple tasks of preparing counterattacks on the mainland and establishing rule in its downsized power base. Most significant of its undertakings was reform and reorganization of the party between 1950 and 1952. As early as 1948, Chiang Kai-shek had begun contemplating how he might learn from "the lesson of the defeat."[111] Reform and reorganization formally started with the establishment of the Guomindang Central Reform Committee (GMDCRC) in July 1950. Consisting of sixteen younger, better-educated members with demonstrated loyalty to Chiang, the GMDCRC became the highest office in the party once the 460-member Central Committee disbanded. Through registration of party members, training of cadres, restructuring party organization, and required regular meetings of each party cell, the Guomindang remade itself and asserted more effective control of the government, military, and society from Taipei down to rural villages.[112] As a result, its reach to overseas Chinese communities was reestablished.

---

110. Top secret, Alexander Grantham to Arthur Creech Jones, February 1, 1950, FO 371/83260, 90–92. Citation from 90.

111. Since the 1970s, works on the Guomindang reform in the early 1950s have begun to appear. It remains a scholarly interest in Taiwan, the mainland, the United States, and Japan. Debate mainly focuses on two issues: the nature of Guomindang rule in Taiwan as the result of the reform and reorganization, and its impact on later democratization processes in Taiwan. For more recent works, see Matsuda; Jiang and Liu, esp. 274–92; and Feng.

112. For the various methods used to reorganize the Guomindang party through the Central Reform Committee between 1950 and 1952, see Dickson. Also see Chao and Myers, esp. chapter 2.

After the United States intervened in the Korean War, radically polarized international relations suddenly boosted the tentative recovery of Guomindang operations in overseas Chinese communities. A personal diary captured the ecstatic mood of celebration in Taiwan on the U.S. entry into the war. "American president Truman ordered the Seventh Fleet in the Pacific, now visiting Hong Kong, to be placed in the Taiwan Strait to prevent any external attack," Lei Zhen (1897–1979), then prominent within Guomindang leadership, wrote on June 28, 1950. "Everyone is exhilarated by the news. Those who intended to migrate to Hong Kong have cancelled their plans, and real estate prices [in Taipei] has jumped five times. ... This is the prelude to the Third World War!"[113] Two days later Lei wrote again, "The American decision this time is a decisive turning point in the Far East and in the world."[114]

Lei had reason to be so attentive to the effect of the Korean War on the movement between Taipei and British Hong Kong: he was not merely an important member of the government and the Guomindang since the 1940s; he had supervised the party's Hong Kong operations during the critical years of its retreat from the mainland. A protégé of two elder statesmen, Dai Jitao and Zhang Ji, Lei began his political career within the Bureau of Laws compiling new laws for the recently established National Government in 1927. Over the next two decades, Lei took a range of important positions within the party, as a member of the Standing Committee of the Nanjing branch of the Guomindang (1931) in charge of propaganda, general director of the Management Department of the Education Ministry (1933), deputy secretary-general of the National Consultative Council (1943), secretary-general of the National Political Consultative Conference (1946), and minister without portfolio (1948).[115] In the years prior to the Guomindang retreat to Taiwan, Lei oversaw the operation of the party's organ, the *Xianggang shibao* (*Hong Kong Times*), in the British colony. The newspaper was in desperate shortage of funds. Often, money to keep it afloat came through loans from commercial banks or even from sales of sugar on international markets.[116]

---

113. Lei, entry for June 28, 1950, 2:134.

114. Lei, June 30, 1950, 2:136.

115. See Fan, passim. Although Fan is not a historian, he did extensive research using original and secondary sources for this first comprehensive biography of Lei Zhen.

116. Lei, vol. 2, entries for March 25, 1950, April 22, 1950, May 28 and 29, 1950, June 4, 1950, September 24, 1950, September 25, 1950, October 3, 1950, November 19, 1950, and November 20, 1950.

Initially, shortage of operation funds troubled the newly established Third Group of the GMDCRC, though it stopped being a problem after the United States entered the Korean War. Headed by Zheng Yanfen (1902–1990), the Third Group dealt with Guomindang organizations and operations in overseas Chinese communities. In one of its first meetings on Hong Kong–Macau affairs, held in Taipei on October 16, 1950, participants noted that "there has been a heightened morale since the Double Ten, so we need to seize the moment and revive party activities." Immediately they noted a dilemma: "how do we respond if party members in Hong Kong and Macao request financial support, given our very limited budget?"[117] In the following years, such worries disappeared while revival and expanded operations in Hong Kong moved to the fore of the group's attention.

Less than five months after the outbreak of the Korean War, the Guomindang Hong Kong–Macau General Branch reestablished itself on December 1, 1950, after a decade-long absence in the British colony. The General Branch commanded 181 cells in Hong Kong and Macau with a total of 2,218 party members. Hong Kong was designated as a directly commanded district (*zhixiaqu*) because of its predominance in the newly formed party organization. Its 164 cells and 2,064 members operated under four committees and one group as follows: Labor Movement Committee, Student Movement Committee, Cultural Movement Committee, Local Work Committee, and Newspaper Group. Primarily targeting labor and youth groups, the Labor Movement Committee had most cells—fifty-four plus six more "directly commanded cells"—under the General Branch. The committee responsible for student mobilization was the second largest, with twenty-six regular cells and three directly commanded cells.[118]

As internal reports by a leader of the GMDCRC's Third Group show, the Hong Kong–Macau General Branch focused on a two-front offensive in the following years: to regain initiative in mass organizations—particularly trade

---

117. 張其昀, 鄭彥棻致蔣中正 Zhang Qijun and Zheng Yanfen to Jiang Zhongzheng, "檢呈黨務座談會記錄" (Report on the discussion meeting for party business), Guomindang gaizao weiyuanhui (Taipei), 海祕 (39) 185.

118. 張其昀, 鄭彥棻 Zhang Qijun and Zheng Yanfen, "港澳總支部一年來重要工作" (Important achievements by the Hong Kong–Macau branch in the past year), December 17, 1950; Guomindang gaizao weiyuanhui (Taipei), 台 (40) 改秘室字第603號.

unions—and to enhance the Guomindang voice through propaganda. For the first task, the Guomindang adopted the tactic of divide (*fenhua*) by creating competing unions within the same industry or trade, particularly the powerful and critical unions within the FTU.[119] The Trade Unions and Trade Disputes Ordinance of 1948, which permitted a union as small as seven members, facilitated such division within organized labor.[120] While rebuilding its Hong Kong organization, leaders of the GMDCRC's Third Group in Taipei recognized that the TUC "always supported our government and made great efforts to attack the deceitful bandits [of Communists]." More importantly, "its leaders such as Feng Haichao [*Ct.* Fung Hoi Chiu] and He Kang [*Ct.* Ho Hong] were all members of our party, though in appearance they have kept us at arm's length so as not to invite suspicion from the Hong Kong Government."[121]

For the purpose of influencing workers in Hong Kong, the Third Group accepted Feng Haichao's proposal for issuing a *Trade Union Daily* (*Gongtuan ribao*) with start-up funds of HK$10,000 and began to "dispatch our comrades secretly to work as its editors." Chiang Kai-shek promptly endorsed the recommendation.[122] The newspaper eventually appeared as the *Laogong bao* (*Lo Kung Weekly News*), not a daily paper as the TUC initially proposed. Its first continuous run started on May 1, 1955, and lasted until June 1958, then resumed in February 1962 and printed its final issue in November 1964. In comparison to occasional publications by FTU-affiliated labor unions, which carried detailed reports on union accounts and local workers' stories about everyday life in Hong Kong, the *Laogong bao* had no such coverage. It focused on anti-

---

119. "港澳總支部一年來重要工作" (Important achievements by the Hong Kong–Macau branch in the past year).

120. See "Trade Unions and Trade Disputes Ordinance, 1948," clause 7. In "Historical Laws of Hong Kong."

121. 張其昀, 鄭彥棻 Zhang Qijun and Zheng Yanfen, "為港九工團擬刊行工團日報請撥開辦費港幣壹萬元" (Application for starting funds of HK$10,000 for the proposed Trade Unions Daily by the TUC), December 1, 1950; Guomindang gaizao weiyuanhui (Taipei), 台(39)改秘室字第0141號. Feng and He were also enlisted by the Hong Kong government as workers' representatives on the Labour Advisory Board in the 1950s.

122. "為港九工團擬刊行工團日報請撥開辦費港幣壹萬元" (Application for starting funds of HK$10,000 for the proposed Trade Unions Daily by the TUC).

Communist propaganda echoing the Guomindang organ in Hong Kong, the *Xianggang shibao*.[123]

Guomindang operatives succeeded in competing with the FTU for influence among workers. According to a General Branch report, it had made "great progress" in regaining influence over labor organizations by 1952. Their operatives were able to infiltrate eleven FTU-affiliated labor unions, persuading some members to leave and form separate "free labor unions." Desertions occurred in the Motor Drivers General Union, the Trade Union of Workers in Foreign-Style Services, and the Seamen's Union, all among the strongest in the FTU. In addition, Guomindang operatives tried to infiltrate ten more FTU-affiliated unions, including the Tramway Union, which they viewed as the "headquarters" of the FTU.[124] The Third Group in Taiwan recognized that "works done by the Hong Kong–Macau General Branch have been most distinctive in the labor movement, followed by that in the cultural and educational circles." It commended Feng Haichao's "most important role" and comparable contributions by He Kang, who had just received training in the eighteenth class of the Revolutionary Practice Institute (Geming shijian yanjiuyuan) in Taipei. The Third Group wished to have both of them as representatives of Hong Kong and Macau to participate in Taiwan's Seventh National People's Congress in 1952, but selected an alternative to keep Feng Haichao's party membership secret.[125]

---

123. The *Laogong bao* (*Lo Kung Weekly News*), issued by the TUC, is not held in the Main Library of the University of Hong Kong, which has a Special Collection of Hong Kong. The only place I found some issues of this newspaper is the archive of the TUC's competitor, the FTU. For publication information, see Kan and Chu (eds.), 89. Comparison between the *Laogong bao* and FTU-affiliated union newspapers is drawn from my survey of the newsletters and monthly journals or annual reports published by four major labor unions: Seamen's Union, the General Union of Motor Drivers, Union of Workers in Foreign-Style Employment, and General Union of Textile Workers.

124. 張其昀, 谷正綱 Zhang Qijun and Gu Zhenggang, "將來反港九匪化工會進展情況" (Prospect of counter-offensive against banditry control of trade unions in Hong Kong and Kowloon), May 2, 1952, Guomindang gaizao weiyuanhui (Taipei), 台(41)改秘室字第0200號.

125. 張其昀, 鄭彥棻 Zhang Qijun and Zheng Yanfen, "第七次全國人民代表大會港澳區代表遴選" (Selection of representatives for Hong Kong–Kowloon dis-

The changes within Hong Kong's labor organizations were not missed by the colonial state. In 1953, the Labour Department reported that several former FTU-affiliated unions had severed their ties to realign themselves with the right-wing TUC, thus becoming "free" trade unions. Most of these unions, the Labour Department quickly added, "are weak in membership and therefore poor financially," implying that money might have played a role in their switch to the right.[126] Unlike the Third Group in Taiwan, the Labour Department made a dismal assessment on these breakaway unions in 1953 that were "tied up politically with the Right":

> The so-called "free" trade union movement has proved a failure. The 26 trade unions which were formed from break-away elements of left-wing unions have an estimated paying membership of only some 2,800. There could be little complaint if these unions were in capable hands and if the interests of their members were the prime consideration. Unfortunately a number of unions have been guilty of all kinds of dubious practices such as gambling on the premises, collection of contributions from the public by doubtful means and spending of welfare funds for other than welfare purposes.[127]

The dubious practices and mismanagement of union funds echoed longstanding practices within GMD-controlled labor unions like the one in the textile industry and the Trade Union of Paint Workers when affiliated with the right-wing TUC. Around the same time, U.S. intelligence in Hong Kong too observed that right-wing labor unions "frequently used" their premises "for gambling purposes in order to raise money for the support of the unions."[128] However unpromising the practice, Guomindang operations had made a vigorous comeback in Hong Kong.

From late 1951 onward, physical attacks highlighted a violent front of General Branch operations. More than fifty physical assaults by Guomindang

---

trict at the seventh national people's assembly), September 22, 1952, Guomindang gaizao weiyuanhui (Taipei), 台(41)改秘室字第0395號, 黨史館.

126. *LDAR* 1952–1953, 32.

127. *LDAR*, 1953–1954, 37.

128. Anonymous, "The Scope and Success of Taiwan Operations in Hong Kong," undated report by staff members of the U.S. Consulate-General in Hong Kong, sent by the U.S. ambassador to Taiwan to George Yeh, foreign minister of the ROC, on June 2, 1955; cited in Chan Man-lok, 117.

agents or sympathizers on workers with left-wing preferences took place in just four months in late 1951. British police took part on one occasion, beating a worker carrying sheet music of a popular mainland song.[129] In the second half of 1952, physical attacks on businesses connected to China and FTU-affiliated unions became frequent occurrences. On July 7 four Guomindang sympathizers "forcibly entered the premises of the Hong Kong branch of the (Communist) Bank of Communication, assaulted a watchman, and destroyed bank documents and records."[130] Severe disturbances broke out in early October when Governor Grantham was on leave in England. During the night of September 30, "an organised demonstration was staged against left-wing workers in a silk mill in the New Territories." The next morning, on the national day of the People's Republic of China, "a gang of 100 [Anti-Communist Anti-Russian Youth] League members began stoning the workers' headquarters." Four similar attacks broke out, but swift police action stopped them from developing into widespread riots. Two days later, eight Anti-Communist Anti-Russian Youth League members made another "pre-arranged attack on decorations erected by Communist employees at Bailey's Yard."[131] On Double Ten, the national day celebrated by the Guomindang, six pro-Communist unions were attacked by mobs. According to Reuters, "a crowd broke down the doors" of the Electrical Workers' Union office, "overpowered Communist officials, damaged office furniture, scattered union documents in the street and tore the red flag to shreds." By evening, at least twelve such clashes had erupted at various locations on the Kowloon Peninsula. By one unofficial

---

129. "香港我居民受迫害, 新華社作翔實報導, 蔣匪殘餘竟被慫容行兇, 四個月來發生事件多達五十多起" (The Xinhua makes detailed report on repression against our Chinese residents in Hong Kong; remnants of the Guomindang bandits were encouraged to carry out physical attacks, more than fifty incidents occurred in the past four months), *Wenhui bao*, November 20, 1951, 4.

130. CO 1023/101, 96. The untitled report appears to be an item in the "Extracted from Weekly Intelligence Report" by the Special Branch, 96–98, as an attachment to "Inward Telegram, from Grantham to the Secretary of State for the Colonies (Secret)," October 14, 1952, CO 1023/101, 99.

131. These incidents were cited by the political adviser at the Colonial Secretariat of Hong Kong. See Secret, G. W. Aldington (Hong Kong) to E. H. Jacobs-Larkcom (Danshui), November 27, 1952, CO 1023/101, 77–78, 80–82, citation from 77.

count, ten people were "seriously injured when beaten up or stones [*sic*]." The authorities mobilized hundreds of armed police wearing helmets and carrying riot shields and called out the Special Hong Kong Volunteer Police Reserve to help maintain order. They "fired tear gas into an angry crowd of 1,000 Chinese Nationalists demonstrating outside the pro-Communist Carpenters Union office in Kowloon." In the end, thirty-five rioters were arrested.[132]

Although the police labeled the events "minor disturbances," an internal report by the Special Branch, forwarded by Grantham to London, indicated that the clashes were carefully engineered in Taiwan. The four men who attacked the Hong Kong branch of the Bank of Communication arrived in Taiwan a month after they were deported from Hong Kong. They were "given a civic welcome in Taipei" and praised by Deng Wenyi, vice-minister of the interior.[133] "Some of these incidents may have been precipitated by left wing organisations' decision to fly Communist flags on this occasion," the report noted, "but demonstrators had in most cases been paid to stir up trouble by Nationalist agents and had been assured that any fines they might incur would be refunded." In particular, "these provocations were organised by the 'anti-Communist anti-Russian Youth Association' which has direct links with Taiwan."[134]

What might have also emboldened Guomindang-directed agents in Hong Kong was an official decision in late 1952 that could have been easily interpreted as Britain's further move to the right in the colony. On October 8, 1952, two days before the attacks on the FTU-affiliated unions, Hong Kong's chief justice delivered his final ruling on thirty-one disputed airplanes in favor of the plaintiff, American Civil Air Transport.[135] This ended a protracted case involving the U.S. purchase of seventy-one airplanes formerly owned by the Central Air Transport Corporation (CATC) and the China National Aviation Corporation (CNAC). The decision reversed an initial ruling by Hong Kong's Supreme Court denying U.S. ownership of the planes after CATC and CNAC managers and staff pledged allegiance to the People's Republic of China in

132. Reuter newsfeed, October 10, 1952, CO 1023/101, 101–7.

133. CO 1023/101, 96–98.

134. "Extract from Weekly Intelligence Report, 14 Oct. 1952," CO 1023/101, 98.

135. "Second Aircraft Case in Hong Kong," *The Times* (London), October 8, 1952, 5.

November 1949.[136] Although Hong Kong did so reluctantly, submission to U.S. pressure invited unwanted troubles to its door. With a professed desire to remain neutral, British quietly deported troublesome Guomindang operatives in Hong Kong. Right-wing lawbreakers were sent to Taiwan to preempt future conflict. The approach soon turned out to be inadequate for preventing disruptive and destructive activities.

The battle against Taiwan-led penetration into Hong Kong became long and entangled, partly because Britain's consul in Taiwan was under constant pressure to approve visa applications to British territories. Since Great Britain's de jure recognition of the People's Republic of China in January 1950, passports issued by the Guomindang-led Republic of China (ROC) had become technically invalid in British-held territories. Concerned with keeping Hong Kong safe from China's partisan conflict, the Executive Council strictly controlled visas to prevent entrance of potentially subversive elements. Only briefly in late 1949 did the British consulate at Danshui (Tamsui) exercise its authority to grant visas to ROC passport holders before "the numbers of applicants" overwhelmed its staff. Hong Kong authorities and the British consul at Danshui made arrangement in January 1950 to route all applications for entry visas from ROC passport holders through travel agencies.[137] Hong Kong immigration authorities thus gained leverage in reviewing applications while limiting the power of the British consul at Danshui.

Immediately, ferocious protests against the visa restrictions erupted in Taiwan. Demonstrations sprang up in front of the British consulate, and officials frequently complained to the British consul. Zheng Yanfen, director of the Third Group of the GMDCRC, applied for a visa to Hong Kong and was refused in late 1952. Subsequently, British consul E. H. Jacobs-Larkcom had to endure a "stormy interview" with a high official in Taiwan. It forced Jacobs-Larkcom to seek help from the U.S. chargé d'affaires in Taipei to mediate on his behalf and pacify angry ROC officials. Constant pressure in Taiwan also

136. "四千員工通電歸向人民，中航央航正式起義" (4,000 employees telegraphed to join the people; CATC & CNAC revolted), *Wenhui bao*, November 10, 1949, 1.

137. Confidential, "Memorandum for Executive Council: Entry into Hong Kong from Formosa," March 31, 1953, CO 1023/101, 35–38, citation from 35. The memo appears to be authored by the commissioner of police.

forced Jacobs-Larkcom to appeal for "a more lenient entry visa policy on the part of the Hong Kong authorities" because it would result in "improving the background atmosphere" and because "95% of our applications relate to Hong Kong."[138] He protested directly to the political adviser at Hong Kong, a representative of the Foreign Office, for rejecting 20–50 percent of entry visa applications from Taiwan.[139]

The visa dispute between Hong Kong and the British consul at Danshui revealed real problems that the Hong Kong police had monitored during the Guomindang revival. In repudiating Jacobs-Larkcom's protest that Hong Kong was too harsh on Taiwan visa applicants, Geoffrey Aldington, political adviser at the Colonial Secretariat of Hong Kong, insisted that the rejections stemmed from concerns for "internal security" in the colony. In 1952, he indicated, "the primary concern of the Hong Kong Government in this matter is not the fear of adverse Communist propaganda which Jacobs-Larkcom suggests," but "a new element of truculence on the part of the pro-Nationalist faction" which manifested itself in the October disturbances.[140] In reply, Aldington detailed organizational links in one of the Guomindang-directed operations in Hong Kong:

> We have known for about the last two years that a pro-Nationalist organization affiliated to the "Anti-Communist, Anti-Russian Youth League" existed in the Colony, but it was not until the beginning of 1952 that its activities went beyond the writing and posting of anti-Communist slogans and the provision, and if necessary invention, of information against known Communist institutions here with the objective of inciting Police raids on their promises. In January and February of this year it became obvious that systematic attempts were being made to penetrate labour and educational circles in the Colony in the Nationalist interest and to establish a form of control in the squatter areas. The director of these operations was Pan Chiu-kit (彭超傑) who in May last visited Taiwan to undergo a short training course.

---

138. Confidential, Jacobs-Larkcom to C. H. Johnston, September 30, 1952, CO 1023/101, citation from 91.

139. Confidential, E. H. Jacobs-Larkcom (Danshui) to G. W. Aldington (Hong Kong), February 25, 1953, CO 1023/101, 71–72.

140. Confidential, Geoffrey Aldington (Hong Kong) to C. E. Johnston (China and Korea Department, Foreign Office), November 4, 1952, CO 1023/101, 87–88.

Then he emphasized that "money was being freely used for the purpose of provoking demonstrations against left-wing headquarters, and that extensive plans in this connection had been made for the Double Tenth."[141]

Guomindang-initiated provocations failed to develop into large-scale riots in October 1952, Aldington revealed, because Hong Kong police received a tip, and "extensive plans were made in advance which enabled the Police to break up individual incidents before the crowds could be worked up." The thirty-two arrested after these attacks, who were deported to Taiwan, "left quietly and without publicity."[142] Having seen ample evidence of the danger of Guomindang-led activities in Hong Kong, the Colonial Office in London endorsed Aldington's position. Writing to the War Office, J. B. Sidebotham, head of the Hong Kong Department, wrote that "the dangers to internal security in Hong Kong do not always arise from Communist activities as such, but that actions of the Anti-Communist element can be fully capable of causing disturbances."[143]

Operating as an underground organization in Hong Kong where political parties were outlawed, the Guomindang Hong Kong–Macau General Branch not only depended on increased financial support from Taiwan but also on a particular kind of local connection. Reliance on secret societies as a tool of social control was steeped in Guomindang history and continued to play a big role in its Hong Kong revival.[144] It is impossible to completely depict the overlap of some secret societies with the Guomindang organization in Hong Kong, although internal correspondence of the Third Group provided glimpses into such continued cooperation. The Yi-an General Association of Industry and Commerce in Kowloon, the Third Group noted, was "a strong organization of

---

141. Secret, G. W. Aldington (Hong Kong) to E. H. Jacobs-Larkcom (Danshui), November 28, 1952, CO 1023/101, 77–78, citation from 77.

142. Aldington to Jacobs-Larkcom, November 27, 1952.

143. Secret, J. B. Sidebotham (Colonial Office) to Major A. E. Tracy (War Office), December 9, 1952, CO 1023/101, 76.

144. The Guomindang's use of the Green Gang in Shanghai during its Communist purge in 1927 was well documented. The study by Frederic Wakeman Jr. added major insights concerning how its Guomindang-led government and municipal management were compromised by significant entanglement with criminal organizations. See Wakeman.

the Triad." Its chair, Mr. Xiang Qian, was not a Guomindang member, "but always eager to help our party's work, especially in recent years he has worked particularly hard." Xiang's attempt from Hong Kong to organize anti-Communist activities on the mainland attracted the attention of Hong Kong authorities. He was deported to Taiwan in June 1953.[145] Even though the colonial state became more vigilant, cooperation between secret societies and Guomindang agents in Hong Kong soon caught it off guard.

1956 Riots

In 1956, Hong Kong's economy regained vibrancy for the first time since the United Nations embargo against China sent it spiraling downward. Industry expanded. Its products found new markets in Southeast Asia and elsewhere, and imports from China also grew. Industrial expansion necessitated land expansion. A major industrial town, Kwun Tong, emerged from reclaimed land by Kowloon Bay.[146] Tsuen Wan, the rural area where He Zhuozhong grew up and spent his youth in the underground resistance, became a growing industrial town as more factories and shops lined its major streets. It was still an outlying area of urban Kowloon without easy public transportation. In contrast, west Kowloon had become densely populated with three large government-subsidized resettlement estates at Li Cheng Uk, Shep Kip Mei, and Tai Hang Tung. Among the more than 125,000 residents were many relocated squatters and civil war refugees newly arrived in Hong Kong. Material comforts in these estates did not compare to those in industrialized societies, but the multistory buildings were far safer than squatter sheds. An average room of 120 square feet housed a family of five, a room of eighty-six square feet sufficed for a smaller family. Each flat consisted of one such room with neither kitchen nor bathroom. Residents shared communal washrooms and cooked, illegally, on narrow verandas that functioned as walkways to the flats.

---

145. 張其昀, 鄭彥棻, 鄭介民 Zhang Qijun, Zheng Yanfen, and Zheng Jiemin, "向前簡歷及工作概略" (A C.V. of Xiang Qian), July 22, 1953, Guomindang gaizao weiyuanhui (Taipei), 台(42)中祕室字第0274號.

146. *LDAR* 1955–1956, 7.

Elsie Tu (formerly Elsie Elliot), a British missionary who arrived in 1951 and worked and lived among squatters, noted that these estates were often described as "rabbit warrens."[147]

Relations with the mainland showed positive signs. Probably resulting from a "private visit" by Grantham and his wife to Beijing the previous fall, travel restrictions were significantly relaxed on both sides of Lowu for the first time since 1950. During the Chinese New Year, the number of Chinese workers going home to Guangzhou or to villages in Guangdong province was so large that it caused anxiety in the poorly paid trades. Employers feared that wages would have to be increased to maintain production.[148] In June, at the invitation of the Chinese Chamber of Commerce, a Chinese folk artists troupe made a month-long visit to perform in Hong Kong, the first such cultural event since 1949.[149] Its first performance attracted an audience of more than 1,400 who cheered and applauded ecstatically. Performances were all sold out. British officials came to watch the show and praised the artists.[150] While folk artists brought excitement to Hong Kong theater, Bishop Ronald Hall was giving reports around Hong Kong on his recent visit to Red China. He had lunched with Premier Zhou Enlai and toured six major cities to investigate churches there. He was impressed that the Chinese government allowed freedom of religion and provided children and the elderly with good care.[151] Professor Chen Junbao, known for his liberalism, had already sent his children to the mainland for higher education. He himself had made extended trips to the

---

147. Tu, 45.

148. HKLB 1955–1956, 7.

149. Chen Junbao, June 21–July 9, 1956, 3:505–10; "中國民間藝術團演出招待香港各界名流" (Chinese Folk Artists Troupe performed and held a party for social celebrities in Hong Kong), *Renmin ribao*, June 25, 1956, 1; "中國民間藝術團離開香港回廣州" (Chinese Folk Artists Troupe left Hong Kong and returned to Guangzhou), *Renmin ribao*, July 20, 1956, 1.

150. "首次獻演, 盛況空前, 藝術團哄動觀眾" (First performance elicited unprecedented enthusiasm; Folk Troupe impressed the audience), *Wenhui bao*, June 22, 1956, 4. The paper carried continuous reports almost daily about the troupe's performance in Hong Kong. For British government officials' attendance, see "藝術團演出更動人, 港府人員蒞場觀看" (More impressive performance by the Folk Troupe; members of HK Government joined the audience), *Wenhui bao*, July 2, 1952, 4.

151. "歷六大城市訪各地教會, 何明華談訪華行" (Bishop Hall visited churches in six cities and spoke about his visit to China), *Wenhui bao*, June 26, 1956, 4.

mainland almost annually since 1950. Early in 1956 Chen organized at least two tour groups to the mainland sponsored by the Chinese Reform Association. He visited Beijing and the northeast for two summer months with another tour group—his third visit to the area since 1950.[152]

Despite relaxation on visits to the mainland, Hong Kong Chinese no longer loudly expressed their emotional attachment to the mainland through public proclamations as they did in late 1949. Mass organizations chose to celebrate the anniversary of the People's Republic relatively quietly within their own circles. A proud Chinese nationalist, Chen Junbao became particularly busy as October approached. On September 30, 1956, he was guest speaker at a luncheon hosted by the Chinese Reform Association at the Jinling Restaurant in the Western District to celebrate the PRC's seventh anniversary. Then he went on to the Guangdong Restaurant, where more than 3,000 teachers held another celebration. In the evening, he was among more than 1,000 guests at a party hosted by the Hong Kong Office of Xinhua News Agency at the Gloucester Hotel in Central.[153] Eleven days later, Chen participated in the celebration hosted by the Chinese Reform Association for the Double Ten. He took the opportunity to comment on the limited achievements of China's 1911 Revolution, which failed to prevent China's terrible fate of being "sliced up like a melon" during the warlord period—an allusion to the country's current division across the Taiwan Strait under the Cold War.[154]

As he spoke, Chen probably had no idea that China's divisions were literally exploding in Hong Kong. Violence engulfed the colony so rapidly that regular police actions were futile. Even the *Sing Tao Jih Bao*, decisively pro-Guomindang in recent years, set aside a whole page to report on the violent clashes that first erupted in west Kowloon.[155]

The Double Ten in 1956 began, as it had over the past few years, with Hong Kong residents awakening to Nationalist blue-sky-white-sun flags everywhere. Flags were far more numerous this time around. At Li Cheng Uk, a

---

152. Chen Junbao, vol. 3, passim.

153. Chen Junbao, September 30, 1956, 3:541.

154. Chen Junbao, October 10, 1956, 3:545.

155. With a headline across the page, "李鄭屋村徙置區昨因懸旗引起大衝突" (Flag caused big clash at Li Cheng Uk resettlement yesterday), *Sing Tao Jih Bao* carried multiple reports on the conflict at Li Cheng Uk, the attacks on the Garden Bakery and other stores, and police response. See *Sing Tao Jih Bao*, October 11, 1956, 14.

resettlement estate in west Kowloon, the housing staff noticed not only small Nationalist flags but two very large symbols marking Double Ten—Chinese characters that consisted of two joined crosses—pasted on the outer wall of Block G facing the street. Observing Urban Council rules, the staff officer had the symbols removed. Soon after, around 11 a.m., a crowd of 300 to 400 gathered at the Resettlement Office demanding replacement of the Double Ten symbol.[156] A small group of police came but failed to disperse them. Although the crowd went away after the housing staff put a few flags back on the wall, it soon returned, swelling to 1,000 by early afternoon. To appease their wrath, rowdies demanded, the housing officer must make public apologies to the crowd and in Chinese newspapers, erect big portraits of Sun Yat-sen and Chiang Kai-shek with a large Nationalist flag, and provide and discharge 100,000 firecrackers. The police noted "at least one agitator" in the crowd rousing tempers. Taking police reluctance to use force as a sign of weakness or acquiescence, some of the mob broke into the Resettlement Office and attacked its staff, to the accompaniment of loud cheers. The crowd turned on the police when they tried to rescue the housing staff and "pelted them with mineral water bottles from a nearby shop." It dispersed only after the police fired tear gas.[157]

The confrontation in Li Cheng Uk was merely a prelude to horrendous riots that engulfed Kowloon for the next two days.[158] Western Kowloon, where the population was dense with former civil war refugees, and Tsuen Wan, a newly emerging industrial town with seventy-five registered factories and workshops, plus unregistered ones, were the bloodiest sites. Pro-Nationalist rioters attacked left-wing union headquarters, factories where left-wing unions had strong influence, stores that carried goods from the mainland or had flown the five-star red flag of the People's Republic of China on October 1, and other pro-mainland mass organizations. For two days, gangs of rioters beat up workers and staff members in pro-mainland establishments, then looted and set fire to shops and factories. The official report counted thirty-

---

156. Hong Kong Government, "Report on the Riots in Kowloon and Tsuen Wan, October 10th to 12th, 1956," CO 1030/389, citation from 6. Hereafter cited as "Report on the Riots, 1956."

157. "Report on the Riots, 1956," 7.

158. If not otherwise noted, the following description is based on "Report on the Riots, 1956."

nine incidents occurring in the Li Cheng Uk estate, the Tai Hang Tung estate, Shamshuipo, Mongkok, Yaumatei, Kowloon City, Hung Hom, Ngau Chi Wan, Ngau Tau Kok, and Ho Man Tin.

Arson, beatings, and looting went hand in hand in these attacks. Seventeen fires broke out in Kowloon alone, but the Fire Brigade was often unable to reach sites of fire because burning vehicles or looted merchandise blocked the streets. One major fire took place at the pro-mainland Heung To School, just a quarter of a mile northeast of the Tai Hang Tung resettlement estate where "settlers of predominantly Nationalist sympathies" lived. Between 3 and 4 a.m. on October 11, "the mob set fire to an adjacent hut and forced their way into the compound, looting the ground floor of the school and setting fire to the furniture etc. outside." When the police arrived, they found about twenty staff members on the upper floor. They had repulsed the first mob attack but failed to stem the second one.[159] A few fortunate defenders were able to withstand attacks with their neighbors' help. At the office of Metal Works Union at Pei Ho Street in Kowloon, for instance, union staff and workers defended themselves with large pots of boiling water, which they held to scare away any rioter who ran upstairs to their office. When the mob threatened to set the building ablaze, neighbors shouted at the rioters and forced them away.[160] Others were less fortunate. Swiss Vice-Consul Irtz Ernst and his wife were in a taxi passing through the main intersection near the Li Cheng Uk estate in the early afternoon of October 11. Rioters stopped their taxi, overturned the car, and set it on fire. The taxi driver escaped but both the Ernsts were trapped inside and severely burned. Days later Mrs. Ernst died in the hospital.[161] Only after this European casualty did the acting commissioner of police permit gun fire to be "used without hesitation where necessary."[162]

In contrast to the "mobile and elusive" mobs in Kowloon, the rioters at Tsuen Wan carried out organized plans by recognized leaders. Located about five miles west of the chief center of rioting in urban Kowloon, in 1956 Tsuen Wan had only a few main roads. Factories provided dormitories so workers

---

159. "Report on the Riots, 1956," 16.

160. Zhou Yi (2002), 129. Zhou was then the secretary of Metal Works Trade Union and among the dozen defenders of the union's office.

161. "Hongkong Riots Subsiding; Curfew Still in Force," *The Times* (London), October 13, 1956, 6.

162. "Report on the Riots, 1956," 20.

need not commute long distances. The pro-mainland FTU and pro-Taiwan TUC had somewhat equal constituency among the workers. Before the riots, right-wing unions held a number of meetings in early October to plan the Double Ten celebration, followed by one special meeting on October 10 of "Nationalist partisans and members of Triad societies."[163]

Riots first broke out at the Pao Hsing Cotton Mill, where management had previously ordered the removal of large, pro-Taiwan slogans from dormitory windows. In the afternoon of October 11, "some men carrying large Nationalist flags on long bamboo poles" arrived outside the factory and planted the flags there, while a crowd of male factory workers dressed in khaki shorts and shirts began to shout abuse at the factory management. The mob attacked passersby on foot, in buses, and in cars. Some rioters tried to overturn and set fire to vehicles, while others put up a barricade of rocks across the road. A subdivisional inspector leading three sections of police and thirty more plainclothes detectives arrived with tear gas and guns in hand but dared not to use them because the mob threatened to burn the bus passengers alive if the police opened fire. When some rioters opened the main factory gate from inside, the mob burst through the police cordon into the building. They set fire to the cotton, poured kerosene on the floors, and torched the factory building. Rioters then broke into the dormitory, looted and smashed things inside, and attacked left-wing workers there.[164]

Once inside the Pao Hsing Cotton Mill, the mob made demands that "the Nationalist flag be flown, left wing workers discharged and the staff official who had ordered the decorations to be removed on October 8 dismissed." The management refused. The mob then brought forth "a stranger who appeared to be in some authority over the rioters"; threatening to burn down the factory, he forced the manager to accept their demands and extorted payment of HK$1,000. Only then did he order the fire to be extinguished and led the mob out of the factory.[165] A similar pattern of actions was repeated in attacks on five other factories. Each mob arrived at the site with Nationalist flag bearers in the lead, attacked left-wing workers with fists and blunt instruments, and looted. Each attack culminated with threats of fire or actual arson and extor-

---

163. "Report on the Riots, 1956," 31.
164. "Report on the Riots, 1956," 34.
165. "Report on the Riots, 1956," 35.

tion. At one of these, the Kowloon Textile Factory, the mob got more greedy and forced its management to pay HK$2,500 for the five Nationalist flags they hoisted on the premises.[166]

Overwhelmed and intimidated, the Tsuen Wan police withdrew to their station without using tear gas or firearms. The rioters ran amok. For nearly seven hours, the main group of rioters, estimated at from 500 to 1,000 strong and "led by men with large Nationalist flags," attacked the Tsuen Wan clinic of the FTU, the welfare center, a cooperative store, the library of the Hong Kong–Kowloon Spinning, Weaving and Dyeing Workers' General Union, and the welfare center of the Hong Kong–Kowloon Silk Weavers General Union. Rioters looted these establishments and set them on fire. They brutally beat the staff and workers they found. At the workers' clinic, rioters beat up the two male staff members, stripped the four nurses, and gang-raped one of them. When the pharmacist tried to shield his female colleagues, he was beaten to death.[167] The mob made a public show outside the Tsuen Wan Theater. Left-wing "prisoners" were brought to a large bamboo structure decorated with anti-Communist slogans and pictures and forced to "bow repeatedly or 'kow-tow'" and shout anti-Communist slogans. The mob then stoned and beat them mercilessly until they lost consciousness.[168]

By midnight, as regular military troops began patrolling the area enforcing a curfew, a total of fifteen violent incidents had shattered this industrial town, leaving eight workers dead and more than one hundred serious casualties requiring hospitalization.[169] Wounds inflicted on Gu Huizhen, who had been gang-raped, were so severe that she was rushed to Guangzhou, along with

---

166. "Report on the Riots, 1956," 62.

167. Zhou Yi (2002), 143, 144. Zhou's account, based on his experiences, his access to FTU-affiliated union staff and officials as well as to FTU documents, differs from the official report, which noted that no rape occurred during the riots. I choose to take Zhou's account, not just because he personally experienced the event at one of the left-wing unions. I do so also because Chinese girls and young women, as well as society at large, viewed such sexual assaults with profound shame and chose not to report them. That choice was similar to those occurred during the Japanese conquest of Hong Kong. British accounts therefore missed, if not ignored, a significant part of the reality.

168. "Report on the Riots," 37. It is here that the official report indicates "there is no evidence of rape."

169. "Report on the Riots," 62.

other severely wounded workers, for medical treatment. In mid-December she had recovered enough to appear in a public rally and speak openly about her trauma and suffering during the riots.[170] Damage caused by looting and arson as well as widespread fear among workers kept factories from resuming normal operation until early November.

The riots of October 1956 had no parallel in Hong Kong's peacetime history, though brutal mob attacks echoed the hellish violence when Hong Kong came under siege and fell to the Japanese in 1941. Even though British official reports invariably labeled grassroots protests as "riots" in the past, never had there been such large-scale, well-coordinated riots like the ones in 1956. The Chinese government quickly discerned its political import and demanded that British authorities take swift measures. The *Renmin ribao* voiced official concerns on October 12 through an "Observer's Comment" on the front page. The next day, Premier Zhou Enlai called the British chargé d'affaires for a formal meeting and made a "strong protest" to British authorities for their failure to stop riots instigated by Guomindang agents, which resulted in significant loss of life and property.[171] Never had an event in Hong Kong aroused the sustained attention of the official *Renmin ribao* as the riots in 1956. It ran coverage continuously for twenty days about the event and its wide repercussions on the mainland and in Hong Kong.

The Kowloon riots, as the event was called officially, had done so much damage to the reputation of the colony as an oasis of "law and order" that the colonial state needed an explanation or an excuse for its neglect. The official report, eventually made public in early 1957, deemphasized the political

---

170. Fang Li (方力), "廣東省和廣州市各界人民集會, 慰問九龍事件中受害同胞, 要求嚴懲國民黨特務份子, 防止再發生暴亂" (People of all circles in Guangzhou and Guangdong Province give their comfort to the victims of the Kowloon Incident; they demanded punishment of special agents of the Guomindang and preventing repetition of the riot), *Renmin ribao*, December 17, 1956; Gu Huizhen, "只要我還有一口氣我就要報仇" (I shall seek retribution as long as I am still breathing), *Renmin ribao*, December 17, 1956.

171. "國民黨特務分子在九龍製造大暴亂" (Special agents of the Guomindang created brutal riots in Kowloon), *Renmin ribao*, October 12, 1956, 1; "對於香港英當局未能制止國民黨特務所組織的暴亂, 周恩來總理提出嚴重抗議" (Regarding British authorities in Hong Kong for failing to stop the riots by Guomindang agents, Prime Minister Zhou Enlai lodged serious protest), *Renmin ribao*, October 14, 1956, 1.

meaning of the riots. Instead, it cited three situations among the Chinese as the causes: the large number of refugees from the mainland who held anti-Communist views and lived in frustration in Hong Kong, the spontaneity of the initial event at Li Cheng Uk estate, and Triad involvement that took advantage of the chaos to sustain the riots. As always, the official report commended the police for responding swiftly and responsibly. Emphasizing the spontaneity of the riots and the role of the criminal Triads did not exonerate the colonial state. Instead, it raised more questions about the riots dominated by numerous and persistent political symbols and messages.

Documents now available at the Guomindang Party History Archive at Taipei contradict British claims that the riots were apolitical. Just as Hong Kong authorities surmised the premeditated nature of the attacks in Tsuen Wan, evidence shows that the whole event in 1956 was planned in (if not executed by) Taiwan. A handwritten draft report dated October 13, 1956, by Zhang Lisheng and Zheng Yanfen, who directed the Third Group and oversaw operations of the Hong Kong–Macau General Branch of Guomindang, indicated that planning for the Double Ten celebration "has been on the way for a long time by us." They estimated that the total number of flags on display "exceeded one million" but claimed that the riots, arson, looting, and clashes with police were all "instigated by the Communist bandits." This, of course, was flatly refuted by British investigations and by the fact that all the victims were workers in left-wing unions.[172]

Other sources confirm that the Guomindang engineered to create a favorable atmosphere for itself in the colony. In late January 1957, weeks after Hong Kong's official report on the riots was published, the Chinese Reform Association issued a public statement, arguing that the report "failed to explain certain known facts," particularly the operation of Guomindang agents. The statement pointed out that "for many years past it has been the practice of the Kuomintang Party headquarters in Taiwan to dispatch crates containing millions of paper flags by ship," while "processions of cyclists provided by Kuomintang organsations have paraded the streets of Hongkong and Kowloon

---

172. 張厲生, 鄭彥棻 Zhang Lisheng and Zheng Yanfen, "關於本年國慶日香港九龍青山道徙置區因懸掛國旗引起之騷動事件" (About the riots in Kowloon Qingshan Road caused by hanging national flags on the day of national day), 2, Guomindang gaizao weiyuanhui (Taipei), 台(45)中秘室登字第228號.

on October 10."[173] The facts in this statement echo those in secret reports by the Special Branch to London on Guomindang-directed operations in Hong Kong. The one million flags on display in the colony mentioned in Zhang Lisheng and Zheng Yanfen's report illustrate the critical role the Guomindang played in this heinous event.

Although the colonial state eventually mobilized regular troops to suppress the riots, left-wing unions did not feel that their calls for help had received a proper response. The Metal Works Union, which survived the mob attack because of neighborhood support, had sent a messenger to the police station for help; the police refused to listen and sent the messenger away.[174] At suburban industrial Tsuen Wan, where systematic attacks were launched on left-wing workers, labor unions, and factories, police refrained from using firearms, possibly motivated by self-protection. Continued violence could have been stopped much earlier than midnight because regular troops arrived in Tsuen Wan at 9:30 p.m. However, they focused on clearing blocked roads and helping the wounded. Not until two hours later did troops confront the mobs and enforce the curfew.[175] The puzzling delay, if not acquiescence to the rioters as journalist Zhou Yi has charged, left troubling questions about the official report and the official attitude toward working Chinese and left-wing labor in the post–Russell Street years.

The violent disturbances in 1956 underscored the profound changes that had taken place since 1948. Colonial Hong Kong's legal environment had been remolded in just two years, not to continue but to reverse and eliminate reforms in labor affairs once desired by London. Labor unions and other civic organizations identified with the People's Republic of China became the targets of official repression and eventually of rioting mobs. From the police action at Russell Street in 1950 to the systemic deportation of labor leaders and social activists, to the trial of the pro-mainland *Dagong bao* and the final deci-

---

173. "October Riots: Chinese Reform Association Statement Issued," *South China Morning Post and the Hongkong Telegraph*, January 31, 1957, 6.

174. Zhou Yi (2002), 129–30.

175. "Report on the Riots," 38–39.

sion on assets of the China National Aviation Corporation and the Central Air Transport Corporation in 1952, these official actions encouraged the rise of a political culture of hostility toward pro-mainland organizations in Hong Kong. To the public, these events clearly signaled British Hong Kong's partiality, not neutrality, which failed to keep a "delicate balance" in China's partisan conflict.[176]

The horrendous events in Hong Kong shocked and aroused questions in London as well. When Secretary of the State for the Colonies Alan Lennox-Boyd made a formal statement in the Parliament about the Kowloon riots on October 24, 1956, members of the House of Lords demanded to know if "the Hong Kong Government did not take due precautions against such a disturbance," or if "the troubles have been inspired from outside the Colony." Lord Lloyd, undersecretary of state for the colonies, defended British authorities in Hong Kong for having taken "every precaution" against disturbances and making "energetic and ... successful steps to restore law and order in the Colony."[177] But John Rankin, labour politician from Glasgow, Scotland, came to a different interpretation. He suggested that the extremely narrow franchise—16,000 out of nearly 3 million, or less than 1 percent of the total population eligible to elect the colony's Urban Council—might be a major cause of discontent.[178]

That criticism alluding to Hong Kong's failed constitutional reform was only a prelude to a more pungent critique of colonial governance in Hong Kong. In the debate on November 8, Rankin presented a lengthy, acerbic criticism of Hong Kong governance, in which he again argued that "poverty, low wages and evil housing conditions were the root causes of the trouble now taking place there." Surprisingly, he brought out a small detail that implicated both London and Hong Kong's colonial regime for the "industrial discontent." He told Parliament that Ken Baker, the labour officer appointed to Hong Kong in 1947, "was robbed of his status and functions and became an ordinary official of the Labour Office" because "the Hong Kong Government

---

176. See Tsang (1997b). Tsang emphasized British efforts in keeping neutrality in what he called a "delicate balance."

177. House of Lords (Britain), Debate, October 24, 1956, 199:989–90.

178. House of Commons (Britain), Debate, October 24, 1956, 5:558, 623–25.

did not like the appointment" and the Colonial Office approved Baker's demotion when the Tory Party returned to power in 1951.[179] Rankin pointed out the political polarity and complexity of Hong Kong society, where "many varied feelings that existed in the crowd" because "in Hong Kong there are people who are anti-European, there are those who are anti-Red, or pro-Red, and those who are anti-police. There are people who are anti-Rich." Without democratizing its political structure to properly channel and address social discontent, he argued, emotion "could be compounded" and "would express itself in the most violent terms."[180] Rankin accused the authoritarian government of Hong Kong as the cause for its failure to address the many problems in the colony because it was "composed entirely of officials and appointed members who are either yesmen or big business representatives." Understandably, Tory MPs strongly disagreed with him. But Rankin's description of the colony, drawn firsthand from a recent visit, was poignant:

> Hong Kong has everything. A lovely situation and squalid, overcrowded homes; riches and poverty that perpetuate a mocking disharmony; monopoly wherever one goes; virtue and vice that rub shoulders at every corner; good hearted men and women seeking to abolish these evils, others thriving on them. On that unstable infrastructure the October riots developed.[181]

Surely, Governor Grantham would strongly disagree. He had presided over reversing the imperial reform initiative and rebalanced leftist and rightist activism to keep Hong Kong safe from the contagious inspiration of a unified China. His term of governorship had been thrice renewed, an unmistakable indication of London's trust. Whenever he went to the United States, he promoted Hong Kong's importance as a beachhead of the anti-Communist free world. In a speech to the American Council on Foreign Relations at a dinner in New York in his honor, he reminded his audience that "Hong Kong is geographically a part of China" but "it has always played a large role in shaping Chinese politics" by presenting "a living example for the Chinese of a free life."[182] The violent riots rolling the colony into chaos could have nothing to

---

179. House of Commons (Britain), Debate, November 8, 1956, 5:560, 411.
180. House of Commons (Britain), Debate, November 8, 1956, 5:560, 412.
181. House of Commons (Britain), Debate, November 8, 1956, 5:410.
182. Grantham (1953).

do with his wise leadership but were caused by criminal elements in Chinese society. These troubles, of course, must be kept under constant watch, but this was the responsibility of his successors. In 1957, Sir Alexander completed his decade-long governorship, retired to England, and became an active member in the China Association, the leading organization of leading businessmen with century-long interests in China.

Conclusion

In 1958, exactly twenty years after Henry R. Butters surveyed labor conditions in Hong Kong, Assistant Labour Advisor Sheila Ann Ogilvie of the Colonial Office came to the colony to investigate labor conditions once again. Inspection at regular intervals had become routine in the 1950s. Ogilvie's visit would have taken place a year or two later if not for an uproar in Parliament over textile dumping from Hong Kong. In the five years between 1951 and 1956, annual imports to Britain of cotton textiles "made by underpaid Hong Kong labour" had risen eleven times, from five million square yards to fifty-five million square yards. Lancashire felt threatened.[1] The issue was brought to the House of Commons on the same day the secretary of state for the colonies first reported on the 1956 riots. Debate sessions followed in June 1957 and May and June 1958. MPs raised questions concerning the very low wages paid to Hong Kong textile workers—one-third to two-fifths of that paid in Britain—and their "excessive" hours of work.[2] Low wages and long hours were key areas of investigation, but Ogilvie discovered far more about labor conditions in Hong Kong.

A former factory inspector with a progressive outlook and a sharp eye for detail, Ogilvie had acquired firsthand experience in Scotland and from textile factories in over twenty British colonies and eight territories ranging from Puerto Rico to Egypt. Hong Kong was the first territory she had set foot in beyond Aden and Mauritius. During Hong Kong's hottest and most humid season, she visited fifty-two industrial workplaces, ranging from "first class to 'awfully scruffy'." Some of her visits occurred during night shifts between ten in the evening and three in the morning to ascertain working conditions on

---

1. House of Commons Debate, June 27, 1957, in House of Commons, 5:572, 382.

2. House of Commons Debate, October 24, 1956, House of Commons, 5:558, 621; House of Commons Debate, June 27, 1957, House of Commons, 5:572, 382; House of Commons Debate, May 15, 1958, House of Commons, 5:588, 595; House of Commons Debate, May 23, 1958, House of Commons, 5:588, 1731–42; House of Commons Debate, June 30, 1958, House of Commons, 5:590, 878–1012.

site.[3] She organized her report in four sections: physical conditions, labor relations, wages, and hours of work. Even though it appeared much shorter and narrower than the Butters report twenty years earlier, Ogilvie's discovery loudly echoed many of the same concerns. Moreover, she brought to light important problems beyond the patterns he had discerned.

Ogilvie captured critical features of industrial operations with an expert eye that compensated for her lack of language and local experience. The physical conditions of these establishments provided clues to technological changes and stubbornly tenacious patterns of practice in industrial Hong Kong. With a focus on textiles, she drew her observations from realities in industrial establishments employing as many as two thousand and as few as five workers. She was impressed by the up-to-date equipment and operating standards in most large factories, but was appalled by the overcrowding and absence of safety measures in the "disproportionately large" number of "scruffy" undertakings. Overcrowding in industrial manufacturing was a serious problem Butters had detailed in 1938, epitomized by a tailoring establishment where a worker suspended from a beam did ironing on a board similarly suspended in front of him. Such extremes did not appear in Ogilvie's report, but she still encountered widespread practice of manufacturing operations in the mezzanines and cocklofts of tenement houses. These establishments were "without through ventilation" due to very low ceilings, and modern motor-driven devices raised temperatures even higher in Hong Kong's sultry summer. In addition to poor air quality within substandard workshops, unguarded power presses and unfenced shafts under sewing machine benches frequently caused accidents. The few installed guards were "of very poor quality and easily removed."[4] Injuries caused by mechanized operations without worker protection, among other problems, had mobilized women workers to unionize after the war. It remained an outstanding problem a decade and a half later, despite the expan-

---

3. Sheila Ann Ogilvie, "Visit to Hong Kong," CO 2030/763, Labour Advisors Visit to Hong Kong (July 1958), 99–118; citation from 100. This twenty-page report to the Colonial Office is the formal one shared with the Hong Kong government, with relatively milder language and detailed data. Ogilvie also submitted a more candid assessment with forthright comments to the Colonial Office for internal circulation, which I cite as well. Citation used is based on file pagination, not the report's.

4. Ogilvie, "Visit to Hong Kong," 100–101.

sion of modern industries and presumed state intervention to reform labor affairs.

Along with poor working conditions, Ogilvie encountered poor wages and, as the MPs argued, excessive work hours, measured not by European standards but compared with other Asian countries. Some wage patterns continued from the old days: workers more often received piece rate compensation, not daily or hourly wages. This gave employers leverage in extracting maximum productivity and profit out of every worker. Skilled or semiskilled workers were best off: highly skilled mechanics could earn as much as HK$20 a day, whereas the daily wage of semi-skilled men and women in cotton spinning and weaving factories was HK$6–8. However, "generally women but not only beginners and young women" earned much less, only HK$2–3 a day. Because rest days were unpaid, taking one day off to rest each week meant their earnings fell to HK$50–70 a month.[5] Moreover, the work week averaged more than sixty or seventy hours. These basic conditions shaped the work and lives of the majority of women workers (more than one-third of the labor force) and close to half of the male workers. Workdays of eleven and a half hours were common, especially in Chinese-owned operations.[6] Nonetheless, Ogilvie's data only reflected the working conditions of a fraction of Hong Kong's industrial labor force: at 170,000 in registered factories and workshops. Official statistics show at least 150,000 more must be counted as industrial labor who worked in "unregistrable" establishments. Together with those working on construction and transportation, they amount to 17 percent (excluding 34,700 workers in government employment) or 18.5 percent in the total population of 2,677,000 (Table 5).[7] Considering the repeated comments in official annual reports attributed increased employment to the rapid growth of light industries, this half million industrial and urban workforce is likely an underestimate, which has overlooked the legion of people working on the fringe for the registered and unregistered industrial establishments.

Why did the majority of the Hong Kong workforce toil for such excessively long hours? In defending "the Hong Kong way" against criticism from the

---

5. Ogilvie, "Visit to Hong Kong," 106.

6. Ogilvie, "Visit to Hong Kong," 109.

7. For population of nearly 2.7 million in 1957, see *HKAR*, 1957, 36.

Table 5. Official estimate of workforce in major lines of employment, 1957–1958

Line		Estimated Workforce
Registered factories/workshops		170,000
Unregistrable establishments		150,000
Construction		120,000
Transportation		21,000
Government		34,700
	Subtotal	495,700
Agriculture		200,000
Fishing		64,200
	Subtotal	264,200
Total		759,900

Source: *LDAR 1957–1958*, 13

MPs, Undersecretary of State for the Colonies John Profumo argued that "long hours of work are a traditional feature of Oriental life."[8] He was not alone at the Colonial Office in taking that view. R. G. D. Houghton, a former assistant labour adviser sent by the Colonial Office to Hong Kong in 1951 to investigate labor conditions, argued in a very long report that "to many Chinese … life and work have become so closely integrated that they are almost one and the same thing."[9] Ogilvie's investigation shattered this official myth. Hong Kong workers had no choice but to work very long hours. They could not survive otherwise. Subsistence-level living for a single person, "taking no account of soap, clothes or any kind of extras at all, required $60 per month." This included HK$45 for basic food and HK$15 for a bed space in a workers' dormitory if the factory provided one. Single workers could choose to rent a bed space elsewhere, while those with families rented cubicles.[10] The pure logic of economics, not cultural habit, forced at least half of the 170,000 industrial workers in registered factories and workshops, and many more among the outworkers, into the vicious circle of low wages and excessively long work-

---

8. House of Commons Debate, May 23, 1958, in House of Commons, 5:588, 1731–42; citation from 1738.

9. R. G. D. Houghton, C.B.E, "Confidential Report to the Commissioner of Labour on the Labour Problems of Hongkong," March 1951, CO 129/626/3, Labour Department: Report to Labour Commissioner, 33–182; citation from 75.

10. Ogilvie, "Visit to Hong Kong," 106.

days.[11] Employment conditions, not cultural habit, ensured that little had changed in the desperate living conditions of laboring Chinese for nearly a century, conditions that had been known to London, if not to the world.

Of course, the colonial state in Hong Kong and the Colonial Office argued (with good reason) that the influx of refugees from a war-torn and then Communist China saturated the labor market and drove wages down. Indeed, China's political and economic failure before 1949 had its share in the population explosion in postwar Hong Kong. Ogilvie recognized, as did her colleagues in Hong Kong and London, that many Chinese workers considered low wages and long hours better than unemployment. However, the debate in the House of Commons suggested a different option: reducing the hours of employed workers to "pool the available jobs and thus find employment for more people."[12] This argument failed to move the industrialists or the colonial state in Hong Kong. Both cited fierce competition from Japan and mainland China in the world export market as an excuse to keep the Hong Kong way.

Nonetheless, Hong Kong's low wages and long hours, described in the House of Commons as "scandalous" and "the worst in Asia," opened Ogilvie's eyes to problems beyond pure economics. Her discussion of labor relations swept the dirt out from under the rug and into the open. The colonial state had been the chief perpetrator if not the source of Hong Kong's enduring pattern of industrial subjugation. Twenty years since Hong Kong's first labour officer made it a key recommendation for reform, the colony had passed no legislation to define the minimum wage, disregarding repeated admonishments by the Colonial Office throughout the 1950s.[13] Ogilvie also noted, as

---

11. This figure of 170,000 workers in registered factories and workshops was only a portion of the industrial workforce. An estimate of 150,000 people "employed in unregistrable and cottage-type industries, as outworkers, and in the under-employed industrial fringe," according to the Labour Department. Based on official statistics, the total urban workforce, including those in industry, construction, and government departments, constituted roughly 17–18.5 percent of the total of population of 2,677,000 in 1957–1958.

12. House of Commons Debate, May 23, 1958, House of Commons, 5:588, 1731–42; citation from 1734.

13. See chapter 1 for Butters's recommendation in 1938. In 1951, the Colonial Office dispatched Assistant Labour Advisor R. G. D. Houghton to Hong Kong, and

did Butters, the Factories and Industrial Undertakings Ordinance still dealt with only industrial establishments of twenty workers or more, leaving a vast number of smaller operations in complete freedom. Furthermore, a permissive Labour Department had abrogated its power to "require an employer to remedy defects" when safety issues occurred. Instead, Hong Kong continued an out-dated practice, as labour inspectors spent much time "in dealing with annual registration of work places which has been discontinued in many other territories to-day."[14] Naturally Hong Kong's radical differences raised questions about the colony's true concerns in the area of labor problems.

In contrast to its relaxed attitude toward employers, the Labour Department had been most vigilant against labor unions. Since the early 1950s, both the governor and the commissioner of labour spared no opportunity in alerting London that Hong Kong's labor unions posed a grave danger to the colony. In 1951, R. G. D. Houghton from the Colonial Office became their ally. His report argued that labor unions were controlled by outside forces and fixing the minimum wage was premature. Governor Grantham underscored these points in his letter to London claiming that labor unions were organized "primarily

---

he returned with a report that echoed the view of the colonial state in Hong Kong. Houghton emphasized on politicization of labor unions in the colony, an issue that both the governor and the commissioner of labour in Hong Kong also highlighted in their response to the Houghton report. On the question of "the possible need for establishment of wage-fixing machinery," E. Parry, an Assistant Labour Adviser in the Colonial Office, noted, "it doesn't appear to me he has done this. In fact I consider his view hesitant and inclusive." Minute by E. Parry, June 20, 1951, CO 129/626/3, Labour Department Report to Labour Commissioner, 11. Both Governor Grantham and Commissioner of Labour B. Hawkins used politicization of trade unions as the scarecrow to deflect London's insistence on establishing wage-fixing legislation. See Alexander Grantham to James Griffith, M. P., September 10, 1951, and B. Hawkins, "Comments by the Commissioner of Labour, Hong Kong, on the Memorandum submitted to the Secretary of State by the Colonial Labour Advisory Committee on Trade Unionism in the Colonies," August 24, 1951, CO 129/626/3. Interestingly, in 1953 the Colonial Office dispatched E. Parry to inspect the three colonies of Malaya, Singapore, and Hong Kong, where he spent ten weeks, but his focus was mostly on Malaya, where he found "the contrast between the rich and poor was striking" amid the ongoing Malayan Emergency. See Report by Mr. Parry on Labour Problems, CO 1022/120, citation from 7.

14. Ogilvie, "Visit to Hong Kong," 100.

for political ends."[15] In 1954, Grantham again wrote to the Colonial Office, emphasizing with his characteristic eloquence the political danger of the "honest, dynamic, cautious and astute" left-wing Federation of Trade Unions and presenting a cynical interpretation of labor union welfare efforts:

> The truth of the matter is that Trade Unionism, as it is known in the Western world, is a mirage in Hong Kong, despite Government's declared policy and the constant efforts of the Labour Department. The Unions themselves are many and various, but they are, one and all, bedeviled by the political direction implicit in their affiliations. The welfare and terms of service of their members are of importance only in their bearing on the major aims of the Unions which are to secure and to hold the political allegiance of the workers. Matters are made worse by the fact that the political issues in question are not related to Hong Kong's problems but are foreign in conception and origin. Furthermore, the Left-wing federation, where the greater potential danger lies, is, at all events by comparison with its rival, honest, dynamic, cautious and astute. A labour dispute in Hong Kong, therefore, is unlikely, except superficially, to be a dispute between labour and management. It is more likely to be, in reality, a dispute involving rival political factions with the absolute control of labour as the ultimate goal.[16]

The governor and the labour commissioner could easily draw in Houghton, who held similar beliefs and preferences regarding industrial relations, and turn his 1951 report into their political mouthpiece.[17] But they failed to convince Ogilvie, a seasoned factory inspector with global experience and reform-

---

15. Alexander Grantham to James Griffins, M. P., September 10, 1951, CO 129/626/3; it is a three-page letter, with its own pagination and placed after page 19 in the file without file pagination. Citation from letter page 1. Also see B. Hawkins, "Comments by the Commissioner of Labour, Hong Kong, on the Memorandum submitted to the Secretary of State by the Colonial Labour Advisory Committee on Trade Unionism in the Colonies," August 24, 1951, which, as an enclosure to Grantham's letter in the same file, elaborated on the need to enforce surveillance of labor unions.

16. A. Grantham to Secretary of State for the Colonies, "Hong Kong: Relations with China," December 22, 1954, FO 371/115063.

17. In 1953, the Malayan Trade Union Council, which had fought for an Employment Ordinance for six years, wrote to the International Labour Office in Geneva, accusing "Mr. R.G.D. Houghton, ex-U.K. Ministry of Labour Official, Commissioner for Labour, Federation of Malaya from 1947 to 1950 and now Secretary of the Malayan Planting Industries Employers' Association," of "engineering" the employers' objection to the draft ordinance. See M. Arokiasamy (General Secretary, Ma-

ist intention. Her formal report was relatively mild in language. It was sent first, according to procedure, to the labour commissioner and Governor Robert Black, who had succeeded to the post at Grantham's recommendation. Even so, she could not but note from the beginning of her assessment: "The simplest thing to say about labour relations in Hong Kong is that there are none. There are the exceptions that prove the rule, but they are few and far between."

In separate comments circulated within the Colonial Office, Ogilvie wrote more candidly and pointed at the obvious causal relationship between practices by the Labour Department and emboldened employer resistance to any reform in labor affairs. The department maintained "a policy of keeping the higher posts in the hands of Europeans,"[18] a practice vigorously pursued after the war under Brian Hawkins's leadership and endorsed by famously "progressive" Governor Mark Young. The colonial state led by Grantham had promulgated anti-union laws, and the Labour Department took no action in industrial mediation. "The labour officer at present in charge of this branch of the work is disinclined to put a great deal of energy into it" and did nothing "to encourage employers to negotiate with workers whether through joint consultation, negotiation of one employer with all his workers, negotiation between an employer and trade union or between groups of employers and groups of unions."[19] Taking note of the various public displays of political partiality by the colonial state, employers simply disregarded labor unions. The Tramway

---

layan Trade Union Council) to L. E. Bodmer, Social Security Division, International Labour Office, Geneva, May 18, 1953, CO 1022/120, 17–18.

18. Sheila Ann Ogilvie, "Comments for the Colonial Office on Some Points in the Report," CO 1030/763, 89–98; citation from 89.

19. Ogilvie, "Comments," 90. Hawkins, who once set up a Labour Department that firmly followed an anti-union policy, had been promoted to the secretary for Chinese affairs in 1955. Major H. F. G. Chauvin, whom Hawkins trusted, remained the mainstay in the branch of industrial relations throughout the 1950s and early 1960s, while other labour officers ranked above him as cadet officers had come and gone during that critical period. In 1962, the annual report by the Commissioner of Labour first specified different branches in the office and listed specific senior Labour Officers in charge of each. Chauvin headed the "Industrial Relations Section," which Ogilvie particularly criticized for its inaction. Kenneth A. Baker headed the "Trade Unions Section," a responsibility he had taken since his arrival in 1947. See *LDAR*, 1954–1955, 1955–1956, 1956–1957, 1957–1958, 1958–1959, 1959–1960, 1960–

Company, for example, had stopped dealing with the Tramway Union, the best organized among labor, since 1950.[20]

Quite the opposite of a vigorously organized, politicized, and subversive labor movement, as Grantham had led London to believe, Ogilvie instead discovered a haphazard group of labor organizations in a pathetic state. Unions were too timid to initiate collective bargaining because workers' "fear of deportation as agitators and their fear that claims for better conditions would result in dismissals, decreased wages and unemployment."[21] The only time labor unions showed "signs of activity," she noted, was "when workers are dismissed (whether individuals or groups and for whatever reason) and are particularly active when some lose employment through redundancy. In such ones they are active until employers agree to pay severance pay."[22] Although union leaders told Ogilvie "with some pride that there had been very few cases of reduction of wages," wages were already below subsistence level in her view.[23] Without a strong union to stand up for their legal rights, some women workers, desperate when facing excessive employer demands, took a novel approach: "When an employer illegally employs women an additional hour at night women often make anonymous telephone calls to the Labour Department to complain about it."[24] Whether any employer was penalized for violating the law is anyone's guess. Adding to the weakened state of organized labor was a subdued Kenneth Baker, who was still responsible for trade unions within the Labour Department. "I think he does what he can," Ogilvie noted

---

1961, 1961–1962, and 1962–1963. "List of Staff" usually appears after the table of contents and before the text of the annual report.

20. Governor Grantham to the Secretary of State for the Colonies, "Hong Kong: Relations with China," December 22, 1954, FO 371/115063.

21. Ogilvie, "Comments," 90.

22. Ogilvie, "Visit to Hong Kong," 103. In fact, "fragmented" labor movement resulted from "the existing colonial system," as well as official partiality to the employers and their widespread use of piece rate that "automatically weeded out older women workers" continued in the 1970s, as observed by anthropologist Janet W. Salaff in her field work in Hong Kong between 1971 and 1976. She found that "the gap between men and women in education, employment, and earnings remains nearly as wide today as in the past." See Salaff. Citations from 13, 18, 101.

23. Ogilvie, "Visit to Hong Kong," 103.

24. Ogilvie, "Comments," 94.

without naming Baker, but "his enthusiasm was dampened in the past and his activities restricted."[25]

In 1958, the rebalance between right-wing and left-wing labor unions had become notable in Ogilvie's visit. The pro-Guomindang Trades Union Council (TUC) invited Ogilvie to their headquarters, where she met its executive council and union officials, "but not workers." The TUC president's prepared speech demanded legislation on maximum hours and minimum wages, revision of the present system of conciliation and arbitration, and elimination of two unions in the same industry. The pro-mainland Federation of Trade Unions (FTU), however, made no attempt to contact Ogilvie. Because the colonial state did not officially recognize the FTU as a labor union federation, it was "difficult for the Labour Department to invite the F.T.U. to meet me," Ogilvie remarked. As a way out of this absurd situation, the Labour Department arranged for Ogilvie to meet representatives from the Hong Kong–Kowloon Spinning, Weaving, and Dyeing Workers' General Union. Formed after the war with encouragement from the Labour Department, this union had grown to become the largest within the FTU with more than 10,000 members. Two women representatives came to see Ogilvie and sought her official support for "more jobs for the many unemployed." Their other recommendations focused on welfare outside the workplace, echoing FTU priorities after the crackdown on Russell Street: employer should provide more workplace dormitories and medical facilities for workers in factories without such benefits.[26] These measures, as one might imagine, would help workers receiving below subsistence-level wages on jobs in unsafe environments, and additional medical facilities might prevent a total collapse of a worker's precarious living should an accident lead to additional medical expenses. But all were patchwork expediency, which could neither achieve systemic change in employment conditions nor make workers "citizens," as Butters first envisioned in 1938.

---

25. Ogilvie, "Comments," 90. She noted that "the Labour Officer who deals with trade unions has not been exclusively in Hong Kong." Baker had been assigned the job since his arrival, and eventually appeared as the lead officer of "Trade Unions section" when the annual report by the commissioner of labour specified different branches within the department in 1962.

26. Ogilvie, "Visit to Hong Kong," 104.

Although labor conditions in late 1950s Hong Kong astonished the Labour Adviser Ogilvie, she would have been less surprised had she recognized that the labor question in Hong Kong was intricately interwoven with the colonial question and ultimately the question of the British Empire. Hong Kong was one of the earliest sites to embrace the imperial initiative of state intervention in labor affairs. But in two decades, the colony had become a battlefield pitting imperial status quo against mobilized Chinese labor. The dramatic turn of events in labor affairs was in large measures related to Hong Kong's status as a restored British colony. The dismal labor situations and the anemic unions observed by Ogilvie in 1958 were fragmented shadows of a vigorous labor activism going from strength to strength in the 1930s and 1940s. Such results cannot be explained by the internal problems of working Chinese, held down by cultural habit or ties to traditional forms of social organization. Instead, it points to at least two fundamental problems in Britain's imperial intervention in colonial labor affairs.

Enforcement of reformist intervention in Hong Kong first revealed the problem of colonial resistance at the level of operation. However radical a departure from past imperial approaches to colonial affairs, the policy of state intervention did not change the age-old British practice of leaving day-to-day colonial governance in the hands of men on the spot. Policy became ever more dependent on these men. There were conscientious British officials in the colony who genuinely worked on improving and reforming industrial relations. But their influence was temporary, their power was limited, and they were ultimately at odds with the defenders of the colonial system on the ground. With these colonial defenders in key positions serving as vital agents to translate London's reformist agenda into local practice, much was lost in the process. Bureaucratic inertia might have built momentum to keep the existing system going. What we have seen in previous chapters, however, was deliberate and determined resistance by leaders of the colonial establishment. Step by step, offices and men who strongly believed in the colonial system deployed various tactics to resist, neutralize, and eventually subvert reform in labor affairs. Hong Kong's Legislative Council killed the first reformist Bill of Trade Unions through neglect. The same Legislative Council, on the other hand, promptly resurrected or promulgated repressive labor laws when opportunities arrived later. Governor Mark Young, famed for his abortive postwar constitutional reform and for abolishing the racist Peak Ordinance, gave no support to reforming labor affairs. With his firm endorsement, a conservative commissioner headed the Labour Department and effectively resisted London's recommendation for progressive institutional modifications. Through appointment or demotion of particular personnel, the Labour Department in the pivotal postwar decade defended the existing system of industrial relations and prevented institutional reforms in labor affairs.

A colonial establishment depending on a reactionary leadership to enforce progressive changes only reveals irony in operation, though the irony had its origin in fundamental contradictions in London's turn to an interventionist approach in colonial affairs. Looking at the West Indies case, political scientist Cary Fraser called London's interventionism within the imperial framework a "redemptive" initiative, which intended to correct—but not eradicate the cause to—past wrongs. The imperial vision of "redemption" came too little and too late. By then peoples in the West Indies had already mobilized to demand greater independence. Ultimately it proved to be "imperial hubris," because the center refused to face the root cause of colonialism, which gave rise to growing local discontent and protest.[27]

The failure of state intervention to reform Hong Kong's notorious labor conditions was also the logical outcome of continued belief in the empire and ongoing efforts to keep local "aliens" under colonial rule. Unlike West Indies and Africa, where the absence of Axis challenge allowed the British to focus on the simpler tasks of extracting resources for the war effort, the fall of British Asia under Japanese attack had effectively put European "imperial hubris" in check, but never completely uprooted it. In fact, the Japanese occupation stimulated the resurgence of British will for the empire, which eventually triumphed in Hong Kong when it crumpled elsewhere. From wartime to peacetime, it was sustained by an impulse to regain British honor, besmirched by losing the colony to an Asian power. In particular, the imperial will was sustained by the economic objectives of keeping British interests in the area and by strategic considerations of protecting British Asia. Resistance to London's reform initiative temporarily placed Hong Kong's tenacious colonial state at

---

27. Fraser.

odds with the imperial center. But the colonial state gained ground as British regional priorities shifted to confront a unified China emerging at the mid-twentieth century. Consensus prioritizing the continued defense of the empire solved any remaining differences between London and Hong Kong regarding organized Chinese labor.

The rise and fall of Chinese labor activism in British Hong Kong in these decades raise the question about the nature of British policy in the large context of Britain's global imperial retreat amid the Cold War. British historian Steve Tsang has argued that British policy was not to aggressively make Hong Kong an anti-Communist base as the "Berlin in the East" but, together with the United States, to take "a purely defensive posture in Asia."[28] Indeed, London's chief concern was "defensive," as both London and Hong Kong were most anxious to defend British overseas interests built over centuries. But the defense was quite aggressive, as recent scholarship shows. It was built on multiple fronts with particular attention to projecting anti-Communist "soft power" in cultural realms.[29] This study takes scholarship to another front and shows a vigorous defense through British state intervention in labor affairs. By remolding Hong Kong's legal framework and the measured use of brute force, the colonial state abandoned its reformist objective and returned to surveillance and suppression of well-organized Chinese labor.

Just as resolve to retain the empire and British Hong Kong persistently motivated the British shift from redemptive reforms to repression in labor affairs, the desire to live a life with dignity propelled the working Chinese in Hong Kong to join civic activism for national salvation, wartime resistance, and postwar collective action. The most obvious continuity in this saga of the rise and fall of Chinese labor activism in Hong Kong had been the divergent orientations held by British leadership and Chinese labor, which crossed paths in these tumultuous decades. In an equally persistent determination, working Chinese retained deep attachment to China, their homeland. Their sense of belonging to this national community was more than just "imagined" through

---

28. Tsang (1997).

29. For colonial control in education, see Wong. An earlier study on Hong Kong education, which took a more official position, also recognized intense surveillance over Chinese schools in Hong Kong. See Sweeting. For state intervention in literary creation, see Lu and Xiong (eds.), vol. I.

a shared idea carried by print media.[30] Working Chinese in Hong Kong put their lives in the nation's defense when China faced grave national peril and rejoiced at the moment of its promising renewal. Their self-conscious membership in a Chinese nation became crystalized by foreign invasion and repeatedly strengthened through collective actions. Labor activism from the 1930s to the 1950s carried forth the anti-imperialist nationalism of the 1920s, when the agenda emerged subtly in the 1922 Seamen's Strike and became outspoken in the General Strike-Boycott of 1925–1926. Their fight renewed in the 1930s. From one person to another, the spirit of activism as well as mobilization and organizational skills were passed from one generation to the next. Through human connections, often arising in a workplace shared among like-minded workers, the well-established tradition of anti-imperialist activism continued.

As the arena of Chinese labor activism moved from civic front to military battlefield and back to the economic realm of collective action in industrial conflicts, a persistent humanist spirit underscored people's sense of belonging to a Chinese nation. Living and working under foreign rule heightened this consciousness and thrust Hong Kong's working Chinese to the forefront of anti-imperialist struggles since the late nineteenth century. But in shifting their target from British imperialism in the 1920s to Japanese imperialism in the 1930s and 1940s, working Chinese demonstrated an unmistakable sense of justice. Their struggle was free of impulsive, indiscriminate xenophobia. Indeed, the catastrophic war was a social leveler, as historian Diana Lary has pointed out.[31] In colonial Hong Kong, it was also a political leveler that brought down former colonial masters. Although anti-imperialist Chinese labor did not rush to British defense when Hong Kong came under Japanese attack, neither did they take advantage of the rapid destruction of British rule to avenge past grievances. Instead, they sustained their anti-imperialist struggle with a deep empathy and included foreigners without racial prejudice in their wartime rescue missions. They extended help to imprisoned former British officials but met frequent rejection because of British distrust. For national leaders, aiding Allied personnel entailed strategic significance. But for working

---

30. For these points in an influential analysis on nationalism, see Benedict Anderson.

31. Lary.

Chinese deployed in rescue operations or intelligence work, these missions cost lives and exacted personal deprivation. These heroic deeds could never have been accomplished without their willing participation, their generosity, and their profound sense of humanity.

With self-perception grounded in the experiences of being Chinese so-journers and members of the working class, searching for association and alliance with mainland political forces was a logical step for working Chinese. Mutual support and other connections between organized labor in Hong Kong and mainland political parties continued a well-established tradition from the founding days of China's oldest modern party, the Guomindang. But changes in mainland politics necessarily led to changes in association. The Guomindang, a principal leader in the national labor movement and a major influence in Hong Kong's organized labor, lost its authority to the more active labor organizations in 1930s Hong Kong. Its political failure before, during, and after the war undercut its appeal to the postwar labor movement. Labor activists instead chose the political opposition, the Chinese Communist Party, which in turn boosted social activism in Hong Kong. An association with the Communists brought logistical support in military training, leadership, and guidance in guerrilla warfare, which taught discipline to inexperienced activists and strengthened postwar collective labor actions.

Of course, the connection between the most active and best-organized Chinese labor organizations and the CCP raises questions about the nature of labor activism in Hong Kong. Forged through the National Salvation Movement, resistance guerrilla warfare, and collective labor actions, this organizational connection had its most outstanding feature not in top-down commands from the party center on the mainland, but in ground-up initiatives from the Chinese in Hong Kong. The Hong Kong initiative demonstrates a different pattern from the top-down, party-mass connection between Communist leadership and northern Chinese peasants during the resistance war, a case famously made by Chalmers Johnson who argued for a more active Communist leadership reaching down to peasants.[32] Labor activists in the city of

---

32. Johnson. Communists as outsiders reaching down to local societies to provide leadership of social change in fact was a predominant pattern shown in several major studies of the Communist movement in China. See, for example, Averill, Benton, Keating, and Selden.

Hong Kong in South China, on the contrary, embraced Communist leadership and reached upward to the party organization on the mainland. Nonetheless, labor activists in Hong Kong were very much like the peasants in North China in making their choice of the Communist Party first and foremost for its defensive nationalist appeal and effective leadership. In other words, the urgent need for national and self-defense here and now, not the remote Communist vision, initially activated and sealed the organizational connection. Later on, proven capability in leading guerrilla warfare and labor action sustained the appeal of Communists as trustworthy leaders to a variety of local Chinese, from eager young activists to social leaders in the New Territories and doubtful workers on factory floors.

Coming from other locales in China as internal migrants and seeking a living in a city of strangers, working Chinese in Hong Kong, like those in other cities such as Shanghai or Beijing, formed bonds with existing forms of social organization before the great wave of labor activism. Regional associations, dialect groups, sworn sisterhoods or brotherhoods, and guilds overlapped with working people's membership in voluntary associations for national salvation, in guerrilla troops, and in labor unions. As this study has shown, the former, "traditional" kinds of social association never quite achieved control over the latter, the activist associations in Hong Kong. Unlike in Shanghai or Beijing, where "politics of place" divided labor, regional or linguistic affinity offered a stepping-stone toward a widened alliance among working people in Hong Kong. It aided the initial formation of the East River guerrilla force. This inclusive, revolutionary organization in turn helped break existing social barriers between landed people and boat people or between the Cantonese and the Hakka. Sworn sisterhoods aided the formation of some labor unions, but that was not a universal pattern of industrial union formation in Hong Kong. More than any other forms of organization, voluntary associations during the National Salvation Movement provided an organizational springboard to future activism in armed resistance and in postwar labor organizations.

Secret societies (sworn brotherhoods), on the other hand, had gone so far in their proclivity for criminal activities as a survival tactic that they often became antagonistic to wartime resistance and postwar labor activism. In postwar times, sworn brotherhood/secret societies continued to exist and engage workers as a form of mutual aid group.[33] Although the Triads' ubiquitous presence continued in grassroots Hong Kong, their influence remained extremely localized in specific neighborhoods. When achieving anything of consequence, they served as an instrument of violence for a partisan force. As this study shows, the pattern of Triad-partisan relations in Hong Kong was one of conflict with the Communists and collaboration with the Guomindang. This pattern persisted during the postwar labor movement in the Triad relationship with labor organizations under the influence of the two parties, and it became most salient in the 1956 riots.

With exuberant democratic spirit, better organization, and recognized efficacy in leading collective actions, active labor unions in Hong Kong in these tumultuous years held critical power in the delicate balance between the Chinese nation and the British Empire. Despite its awareness of workers' genuine desire to improve their economic lot and the legitimacy of achieving such a goal through collective action, the restored colonial state in Hong Kong became increasingly unwilling to tolerate vibrant, legal labor unions closely connected with their homeland. Although the colonial state and mobilized workers had cooperated and helped one another achieve a mutually desired economic recovery in the wake of the war, they were merely fellow travelers for a short-term objective. Their orientations and their desired destinations diverged so widely that any long-term companionship became impossible. In retrospect, colonial state repression of collective action by Chinese labor in early 1950 was not too different from earlier state actions against popular protest by Chinese in support of their homeland. But in 1950 state repression

---

33. In some local branches of unions affiliated to the FTU, leading members were also members of the neighborhood/area Triads. Known membership in local Triads among union leaders included those in the Painters Union and Caulkers' Union. But labor unions could also clash with the local Triads. One such case involved the Carpenters Union and a Triad band "Ho Ho To" (和合桃) in Sai Wan around 1947. After an unsuccessful negotiation at a local restaurant where the Carpenters Union tried to gain Ho Ho To's agreement allowing union-affiliated carpenters to work in the area, the two sides came to blows. In the fight, the chairman of the Carpenters Union led the charge. Workers from the union defeated the gangsters, and thus won the right to work in Sai Wan. The three bravest workers were rewarded with lifetime union membership with the waiver of their union dues. Author's communications with Zhou Yi, March 2017. Zhou refers to his interview notes with several union leaders in the early 2000s.

of mobilized labor became all the more necessary, not because Cold War anti-Communism legitimized it but because of the potent force of Chinese identity expressed by organized Chinese labor. Their sentiment had also evoked a loud, frightening echo in the demonstrated sympathy to workers among ordinary Chinese in Hong Kong. Continued identification with China was a subtle form of opposition to the illegitimate colonial restoration, short of explicit demands for decolonization. Redirecting its course from reform toward repression of labor was the only logical choice for the restorative colonial regime, which became the first critical step toward making a depoliticized culture in Hong Kong.[34]

Placing their long-held hopes for a strong China in the Communist Party also meant that the most active workers in Hong Kong in these turbulent decades had to wait on the sidelines for a very long time. Governing a vast country emerging from incessant wars and in economic bankruptcy, the Communist leadership chose to focus on core tasks and core regions in the north. This national strategy developed at the end of the war when the party decided to "defense in the South." The choice became more salient when the People's Liberation Army halted its southward advance at Shenzhen in October 1949, and solidified once the Korean War broke out and the UN embargo began at the end of 1950. In leading a national struggle to survive, the Central People's Government in Beijing, like the earlier National Government in Nanjing, took a conservative approach to colonial rule in Hong Kong. Discouraging militant confrontation with British authorities became guiding policy to all organizations under its influence, including labor unions.

Under Beijing's restrained approach, a united China could not meet the expectations of mobilized labor in Hong Kong, who had loudly expressed anticolonialist sentiment in hoisting their national flags, in their visits to the People's Liberation Army in Shenzhen, and in singing the Chinese national anthem when defying police action in Hong Kong. As homeland China remained weak and unable to offer support beyond verbal denunciation of colonial violence and material aid in times of local disasters, retreat from activism

---

34. The Hong Kong–based political scientist Lam Wai-man, in her study of political activism from the late 1950s and 1970s, argues that the colonial state had energetically confronted leftwing activism in its effort to depoliticize the culture in the colony. See Lam.

became the only option for mobilized labor. As their leadership refrained from actively seeking improvements on employment conditions, working Chinese had no choice but to cope with the existing low wages, excessive working hours, unsafe working conditions, and cramped living quarters that astonished Ogilvie in 1958. Those labor conditions existed well before Butters observed and summarized them in 1938. They not only embodied the failure of London's reformist intervention. They also underscored the crucial importance of international and national politics in shaping the particulars of Hong Kong's labor movement.

Despite a few alarming rumors that China was about to take back Hong Kong, London became confident by the late 1950s that Beijing had no short-term intention of reclaiming the territory. Nor did London view refugees from China as troublesome anymore. On the contrary, candid discussions within the Colonial Office indicated that they brought "economic benefits to the Colony as a whole. The influx of new labour keeps down labour costs, the needs of food, clothing, housing etc., even if paid for by the Government, are a profit to many citizens."[35] Although labeled "refugees," these people were economic migrants, a phenomenon that Hong Kong had witnessed for more than a century. What continued to worry London, and Hong Kong's colonial state, was the emotional attachment of these economic migrants to their homeland—that they "in a sense may well have their first loyalty to China."[36]

Eliminating labor activism in the 1950s did not completely uproot such loyalty, much less to solve industrial problems. Less than ten years after Ogilvie's investigation, working Chinese erupted in another colony-wide protest and loudly voiced their solidarity with revolutionary China. Unlike labor activists before them, however, the 1967 protesters resorted to violence to voice discontent and hence failed to gain popular sympathy.[37] Even so, their identi-

---

35. Brief for the Secretary of State for the Colonies, November 24, 1959, CO 1030/769, Departmental Briefs on Hong Kong, 15–16; citation from 15. No full name appears for the author, except an abbreviation "P."

36. Brief for the Secretary of State for the Colonies, November 24, 1959.

37. The protest is the topic of one monograph by a political scientist, a collection of essays by Hong Kong– and Britain-based scholars, and a book in the Chinese language by a journalist. But no historian has written a definitive analysis of the event, except for one unpublished dissertation. See Scott, Cheung, Bickers and Yip (eds.), and Waldron (1976).

fication with homeland China did not die. Students in the 1970s again looked toward China for inspirations as they searched a different mode of life beyond the British colony. It is beyond the scope of this book to investigate the causes of this continued attachment to homeland China and why it did not disappear in later decades. But it may not be too far from reality to suggest, as this study of labor activism does, that identification with an independent China free of foreign control reveals the persistent desire among Chinese in Hong Kong to live a life of respect and dignity, equal to others. This desire mobilized tens of thousands of working Chinese in Hong Kong, who rose above local loyalties to fight for national and international causes. The same desire mobilized millions around the world to achieve self-government. The desire not only linked labor activism from the 1930s and 1950s to labor protests and student activism decades later; it also made them active contributors to the making of history. Despite the dismal outcome of the activism chronicled here, that deep-rooted desire, with its power to mobilize mass movements, eventually forced the colonial state to attempt social intervention and economic improvement with greater commitment. Ultimately, the motivating power of identity, which loomed large in Hong Kong's past, must force any governing power to look deep into the social roots of cultural expression and respond accordingly, should it wish to remain legitimate and relevant in history.

List of Names and Terms

Ai Siqi　艾思奇
Angsheng lianyishe　昂聲聯誼社

Bai Chen　白沉
Bao Lichu (Richard Bow)　鮑立初
Bi Ke　畢克

Cai Bingru　蔡冰如
Cai Chusheng　蔡楚生
Cai Guoliang (Tsoi Kwok Leung)　蔡國樑
Cai Shunfa　蔡順法
Cai Songying　蔡松英
Cai Tingkai　蔡廷鍇
Cai Zhongmin　蔡钟敏
Chen Ce (Chan Chak)　陳策
Chen Hualong　陳華龍
Chen Junbao　陳君葆
Chen Wenhan　陳文漢
Chengwei　城委
chenji facai　趁機發財

Dai Jitao　戴季陶
Dasheng　大盛 (alias of Li Fuchun)
Dazhong ribao　大眾日報
Danjia (Tanka)　蜑家
Deng Wenyi　鄧文儀
Di Fan　狄梵
Diandeng gongsi Huayuan xiejinhui　電燈公司華員協進會
Dianche cun'aihui　電車存愛會
Du Yuesheng　杜月笙

Fang Fang　方方
Fang Lan　方蘭
Fazhui ju　法制局

feixing jihui　飛行集會
Fei Yimin　費彝民
fenhua　分化
Feng Haichao (Fung Hoi Chiu)　馮海潮
Feng Qin　馮欽
gaishan daiyu　改善待遇

GangJiu gexie　港九歌協
GangJiu gonglianhui　港九工聯會
Geming shijian yanjiuyuan　革命實踐研究院
Gongtuan ribao　工團日報
Gongwei　工委
GangYue chengwei　港粵城委
guochou jiahen　國仇家恨
Guomindang minzhu cujinhui　國民黨民主促進會
guzhi　固執
Gongtuan lianhehui　工團聯合會
gongzheng yanming　公正嚴明
Gu Huizhen　古惠貞
guanxin qunzhong jiku,chuangban gongren fuli　关心群众疾苦,创办工人福利

Haihua School　海華學校
He Jiari　何家日
He Kang (Ho Hong)　何康
He Pei　何培
He Sijing　何思敬
He Xiangning　何香凝
He Zhuozhong　何卓忠
Heung To School　香島中學
Han Wenhui (Hon Man-wai)　韓文惠
Huo De　霍德
Hong Biao　洪標 (aka Zhou Nan)
Honghong geyongtuan　虹虹歌詠團

343

Huiyang qingnianhui　惠陽青年會
Hongji　宏記
Hu Die　胡蝶
Huang Dengming　黃燈明
Huang Guanfang　黃冠芳
Huang Zuomei (Raymond Wong Chok-
　　mui)　黃作梅
Huanran gongshe (Wun Yin Kung She)
　　煥然工社
Huo De　霍德
Huanan jiuguohui　華南救國會

Jiang Guangnai　蔣光鼐
Jiang Wei　蔣偉
jijin huihuang　極盡輝煌
Jin Yaoru　金堯如
Jinling jiujia　金陵酒家
jiu-guo ya　救國呀
Jiulong Chuanwu zhigong peixinshe
　　九龍船塢職工培新社
Jiuwu laogong lianhehui　九塢勞工
　　聯合會
Juemin xiaoxue 覺民小學

kangyi　抗議
kangle　康樂
Kong Xiufang　孔秀芳

Lei Zhen　雷震
Li Boyuan　李伯元
Li Cheng Uk　李鄭屋
Li Fuchun　李富春
Li Huaqing　李华清
Li Jishen　李濟深
Li Shi　李石
Li Shufen　李樹芬
Li Song　李崧
Li Wenhai　李文海
Li Wenhui　李文輝
Li Wenxing　李文興
Li Xifen (Lai Sek-fan)　黎錫芬

Li Yimei　李義梅
Li Zongying (Lee Tsung-ying)
　　李宗瀛
Lian Guan　連貫
Liang Guang　梁廣
Liao Chengzhi　廖承志
Liao Mosha　廖沫沙
Lin Guanrong　林冠榮
Lin Yuying　林育英
Lin Zhongdan　林仲丹
Lingsheng she　鈴聲社
Liu Fa　劉法
Liu Fochang　劉佛昌
Liu Jieyun　劉潔雲
Liu Jinjin　劉錦進
Liu Heizai　劉黑仔
Liu Shaoqi　劉少奇
Liu Qiong　劉瓊
Liu Xuan　劉宣
Liu Yazi　柳亞子
Lou Songping　樓頌平
Luo Wenjin (Man Kam Lo)　羅文錦
Luosujie xue'an　羅素街血案
Lu Dong　盧動
Lu Weiliang　盧偉良
Luo Fu　洛甫
shanggong　賞工

Ma Chaojun　馬超俊
Ma Guoliang　馬國亮
Ma Hong Ji jiqichang　馬宏記機器廠
Mai Haien　麥海恩
Mai Hezhi　麥河志
Mai Yaoquan (Mak Eu-chuen)
　　麥耀全
Mao Dun　茅盾
Mei Lanfang　梅蘭芳
Minzheng jiguan ji zhengfu gongtuan
　　yaoqiu gaishan daiyu zhigong
　　daibiaohui　民政機關暨

政府工團要求改善待遇職
工代表會

Mo Shubao　莫叔寶

Mo Yinggui (Mok Ying-kuai)　莫應溎

Motuoche yanjiu zonggonghui
摩托車研究總工會

Ouyang Shaofeng　歐陽少峰

Pan Hannian　潘漢年

Peng Chaojie (Pan Chiu-kit)　彭超傑

Puqing xiyuan　普慶戲院

Qi Guozhao　齊國昭

Qi Yun　戚雲

Qiao Guanhua　喬冠華

Qian Ying　錢瑛

QiaoGang Taishan qingnianhui
僑港台山青年會

Qingnian huzhuhui　青年互助會

Qingnian tongleshe　青年同樂社

Qiufeng geyongtuan　秋風歌詠團

Sa Kongliao　薩空了

Sanmin zhuyi tongzhi lianhehui
三民主義同志聯合會

Sikebi weixian　斯科比危險

Sham Chung　深涌

Shan Liu　山寮

shanggong　賞工

Shen Ji　沈寂

Shep Kip Mei　石硤尾

Shu Shi　舒適

Sima Wensen　司馬文森

Situ Huimin　司徒慧敏

shiji xingdong　實際行動

Shi Jue　石覺

Song Meiling　宋美齡

Song Qingling　宋慶齡

Song Ziwen (T.V. Soong)　宋子文

Su Yun (So Wan)　蘇雲

Sun Liren　孫立人

Tai Hang Tung　大坑東

Tai Mo Shan　大帽山

Tan Tian (Francis)　譚天

Tan Tiandu　譚天度

Wang Zuoyao　王作堯

Wong Mo Ying　黃毛應

Wu Guo-an　吳國安

Wu Guo-quan　吳國全

Wu Kau Tang　烏蛟騰

Wu Tiecheng　吳鐵城

Wu Yaguang　伍亞光

Wu Youheng　吳有恒

Wu Zhan　吳展

Xia Yan　夏衍

Xian Peilin　冼佩玲

Xiang Qian　向前

Xiangang chengshi weiyuanhui　香港
城市委員會

Xianggang fenju　香港分局

Xianggang gongzuo weiyuanhui　香港
工作委員會

Xianggang haijun chuanwu huayuan
xiejinhui　香港海軍船塢
華員協進會

Xianggang Jiulong fangzhi zonggonghui
香港九龍紡織總工會

Xianggang kang-Ri jiuguohui
香港抗日救國會

Xianggang shibao　香港時報

Xu Guansheng　徐觀生

Xu Heng　徐亨

Xuede lizhishe　學德勵志社

Yang Hua　楊華

Yang Ji　楊績

Yao Jian　姚堅

Ye Guang　葉光

Jiulong Yi-an gongshang lianhe zonghui
    九龍義安工商聯合總會
Yin Linping　尹林平
Yingshang Zhonghua xiehui　英商中
    華協會
Yu Hanmou　余漢謀
Yuan Rongjiao　袁容姣
Yuxian yueshe　餘閒樂社

Zeng Hongwen　曾鴻文
Zeng Sheng　曾生
Zeng Shoulong　曾壽隆
Zhang Dongquan　張東荃
Zhang Hanfu　章漢夫
Zhang Hao　張浩
Zhang Ji　張继
Zhang Lisheng　張屬生
Zhang Sheng　張生
Zhang Wentian　張聞天
Zhang Yongxian　張咏賢
Zhang Zhennan (Cheung Chun Nam)
    張振南
Zheng Bin　鄭斌

Zheng Jin　鄭晉
Zheng Tianbao　鄭天保
Zheng Yanfen　鄭彥棻
zhengtong　正統
ZhiHua tiyuhui　智華體育會
Zhigong Tang　致公堂
zhixiaqu　直轄區
Zhongguo yanji shushu
    中國研機書塾
Zhonghua minzu geming tongmeng
    中華民族革命同盟
Zhou Boming　周伯明
Zhou Nan　周楠
Zhou Zhang　周璋
Zou Taofen　鄒韜奮
Zhu Fu　朱復
Zhu Jingwen　朱敬文
Zhu Yamin　朱亞民
ZhuGang tepai junshi daibiao
    駐港特派軍事代表

Works Cited

Primary Sources

Archival Documents

Bureau of Asia & the Pacific, Waijiaob. #11-01-19-04-03-011. Modern History Institute, Academia Sinica, Taipei.

Cabinet (Britain). CAB 28 (38). Public Records Office, London.

————. CAB 36 (38). Public Records Office, London.

————. CAB 129/31/29. Public Records Office, London.

————. CAB 129/33/27. Public Records Office, London.

————. CAB 129/35/9. Public Records Office, London.

————. CAB 129/35/10. Public Records Office, London.

————. CAB 129/35/24. Public Records Office, London.

————. CAB 129/36/27. Public Records Office, London.

————. CAB 129/36/30. Public Records Office, London.

Colonial Office (Britain). CO 129. Public Records Office, London.

————. CO 1022. Public Records Office, London.

————. CO 1023. Public Records Office, London.

————. CO 1030. Public Records Office, London.

————. CO 2030. Public Records Office, London.

Foreign Office (Britain). FO 371. Public Records Office, London.

Guomindang gaizao weiyuanhui (Taipei). 海祕 (39) 185 (Haimi [39] 185). Guomindang History Archive.

————. 臺 (40) 改秘室字第603號 (Tai [40] gai mi shi zi di 603 hao). Guomindang History Archive.

————. 臺 (39) 改秘室字第0141號 (Tai [39] gai mi shi zi di 0141 hao). Guomindang History Archive.

————. 臺 (41) 改秘室字第0200號 (Tai [41] gai mi shi zi di 0200 hao). Guomindang History Archive.

————. 臺 (41) 改秘室字第0395號 (Tai [41] gai mi shi zi di 0395 hao). Guomindang History Archive.

————. 臺 (42) 中秘室字第0274號 (Tai [42] zhong mi shi zi di 0274 hao). Guomindang History Archive.

————. 臺 (45) 中秘室登字第228號 (Tai [40] zhong mi shi deng zi di 228 hao). Guomindang History Archive.

Hong Kong Government. "Historical Laws of Hong Kong." http://oelaw.lib.hku.hk.

————. *Hong Kong Government Gazette.*

————. *Hong Kong Hansard: Reports of the Meetings of the Legislative Council.* Various years.

————. "Report on the Census of the Colony of Hong Kong, 1931."

————. HKRS 843-1-52, "Monthly Reports." Hong Kong Public Records Office.

Published Official Documents

Army Map Service (U.S.). "Hong Kong and New Territory." Washington, DC, 1945.

Butters, H. R. *Report on Labour and Labour Conditions in Hong Kong.* Hong Kong: Noranha, 1939.

Chen Ce (Chan Chak). "協助香港抗戰及率英軍突圍經過總報告" Xiezhu Xianggang kangzhan ji shuai Yingjun tuwei zongbaogao (Final report on assisting defense of Hong Kong and leading successful escape of British troops). In Xu Heng, *Xu Heng xiangsheng fangtanlu.* 163–82.

Colonial Office (Britain). *The Colonial Empire in 1937–1938: Statement to Accompany the Estimate for Colonial and Middle Eastern Services.* London: His Majesty's Stationery Office, 1938.

————. *The Dominions Office and Colonial Office List, 1939.* London: Waterlow, 1939.

————. *Statement of Policy on Colonial Development and Welfare Presented by the Secretary of State for the Colonies to Parliament by the Command of His Majesty.* London: His Majesty's Stationery Office, 1940.

————. *Labour Supervision in the Colonial Empire, 1937–1943.* London: His Majesty's Stationery Office, 1943.

————. *The Colonial Office List 1948.* London: His Majesty's Stationery Office, 1948.

Colonial Secretary's Office (Hong Kong). *The Hong Kong Civil Service List.* Hong Kong, Government Printers & Publishers, 1941.

Commissioner of Labour (Hong Kong). *Annual Departmental Report of the Commissioner of Labour.* Various years. (*LDAR*)

Department of State (United States). *Foreign Relations of the United States.* (*FRUS*)

————. *United States Relations with China: With Special Reference to the Period 1944–1949.* Stanford, CA: Stanford University Press, 1967.

Hambro, Edvard. *The Problem of Chinese Refugees in Hong Kong: Report Submitted to the United Nations High Commissioner for Refugees.* Leyden: A. W. Sijthoff, 1955.

Hong Kong Government. *Annual Report of Hong Kong.* Various years. (*HKAR*)

House of Commons (Britain). *Hansard Parliamentary Debates: House of Commons.* Various years.

House of Lords (Britain). *Hansard Parliamentary Debates: House of Lords.* Various years.

Labour Office (Hong Kong). *Labour Office Report (Covering the Period 1st May 1946 to 31st March 1947).*

U.S. Consulate General (Hong Kong). *Review of Hongkong Chinese Press.* Various years.

Zhonggong Guangdong shengwei zuzhibu, Zhonggong Guangdong shengwei dangshi yanjiushi, and Guangdong sheng dang'anguan (eds.).《中國共產黨廣東省組織史資料》 *Zhongguo Gongchandang Guangdong sheng zuzhishi ziliao* (*Historical materials on the organization of Chinese Communist Party in Guangdong province*). Beijing: Zhonggong dangshi chubanshe, 1994–1996. 2 volumes. (*GDZZSZL*)

Zhonggong Jiangsu shengwei dangshi gongzuo weiyuanhui et al. (eds.).《中共中央南京局》 *Zhonggong zhongyang Nanjingju* (*The Nanjing Bureau of Chinese Communist Party*). Beijing: Zhonggong dangshi chubanshe, 1990. (*ZGZYNJJ*)

Zhonggong zhongyang tongyi zhanxian gongzuobu and Zhonggong zhongyang wenxian yanjiushi (eds.).《周恩來統一戰線文選》 *Zhou Enlai tongyi zhanxian wenxuan* (*Selected articles by Zhou Enlai on the United Front*). Beijing: Renmin chubanshe, 1984. (*ZELWX*)

Zhonggong zhongyang shujichu (ed.).《六大以來》 *Liuda yilai: Dangnei mimi wenjian* (*Since the sixth conference: secret documents for internal circulation of the [Communist] party*). Beijing: Renmin chubanshe, 1981. 2 volumes.

Zhongyang dang'anguan (ed.).《中共中央文件選集》 *Zhonggong zhongyang wenjian xuanji* (Selected documents by the central committee of the CCP). Beijing: Zhonggong zhongyang dangxiao chubanshe, 1982–1991. 18 volumes. (*ZGZYWJXJ*)

Zhongyang dang'anguan and Guangdongsheng dang'anguan (eds.). *Guangdong geming lishi wenjian huiji*《廣東革命歷史文件彙集》 *Guangdong geming lishi wenjiann huiji* (*Collection of historical documents of revolution in Guangdong*). Beijing: Zhongyang dang'anguan, 1982–89. 60 volumes. (*GDGM*)

———.《中共中央香港分局文件彙集1947.5–1949.3》 *Zhonggong zhongyang Xianggang fenju wenjian huiji, 1947.5–1949.3* (*Collection of documents at Hong Kong branch bureau of the Chinese Communist Central Committee*). Beijing: Zhongyang dang'anguan, 1989. (*XGFJWJ*)

Diaries, Speeches, Memoirs, Interviews

Bertram, James. *North China Front*. London: Macmillan, 1939.

———. *Capes of China Slide Away: A Memoir of War and Peace, 1910–1980*. Auckland: Auckland University Press, 1993.

Chen Daming.《香港抗日游擊隊》 *Xianggang kangRi youjidui* (*Hong Kong's resisting-Japan guerrilla force*). Hong Kong: Huanqiu guoji chuban youxian gongsi, 2000.

Chen Junbao.《陳君葆日記全集》 *Chen Junbao riji quanji* (*Diary by Chen Junbao*), ed. Xie Ronggun. Hong Kong: Shangwu yinshuguan, 2004. 6 volumes.

Chen, Percy. *China Called Me: My Life Inside the Chinese Revolution*. Boston: Little, Brown, 1979.

Deng Guangyin.《我的父親鄧文劍》 *Wo de fuqin Deng Wenzhao* (*My father Deng Wenzhao*). Beijing: Zhongguo wenshi chubanshe, 1996.

Epstein, Israel. *My China Eye: Memoirs of a Jew and a Journalist.* San Francisco: Long River Press, 2005.

Fang Jun, Mai Xiaolin, and Xiong Xianjun 方駿, 麥肖玲, 熊賢君 (eds.). 《香港早期報紙教育資料選萃》 Xianggang zaoqi baozhi jiaoyu ziliao xuancui (Selection of articles on education from early newspapers in Hong Kong). Changsha: Hunan renmin chubanshe, 2006. (*XGBZJYZL*)

Fang Shaoyi 方少逸. "憶學生運動片斷" (Moments in youth movement). In 《廣東青年運動回憶錄》 Guangdong qingnian yundong huiyilu (Recollections of youth movement in Guangdong). Guangzhou: Guangdong renmin chubanshe, 1986. 100–109.

Fujian sheng dang'anguan (ed.). 《福建事變檔案資料 (1933.11–1934.1)》 Fujian shibian dang'an ziliao (Archival materials of the Fujian Incident, 1933.11–1934.1). Fuzhou: Fujian renmin chubanshe, 1984.

Grantham, Alexander. "China as Seen from Hong Kong," talk to the Council on Foreign Relations, New York, September 29, 1953. Transcribed by David F. Weller in "The Papers of Hamilton F. Armstrong." Mudd Manuscript Library, Princeton University.

———. "Hong Kong." *Journal of the Royal Central Asian Society*, 46 (1959), 119–29.

———. *Via Ports.* Hong Kong: Hong Kong University Press, 1965/2012.

———. "Grantham Interview." By D. J. Crozier, August 21, 1968; transcript in Manuscripts Archive, Rhodes House, Oxford University.

Guangdong funü yundong lishi ziliao bianzuan weiyuanhui (ed.). 《香港婦女運動資料彙編, 1937–1949》 Xianggang funü yundong ziliao huibian (Collection of materials on women's movement in Hong Kong, 1937–1949). Guangzhou: Guangdong funü yundong lishi ziliao bianzuan weiyuanhui, 1994. (*XGFYZL*)

Guangdong qingyunshi yanjiu weiyuanhui yanjiushi (ed.). 《青春進行曲: 回憶香港虹虹歌詠團》 Qingchun jinxingqu: huiyi Xiangang Honghong geyongtuan (The March of Youth: Recollections of the Rainbow Choir in Hong Kong). Guangzhou: Guangdong renmin chubanshe, 1988. (*QCJXQ*)

Guangdong qingyunshi yanjiu weiyuanhui yanjiushi and Dongzong GangJiu dadui duishi zhengbianzu (eds.). 《回顧港九大隊》 Huigu GangJiu dadui (Recollections of the Hong Kong–Kowloon Independent Brigade). Guangzhou: Guangdong shengwei bangongting laodong fuwu gongsi, 1987. 2 volumes. (*HGGJDD*)

Guo Tingyi, Wang Yujun, and Liu Fenghan. "馬超俊口述自傳" Ma Chaojun koushu zizhuan (Oral History by Ma Chaojun), in Liu Fenghan et al., 《馬超俊傅秉常口述自傳》 (Ma Chaojun, Fu Bingchang koushu zizhuan [Oral Histories by Ma Chaojun and Fu Bingchang]). Beijing: Zhongguo dabaike quanshu chubanshe, 2009.

He Jinzhou 何錦洲. "民主革命時期周楠同志在香港、廣州的革命鬥爭" Minzhu geming shiqi Zhou Nan tongzhi zai Xianggang, Guangzhou de geming douzheng (The revolutionary endeavors by comrade Zhou Nan during the period

for democratic revolution). http://www.gzzxws.gov.cn/gzws/cg/cgml/cg1/200
808/t20080825_3742_7.htm (accessed October 27, 2012).

He Sijing 何思敬. "回憶李章達先生" Huiyi Li Zhangda xiansheng (In memory of
Mr. Li Zhangda), 《廣東文史資料》 Guangdong wenshi zijiao, no. 10 (1963).

He Xiaolin and Guo Ji (eds.). 《勝利大營救》 Shengli da yingjiu (Victorious rescue mission). Beijing: Jiefangjun chubanshe, 1999.

He Zhuozhong 何卓忠. "He Zhuozhong Huiyilu" (Reminiscences by He Zhuozhong).
Handwritten manuscript. Photocopy in the author's possession.

Huang Qiuyun 黃秋耘 et al. 《秘密大營救》 Mimi dayingjiu (Secret rescue mission).
Beijing: Jiefangjun chubanshe, 1986.

Huang Yeheng 黃業衡. 《鐸吧往事》 Duoye wangshi (Recollection of the dockyard). Hong
Kong: Tianma tushu youxian gongsi, 2009.

Huang Zuocai. "香港新華社誕生的來龍去脈" Xianggang Xinhuashe dansheng de
lailong qumai (The origins of the Xinhua News Agency in Hong Kong). Unpublished manuscript in the author's possession.

Jin Yaoru 金堯如. 《香江五十年憶往》 Xiangjiang wushinian yiwang (Recollections of
fifty years in Hong Kong). Hong Kong: Jin Yaoru jinian jijin, 2005.

———. 《中共香港政策祕聞實錄》 Zhonggong Xianggang zhengce miwen shilu (An au-
thentic record of secretly transmitted policy of Hong Kong by the Chinese Communist Party). Hong
Kong: Tianyuan shuwu, 1998.

Kerr, Donald. "I Bring You Go Home Now." In Dongjiang zongdui lishi yanjiuhui
(ed.),《克爾日記：香港淪陷時期東江縱隊營救美軍飛行員紀實》 Kere
riji: Xianggang lunxian shiqi Dongjiang zongdui yingjiu Meijun feixingyuan jishi (Kerr's diary:
A record of rescuing an American pilot by the East River Column in Hong Kong under Japanese
occupation). Hong Kong: Xianggang keji daxue Huanan yanjiu zhongxin, 2015.
159–269.

Koo, Wellington V. K. The Wellington Koo Memoir. New York: Columbia University Press,
1976. Interviewed by Kai-fu Tsao, ed. James D. Seymour. Microfilm 4 reels.

Laufer, E. M. "Interview with Mr. E. M. Laufer of the Hong Kong China Light and
Power Limited (1938–1980)," by Steve Tsang, June 12, 1990. Transcript (edited
by Laufer) in Manuscripts Archive, Rhodes House, Oxford University.

Lei Zhen. 《雷震日記：第一個十年（二）》 Lei Zhen riji: diyige shinian (Diary of
Lei Zhen: the first ten years), vol. 2. Taipei: Guiguan tushu youxian gongsi, 1989.

Li Shufen (Li Shu-fan). Hong Kong Surgeon. New York: Dutton, 1964.

———. 《香港外科醫生》 Xianggang waike yisheng (Hong Kong surgeon). Hong Kong:
Li Shufen yixue jijinhui, 1965.

Li Song. 《李崧回憶錄》 Li Song huiyilu (Recollections by Li Song). Hong Kong: Xianggang shangbao, 1987.

Lian Guan tongzhi jinian wenji bianxiezu (ed.).《賢者不朽：連貫同志紀念文集》
Xianzhe buxiu: Lian Guan tongzhi jinian wenji (The wise lives forever: recollections about comrade
Lian Guan). Beijing: Zhongguo huaqiao chubanshe, 1995.

Liao Chengzhi Wenji Bianji bangongshi (ed.). 《廖承志文集》 *Liao Chengzhi Wenji (A collection of works by Liao Chengzhi)*. Hong Kong: Sanlian shudian, 1990. 2 volumes.

Liu Jieyun 劉潔雲. "在港九抗日游擊隊的歲月" Zai Gangjiu KangRi youjidui de suiyue (Resisting Japan with the guerrillas of Hong Kong–Kowloon Brigade). *Liwan Wenshi*, no. 7 (January 2012a), http://www.lw.gov.cn/zx/lwws7/201201 (accessed November 15, 2012).

———. "參加港九工運回憶錄" Canjia GangJiu gongyun huiyilu (Recollections of my experiences in the labor movement in Hong Kong and Kowloon). *Liwan wenshi*, no. 7 (January 2012b), http://www.gzzxws.gov.cn/lwws7/201201 (accessed November 15, 2012).

Lu Weiluan and Xiong Zhiqing (eds.). 《香港文化众聲道》 *Xianggang wenhua zhongshengdao (Multi-voice channel of culture in Hong Kong)*. Hong Kong: Sanlian shudian, 2014.

MacDougall, David Mercer. "Transcript of an Interview with Brigadier David Mercer MacDougall, CMG, MA of the Cadet Service of Hong Kong (1928–1949) (Colonial Secretary 1946–1949)," by Steven Tsang, February 26, 1987. Manuscripts Archive, Rhodes House, Oxford University.

Mao Zedong. *Mao Zedong xuanji*. Beijing: Renmin chubanshe, 1969.

Pan Jiangwei 潘江偉. "抗日戰爭時期的香港工會運動" KangRi zhanzheng shiqi di Xianggang gonghui yundong (Labor union movement in Hong Kong during the war of resisting Japan). Unpublished manuscript, Hong Kong Federation of Trade Unions.

Priestwood, Gwen. *Through Japanese Barbed Wire*. New York: Appleton-Century, 1943.

Qiao Guanghua. "口述自傳" Koushu zizhuan (Autobiography verbally recorded). In Qiao Guanhua and Zhang Hanzhi, 《那隨風飄去的歲月》 *Na suifeng piaoqu de suiyue (Years gone with the wind)*. Shanghai: Xuelin chubanshe, 1997.

Sa Kongliao. 《香港淪陷日記》 *Xianggang lunxian riji (Diary written in days when Hong Kong fell)*. 1946; Beijing: Sanlian shudian, 1985.

Selwyn-Clarke, Selwyn. *Footprints: The Memoirs of Sir Selwyn Selwyn-Clarke*. Hong Kong: Sino-American Publishing, 1975.

Shi Jue. 《石覺先生訪問紀錄》 *Shi Jue xiansheng fangwei jilu (Transcript of interviews with Mr. Shi Jue)*. Taipei: Modern History Institute, Academia Sinica, 1986.

Song Qingling Jijinhui and Zhongguo Fulihui (eds.). 《宋慶齡書信集》 *Song Qingling shuxinji (A collection of Song Qingling's correspondence)*. Beijing: Renmin chubanshe, 1999.

Stillwell, Joseph W. *The Stilwell Papers*. New York: William Sloane Associates, 1948.

Tan Tiandu. "抗戰勝利時我與港督代表的一次談判" Kangzhan shengli shi wo yu Gangdu daibiao de yici tanpan (My negotiations with the Representative of Hong Kong Governor in the Wake of the Resistance War's Victory). In Zhonggong zhongyang dangshi yanjiushi and Zhongyang dan'anguan (eds.). *Zhonggong dangshi ziliao*. Beijing: Zhonggong dangshi chubanshe, 1997. 62:56–69.

Tang Hai 唐海. 《香港淪陷記: 十八天的戰爭》 *Xianggang lunxianji: shi-ba-tian de zhanzheng* (*The fall of Hong Kong: an eighteen-day war*). Shanghai: Xinxin chubanshe, 1946.

Tu, Elsie. *Colonial Hong Kong in the Eyes of Elsie Tu*. Hong Kong: Hong Kong University Press, 2003.

Wu Weichi 吳渭池. "吳渭池傳略" Wu Weichi zhuanlue (A biography of Wu Weichi). Transcribed by Liang Xilin. *Tianye yu wenxian* (*Fieldwork and documents*), no. 45 (October 2006), 12–24.

Wu Youheng. "把握风光唱晚晴" Bawo fengguang changwanqing (Seizing the moment to celebrate sunset years). In Wu Youheng, *Wu Youheng Wenxuan* (*Selected Works by Wu Youheng*). Guangzhou: Huacheng chubanshe, 1993. 2:243–47.

Xia Yan. "走險記" Zouxian ji (Journey through dangerous paths). In 《夏衍雜文隨筆集》 *Xia Yan zawen suibiji* (*A collection of essays by Xia Yan*). Beijing: Sanlian shudian, 1980. 189–202.

———. 《懶尋舊夢錄》 *Lanxun jiumeng lu* (*Recollections in reluctance of old dreams*). Beijing: Sanlian shudian, 1985.

Xianggang Gonglianhui. 《夏季課程 2008》 *Xiaji kecheng 2008* (*Summer courses catalog 2008*). Hong Kong: FTU, 2008.

Xu Heng 徐亨. 《徐亨先生訪談錄》 *Xu Heng xiansheng fangtanlu* (*Interview with Mr. Xu Heng*). Transcribed by Chi Jingde and Lin Qiumin. Taipei: Guoshiguan, 1998.

Xu Yueqing 徐月清 (ed.). 《活躍在香江: 港九大隊西貢地區抗日實錄》 *Huoyue zai Xiangjiang: GangJiu dadui Xigong diqu kangRi shilu* (*Active in Hong Kong: Recollections of Hong Kong–Kowloon Brigade's wartime resistance in Sai Kung*). Hong Kong: Sanlian shudian, 1993.

Ye Dewei (ed.). 《香港淪陷史》 *Xianggang Lunxianshi* (*A history of Hong Kong under occupation*). Hong Kong: Guangjiaojing chubanshe, 1982.

Yuan Xianggang wenhua jiaoyu yishu shetuan qingzhu Xianggang huigui zuguo (ed.). 《光輝的足跡》 *Guanghui de zuji* (*Brilliant footprints*). Guangzhou: Guangzhou shiwei dangxiao yinshuachang, 1997. (*GHZJ*)

Zeng Sheng. 《曾生回憶錄》 *Zeng Sheng Huiyilu* (*Recollections by Zeng Sheng*). Beijing: Jiefangjun chubanshe, 1992.

Zhang Hanzhi 章含之. 《我與喬冠華》 *Wo yu Qiao Guanhua* (*Qiao Guanhua and I*). Beijing: Zhongguo qingnian chubanshe, 1994.

Zhang Huizhen and Kong Qiangsheng 張慧真 & 孔強生 (eds.). 《從十一萬到三千: 淪陷時期香港教育口述歷史》 *Cong shiyiwan dao sanqian: lunxian shiqi Xianggang jiaoyu koushu lishi* (*From one hundred and ten thousand to three thousand: Oral history of education in Hong Kong under Japanese occupation*). Hong Kong: Oxford University Press, 2005.

Zhong Zi 鍾紫 (ed.). 《香港報業春秋》 *Xianggang baoye chunqiu* (*A history of print media in Hong Kong*). Guangzhou: Guangdong renmin chubanshe, 1991.

Zhongguo Guomindang zhongyang weiyuanhui disanzu (ed.). 《中國國民黨在海外各地黨部史料初稿彙編》 *Zhongguo Guomindang zai haiwai gedi dangbu shiliao chugao huibian* (*A preliminary collection on the overseas party branches of the Chinese Guomindang*). Taipei: Zhongguo Guomindang zhongyang weiyuanhui, 1961.

Zhonghua quanguo zonggonghui Zhongguo gongren yundongshi yanjiushi (ed.). 《張浩紀念集》 *Zhang Hao jinianji* (*Recollections about Zhang Hao*). Shanghai: Shanghai renmin chubanshe, 1986.

Zhu Yamin 朱亞民. "我早期的工人生活和鬥爭" *Wo zaoqi de gongren shenghuo he douzheng* (*My life and struggle as a worker in my youth*). In Zhu Yamin, 《我與浦東抗日游擊隊》 *Wo yu Pudong kangRi youjidui* (*Resisting Japan guerrillas in Pudong and I*). Shanghai: Shanghai renmin buchanshe, 1996. 252–67.

Newspapers

China Mail. Hong Kong.

Dagong bao 大公報. Hong Kong.

Kung Sheung Daily News 工商日報 (*Industrial and Commercial Daily News*). Hong Kong.

Huashang bao 華商報. Hong Kong.

Renmin ribao 人民日報 (*People's Daily*). Beijing.

Sing Tao Jih Bao 星島日報 (*Sing Tao Daily*). Hong Kong.

South China Morning Post. Hong Kong. (*SCMP*)

South China Morning Post and the Hongkong Telegraph. Hong Kong.

South China Sunday Post. Hong Kong.

The Times. London.

Wah Kiu Yat Po 華僑日報 (*Overseas Chinese Daily*). Hong Kong. (*WKYP*)

Wenhui bao 文匯報. Hong Kong.

Xianggang shibao 香港時報 (*Hong Kong Times*). Hong Kong.

Labor Union Publications

GangJiu fangzhiranye zonggonghui 港九紡織染業總工會 (ed.). 《紡織染業總工會三週年紀念特刊》 *Fangzhiranye zonggonghui san zhounian jinian tekan* (*Special issue for the third anniversary of Textile Workers General Union*). June 25, 1950.

——— (ed.). 《港九紡織染業總工會五週年紀念特刊》 *Fangzhiranye zonggonghui wu zhounian jinian tekan* (*Special issue for the fifth anniversary of Textile Workers General Union*). Hong Kong, June 1952.

Gangjiu funü zhigong zonghui (ed.). 《婦女織工》 *Funü zhigong* (*Female Knitters*). Irregular publications.

Gongren wenhuashe (ed.). 《工人的活路》 *Gongren the huolu* (*The Hope for Workers*). Hong Kong: Gongren wenhuashe, 1948.

Laogong bao 勞工報 (*Lo Kung Weekly News*). Hong Kong.

Motuoche yanjiu zonggonghui 摩托車研究總工會. 《復刊號》 *Fukan hao* (*Resumption Newsletter*). February 1947.

Motuocheye zhigong zonggonghu 摩托車業職工總工會. 《摩托車業職工總會會刊: 一九四九年港九的士工潮特刊》 *Motuocheye zhigong zonghui huikan: 1949 nian GangJiu dishi gongchao tekan (Journal of Motor Drivers General Union: Special issue for taxi drivers' strike in 1949)*. September 1, 1949.

Motuocheye zhigong zonghui. 《摩總通讯》 *Mozong tongxun (Motor Newsletter)*. Irregular publications.

Qiche jiaotong yunshuye zonggonghui chengli bashi zhounian jinian tekan 1920–2000 (Special issue in commemoration of the eightieth anniversary of the General Union of Motorized Transportation Industry, 1920–2000). Hong Kong, 2000.

Xianggang haiyuan gonghui (Hong Kong Seamen's Union). 《香港海員》 *Xianggang haiyuan (Hong Kong Seamen)*. Irregular publications.

Xianggang yangwu gonghui 香港洋務工會. 《香港洋務》 *Xianggang yangwu (Foreign-Style Employment in Hong Kong)*. Irregular publications.

Secondary Sources

Anderson, Benedict. *Imagined Communities: Reflections on the Origin and Spread of Nationalism.* 1983; London: Verso, 1991.

Anderson, E. N. *The Floating World of Castle Peak Bay.* Washington, DC: American Anthropological Association, 1970.

———. *Essays on South China's Boat People.* Taipei: Orient Cultural Service, 1972.

Averill, Stephen C. *Revolution in the Highlands: China's Jinggangshan Base Area.* Lanham, MD: Rowman & Littlefield, 2006.

Beinin, Joel, and Zachary Lockman. *Workers on the Nile: Nationalism, Communism, Islam, and the Egyptian Working Class, 1882–1954.* Princeton: Princeton University Press, 1987.

Benton, Gregor. *Mountain Fires: The Red Army's Three-Year War in South China, 1934–1938.* Berkeley: University of California Press, 1992.

Bickers, Robert, and Ray Yip (eds.). *May Days in Hong Kong: Riot and Emergency in 1967.* Hong Kong: Hong Kong University Press, 2009.

Blyth, Sally, and Ian Wotherspoon (eds.). *Hong Kong Remembers.* Hong Kong: Oxford University Press, 1996.

Braga, Stuart. "Making Impressions: The Adaptation of a Portuguese Family to Hong Kong, 1700–1950." Ph.D. dissertation, Australian National University, 2012.

Bullock, Alan. *Ernest Bevin: Foreign Secretary, 1945–1951.* New York: Norton, 1983.

Cai Rongfang (Tsai Jung-fang). 《香港人之香港史, 1841–1945》 *Xianggangren zhi Xianggangshi, 1841–1945 (The Hong Kong people's history of Hong Kong, 1841–1945)*. Hong Kong: Oxford University Press, 2001.

Cai Shaoqing 蔡少卿. 《中國近代會黨史研究》 *Zhongguo jindai huidangshi yanjiu (Studies on modern secret societies in China)*. Beijiing: Zhongguo renmin daxue chubanshe, 2009.

Carroll, John M. *Edge of Empires: Chinese Elites and British Colonials in Hong Kong.* Cambridge, MA: Harvard University Press, 2005.

Cell, John. *Hailey: A Study in British Imperialism, 1872–1969.* Cambridge: Cambridge University Press, 1992.

Chan Lau Kit-ching. *Britain, China and Hong Kong, 1895–1945.* Hong Kong: Chinese University Press, 1990.

———. *From Nothing to Nothing: The Chinese Communist Movement in Hong Kong, 1921–1936.* New York: St. Martin's, 1999.

———. "The Perception of Chinese Communism in Hong Kong 1921–1934." *China Quarterly,* no. 164 (December 2000), 1044–61.

Chan Man-lok. "Between Red and White: Chinese Communist and Nationalist Movements in Hong Kong, 1945–1958." MPhil. thesis, University of Hong Kong, 2011.

Chan, Ming K. "Labor and Empire: The Chinese Labor in the Canton Delta, 1895–1927," Ph.D. dissertation, Stanford University, 1975.

——— (ed.). 《中國與香港工運縱橫》 *Zhongguo yu Xianggang gongyun zongheng (Dimensions of the Chinese and Hong Kong labor movement).* Hong Kong: Xianggang Jidujiao gongye weiyuanhui, 1986.

Chan Sui-jeung. *East River Column: Hong Kong Guerrillas in the Second World War and After.* Hong Kong: Hong Kong University Press, 2009.

Chan Wai Kwan. *The Making of Hong Kong Society: Three Studies of Class Formation in Early Hong Kong.* Oxford: Clarendon, 1991.

Chan-Yeung, Moira M. W. *The Practical Prophet: Bishop Ronald O. Hall of Hong Kong and His Legacies.* Hong Kong: Hong Kong University Press, 2015.

Chao, Linda, and Ramon H. Myers. *The First Chinese Democracy: Political Life in the Republic of China on Taiwan.* Baltimore: Johns Hopkins University Press, 1998.

Chen Boda 陳伯達. 《評<中國之命運>》 *Ping "Zhongguo zhi mingyun" (A commentary on "China's destiny").* Shanghai: Xinhua shudian, 1949.

Chen Da 陳達. 《中國勞工問題》 *Zhongguo laogong wenti (China's Labor Problems).* 1929; Shanghai: Shanghai shudan, 1990.

Chen Datong and Chen Wenyuan 陳大同, 陳文元 (eds.). 《百年商業》 *(A century of commerce).* Hong Kong: Guangming wenhua shiye gongsi, 1941.

Chen Lifeng and Mao Lijuan. 《上海抗日救亡運動》 *Shanghai kang-Ri jiuwang yundong (The movement of resisting Japan for national salvation in Shanghai).* Shanghai: Shanghai renmin chubanshe, 2000.

Chen Xihao 陳希豪.《過去三十五年中之中國國民黨》 *Guoqu sanshiwu nian zhong zhi Zhongguo Guomindang (China's Guomindang during the past thirty-five years).* Shanghai: Commercial Press, 1929.

Cheng, T. C. "Chinese Unofficial Members in Legislative and Executive Councils in Hong Kong up to 1941." *Journal of the Royal Asian Society Hong Kong Branch,* 9 (1969), 7–30.

Chesneaux, Jean. *The Chinese Labor Movement, 1919–1927.* Trans. H. M. Wright. Stanford, CA: Stanford University Press, 1968.

Cheung Ka Wai. 《香港六七暴動內情》 *Xianggang liuqi baodong neiqing (Inside Story of 1967 Riot in Hong Kong).* Hong Kong: Pacific Century Press, 2000.

Chow, Pauline. "一九四九年前華機會與港府關係" (Chinese Mechanics Union's relation with the government in Hong Kong before 1949). In Ming K. Chan (ed.), 《中國與香港工運縱橫》 *Zhongguo yu Xianggang gongyun zongheng (Dimensions of the Chinese and Hong Kong Labor Movement).* Hong Kong: Xianggang Jidujiao gongye wenyuanhui, 1986. 116–26.

Chung, Stephanie Po-yin. *Chinese Business Groups in Hong Kong and Political Change in South China, 1900–1925.* New York: St. Martin's, 1998.

Coates, Austin. "Rizal in Hongkong." In *Proceedings of the International Congress on Rizal,* 12 (December 1961), 4–8.

Coble, Parks M. "Chiang Kai-shek and the Anti-Japanese Movement in China: Zou Tao-fen and the National Salvation Association, 1931–1937." *Journal of Asian Studies,* 44:2 (February 1985), 293–310.

Constantine, Stephen. *The Making of British Colonial Development Policy, 1914–1940.* London: Frank Cass, 1984.

Cooper, Frederick. *Decolonization and African Society: The Labor Question in French and British Africa.* Cambridge: Cambridge University Press, 1996.

Cunich, Peter. *A History of the University of Hong Kong, Volume 1, 1911–1945.* Hong Kong: Hong Kong University Press, 2012.

Daniel, George T. "Labor and Nationalism in the British Caribbean." *Annals of the American Academy of Political and Social Science,* 310 (March 1957), 162–71.

Darwin, John. "Hong Kong in British Decolonisation." In Judith M. Brown and Rosemary Foot (eds.), *Hong Kong's Transition, 1842–1997.* New York: St. Martin's Press, 1997. 16–32.

———. *The Empire Project: The Rise and Fall of the British World-System, 1830–1970.* Cambridge: Cambridge University Press, 2009.

Davis, S. G. *Hong Kong in Its Geographical Setting.* London: Collins, 1949.

Deng Zhongxia 鄧中夏. 《中國職工運動簡史》 *Zhongguo zhigong yundong jianshi (A short history of Chinese labor movement).* 1948; Shanghai: Shanghai shudian, 1990.

Dickson, Bruce. "The Lessons of Defeat: The Reorganization of the Kuomintang on Taiwan, 1950–52." *China Quarterly,* no. 133 (March 1993), 56–84.

Dongjiang zongduishi bianxiezu (ed.). 《東江縱隊史》 *Dongjiang Zongduishi (A history of East River Column).* Guangzhou: Guangdong renmin chubanshe, 1985.

Donnison, F. S. V. *British Military Administration in the Far East, 1943–46.* London: Her Majesty's Stationery Office, 1956.

Ebury, Sue J. "Sir Lindsay Tasman Ride." In May Holdsworth and Christopher Munn (eds.), *Dictionary of Hong Kong Biography.* Hong Kong: Hong Kong University Press, 2012. 367–69.

Endacott, G. B., and Alan Birch. *Hong Kong Eclipse*. Hong Kong: Oxford University Press, 1978.

England, Joe, and John Rear. *Chinese Labour under British Rule: A Critical Study of Labour Relations and Law in Hong Kong*. Hong Kong: Oxford University Press, 1975.

Fan Hong 范泓. 《風雨前行: 雷震的一生》 *Fengyu qianxing: Lei Zhen de yisheng (March forward in adversity: The life of Lei Zhen)*. Guilin: Guangxi shifan daxue chubanshe, 2004.

Faure, David. *Colonialism and the Hong Kong Mentality*. Hong Kong: Centre of Asian Studies, University of Hong Kong, 2003.

Fedorowich, Kent. "Decolonization Deferred? The Re-establishment of Colonial Rule in Hong Kong, 1942–1945." *Journal of Imperial and Commonwealth History*, 28:3 (2000), 25–50.

Feng Lin 馮琳. 《中國國民黨在台改造研究 (1950–1952)》 *Zhongguo Guomindang zaiTai gaizao yanjiu (A study on the reform by Guomindang in Taiwan [1950–1952])*. Nanjing: Fenghuang chubanshe, 2013.

Ford, Stacilee. "'Reel Sisters' and Other Diplomacy: Cathay Studios and Cold War Cultural Production," in Priscilla Robinson and John Carroll (eds.), *Hong Kong in the Cold War*. Hong Kong: Hong Kong University Press, 2016. 183–210.

Fraser, Cary. "The Twilight of Colonial Rule in the British West Indies: Nationalist Assertion vs. Imperial Hubris in the 1930s." *Journal of Caribbean History*, no. 30 (1996), 1–27.

Fung Chi-ming. *Reluctant Heroes: Rickshaw Pullers in Hong Kong and Canton: 1874–1954*. Hong Kong: Hong Kong University Press, 2005.

GangAo yu jindai Zhongguo xueshu yantaohui lunwenji bianji weiyuanhui (ed.). 《港澳與近代中國學術研討會論文集》 *GangAo yu jindai Zhongguo xueshu yantaohui lunwenji (Essays from the Symposium on Hong Kong–Macau and modern China)*. Taipei: Guoshiguan, 2000.

GangJiu duli daduishi bianxiezu (ed.). 《港九獨立大隊史》 *GangJiu duli dadui shi (A history of Hong Kong–Kowloon Independent Brigade)*. Guangzhou: Guangdong renmin chubanshe, 1989.

Ge Jianxiong et al. 《中國移民史》 *Zhongguo yimin shi (A history of Chinese migration)*. Fuzhou: Fujian renmin chubanshe, 1997.

Goodman, Bryna. "New Culture, Old Habits: Native-Place Organization and the May Fourth Movement," in Frederic Wakeman Jr. and Wen-hsin Yeh (eds.), *Shanghai Sojourners*. Berkeley: Institute of East Asian Studies, University of California, 1992. 76–107.

———. *Native Place, City, and Nation: Regional Networks and Identities in Shanghai 1853–1937*. Berkeley: University of California Press, 1995.

Gordon, Andrew. *A Modern History of Japan*. New York: Oxford University Press, 2009.

Guan Lixiong. 《日佔時期的香港》 *Rizhan shiqi de Xianggang (Hong Kong under Japanese Occupation)*. Hong Kong: Sanlian shudian, 1993.

Gutkind, Peter C. W., Robin Cohen, and Jean Copans (eds.). *African Labor History*. Beverly Hills, CA: Sage, 1978.

H. L. "The End of Extraterritoriality in China." *Bulletin of International News*, 20:2 (January 23, 1943), 49–56.

Hailey, William Malcolm. "Some Problems Dealt with in the 'African Survey.'" *International Affairs*, 18:2 (March–April 1939), 194–210.

Harrison, Robert T. *Britain in the Middle East, 1619–1971*. London: Bloomsbury Academic, 2016.

Hart, Richard. "Labour Rebellions of the 1930s in the British Caribbean Region Colonies." Caribbean Labour Solidarity and Socialist History Society, Occasional Papers Series No. 15. 2002.

Hase, Patrick H. *Custom, Land, and Livelihood in Rural South China: the Traditional Land Law of Hong Kong's New Territories, 1750–1950*. Hong Kong: Hong Kong University Press, 2013.

He Lang 贺朗. 《吴有恆傳》 *Wu Youheng zhuan* (*A biography of Wu Youhenag*). Guangzhou: Huacheng chubanshe, 1993.

Henderson, Ian. "Early African Leadership: the Copperbelt Disturbances of 1935 and 1940." *Journal of Southern African Studies*, 2:1 (October 1975), 83–97.

Henriot, Christian. *Scythe and the City: A Social History of Death in Shanghai*. Stanford, CA: Stanford University Press, 2016.

Hershatter, Gail. *The Workers of Tianjin, 1900–1949*. Stanford, CA: Stanford University Press, 1986.

Hinder, Eleanor M. *Life and Labour in Shanghai: A Decade of Labour and Social Administration in the International Settlement*. New York: Institute of Pacific Relations, 1944.

Holt, Thomas C. *The Problem of Freedom: Race, Labor, and Politics in Jamaica and Britain, 1832–1938*. Baltimore: Johns Hopkins University Press, 1992.

Hong Kong's Who's Who & Residents Register 1947/48. N.p., n.d. [Likely published in 1948, available at the Hong Kong Special Collection at the University of Hong Kong.]

Honig, Emily. *Sisters and Strangers: Women in the Shanghai Cotton Mills, 1919–1949*. Stanford, CA: Stanford University Press, 1986.

Howard, Joshua H. *Workers at War: Labor in China's Arsenals, 1937–1953*. Stanford, CA: Stanford University Press, 2004.

Hughes, Richard. *Hong Kong: Borrowed Place, Borrowed Time*. New York: Praeger, 1968.

Ingrams, Harold. *Hong Kong*. London: Her Majesty's Stationery Office, 1952.

Israel, John. *Student Nationalism in China, 1927–1937*. Stanford, CA: Stanford University Press, 1966.

Jansen, Marius B. *Japan and China: From War to Peace, 1894–1972*. Chicago: Rand McNally, 1975.

Jarvie, I. C., and Joseph Agassi (eds.). *Hong Kong: A Society in Transition*. London: Routledge and Kegan Paul, 1969.

Jiang Ping and Luo Kexiang 姜平, 羅克祥. 《李濟深傳》 *Li Jishen zhuan* (*A biography of Li Jishen*). Beijing: Dang'an chubanshe, 1993.

Jiang Yongjing and Liu Weikai. 《蔣介石與國共內戰》 *Jiang Jieshi yu GuoGong neizhan* (*Jiang Jieshi and the civil war*). Taipei: Shangwu yinshuguan, 2011.

Jin Guangyao 金光耀. "1949–1950 英國對新中國的承認" 1949–1950 Yingguo dui xin Zhongguo de chengren (Britain's recognition of the new China, 1949–1950). *Lishi yanjiu*, 5 (1994), 119–31.

Johnson, Chalmers. *Peasant Nationalism and Communist Power: The Emergence of Revolutionary China*. Stanford, CA: Stanford University Press, 1962.

Jones, Margaret. "Tuberculosis, Housing and the Colonial State: Hong Kong, 1900–1950." *Modern Asian Studies*, 37:3 (July 2003), 653–82.

Kan Lai-bing and Grace H. L. Chu (eds.). *Newspapers of Hong Kong, 1841–1979*. Hong Kong: Chinese University of Hong Kong, 1981.

Katznelson, Ira. "Working Class Formation: Constructing Cases and Comparison." In Ira Katznelson and Aristide R. Zolberg (eds.), *Working-Class Formation: Nineteenth-century Patterns in Western Europe and the United States*. Princeton, NJ: Princeton University Press, 1986. 3–41.

Keating, Pauline B. *Village Reconstruction and the Cooperative Movement in Northern Shaanxi, 1934–1945*. Stanford, CA: Stanford University Press, 1997.

Keswick, Maggie (ed.). *The Thistle and the Jade: A Celebration of 175 Years of Jardine Matheson*. Rev. Clara Weatherall. London: Francis Lincoln, 2008.

King, Frank H. H. "Arthur Morse." In *Oxford Dictionary of National Biography*, http://www.oxforddnb.com.libproxy.unh.edu (accessed February 4, 2013).

Kuhn, Philip A. *Chinese among Others: Emigration in Modern Times*. Lanham, MD: Rowman & Littlefield, 2008.

Kuo Tai-chun and Hsiao-ting Lin. *T. V. Soong in Modern Chinese History: A Look at His Role in Sino-American Relations in World War II*. Stanford, CA: Hoover Institution, 2006.

Kwan, Daniel Y. K. *Marxist Intellectuals and the Chinese Labor Movement: A Study of Deng Zhongxia (1894–1933)*. Seattle: University of Washington Press, 1997.

Lam Wai-man. *Understanding the Political Culture of Hong Kong: The Paradox of Activism and Depoliticization*. Armonk, NY: M. E. Sharpe, 2004.

Lary, Diana. *Chinese People at War: Human Suffering and Social Transformation, 1937–1945*. Cambridge: Cambridge University Press, 2010.

Lebra, Joyce. *Japanese Trained Armies in Southeast Asia: Independence and Volunteer Forces in World War II*. New York: Columbia University Press, 1977.

Lee, Bradford A. *Britain and the Sino-Japanese War, 1937–1939*. Stanford, CA: Stanford University Press, 1973.

Lee, J. M. *Colonial Development and Good Government: A Study of the Ideas Expressed by the British Official Classes in Planning Decolonization, 1939–1964*. Oxford: Clarendon Press, 1967.

Lee, J. M., and Martin Petter. *The Colonial Office, War, and Development Policy: Organization and the Planning of a Metropolitan Initiative, 1939–1945*. London: Maurice Temple Smith, 1982.

Lee, P. C. *Hongkong Album*. Hong Kong: Sin Poh, 1960.

Lethbridge, Henry J. "Hong Kong under Japanese Occupation." In I. C. Jarvie and Joseph Agassi (eds.), *Hong Kong: A Society in Transition*. London: Routledge and Kegan Paul, 1969. 77–127.

———. "Hong Kong Cadets." in Henry Lethbridge, *Hong Kong: Stability and Change*. Hong Kong: Oxford University Press, 1978a. 31–51.

———. "A Chinese Association in Hong Kong: the Tung Wah." In Henry Lethbridge, *Hong Kong: Stability and Change*. Hong Kong: Oxford University Press, 1978b. 52–70.

———. "The Evolution of a Chinese Voluntary Association in Hong Kong: the Po Leung Kuk." In Henry Lethbridge, *Hong Kong: Stability and Change*. Hong Kong: Oxford University Press, 1978c. 71–103.

———. "The District Watch Committee: the Chinese Executive Council of Hong Kong?" In Henry Lethbridge, *Hong Kong: Stability and Change*. Hong Kong: Oxford University Press, 1978d. 104–29.

Li Boyuan and Ren Gongtan. 《廣東機器工人奮鬥史》 *Guangdong jiqi gongren fendoushi* (*A history of the struggle by Guangdong mechanics*). Taipei: Zhongguo laogong fuli chubanshe, 1955.

Li Yunhan. 《抗戰前中國知識份子的救國運動》 *Kangzhan qian Zhongguo zhishi fenzi de jiuguo yundong* (*The National Salvation Movement of Chinese intellectuals before the War of Resistance*). Taipei: Jiaoyubu shehuisi, 1977.

Liang Keping 梁柯平. 《抗日戰爭時期的香港學運》 *KangRi zhanzheng shiqi de Xianggang xueyun* (*Student movement in Hong Kong during the War of Resisting Japan*). Hong Kong: Hong Kong Organizing Committee for the Activities of Commemoration of the Sino-Japanese War Co. Ltd., 2005.

Lindsay, Oliver. *The Lasting Honour: the Fall of Hong Kong, 1941*. London: Hamish Hamilton, 1978.

Liu Shaoqi 劉少奇. 《中國職工運動史》 *Zhongguo zhigong yundongshi* (*A history of Chinese labor movement*). N.p.: Zhenli she, 1947.

Liu Weikai 劉維開. "淪陷期間中國國民黨在港九地區的活動" *Lunxian qijian Zhongguo Guomindang zai GangJiu diqu de huodong* (The activities of the Guomindang in Hong Kong and Kowloon). In *GangAo yu jindai Zhongguo xueshu yantaohui lunwenji* bianji weiyuanhui (ed.), *GangAo yu jindai Zhongguo xueshu yantaohui lunwenji* (*Essays from the Symposium on Hong Kong, Macau, and modern China*). Taipei: Guoshiguan, 2000. 477–500.

Liu Xiaoyuan. *A Partnership for Disorder: China, the United States, and Their Policies for Postwar Disposition of the Japanese Empire, 1941–1945*. Cambridge: Cambridge University Press, 1996.

Liu Zhipeng and Zhou Jiajian. 劉智鵬, 周家建.《吞聲忍語: 日治時期香港人的集體回憶》 Tunsheng renyu: Rizhi shiqi Xianggangren de jiti huiyi (Hold breath and keep silent: collective memories of residents in Hong Kong during the Japanese occupation). Hong Kong: Zhonghua shuju, 2009/2010.

Lo Ah 羅亞.《政治部回憶錄》 Zhengzhibu huiyilu (Recollections about the Special Branch). Hong Kong: Chinese University of Hong Kong, 1997.

Lo Koon-Cheung (Lao Guanxiang) 老冠祥. "國民政府與香港抗戰" Guomin zhengfu yu Xianggang kangzhan (The national government and Hong Kong in the War of Resisting Japan). In Chen Jingtang, Qiu Xiaojin, and Chen Jialiang (eds.).《香港抗戰》 Xianggang kangzhan (The Defence of Hong Kong). Hong Kong: Kangle ji wenhua shiwushu, 2004. 88–123.

Lockman, Zachary. Comrades and Enemies: Arab and Jewish workers in Palestine, 1906–1948. Berkeley: University of California Press, 1996.

Louis, William Roger. Imperialism at Bay: the United States and the Decolonization of the British Empire, 1941–1945. New York: Oxford University Press, 1978.

Lu Xun. "The American Cold War in Hong Kong, 1949–1960: Intelligence and Propaganda." In Priscilla Robinson and John Carroll (eds.), Hong Kong in the Cold War. Hong Kong: Hong Kong University Press, 2016. 117–40.

Lu, Yan. "Together with the Homeland: Civic Activism for National Salvation in British Hong Kong." Modern China, 40:6 (2014a), 639–74.

———. "In the Wake of Political Intervention: British Hong Kong and the Lingnan Macroregion." Frontiers of History in China, 9:3 (September 2014b), 449–71.

Luzzatto, Rola, and Rennie Remedios (eds.). Hong Kong Who's Who: An Almanac of Personalities and Their History, 1958–1960. Hong Kong: Ye Holde Printerie, 1960.

Malmsten, Neal R. "The British Labour Party and the West Indies, 1918–39." Journal of Imperial and Commonwealth History, 5:2 (January 1977), 172–205.

Manela, Erez. The Wilsonian Moment: Self-Determination and the International Origins of Anti-Colonial Nationalism. Oxford: Oxford University Press, 2007.

Mark, Chi-kwan. Hong Kong and the Cold War: Anglo-American Relations, 1949–1957. Oxford: Clarendon, 2004.

Martin, Brian G. "'The Pact with the Devil': The Relationship between the Green Gang and the Shanghai French Concession Authorities, 1925–1935." In Frederic Wakeman Jr. and Wen-hsin Yeh (eds.), Shanghai Sojourners. Berkeley: Institute of East Asian Studies, University of California, Center for Chinese Studies, 1992. 266–304.

———. "The Green Gang and the Guomindang State: Du Yuesheng and the Politics of Shanghai, 1927–1937." Journal of Asian Studies, 54:1 (February 1995), 64–92.

———. The Shanghai Green Gang: Politics and Organized Crime, 1919–1937. Berkeley: University of California Press, 1996.

Matsuda Yasuhiro. Taiwan ni okeru ittō dokusai no taisei no seiritsu (The establishment of one-party dictatorship in Taiwan). Tokyo: Keio Gijuku Daigaku Shuppankai, 2006.

Mazower, Mark. Inside Hitler's Greece. New Haven, CT: Yale University Press, 1993.

Miners, Norman J. "Henry Robert Butters." In May Holdsworth and Christopher Munn (eds.), *Dictionary of Hong Kong Biography*. Hong Kong: Hong Kong University Press, 2012. 54–55.

Morgan, W. P. *Triad Societies in Hong Kong*. Hong Kong: Government Press, 1960.

Munn, Christopher. *Anglo-China: Chinese People and British Rule in Hong Kong, 1841–1880*. Hong Kong: Hong Kong University Press, 2001/2009.

Ngo Tak-Wing. "Industrial History and the Artifice of *Laissez-Faire* Colonialism." In Tak-Wing Ng (ed.), *Hong Kong's History: State and Society under Colonial Rule*. London: Routledge, 1999. 119–40.

O'Sullivan, Christopher D. *Sumner Welles, Postwar Planning, and the Quest for a New World Order, 1937–1943*. New York: Columbia University Press, 2008.

Ozorio, Anne. "The Myth of Unpreparedness: The Origins of Anti-Japanese Resistance in Prewar Hong Kong." *Journal of the Royal Asiatic Society Hong Kong Branch*, 42 (2002), 161–86.

Parpart, Jane L. *Labor and Capital on the African Copperbelt*. Philadelphia: Temple University Press, 1983.

Paulés, Xavier. "Book Review." *Frontiers of History in China*, 12:1 (2017), 145–48.

Pratt, Mary Louise. "Arts of the Contact Zone." *Profession* (1991), 33–40.

———. *Imperial Eyes: Travel Writing and Transculturation*. London: Routledge, 1992.

Pepper, Suzanne. *Civil War in China: The Political Struggle, 1945–1949*. Berkeley: University of California Press, 1978.

———. *Keeping Democracy at Bay: Hong Kong and the Challenge of Chinese Political Reform*. Lanham, MD: Rowman & Littlefield, 2008.

Perry, Elizabeth J. *Shanghai on Strike: The Politics of Chinese Labor*. Stanford, CA: Stanford University Press, 1993.

Peterson, Glen. "Crisis and Opportunity: The Work of Aid Refugee Chinese Intellectuals (ARCI) in Hong Kong and Beyond." In Priscilla Robinson and John Carroll (eds.), *Hong Kong in the Cold War*. Hong Kong: Hong Kong University Press, 2016. 141–59.

Post, Ken. *Arise Ye Starvelings: The Jamaican Labour Rebellion of 1938 and Its Aftermath*. The Hague: Internationaal Instituut, 1978.

Ride, Edwin. *BAAG: Hong Kong Resistance, 1942–45*. Hong Kong: Oxford University Press, 1981.

Salaff, Janet W. *Working Daughters of Hong Kong: Filial Piety or Power in the Family?* London: Cambridge University Press, 1981.

Scott, Ian. *Political Change and the Crisis of Legitimacy in Hong Kong*. Honolulu: University of Hawaii Press, 1989.

Selden, Mark. *China in Revolution: The Yanan Way Revisited*. Armonk, NY: M. E. Sharpe, 1995.

Sewell, Sharon. *Decolonization and the Other: The Case of the British West Indies*. Newcastle upon Tyne: Cambridge Scholars Publishing, 2010.

Sinn, Elizabeth. *Power and Charity: A Chinese Merchant Elite in Colonial Hong Kong.* Hong Kong: Hong Kong University Press, 1989/2003.

———. "Moving Bones: Hong Kong's Role as an 'In-between Place' in the Chinese Diaspora." In Sherman Cochran and David Strand (eds.), *Cities in Motion.* Berkeley: Institute of East Asian Studies at the University of California, 2007. 247–71.

Smith, S. A. *Like Cattle and Horses: Nationalism and Labor in Shanghai, 1895–1927.* Durham, NC: Duke University Press, 2002.

Snow, Philip. *The Fall of Hong Kong: Britain, China and the Japanese Occupation.* New Haven, CT: Yale University Press, 2003.

———. "David Mercer MacDougall." In May Holdsworth and Christopher Munn (eds.), *Dictionary of Hong Kong Biography.* Hong Kong: Hong Kong University Press, 2012. 297–99.

Stichter, Sharon. "Trade Unionism in Kenya, 1947–1952, the Militant Phase." In Peter C. W. Gutkind, Robin Cohen, and Jean Copans (eds.), *African Labor History.* Beverly Hills: Sage, 1978. 155–74.

Stockard, Janice E. *Daughters of the Canton Delta: Marriage Patterns and Economic Strategies in South China, 1860–1930.* Stanford, CA: Stanford University Press, 1989.

Stranahan, Patricia. *Underground: The Shanghai Communist Party and the Politics of Survival, 1927–1937.* Lanham, MD: Rowman & Littlefield, 1998.

Strand, David. *Rickshaw Beijing: City People and Politics in the 1920s.* Berkeley: University of California Press, 1989.

Sweeting, Anthony. *A Phoenix Transformed: The Reconstruction of Education in Post-war Hong Kong.* Hong Kong: Oxford University Press, 1993.

Tilly, Charles. "Demographic Origins of the European Proletariat." In David Levine (ed.), *Proletarianization and Family History.* Orlando: Academic Press, 1984. 1–85.

Tsai Jung-fang. *Hong Kong in Chinese History: Community and Social Unrest in the British Colony, 1842–1913.* New York: Columbia University Press, 1993.

Tsang, Steve. *Democracy Shelved: Great Britain, China, and Attempts at Constitutional Reform in Hong Kong, 1945–1952.* Hong Kong: Oxford University Press, 1988.

———. *Hong Kong: Appointment with China.* London: Tauris, 1997a.

———. "Strategy for Survival: The Cold War and Hong Kong's Policy towards Kuomintang and Chinese Communist Activities in the 1950s." *Journal of Imperial and Commonwealth History,* 25:2 (1997b), 294–317.

Tuchman, Barbara W. *Stilwell and the American Experience in China, 1911–1945.* New York: Macmillan, 1970.

Tucker, Nancy B. *Patterns in the Dust: Chinese-American Relations and the Recognition Controversy, 1949–1950.* New York: Columbia University Press, 1983.

———. *Taiwan, Hong Kong, and the United States, 1945–1992.* New York: Twayne, 1994.

Ure, Gavin. *Governors, Politics, and the Colonial Office: Public Policy in Hong Kong, 1918–58.* Hong Kong: Hong Kong University Press, 2012.

Wakeman, Frederic, Jr. *Policing Shanghai, 1927–1937.* Berkeley: University of California Press, 1995.

Wakeman, Frederic, Jr., and Wen-hsin Yeh (eds.). *Shanghai Sojourners*. Berkeley: Institute of East Asian Studies, University of California, Center for Chinese Studies, 1992.

Waldron, Stephen Edward. "Fire on the Rim: A Study in Contradictions in Left-wing Political Mobilization in Hong Kong 1967." Ph.D. dissertation, Syracuse University, 1976.

Weiler, Peter. *Ernest Bevin*. Manchester: Manchester University Press, 1993.

Wesley-Smith, Peter. "Anti-Chinese Legislation in Hong Kong." In Ming K. Chan (ed.), *Precarious Balance: Hong Kong between China and Britain, 1842–1992*. Armonk, NY: M. E. Sharpe, 1994. 91–105.

Wicker, E. R. "Colonial Development and Welfare, 1929–1957: The Evolution of a Policy." *Social and Economic Studies*, 7:4 (December 1958), 170–92.

Wilson, Theodore A. *The First Summit: Roosevelt and Churchill at Placentia Bay, 1941*. Lawrence: University Press of Kansas, 1991.

Wolton, Suke. *Lord Hailey, the Colonial Office and the Politics of Race and Empire in the Second World War: The Loss of White Prestige*. London: Macmillan, 2000.

Wong, Ting-hong. *Hegemonies Compared: State Formation and Chinese School Politics in Postwar Singapore and Hong Kong*. New York: Routledge Falmer, 2002.

Wu Minggang 吳明剛. 《1933 福建事變始末》 *1933 Fujian shibian shimo (A narrative of the Fujian Incident of 1933)*. Wuhan: Hubei renmin chubanshe, 2006.

Xiang Lanxin. *Recasting the Imperial Far East: Britain and America in China, 1945–1950*. Armonk, NY: M. E. Sharpe, 1995.

Xiangganggonghui lianhui. 《光輝歲月薪火相傳》 *Guanghui suiyue xinhuo xiangchuan (Flickers of fire continue from the years of glory)*. Hong Kong: Xinhua shudian, 2008.

—— (ed.). 《工聯會與您同行: 60週年歷史文集》 *Gonglianhui yu nin tongxing: 60 zhounian lishi wenji (FTU marches with you: Collection of historical writings in 60 years)*. Hong Kong: Zhonghua shuju, 2013.

Xie Yongguang 謝永光. 《香港淪陷: 日軍攻港十八天戰爭紀實》 *Xianggang lunxian: Rijun gongGang shibatian zhanzheng jishi (Fall of Hong Kong: A record of eighteen-day war by the Japanese army)*. Hong Kong: Shangwu yinshuguan, 1995.

Yuan Xiaolun. 《戰後初期中共與香港進步文化》 *Zhanhou chuqi Zhonggong yu Xianggang jinbu wenhua (Chinese Communist Party and the progressive culture in postwar Hong Kong)*. Guangzhou: Guangdong jiaoyu chubanshe, 1999.

Zhai Qiang. *The Dragon, the Lion, and the Eagle: Chinese/British/American Relations: 1949–1958*. Kent, OH: Kent State University Press, 1994.

Zhang Yang. "亞洲基金會: 香港中文大學創建背後的美國推手" *Yazhou jijinhui: Xianggang Zhongwen daxue chuangjian beihou de Meiguo tuishou (The Asia Foundation: America as the driving force behind the establishment of the Chinese University of Hong Kong)*. *Contemporary China Studies*, 22:2 (March 2015). 91–102.

Zheng Hongtai and Huang Shaolun. 《香港身份證透視》 *Xianggang shenfenzheng toushi (A perspective on Hong Kong ID)*. Hong Kong: Sanlian shudian, 2004.

Zheng Jinyu 鄭錦玉. 《一代戰神孫立人》 *Yidai zhanshen Sun Liren* (*Sun Liren: A military genius of his times*). Taipei: Shuiniu chubanshe, 2004.

Zhongguo minyong hangkongju sixiang zhengzhi gongzuo bangongshi (ed.). 《兩航起義始末》 *Lianghang qiyi shimo* (*A narrative of the revolt by two aviation companies*). Beijing: Zhongguo minhang chubanshe, 2009.

Zhou Jiarong, Zhong Baoxian, and Huang Wenjiang 周佳榮, 鐘寶賢, 黃文江 (eds.). 《香港中華總商會百年史》 *Xianggang Zhonghua zongshanghui bainianshi* (*A centennial history of Chinese Chamber of Commerce in Hong Kong*). Hong Kong: Xianggangn Zhonghua zongshanghui, 2002.

Zhou Shuzhen. 《1949 飄搖港島》 *1949 Piaoyao Gangdao* (*Hong Kong adrift in 1949*). Beijing: Shishi chubanshe, 1996.

Zhou Yi (Chau Yick). 《香港左派鬥爭史》 *Xianggang zuopai douzhengshi* (*A history of leftist struggles in Hong Kong*). Hong Kong: Liwen chuban, 2002.

———. 《香港工運史》 *Xianggang gongyunshi* (*A history of labor movement in Hong Kong*). Hong Kong: Lixun chubanshe, 2009.

Index

CORNELL
East Asia Series

eap.einaudi.cornell.edu/publications

CPSIA information can be obtained
at www.ICGtesting.com
Printed in the USA
LVHW081937201119
638038LV00009B/34/P